Economics and Capitalism in the Ottoman Empire

Is it possible to generate "capitalist spirit" in a society, where cultural, economic and political conditions did not unfold into an industrial revolution, and consequently into an advanced industrial-capitalist formation? This is exactly what some prominent public intellectuals in the late Ottoman Empire tried to achieve as a developmental strategy; long before Max Weber defined the notion of capitalist spirit as the main motive behind the development of capitalism.

This book demonstrates how and why Ottoman reformists adapted (English and French) economic theory to the Ottoman institutional setting and popularized it to cultivate bourgeois values in the public sphere as a developmental strategy. It also reveals the imminent results of these efforts by presenting examples of how bourgeois values permeated into all spheres of sociocultural life, from family life to literature, in the late Ottoman Empire.

The text examines how the interplay between Western European economic theories and the traditional Muslim economic cultural setting paved the way for a new synthesis of a Muslim-capitalist value system; shedding light on the emergence of capitalism—as a cultural and an economic system—and the social transformation it created in a non-Western, and more specifically, in the Muslim Middle Eastern institutional setting. This book will be of great interest to scholars of modern Middle Eastern history, economic history, and the history of economic thought.

Deniz T. Kılınçoğlu received his PhD from Princeton University in 2012. He currently teaches economics and history at the Middle East Technical University-Northern Cyprus Campus, Cyprus.

Routledge studies in the history of economics

1 **Economics as Literature**
Willie Henderson

2 **Socialism and Marginalism in Economics 1870–1930**
Edited by Ian Steedman

3 **Hayek's Political Economy**
The socio-economics of order
Steve Fleetwood

4 **On the Origins of Classical Economics**
Distribution and value from William Petty to Adam Smith
Tony Aspromourgos

5 **The Economics of Joan Robinson**
Edited by Maria Cristina Marcuzzo, Luigi Pasinetti and Alesandro Roncaglia

6 **The Evolutionist Economics of Léon Walras**
Albert Jolink

7 **Keynes and the 'Classics'**
A study in language, epistemology and mistaken identities
Michel Verdon

8 **The History of Game Theory, Vol 1**
From the beginnings to 1945
Robert W. Dimand and Mary Ann Dimand

9 **The Economics of W. S. Jevons**
Sandra Peart

10 **Gandhi's Economic Thought**
Ajit K. Dasgupta

11 **Equilibrium and Economic Theory**
Edited by Giovanni Caravale

12 **Austrian Economics in Debate**
Edited by Willem Keizer, Bert Tieben and Rudy van Zijp

13 **Ancient Economic Thought**
Edited by B. B. Price

14 **The Political Economy of Social Credit and Guild Socialism**
Frances Hutchinson and Brian Burkitt

15 **Economic Careers**
Economics and economists in Britain 1930–1970
Keith Tribe

16 **Understanding 'Classical' Economics**
Studies in the long-period theory
Heinz Kurz and Neri Salvadori

17 **History of Environmental Economic Thought**
E. Kula

18 **Economic Thought in Communist and Post-Communist Europe**
Edited by Hans-Jürgen Wagener

19 **Studies in the History of French Political Economy**
From Bodin to Walras
Edited by Gilbert Faccarello

20 **The Economics of John Rae**
Edited by O. F. Hamouda, C. Lee and D. Mair

21 **Keynes and the Neoclassical Synthesis**
Einsteinian versus Newtonian macroeconomics
Teodoro Dario Togati

22 **Historical Perspectives on Macroeconomics**
Sixty years after the 'General Theory'
Edited by Philippe Fontaine and Albert Jolink

23 **The Founding of Institutional Economics**
The leisure class and sovereignty
Edited by Warren J. Samuels

24 **Evolution of Austrian Economics**
From Menger to Lachmann
Sandye Gloria

25 **Marx's Concept of Money**
The God of Commodities
Anitra Nelson

26 **The Economics of James Steuart**
Edited by Ramón Tortajada

27 **The Development of Economics in Europe since 1945**
Edited by A. W. Bob Coats

28 **The Canon in the History of Economics**
Critical essays
Edited by Michalis Psalidopoulos

29 **Money and Growth**
Selected papers of Allyn Abbott Young
Edited by Perry G. Mehrling and Roger J. Sandilands

30 **The Social Economics of Jean-Baptiste Say**
Markets and virtue
Evelyn L. Forget

31 **The Foundations of Laissez-Faire**
The economics of Pierre de Boisguilbert
Gilbert Faccarello

32 **John Ruskin's Political Economy**
Willie Henderson

33 **Contributions to the History of Economic Thought**
Essays in honour of R. D. C. Black
Edited by Antoin E. Murphy and Renee Prendergast

34 **Towards an Unknown Marx**
A commentary on the manuscripts of 1861–63
Enrique Dussel

35 **Economics and Interdisciplinary Exchange**
Edited by Guido Erreygers

36 **Economics as the Art of Thought**
Essays in memory of G. L. S. Shackle
Edited by Stephen F. Frowen and Peter Earl

37 **The Decline of Ricardian Economics**
Politics and economics in post-Ricardian theory
Susan Pashkoff

38 **Piero Sraffa**
His life, thought and cultural heritage
Alessandro Roncaglia

39 **Equilibrium and Disequilibrium in Economic Theory**
The Marshall–Walras divide
Michel de Vroey

40 **The German Historical School**
The historical and ethical approach to economics
Edited by Yuichi Shionoya

41 **Reflections on the Classical Canon in Economics**
Essays in honour of Samuel Hollander
Edited by Sandra Peart and Evelyn Forget

42 **Piero Sraffa's Political Economy**
A centenary estimate
Edited by Terenzio Cozzi and Roberto Marchionatti

43 **The Contribution of Joseph Schumpeter to Economics**
Economic development and institutional change
Richard Arena and Cecile Dangel

44 **On the Development of Long-run Neo-Classical Theory**
Tom Kompas

45 **F. A. Hayek as a Political Economist**
Economic analysis and values
Edited by Jack Birner, Pierre Garrouste and Thierry Aimar

46 **Pareto, Economics and Society**
The mechanical analogy
Michael McLure

47 **The Cambridge Controversies in Capital Theory**
A study in the logic of theory development
Jack Birner

48 **Economics Broadly Considered**
Essays in honour of Warren J. Samuels
Edited by Steven G. Medema, Jeff Biddle and John B. Davis

49 **Physicians and Political Economy**
Six studies of the work of doctor-economists
Edited by Peter Groenewegen

50 **The Spread of Political Economy and the Professionalisation of Economists**
Economic societies in Europe, America and Japan in the nineteenth century
Massimo Augello and Marco Guidi

51 **Historians of Economics and Economic Thought**
The construction of disciplinary memory
Steven G. Medema and Warren J. Samuels

52 **Competing Economic Theories**
Essays in memory of Giovanni Caravale
Sergio Nisticò and Domenico Tosato

53 **Economic Thought and Policy in Less Developed Europe**
The nineteenth century
Edited by Michalis Psalidopoulos and Maria-Eugenia Almedia Mata

54 **Family Fictions and Family Facts**
Harriet Martineau, Adolphe Quetelet and the population question in England 1798–1859
Brian Cooper

55 **Eighteenth-Century Economics**
Peter Groenewegen

56 **The Rise of Political Economy in the Scottish Enlightenment**
Edited by Tatsuya Sakamoto and Hideo Tanaka

57 **Classics and Moderns in Economics, Volume I**
Essays on nineteenth and twentieth century economic thought
Peter Groenewegen

58 **Classics and Moderns in Economics, Volume II**
Essays on nineteenth and twentieth century economic thought
Peter Groenewegen

59 **Marshall's Evolutionary Economics**
Tiziano Raffaelli

60 **Money, Time and Rationality in Max Weber**
Austrian connections
Stephen D. Parsons

61 **Classical Macroeconomics**
Some modern variations and distortions
James C. W. Ahiakpor

62 **The Historical School of Economics in England and Japan**
Tamotsu Nishizawa

63 **Classical Economics and Modern Theory**
Studies in long-period analysis
Heinz D. Kurz and Neri Salvadori

64 **A Bibliography of Female Economic Thought to 1940**
Kirsten K. Madden, Janet A. Sietz and Michele Pujol

65 **Economics, Economists and Expectations**
From microfoundations to macroeconomics
Warren Young, Robert Leeson and William Darity Jnr.

66 **The Political Economy of Public Finance in Britain, 1767–1873**
Takuo Dome

67 **Essays in the History of Economics**
Warren J. Samuels, Willie Henderson, Kirk D. Johnson and Marianne Johnson

68 **History and Political Economy**
Essays in honour of P. D. Groenewegen
Edited by Tony Aspromourgos and John Lodewijks

69 **The Tradition of Free Trade**
Lars Magnusson

70 **Evolution of the Market Process**
Austrian and Swedish economics
Edited by Michel Bellet, Sandye Gloria-Palermo and Abdallah Zouache

71 **Consumption as an Investment**
The fear of goods from Hesiod to Adam Smith
Cosimo Perrotta

72 **Jean-Baptiste Say and the Classical Canon in Economics**
The British connection in French classicism
Samuel Hollander

73 **Knut Wicksell on Poverty**
No place is too exalted
Knut Wicksell

74 **Economists in Cambridge**
A study through their correspondence 1907–1946
Edited by M. C. Marcuzzo and A. Rosselli

75 **The Experiment in the History of Economics**
Edited by Philippe Fontaine and Robert Leonard

76 **At the Origins of Mathematical Economics**
The Economics of A. N. Isnard (1748–1803)
Richard van den Berg

77 **Money and Exchange**
Folktales and reality
Sasan Fayazmanesh

78 **Economic Development and Social Change**
Historical roots and modern perspectives
George Stathakis and Gianni Vaggi

79 **Ethical Codes and Income Distribution**
A study of John Bates Clark and Thorstein Veblen
Guglielmo Forges Davanzati

80 **Evaluating Adam Smith**
Creating the wealth of nations
Willie Henderson

81 **Civil Happiness**
Economics and human flourishing in historical perspective
Luigino Bruni

82 **New Voices on Adam Smith**
Edited by Leonidas Montes and Eric Schliesser

83 **Making Chicago Price Theory**
Milton Friedman–George Stigler correspondence, 1945–1957
Edited by J. Daniel Hammond and Claire H. Hammond

84 **William Stanley Jevons and the Cutting Edge of Economics**
Bert Mosselmans

85 **A History of Econometrics in France**
From nature to models
Philippe Le Gall

86 **Money and Markets**
A doctrinal approach
Edited by Alberto Giacomin and Maria Cristina Marcuzzo

87 **Considerations on the Fundamental Principles of Pure Political Economy**
Vilfredo Pareto (Edited by Roberto Marchionatti and Fiorenzo Mornati)

88 **The Years of High Econometrics**
A short history of the generation that reinvented economics
Francisco Louçã

89 **David Hume's Political Economy**
Edited by Carl Wennerlind and Margaret Schabas

90 **Interpreting Classical Economics**
Studies in long-period analysis
Heinz D. Kurz and Neri Salvadori

91 **Keynes's Vision**
Why the great depression did not return
John Philip Jones

92 **Monetary Theory in Retrospect**
The selected essays of Filippo Cesarano
Filippo Cesarano

93 **Keynes's Theoretical Development**
From the tract to the general theory
Toshiaki Hirai

94 **Leading Contemporary Economists**
Economics at the cutting edge
Edited by Steven Pressman

95 **The Science of Wealth**
Adam Smith and the framing of political economy
Tony Aspromourgos

96 **Capital, Time and Transitional Dynamics**
Edited by Harald Hagemann and Roberto Scazzieri

97 **New Essays on Pareto's Economic Theory**
Edited by Luigino Bruni and Aldo Montesano

98 **Frank Knight & the Chicago School in American Economics**
Ross B. Emmett

99 **A History of Economic Theory**
Essays in honour of Takashi Negishi
Edited by Aiko Ikeo and Heinz D. Kurz

100 **Open Economics**
Economics in relation to other disciplines
Edited by Richard Arena, Sheila Dow and Matthias Klaes

101 **Rosa Luxemburg and the Critique of Political Economy**
Edited by Riccardo Bellofiore

102 **Problems and Methods of Econometrics**
The Poincaré lectures of Ragnar Frisch 1933
Edited by Olav Bjerkholt and Ariane Dupont-Keiffer

103 **Criticisms of Classical Political Economy**
Menger, Austrian economics and the German historical school
Gilles Campagnolo

104 **A History of Entrepreneurship**
Robert F. Hébert and Albert N. Link

105 **Keynes on Monetary Policy, Finance and Uncertainty**
Liquidity preference theory and the global financial crisis
Jorg Bibow

106 **Kalecki's Principle of Increasing Risk and Keynesian Economics**
Tracy Mott

107 **Economic Theory and Economic Thought**
Essays in honour of Ian Steedman
John Vint, J. Stanley Metcalfe, Heinz D. Kurz, Ner Salvadori and Paul Samuelson

108 **Political Economy, Public Policy and Monetary Economics**
Ludwig von Mises and the Austrian tradition
Richard M. Ebeling

109 **Keynes and the British Humanist Tradition**
The moral purpose of the market
David R. Andrews

110 **Political Economy and Industrialism**
Banks in Saint-Simonian economic thought
Gilles Jacoud

111 **Studies in Social Economics**
By Leon Walras
Translated by Jan van Daal and Donald Walker

112 **The Making of the Classical Theory of Economic Growth**
By Anthony Brewer

113 **The Origins of David Hume's Economics**
By Willie Henderson

114 **Production, Distribution and Trade**
Edited by Adriano Birolo, Duncan Foley, Heinz D. Kurz, Bertram Schefold and Ian Steedman

115 **The Essential Writings of Thorstein Veblen**
Edited by Charles Camic and Geoffrey Hodgson

116 **Adam Smith and the Economy of the Passions**
By Jan Horst Keppler

117 **The Analysis of Linear Economic Systems**
Father Maurice Potron's pioneering works
Translated by Christian Bidard and Guido Erreygers

118 **A Dynamic Approach to Economic Theory: Frisch**
Edited by Olav Bjerkholt and Duo Qin

119 **Henry A. Abbati: Keynes' Forgotten Precursor**
Serena Di Gaspare

120 **Generations of Economists**
David Collard

121 **Hayek, Mill and the Liberal Tradition**
Edited by Andrew Farrant

122 **Marshall, Marshallians and Industrial Economics**
Edited by Tiziano Raffaelli

123 **Austrian and German Economic Thought**
Kiichiro Yagi

124 **The Evolution of Economic Theory**
Edited by Volker Caspari

125 **Thomas Tooke and the Monetary Thought of Classical Economics**
Matthew Smith

126 **Political Economy and Liberalism in France**
The contributions of Frédéric Bastiat
Robert Leroux

127 **Stalin's Economist**
The economic contributions of Jenö Varga
André Mommen

128 **E.E. Slutsky as Economist and Mathematician**
Crossing the limits of knowledge
Vincent Barnett

129 **Keynes, Sraffa, and the Criticism of Neoclassical Theory**
Essays in honour of Heinz Kurz
Neri Salvadori and Christian Gehrke

130 **Crises and Cycles in Economic Dictionaries and Encyclopaedias**
Edited by Daniele Bensomi

131 **General Equilibrium Analysis: A Century After Walras**
Edited by Pascal Bridel

132 **Sraffa and Modern Economics, Volume I**
Edited by Roberto Ciccone, Christian Gehrke and Gary Mongiovi

133 **Sraffa and Modern Economics, Volume II**
Edited by Roberto Ciccone, Christian Gehrke and Gary Mongiovi

134 **The Minor Marshallians and Alfred Marshall: An Evaluation**
Peter Groenewegen

135 **Fighting Market Failure**
Collected essays in the Cambridge tradition of economics
Maria Cristina Marcuzzo

136 **The Economic Reader**
Edited by Massimo M. Augello and Marco E. L. Guido

137 **Classical Political Economy and Modern Theory**
Essays in honour of Heinz Kurz
Neri Salvadori and Christian Gehrke

138 **The Ideas of Ronald H. Coase**
Lawrence W. C. Lai

139 **Anticipating the Wealth of Nations**
Edited by Maren Jonasson and Petri Hyttinen, with an Introduction by Lars Magnusson

140 **Innovation, Knowledge and Growth**
Edited by Heinz D. Kurz

141 **A History of *Homo Economicus***
The nature of the moral in economic theory
William Dixon and David Wilson

142 **The Division of Labour in Economics**
A history
Guang-Zhen Sun

143 **Keynes and Modern Economics**
Edited by Ryuzo Kuroki

144 **Macroeconomics and the History of Economic Thought**
Festschrift in honour of Harald Hagemann
Edited by Hagen M. Krämer, Heinz D. Kurz and Hans-Michael Trautwein

145 **French Liberalism in the 19th Century**
An anthology
Edited by Robert Leroux

146 **Subjectivisim and Objectivism in the History of Economic Thought**
Edited by Yukihiro Ikeda and Kiichiro Yagi

147 **The Rhetoric of the Right**
Language change and the spread of the market
David George

148 **The Theory of Value and Distribution in Economics**
Discussions between Pierangelo Garegnani and Paul Samuelson
Edited by Heinz Kurz

149 **An Economic History of Ireland Since Independence**
Andy Bielenberg

150 **Reinterpreting the Keynesian Revolution**
Robert Cord

151 **Money and Banking in Jean-Baptiste Say's Economic Thought**
Gilles Jacoud

152 **Jean-Baptiste Say**
Revolutionary, entrepreneur, economist
Evert Schoorl

153 **Essays on Classical and Marxian Political Economy**
Samuel Hollander

154 Marxist Political Economy
Essays in retrieval: selected works of Geoff Pilling
Edited by Doria Pilling

155 Interdisciplinary Economics
Kenneth E. Boulding's engagement in the sciences
Edited by Wilfred Dolfsma and Stefan Kesting

156 Keynes and Friedman on Laissez-Faire and Planning
'Where to draw the line?'
Sylvie Rivot

157 Economic Justice and Liberty
The social philosophy in John Stuart Mill's utilitarianism
Huei-chun Su

158 German Utility Theory
Analysis and Translations
John Chipman

159 A Re-Assessment of Aristotle's Economic Thought
Ricardo Crespo

160 The Varieties of Economic Rationality
From Adam Smith to contemporary behavioural and evolutionary economics
Michel S. Zouboulakis

161 Economic Development and Global Crisis
The Latin American economy in historical perspective
Edited by José Luís Cardoso, Maria Cristina Marcuzzo and María Eugenia Romero

162 The History of Ancient Chinese Economic Thought
Edited by Cheng Lin, Terry Peach and Wang Fang

163 A History of Economic Science in Japan
The internationalization of economics in the twentieth century
Aiko Ikeo

164 The Paretian Tradition during the Interwar Period
From dynamics to growth
Mario Pomini

165 Keynes and his Contemporaries
Tradition and enterprise in the Cambridge School of Economics
Atsushi Komine

166 Utilitarianism and Malthus' Virtue Ethics
Respectable, virtuous and happy
Sergio Cremaschi

167 Revisiting Classical Economics
Studies in long-period analysis
Heinz Kurz and Neri Salvadori

168 The Development of Economics in Japan
From the inter-war period to the 2000s
Edited by Toichiro Asada

169 Real Business Cycle Models in Economics
Warren Young

170 Hayek and Popper
On rationality, economism, and democracy
Mark Amadeus Notturno

171 **The Political and Economic Thought of the Young Keynes**
Liberalism, markets and empire
Carlo Cristiano

172 **Richard Cantillon's Essay on the Nature of Trade in General**
A Variorum Edition
Richard Cantillon
Edited by Richard van den Berg

173 **Value and Prices in Russian Economic Thought**
A journey inside the Russian synthesis, 1890–1920
François Allisson

174 **Economics and Capitalism in the Ottoman Empire**
Deniz T. Kılınçoğlu

Economics and Capitalism in the Ottoman Empire

Deniz T. Kılınçoğlu

LONDON AND NEW YORK

First published 2015
by Routledge

2 Park Square, Milton Park, Abingdon, Oxfordshire OX14 4RN
52 Vanderbilt Avenue, New York, NY 10017

Routledge is an imprint of the Taylor & Francis Group, an informa business

First issued in paperback 2019

British Library Cataloguing in Publication Data
A catalogue record for this book is available from the British Library

Library of Congress Cataloging in Publication Data
Kilincoglu, Deniz T.
Economics and capitalism in the Ottoman Empire / Deniz T. Kilincoglu.
pages cm
1. Turkey–Economic conditions–19th century. 2. Turkey–Economic conditions–20th century. 3. Capitalism–Turkey–History. 4. Turkey–History–Ottoman Empire, 1288–1918. I. Title.
HC492.K554 2015
330.956'015–dc23 2015000652

ISBN: 978-1-138-85406-2 (hbk)
ISBN: 978-0-367-87244-1 (pbk)

Typeset in Times New Roman
by Wearset Ltd, Boldon, Tyne and Wear

To Sevil and Bahar

Contents

Acknowledgments

Writing is usually not a process of cooperation and division of labor, unlike most other production processes. A book-length study—especially in history—is mostly a product of a lonely author who is trying to make sense of a large amount of introvert primary sources that do not give away their secrets and interconnections easily. As one such author, I was fortunate to find many people who eased the pains and shared the joys in every stage of this rather long journey of reading, reflecting, and writing.

I am grateful to M. Şükrü Hanioğlu, Michael A. Cook, Michael A. Reynolds, and Holly A. Shissler who read the early versions of the entire manuscript carefully, offering numerous suggestions to improve it. I would also like to thank Bernard Haykel and Abraham Udovitch for their mentorship during my studies about medieval and modern Middle Eastern history. All these people have a deep mark in the positive aspects of this book. Bill Blair, Alex Balistreri, Yaşar Tolga Cora, and Alp Yücel Kaya were extremely generous with their time and energy as they read the early drafts of the entire manuscript and offered invaluable corrections and suggestions. Osman Aray not only shared his views about the text, but also was exceptionally encouraging at every stage of the preparation of this book. Robert P. Finn, Kathi Ivanyi, Luke Yarbrough, Agnes Sherman, Aliye Mataracı, and Aytek Soner Alpan carefully read and commented on various chapters at different stages. Their assistance and friendship are greatly appreciated. I was very fortunate to have two diligent assistants, Burcu Ermeydan and Joseph Kim, who contributed to the production of the manuscript in various ways.

I want to thank the staff of Beyazıt Library, Atatürk Library, ISAM Library, and the Başbakanlık Ottoman Archives in Istanbul, and especially the Firestone Library of Princeton University for their assistance. Throughout the entire period of research and writing of this manuscript, I have received financial support from Princeton University, where I was a PhD student, and at Middle East Technical University-Northern Cyprus Campus, where I have been teaching. Thanks to the support of these institutions, I had the chance to focus on doing research, rather than having financial worries about it. Starting from the first email exchange about the project until the end of the production process, Routledge staff have been very professional and prompt. I would especially like to thank Emily Kindleysides and Laura Johnson in this regard.

Last and definitely the most, I am grateful to my best friend and the love of my life, Sevil Çakır-Kılınçoğlu. During the entire process, not only did she provide unlimited love and encouragement, she was also the only person who truly saw what is happening in the labyrinths of my mind, and helped me reveal it as effectively as possible. She skillfully moderated my many ups and downs during research and writing, and organized our life with her sharp yet serene mind. Thanks to her truly exceptional parenthood skills—based on a continuous and extensive research that deserves a PhD on its own—the miraculous addition to our family, "Bahar Hanım," has been an intellectual as well as emotional contribution to my work, rather than creating any obstacle to it. Sevil read the whole manuscript at different stages and discussed every single detail about my project as if it was her own. Dedicating this work to her with admiration and love is the least that I can do in return for her existence in my life.

Needless to say, no one but me can be held responsible for the inadequacies and errors of this book. But I do not want to end this part with this usual disclaimer. Instead, I would like to finish with a sincere note, defying habitual academic pretensions under an increasingly—and irrationally—demanding university system: this work could have probably been much better if I spent less time with my family and friends. But I unashamedly did not do it. I may have missed a few errors, but I have not missed my daughter's first steps, first tooth, and first calling me "daddy." And I am totally fine with this.

Note on translation, transliteration, and dates

Arabic and Persian words are transliterated according to the *IJMES* (*International Journal of Middle East Studies*) Guide. Ottoman Turkish words, regardless of their origin, are rendered according to a modified version (to be able to denote *hamza*, the letter *ʿayn*, and long vowels) of modern Turkish orthography. In most cases, I prefer to use the original names of Ottoman institutions and provide the English translation in parenthesis when the name first appears. I use the Gregorian calendar throughout the text for dating. However, when my sources are dated in the Hijrī or Rumi calendars, I provide the original dates preceding the Gregorian one in the bibliography.

Abbreviations

BOA	Başbakanlık Osmanlı Arşivi
CUP	Committee of Union and Progress
H	Hijrī Calendar
İA	İslam Ansiklopedisi, Türkiye Diyanet Vakfı
IJMES	International Journal of Middle East Studies
R	Rumi Calendar
TOEM	Tarih-i Osmânî Encümeni Mecmuası
YEE	Yıldız Esas Evrakı

Introduction

"An unending dialogue between the present and the past"[1]

> Christians invest whatever they have in commerce. Muslims, on the other hand, invest in landholding, thereby reserving lands exclusively for agriculture. Since making a big profit out of small capital is only possible through commerce and not agriculture, Christians get wealthier.[2]
>
> (Ali Suâvi, 1869)

> When I was the mayor [of Istanbul] I studied [the Jews of Istanbul]. Most of them do not buy real estate. They rent places in the best districts. Why? Because if they become landholders, their money is lost. But if they invest their money [in business], they can still rent the best places and live therein … and their money remains productive. We [the Muslims], on the other hand, invest all our wealth in land. We don't participate in commercial life. We should carefully assess this situation and guide future generations [accordingly].[3]
>
> (Recep Tayyip Erdogan, 2009)

One hundred and forty years after Ali Suâvi voiced his concerns about Muslim indifference to commerce and non-Muslim dominance in the Ottoman economy—and even after decades-long state-led efforts to create a (Muslim) national bourgeoisie in the Turkish Republic—the words of the Prime Minister of Turkey continue to echo Young Ottoman discourse. Determining whether social memory or material reality is more relevant in the resonance between the two discourses is beyond the scope of this book. Nonetheless, this is an example of continuity in economic thought and discourse in the *longue durée*. This book takes a momentous era, the reign of Abdülhamid II (1876–1909), out of the continuous evolution of Ottoman-Turkish economic thought, investigating its historical context and its connections with the preceding and subsequent periods. More broadly, it aims at examining the role that ideas play in historical change through a case study of the impact of bourgeois economic ideas and values on Ottoman modernization.

Economics and modernization

> The ideas of economists…, both when they are right and when they are wrong, are more powerful than is commonly understood. Indeed the world

> is ruled by little else. Practical men, who believe themselves to be quite exempt from any intellectual influence, are usually the slaves of some defunct economist.[4]

Inspired by this well-known quote from Keynes on the importance of ideas, this book examines how the nineteenth-century classical political economy and bourgeois economic values permeated into sociocultural and political spheres and influenced late nineteenth-century Ottoman modernization. The book focuses especially on the reign of the most controversial ruler of late Ottoman history, Sultan Abdülhamid II (r. 1876–1909). The importance of the Hamidian era lies in the fact that it was the most prolific era of the Ottoman economic literature. Moreover, Ottoman elite of the period, and especially the sultan himself, put the emphasis on economic development as the main path to modernity.[5] The government prepared and implemented economic development plans, and these plans significantly altered the socio-economic infrastructure of the country—from transportation to education. Meanwhile, prominent Ottoman intellectuals of the era joined the government's efforts by popularizing the modern principles and notions of economics, with an eye on social change through reshaping popular economic mentality and behavior in Ottoman society.

The Hamidian era was also the formative period for the "founding fathers" of the post-Ottoman Middle Eastern nation-states. Many intellectuals and statesmen who led nation-building processes—after the dissolution of the empire in 1922—in the Middle East were formal students at Hamidian schools and informal students of influential public intellectuals of the Hamidian era. Therefore, economic ideas as well as the actual economic development experience of the Ottoman state made a considerable impact on economic ideologies and governmental policies in the post-Ottoman Middle East, especially in the Turkish Republic. In this respect, a careful analysis of late nineteenth-century Ottoman economic thought is a key to understanding the roots of twentieth-century nation-building and economic development efforts in the Middle East and the Southern Balkans. Despite its importance, however, economic ideas and discussions that marked this period has not been studied thoroughly in a book-length study. Focusing on this particular era, this book aims to explore three main questions: How did economics as a new interpretation of the world (and its history) influence the Ottoman intellectual sphere? What impact did this new perception of the world have on the Ottoman strategy of survival within the capitalist modernity of the late nineteenth century? And, how were economic ideas and bourgeois values popularized to materialize social change in accordance with modernization efforts?

This study in its entirety is not a catalogue of economists and their ideas in the late Ottoman Empire. Instead, it suggests a new perspective on late Ottoman history through an analysis of the economic ideas that shaped this era. It is equally worth noting that this book is not a book on the development of capitalism in the Ottoman Empire, but rather discursive practices about it. It focuses on economic ideas about capitalism and development, and on the cultural and intellectual impact of global capitalism (through economic literature) in the Ottoman Empire. The book, thereby, aims at shedding light on the social and cultural change as a result of the integration of the empire into global capitalist modernity, rather than more technical economic dynamics of the integration process itself.

Modernity, capitalist modernity, modernization, modernist: a note on the conceptual framework

A note about the conceptual framework that I used in the book is necessary for a better understanding of the arguments. In this book, I follow the definition of "modernity" as "one specific type of civilization that originated in Europe [over two centuries ago] and spread throughout the world."[6] Besides, I use the concept "capitalist modernity" interchangeably with "modernity" to emphasize its predominantly capitalistic economic nature. Broadly speaking, the modern age or modernity is often associated with the capitalist mode of production, industrialization, secularization, and the nation-state, among other economic and political formations. In this respect, I use the word "modern" to indicate belonging to this particular civilization and its institutional framework. In a similar vein, I define "modernization" as a process of adaptation to capitalist modernity through a comprehensive institutional transformation. In addition to this definition, modernization has also meant, in the everyday political and economic jargon, a general updating of the political, economic, and even military system, which in the late Ottoman context also holds without an essential conflict with the earlier definition.

The modernization theory has been rightly criticized for its simplistic and Eurocentric core assumption that modernization is basically imitating the Western European patterns in the process of transition from the so-called "traditional" society to a modern (meaning Western-European type) one. Thanks to numerous case studies that has been done for years, we now know that each case of social change has its own unique features—along with some common goals and patterns—and modernization (however it is defined) cannot be simply explained with imitation of European patterns. In any case, although the basic assumptions and implications of the "modernization school" have been considered misleading and obsolete, this should not let us abandon using the useful concept of "modernization" all together. First of all, if it is still being used by policy makers to express their main goals, it should be taken seriously as a unit of analysis, instead of branding it with its bad connotations.[7] Despite our relatively recent scholarly objections to this approach, countries in the capitalist periphery, including those in Southern and Eastern Europe, have looked at North-Western European and more recently American examples in their efforts to update their domestic institutional setup. Second, particularly in the nineteenth century context, the notion of modernization—with all its Eurocentric connotations—is still the best term which reflects policy-makers' and other reformists' approach to the question of social and political change. In this regard, despite being a highly problematic and controversial term, I believe that my use of the term modernization (in various meanings stated above) encapsulates how Ottoman reformists regarded their own efforts to build a "civilized" (*medenî*) society and to attain "civilization" (*medeniyet*).

Regarding the intellectuals and statesmen who are subjects of this study, I use the terms "reformist" and "modernist" interchangeably to define intellectuals who championed reforms in the socio-economic and/or political system in the Ottoman Empire, inspired by Western-European patterns. Needless to say, such an approach may obscure differences in the views of various groups in the late Ottoman Empire. After all, reformism of Ahmed Midhat (1844–1912) and the Young Turks, for example, are significantly different from each other. However, since I particularly focus on the socio-economic aspects of modernization, I claim that there is not much difference (at the macro level) in that respect among various strands of late Ottoman reformism. Building a modern economy, which would be shaped by the latest technology and production methods, and a society organized around such an economy were the main shared objectives of late Ottoman modernism in very broad terms. In this respect, Ahmed Midhat, Münif Pasha (1830–1910), the Young Turks, and even the sultan, Abdülhamid II, should be defined as "modernist" as an umbrella category. The main difference between these modernists, I claim, lies in their different strategies to achieve their goals. Recognizing the potentially controversial character of my definition and categorization, I insist that keeping political disputations among these figures at bay provides us with a better perspective in understanding the ideas and efforts for socio-economic change in the late Ottoman Empire.

Approach, methods, and sources

Looking retrospectively, history is chaotic, multidimensional, continuous, and a dynamic flow, in which countless agents, from individual humans and animals to atmospheric changes and geological movements, play various roles. Although, focusing on the actions or ideas of some agents in a certain period, separating from earlier and later periods, is liable to distort what actually happened, it is inevitable nonetheless. This study does take a period out of the continuous flow of history and attempt to analyze it with regard to the past that created it and the future which it paved the way for. However, being aware of this rather unnatural process, I have tried to be as cautious as possible in order not to break the strings of time between periods, which are conceptually distinguished by historians for practical analytical purposes. In other words, although this study focuses on a certain period (*c.*1876–1909), this is not because there are ruptures (in terms of economic thought) at both ends, but simply because of the necessity to put limits for such a study. This does not mean, however, that the era in question did not have special characteristics of its own. It was marked by the reign of a particular sultan and the economic, political, and social policies of his regime. These policies and the sultan himself were both products of certain historical trends and in turn pave the way for subsequent historical trends. In short, this book is a study of certain dimensions of a complex and continuous evolutionary pattern (i.e., the development of Ottoman-Turkish bourgeois economic thinking) intended to shed light on the working of this complexity and the meaning of it for our understanding of how humans think, how they influence each other, how ideas circulate, and how material factors, especially in periods of socio-economic and political transformation, impact human thinking and synthesis of ideas.

Understanding Ottoman economic thinking requires efforts beyond a basic reading of the economic literature of the era. One has to take into account psychological factors, cultural traits, religious concerns, and sociological complexities that shaped ideas and discussions in certain ways. Besides, economic ideas reveal themselves in various forms of intellectual activity, from official documents to fiction. This book, as a result, is an interdisciplinary historical study informed by insights and analytical tools from various fields of the social sciences and humanities, such from the history of economic thought to the literary theory. This variety of analytical tools enables me to explore economic ideas in a specific period, but in a broader historical and theoretical context. In my examination of the Ottoman novel as a source for understanding socio-economic change, for example, I benefitted from the perspective of the New Historicism, which "entails reading literary and nonliterary texts as constituents of historical discourses that are both inside and outside of texts."[8] A parallel reading of literary and non-literary texts for their economic content produced new insights for understanding both the popularization of bourgeois ideas and the instrumentality of the novel in the late Ottoman modernization process.

The historical approach of this book is based on the idea that Ottoman-Turkish modernization has been a continuous evolutionary process of social, economic, and political change rather than a loosely connected array of events, people, and periods. It thereby puts Hamidian-era intellectuals and ideas in their historical context and in dialogue with those of the preceding and succeeding eras. In this respect, it shows, for example, how ideas of Münif Pasha (1830–1910) in the 1860s and 70s, and especially the works of Ahmed Midhat Efendi (1844–1912) in the 1880s, paved the way for the post-1908 National Economy program (*Millî İktisat*) of the Committee of Union and Progress (CUP) leaders, and the nation-building project of the early Turkish Republic in the 1920s and 30s.

Earlier trendsetting works on Ottoman economic thinking, such as those of Sabri Ülgener and Mehmet Genç,[9] embarked to find explanations for Ottoman failure in catching up with capitalist modernity in the late eighteenth and nineteenth century. This way of thinking led them to miss the fact that industrialization was the product of a rather unique stage in the economic and social history of North-Western Europe in the last centuries, and not a natural result of the unfolding of human history in a Hegelian sense. Accordingly, an apologetic discourse on Ottoman backwardness, itself inherited from nineteenth century Ottoman modernist discourse, dominated the literature on Ottoman intellectual history, especially the studies by Turkish scholars. In a similar vein, arguments attributing Ottoman failure to allegedly imitative and primitive features of

Ottoman economic thought have dominated the same literature. Such arguments are clearly informed by the modernization theory of the twentieth century. Thus, the underlying analytical framework in many studies on Ottoman economics is based on the idea that Ottoman economists' ideas were merely caricatures of European theories. An important example is the case of Ahmed Midhat Efendi, who was perhaps the most influential intellectual of the era. Ahmed Midhat has been considered a vulgarizer of often ill-understood ideas from Europe, rather than a pragmatic reformist intellectual who rested his understanding of modernization upon an eclectic intellectual base.

In this book, I challenge the discourse of primitiveness and imitation through two arguments. First, we cannot assume that British and French economists produced their ideas in an intellectual vacuum. So, they too imitated their predecessors in some sense. It is a simple fact that every intellectual activity depends on imitation, yet some thinkers achieve some sort of originality by contributing some unprecedented ideas to their fields. In short, imitation does not always imply a general inferiority or primitiveness. Second, instead of dismissing all efforts of Ottoman economists as primitive or imitative, I regard their endeavor to transplant European economic knowledge into their own cultural and intellectual setting as an important phenomenon in global as well as Middle Eastern intellectual history. The intellectuals who are the subjects of this book aimed at using the instruments of a new discipline to analyze and solve the problems of their people, not merely by copying, but by adapting it into the Ottoman episteme and creating a synthesis of Ottoman economic toolbox. This, naturally, does not mean that I support these ideas or that I ignore their top-down modernist approach, which paved the way for the Turkish modernist model of the early twentieth century, namely, "for the people, despite the people." However, writing about the ideas of Ottoman economists requires the utmost attention to the extreme complexity of intellectual as well as political conditions in the late nineteenth century. As I emphasize throughout the book, Ottoman intellectuals of the era were the pioneers of a native synthesis of economic thought and policy in the Middle East, and they went through what every pioneer would: inexperience, imitation of previous examples, confusion, and other ills, along with originalities of first attempts.

Moreover, imitation is the basis of education and the transmission of knowledge from generation to generation and from one culture to another.[10] Therefore, even if the term "imitation" was used in this book as a central unit of analysis, it would not have a negative connotation. On the contrary, in the context of economic development, imitation is considered a practical instrument for "backward economies" as Alexander Gerschenkron (1962) argues regarding the imitation of technology:

> Borrowed technology, so much and so rightly stressed by Veblen, was one of the primary factors assuring a high speed of development in a backward country entering the stage of industrialization. There always has been the inevitable tendency to deride the backward country because of its lack of

> originality. German mining engineers of the sixteenth century accused the English of being but slavish imitators of German methods, and the English fully reciprocated these charges in the fifties and sixties of the past [i.e., the nineteenth] century.[11]

Therefore, a backward economy imitates an advanced example so that it can leapfrog early stages and does not repeat the same mistakes. Imitation thereby speeds up the development process. This book liberally expands this analysis to the context of economic ideas by emphasizing that borrowing tested methods and ideas for economic development is rational behavior for economically backward countries.

In any case, Ottoman reformists did not merely imitate everything but rather adopted foreign ideas and institutions as they deemed necessary, and that they also strove to adapt their traditional institutions to capitalist modernity. The words of a prominent Ottoman intellectual, Ebüzziya Tevfik (1849–1913), provide us a succinct summary of the Ottoman reformists' take on the question of modernization and imitation: "If something that does not exist in a country is procured through imitation, does it diminish its virtues?"[12] The result of the efforts of Ottoman modernists, who dominantly adopted such a pragmatic approach to the problem of modernization, was an Ottoman modernity, not a replica of other modernities in Europe. This book, therefore, puts the emphasis on the pragmatism of Ottoman modernism rather than the alleged shallowness of the late Ottoman intellectual sphere and the imitative character of Ottoman modernization.

As for the Ottomans and others, another objective of this book is to situate late Ottoman economic thinking in a global historical context instead of assessing it in isolation. Ottoman economic thought of the late nineteenth century, just like other examples in Europe as well as the non-European world, was a product of the industrial age and its "worldly philosophers," i.e., economists.[13] However, it would be wrong to assume that Ottoman economic thought was merely a translation activity and did not have distinct flavors and internal dynamics of evolution. Therefore, the ideas and intellectuals discussed in this book are regarded as interrelated parts of the same body (i.e., modern Ottoman economic thought), which is connected to a global intellectual world-system (i.e., modern European classical political economy). By exploring the emergence of Ottoman syntheses of political economy—with its European as well as Islamic features—this study aims at presenting an illuminating case study of the expansion of the modern capitalist economic and cultural system into the Middle East.

The age-old and now obsolete question of why the Ottomans failed to realize an industrial revolution on their soil—following suit the British example—was constructed in the context of nineteenth-century paradigms with a clear anachronistic and teleological perspective. From Max Weber's cultural deterministic thesis,[14] to recent approaches which place more emphasis on natural resource endowments and geography,[15] there are myriad competing theses about the rise of Western Europe and the growing economic gap with the rest of the world. All in all, all these theses have some truth in them, and from formal and informal institutions (including everyday cultural practices) to population sizes, many factors contributed to the so-called the industrial revolution and the rise of the West.

Recently, institutional approaches to the question of economic development and the capitalist system itself regained popularity thanks to the works of economists such as Daron Acemoğlu and James Robinson, and Thomas Piketty.[16] In a similar vein, Timur Kuran has suggested an institutional perspective in a narrower sense—focusing on the Islamic law—to explain the reasons of economic backwardness in the Islamic Middle East.[17] My study also follows the institutional approach, but it has a radical difference from these aforementioned works, suggesting an alternative perspective. These scholars scrutinize their cases from outside—and mostly retrospectively—with an economist's approach. This book however presents insiders' discussions about the institutional aspects of economic development in the case of the late Ottoman Empire. In other words, instead of making an external and retrospective institutional analysis of Ottoman economic history, the book presents an internal and contemporaneous perspective, putting together various institutional analyses of the Ottoman economists of the age regarding the question of capitalist development and the problem of Ottoman economic backwardness in the intellectual and economic context of the late nineteenth century.

Finally, this book focuses on reformist intellectuals of the era. In other words, it aims to reveal the blueprints of a modern society according to Hamidian-era Ottoman modernist economic perspective. Thus, conservative reactions and alternative models (Islamic or otherwise) for social change in the same age are left to be explored in other studies.[18] However, even within reformists, a selection was necessary, and the primary selection criteria were (relative) originality and popular influence. If liberal Ottoman economists, in this respect, may have remained in the shadows, compared to protectionists, this is not due to my ideological preferences, but the abovementioned criteria. Liberals, in general, defended the universal validity of the *laissez-faire* approach, whereas protectionists adopted a more historical and evolutionary approach, and scrutinized the traditional Ottoman economic and social formation in developing their country-specific policy suggestions. Besides, although textbooks and university professors were almost exclusively liberal, among the public intellectuals who wrote on economic issues and introduced this discipline of inquiry to the public, the most influential were protectionists. Therefore, despite all efforts to produce a balanced presentation, these factors may have skewed the current work towards the writings of the latter group.

Outline of the study

Although the chapters of this book form a coherent whole and follow a logical sequence to depict a multidimensional picture of the subject matter, each chapter stands on its own by focusing on certain aspects of the topic and providing relevant historical background. Thus, the readers can benefit from the book in its entirety or just selectively, depending on their needs and interests. It is also worth noting that this book is intended for scholars of a wide range of areas from the history of economic thought to Middle Eastern studies. Although the primary subject matter is the Ottoman Empire, it was not only written exclusively for the Ottomanists. Therefore, each chapter provides non-Ottomanists with basic historical background on the relevant aspects of the socio-economic and intellectual transformation in last century of the Ottoman Empire. This might cause some overlaps and occasional repetitions of certain points in different chapters, but it will hopefully help the reader when referring to individual chapters for specific interests.

The first chapter sets the scene through an overview of the Ottoman economic institutions and economic thought before the 1870s, to provide the reader with a basic understanding of the intellectual and economic context which shaped late nineteenth-century Ottoman modernization efforts. The second chapter explores the Ottoman economic literature in its most prolific period, the Hamidian era (1876–1909). The close textual analysis of books and popular manuals about economics and economy-related matters presents insights into the cultural, linguistic, and intellectual dynamics of translation from European sources, thereby studying the patterns of the Ottomanization of economics through Ottoman intellectuals' adaptation of the conceptual framework of classical political economy into the Ottoman socio-economic and cultural context.

The third chapter focuses on the ideas on redesigning the Ottoman society and its citizens according to the parameters provided by modern economics and the dominant industrial-capitalist paradigm of the nineteenth century. It scrutinizes the economic writings of influential Ottoman intellectuals of a wide range of political and ideological standing, from a loyal statesman, Münif Pasha, to the Young Turks, and analytically juxtapose diverse ideas on changing Ottoman society as an essential component of economic development. In addition to revealing and historicizing various late Ottoman envisionings of an ideal economy-driven society and its citizens in capitalist standards, this chapter also demonstrates how some public intellectuals decisively promoted bourgeois economic values for soft social engineering of the economic mentality and behavior of the Ottoman masses.

The fourth chapter is an examination of the question of economic development in late nineteenth-century Ottoman economic thought, and the emergence of Muslim-Turkish proto-nationalism in the context of capitalist development. It starts with an investigation of the economic writings of the Young Ottomans in the 1860s, and connects their proto-nationalist economic discourse to those of the Young Turks of the subsequent period, and more importantly to the economic ideas of the sultan Abdülhamid II—who was the arch-enemy of Young Ottoman–Young Turk reformist political line of thought. It offers a multifaceted analysis of the evolution of the idea of economic development in late Ottoman thought, and it sheds light on the late nineteenth-century roots of Muslim-Turkish nationalism, which shaped the Turkish Republic in the twentieth century.

The fifth chapter focuses on economic thought in late Ottoman fiction. It traces and analyzes economic ideas and messages in the popular novels and short stories of influential intellectuals of the era, thereby revealing the connections between fiction and economic thought. In this sense, this last chapter aims at demonstrating how modern economic ideas permeated into all spheres of Ottoman social and cultural life thanks to the deliberate efforts of Ottoman reformists for social change.

Notes

1 From E.H. Carr's answer to the question, "What's History?" (Edward H. Carr, *What Is History?* (New York: Vintage Books, 1961), 35).

2 Suâvi, "Memalik-i Osmaniye'de Ticaret," *Ulûm* 12 (1869), 735; quoted in İsmail Doğan, *Tanzimatın İki Ucu: Münif Paşa ve Ali Suavi: Sosyo-Pedagojik Bir Karşılaştırma* (İstanbul: İz Yayıncılık, 1991), 295.

3 Recep Tayyip Erdogan, "Yahudiler Bilgiyi ve Parayı İyi Yönetiyor" ("The Jews Manage Knowledge and Money Well"), *Milliyet*, October 8, 2009, last accessed December 14, 2014, www.milliyet.com.tr/Siyaset/HaberDetay.aspx?aType=HaberDetayArsiv&ArticleID=1147787&Kategori=siyaset&b=Yahudiler%20bilgiyi%20ve%20parayi%20iyi%20yonetiyor.

4 John M. Keynes, *The General Theory of Employment, Interest and Money* (London: Macmillan, 1973), 383–4.

5 I use the broader definition of "economic development," which denotes not only quantitative growth in the gross domestic product (GDP), but also increases in the standards of living of a population, including improvement in social as well as technological aspects of life from education to health care.

6 S.N. Eisenstadt, *Comparative Civilizations and Multiple Modernities* (Leiden: Brill, 2003), 24.

7 As one recent example, see "Putin Reaffirms Commitment to Military Modernization in Speech to Officers," *The Moscow Times*, November 4, 2014, www.themoscowtimes.com/business/article/putin-reaffirms-commitment-to-military-modernization-in-speech-to-officers/510601.html.

8 Catherine Gallagher, "Marxism and the New Historicism," in *The New Historicism*, ed. H. Aram Veeser (New York: Routledge, 1989), 37.

9 Sabri F. Ülgener, *İktisadî İnhitat Tarihimizin Ahlâk ve Zihniyet Meseleleri* (İstanbul: İstanbul Üniversitesi İktisat Fakültesi, 1951); Mehmet Genç, *Osmanlı İmparatorluğu'nda Devlet ve Ekonomi* (İstanbul: Ötüken Neşriyat, 2000).

10 As an example in the opposite direction, I can mention Fibonacci's book, *Liber Abaci* (1202). His work was mostly a summary of what he learned from Arab scholars. If it had been dismissed in his age as merely a work of imitation, Europe would not have learned Arabic numerals, which were to be a fundamental to modern capitalism with their potential for bookkeeping, in addition to their other practical and theoretical mathematical applications.

11 Alexander Gerschenkron, *Economic Backwardness in Historical Perspective, a Book of Essays* (Cambridge, MA: Belknap Press of Harvard University Press, 1962), 8.

12 Ebüzziya Tevfik, "Biz Nasıl Çalışıyoruz, Başkaları Nasıl Çalışıyor ve Ahmed Midhat Efendi," *Mecmua-yı Ebüzziya*, no. Supplement to no. 80 (1898): 2.

13 The term "worldly philosophers" is due to Robert L. Heilbroner, see Robert L. Heilbroner, *The Worldly Philosophers: The Lives, Times, and Ideas of the Great Economic Thinkers*, seventh edition (New York: Touchstone, 1999).

14 Max Weber, *The Protestant Ethic and the Spirit of Capitalism*, trans. Talcott Parsons (New York: Charles Scribner's Sons, 1958).

15 Such as Kenneth Pomeranz, *The Great Divergence: Europe, China, and the Making of the Modern World Economy*, The Princeton Economic History of the Western World (Princeton, N.J: Princeton University Press, 2000); Robert C. Allen, *The British Industrial Revolution in Global Perspective* (Cambridge University Press, 2009).

16 Daron Acemoglu and James Robinson, *Why Nations Fail: The Origins of Power, Prosperity, and Poverty*, 1st ed. (Crown Business, 2012); Thomas Piketty and Arthur Goldhammer, *Capital in the Twenty-First Century* (Cambridge, MA: Belknap Press, 2014).

17 Timur Kuran, *The Long Divergence: How Islamic Law Held Back the Middle East* (Princeton: Princeton University Press, 2011).

18 As an example of such a study, see Charles Tripp, *Islam and the Moral Economy: The Challenge of Capitalism* (Cambridge: Cambridge University Press, 2006). For an unpublished MA thesis related to this subject, see Kenan Göçer, "Cumhuriyet Öncesi İslamcı Akımın İktisadi Görüşleri – Kavramsal Bir Yaklaşım" (Unpublished MS Thesis, Marmara University, 1993).

1 Ottoman society, economy, and economics in the nineteenth century

Enemies were strong, fortune was weak,
Treasury was empty, debt was plenty.
In this situation he found the state,
Is it really necessary to explain what is obvious?
...
Numerous schools were established,
Government debts were regulated.
Thanks to his majestic efforts,
Order and security emerged.[1]

(Münif Pasha, 1882)

When Abdülhamid II ascended to the Ottoman throne in 1876, the empire was in great fiscal and economic (in addition to political) difficulties amidst global financial and economic crises during the Long Depression (1873–96). Although Münif Pasha's eulogy above exaggerates the improvement in the economic and fiscal conditions of the empire during his reign (1876–1909), economic development was placed at the focus of the modernization efforts of his governments. Economics was considered an indispensable instrument of state administration, and became an important topic in popular education. Accordingly, late Ottoman economic thinking produced its most important works in (especially the first two decades of) the Hamidian era.

Intellectual tools for coping with economic and fiscal problems had not been totally absent in the earlier decades, however. On the contrary, publications on economics and economic education in schools had begun in the first half of the century, as the Ottoman elite realized that the nineteenth century was an economy-centered age. Ottoman statesmen as well as intellectuals had begun to study and discuss this new instrument of government through various (rather unsystematic) publications in periodicals as well as in the form of books. Many of these publications and discussions in the popular periodicals provided an intellectual, as well as a linguistic, basis for discussions on economic development in the Hamidian and subsequent periods.

As the Ottomans began to study economics, the failure of state-led industrialization efforts in the first half of the century also taught important (albeit bitter) lessons to the Ottoman elite about how capitalism works, influenced their approach to the question of economic development—in the context of the broader issue of modernization. The realization of the socio-economic institutional factors behind this failure (from the popular work ethic to the legal framework) changed their approach also to the discipline of economics as a guide to economic development.

This chapter provides a historical overview of the economic and intellectual factors that shaped the primary concerns and discussions in Ottoman economic thinking in the final decades of the empire. The first section is a concise reassessment of pre-modern Ottoman economic institutions and economic thought in its global historical context. The second section deals with the economic and social change as a result of the challenge of capitalist modernity and the integration of the Ottoman Empire to this new global world order. Finally, the last section provides an overview of the evolution of Ottoman economic literature until the Hamidian era, and the emergence of main fault lines in Ottoman economic thought—which were to shape economic thought and policies in the last decades of the empire and the early decades of the Turkish Republic.

Ottoman economy and economic mind before the birth of economics

Historians of economic thought usually consider the publication of Adam Smith's *An Inquiry into the Nature and Causes of the Wealth of Nations* (1776) the birth of modern economics as an independent field of social inquiry. Diane Wood, in her *Medieval Economic Thought*, notes that her title is actually a misnomer, since it did not exist.[2] This, of course, does not imply that economic ideas did not exist before the modern era. Yet in the pre-modern world, economic matters were examined within the boundaries of theology and philosophy, and not as distinct phenomena with their own governing rules.

This is the theoretical side of the story. On the practical level, however, agents in the marketplace acted according to implicit everyday rules of economic life, which might conflict with ideals and principles determined by theology. Such conflicts at times produced severe restrictions on business practices—as in the case of the ban on usury in both Christian and Muslim traditions. Market agents, however, devised alternative ways to overcome legal and religious limitations and to expand and protect their space of maneuver. In the context of medieval Islamic economy, for example, merchants had recourse to *hiyal* whenever theological rulings created an obstacle for certain economic transactions.[3] *Hiyal* were the use of legal devices and the legal literature to circumvent Islamic prohibitions on certain economic activities (e.g., *riba* or usuary). The use of such practices was so widespread that there were lawyers who specialized in *hiyal*.[4] At the market level, therefore, practical economic knowledge ruled, at times defying the restrictions of theory.

Conflicts between economic theory and practice was not a result of theorists' isolation from and ignorance of economic practice. On the contrary, many prominent medieval Muslim jurists and theologians who wrote on economic issues, such as Ibn Taymiyyah (1263–1328) and al-Maqrizi (1364–1442), served as *muhtasib*s.[5] *Muhtasib* was an official local administrator who was in charge with the orderly functioning of the market in both moral-religious and economic standards. He controlled weights and measures, prices, quality standards, and even the overall cleanliness of the market place. *Muhtasib* assumed a supervisory role and was in close contact with local religious authorities in his responsibilities. Pre-modern Islamic economic thought, therefore, was considerably buttressed by the theorists' practical experience and concrete observations in the market place, as well as their meticulous studies on the scripture.[6]

Having mentioned pre-modern Islamic economic theories and practices, it should be noted that we are still far from having an adequate understanding of the dynamics of pre-modern Islamic economic thinking in its various geographical and institutional variations.[7] Mainstream historiography of economic thought is still largely Eurocentric, and non-Western traditions of economic analyses continue to remain in the margins of the scholarship on the global historical evolution and transmission of economic ideas. In a similar vein, our knowledge of pre-modern Ottoman economic thought is still very limited.[8] Based on limited research, however, we know that the political administration of the Ottoman Empire in the "classical age" (*c.*1300–1600) was usually business-friendly and economy-conscious:[9]

> Following a very old tradition of Middle Eastern states, the Ottoman government must have believed that merchants and artisans were indispensable in creating a new metropolis. It used every means to attract and settle them in the new capitals. By granting tax exemptions and immunities the imperial government encouraged them to come and settle or in a summary fashion forcibly exiled them to the capital.[10]

Moreover, through the *waqf* (pious foundation) system, the state ensured the establishment and maintenance of economic institutions that served local and trans-regional markets, such as *bedestan*s, caravanserais, and bazaars.[11] The *waqf* system did not only provide (market-related or otherwise) public services, they were also active economic agents in various capacities. Besides, they served to provide *hiyal* opportunities for capital accumulation and circulation in the Ottoman economy. The Ottoman State exploited the Islamic law to make sure that it was the sole owner of all property (in the name of God). The central state used the practice of confiscation to stop alternative dynasties appear through capital accumulation. The state could—and did—confiscate family fortunes, especially following the death of the head of the family who acquired his wealth during official service.[12] Although all property could belong to the state, the state, according to the Islamic law, had no right to touch *waqf* assets under normal conditions. This opened a major window of opportunity for capital accumulation and bequeathing accumulated wealth to subsequent generations. Founding *waqf*s, therefore, became an indispensable way for the local and central elites to bypass political and bureaucratic restrictions on capital accumulation, and keep it over generations through the control of the board of trustees by family members. Another exceptional and controversial role that *waqf*s played was in the case of the "cash *waqf*s." These institutions lent money on interest, on the principle of using the resulting profit in charity. The controversial aspect of this operation was that usury was strictly prohibited by the Islamic law. Where ordinary Muslims could not (in theory) even think about it, these Islamic-law based institutions were operating on the verges of defying this very prohibition.[13] *Waqf*s, therefore, played an important role in the everyday working of the economy, thanks to their central role in capital accumulation and circulation in the empire, well into the nineteenth century.

Since the state treasury depended upon taxes, including those on trade, the primary economic concern of the state was to protect and expand commercial activity within the empire. A careful reading of Ottoman historical and political treatises from the sixteenth century, for example, shows that the Ottoman elites were fully aware of internal and external economic challenges, although they did not conceptualize their ideas in modern economic terms.[14] Moreover, the bureaucratic and military classes were not aloof from commercial life, as the classic theoretical division (i.e., the *erkân-ı erbaʿa*—religious, commercial, military, and agricultural classes) of Ottoman society might deceptively imply. From the early days of Islam, the Muslim political elite—including the prophet himself—had been involved in commerce in various degrees, and the members of the Ottoman military class were no exception.

Rüstem Pasha (1500–61), the well-known grand vizier of Süleyman the Magnificent, for example, was a rich man thanks to his many business transactions in addition to rent revenue.[15] An outstanding example from the seventeenth-century was a later grand vizier (1653–54) Derviş Mehmed Pasha (d. 1655). Before assuming this highest position, he served as the governor of many provinces, including Damascus, Aleppo, Diyarbakir, Mosul, and Baghdad, from 1636 to 1652, and during his term he was also an active and considerably rich entrepreneur.[16] In addition to his many commercial transaction within the region, he imported—through his network of commercial agents—luxury goods from India and sold it in the domestic markets. In his long-distance commercial enterprises he did not fail to enjoy customs duties privileges as a high-ranking official. In addition to commerce, he was also an entrepreneur in large-scale grain production whose product was processed in his own bakeries.[17] It is worth noting that, "many Ottoman officials [of the age] subscribed to the Ibn Khaldunian notion that the ruler and his entourage should not engage in commerce or similar money-making activities."[18] Obviously, this theoretical advice did not stop entrepreneurially-minded Ottoman elite to put their business energy and ambitions in action, while exploiting their official privileges. All in all, the Ottoman state and its central and local members had held active roles in monitoring of and participating in the economic sphere until the end.

With regard to the main principles that shaped pre-nineteenth-century Ottoman economic policy, Mehmet Genç's well-known tripartite model provides a neat summary: provisionism, fiscalism, and traditionalism[19] Provisionism refers to prioritizing the provision of cities, and especially the capital to secure order and stability throughout the empire.[20] Since supply and price fluctuations in basic commodities can lead to social and political upheavals, Ottoman statesmen gave priority to securing the provision of the political centers over other economic concerns. Since supplying markets, at times, necessitated putting limits on exports whereas encouraging imports, this principle could stand as an opposite to mercantilism. This, however, does not imply that the Ottoman statesmen ignored fiscal balances. On the contrary, fiscalism, as Mehmet Genç put it, constituted the second principle that shaped Ottoman economic policies. It refers to the priority of fiscal policy in economic decisions, thereby taking every measure to maximize state revenues and minimize expenditures in order to keep state finances as strong as possible.[21] The third principle was traditionalism, which had two dimensions. First, keeping the socio-economic structure stable without any substantial horizontal and vertical mobility among social classes; and second, not deviating from the traditional socio-economic principles defined by the *shari'a* and the customary law.[22]

Although the Ottoman state had usually business-friendly policies for fiscal reasons, preserving the socio-economic—thereby political—status quo through social immobility constituted a conspicuous objective of Ottoman economic policies.[23] It is important to note also that the Ottomans were not alone in such concerns. The same principle marked medieval Christian economic thought as well.[24] All in all,

> medieval Arab-Islamic and Latin-European Scholastics never visualized solutions to economic problems strictly through the functioning of the free market, 'invisible hand' approach. Administrative control through public policy and social intervention was always advocated in order to ensure social well-being and common good.[25]

Guilds, in the Ottoman Empire as well as in other European empires, was a reliable institution to ensure the functioning of the market according to the abovementioned principles.[26] Craftsmen operated under strict regulations. Starting from the initial enrollment to the guild as an apprentice to being accepted as a master in particular branch of industry, everything ran under strict guidelines and continuous monitoring. Once in business, the production process was closely supervised by the guild administration from the procurement of input materials to the quality and prices of the final products.

In the latter half of the eighteenth century, Ottoman guilds went through a radical transformation process, particularly as a result of the *gedik* system. "By the dawn of the nineteenth century *gedik* had come to mean the right to practice a particular trade at a specific work premise equipped with the means and tools necessary to practice that trade."[27] The *gedik* certificates allowed craftsmen to operate relatively independently and free from the guild restrictions. Moreover, since these certificates could be bought and sold freely, strict and hierarchical control of guilds on the entrance into the market were partly abolished with this new institution, thereby paving the way for a transformation of the urban manufacturing system.[28]

One aspect of the eighteenth-century transformation was "the 'militarization' or the 'bureaucratization' of the Ottoman economy" with "the widespread penetration of the lower-ranking members of the military into areas of economic activity."[29] The symbiotic relationship between the guilds and the janissaries were consolidated in time, as business partnerships provided the former with bureaucratic advantages, while the latter benefitted financially. In the early nineteenth century, this alliance constituted the main resistance to the opening of the Ottoman market to European (particularly British) manufactures.

The Ottoman economy was never closed or self-sufficient. On the contrary, international trade was always vital for the provisioning of the cities, and a major source of taxation for the government. The British Industrial Revolution, however, changed the quality of commercial relations between Western Europe and the Ottoman Empire. As the British manufactures and capital began to flow into the domestic market, the Ottoman economy was gradually integrated into the new international division of labor, whose rules set by European industrial and commercial capitalism. Although the Janissary-guild alliance tried to resist to this trend, this resistance survived until the abolition of the janissary corps in 1826.[30] The loss of their Janissary allies jeopardized guilds' resistance to the further opening of the Ottoman market to European capital.[31] The next and more decisive step towards liberalization came in 1838 with the Anglo-Ottoman Convention, which eliminated state monopolies and removed all official barriers to European merchants.

The challenge of capitalist modernity and economic reform

In the early decades of the nineteenth century, two factors caused the waning of the three-pillared system of economic policy. First, the military and economic superiority of the Western European rivals led Ottoman elites to question military, political, and economic institutions of the empire. Second, Ottomans met modern (post-Smithian) economics as a discipline set of principles which explained the rise of Europe and the relative backwardness of the empire in an economy-centered age.

As it is stated in the first known Ottoman treatise on economics from the 1830s, economics offered new and "scientific" rules for success in the new global order. In old ages, according to the author, military might, and therefore conquests and booty, was the basis of political power for any state. In the new age, however, the welfare of the nation and the economic development of the country constituted the basis for both military and political might.[32] As a result, traditionalism was the first—of the three traditional economic principles—to disappear, while reformism, the idea that marked the last century of the empire, gained prominence. Provisionalism was also gradually replaced by liberal ideas. So much so that even state industries, established partly with provisionalist concerns in the 1830s, were not protected behind customs walls, and were left to operate in free market both domestically and internationally.[33] This continued until the rise of protectionism in the Ottoman Empire, as well as in Europe, in the last decades of the century. Fiscalism, however, sustained its role at various degrees in shaping Ottoman economic policies thanks to the never-ending budgetary crises of the central government until the end of the empire.[34]

At the turn of the nineteenth century, the Ottoman Empire had a population of an estimated 30 million, which was remarkably diverse in ethnic and denominational terms. The overwhelming majority of the population was rural and illiterate.[35] The Ottoman economy was predominantly agricultural, and agricultural production was dominated by self-sufficient small producers who had limited access to markets largely due to the scarcity of roads and means of transport.[36] These characteristics did not change radically for most of Anatolia, while the population of major coastal cities swelled as a result of increasing integration into European capitalist world-economy and the resultant boom in manufacturing and agricultural sectors, especially in the last quarter of the century.[37]

In legal terms, the state was the sole owner of all arable land—until the issue of the Ottoman Land Code of 1858 which legalized private property on land. State control over production and trade of agricultural surplus and taxes on peasantry (such as the tithe) were vital sources for the imperial order, while constituting further constraints on the development of independent agricultural enterprise and development.[38]

Following the abolition of the Janissaries in 1826 and the signing of the Anglo-Ottoman Commercial Convention in 1838, the Tanzimat period (*c.*1839–76) witnessed the efforts of the central government to change the traditional self-sufficient and heavily controlled structure towards a market-oriented economy. As it is clearly seen in the cases of the two leading statesmen of the Tanzimat, Âlî Pasha (1815–71) and Keçecizade Fuad Pasha (1814–69), Smithian economic principles played a key role in this transition. In their separate political testaments, which are submitted directly to Sultan Abdülaziz (1861–76), both former grand viziers emphasized the importance of private enterprise for economic development, and gave their accounts of how they pursued liberal policies during their terms.[39] These documents testifies to the fact that *laissez-faire* principles was very influential in Ottoman political and economic policy-making in the former half of the century.

Along with the abolition of monopolies and many restrictions on trade, the importation of new agricultural production technologies and the production of certain market-oriented commodities (such as cotton) were promoted through tax exemptions and other financial incentives. An agricultural bureaucracy was established to determine and manage agricultural policies as well as coordinate efforts for agricultural development.[40] For example, a Commission for Industry and Agriculture (*Sanâyi ve Ziraat Meclisi*) was formed in 1838, and it was followed by the establishment of a separate Agricultural Commission (*Ziraat Meclisi*) in 1843.[41] Another important attempt to support Ottoman agricultural producers came in the 1860s with the foundation of the District Funds (*Memleket Sandıkları*) in the Balkan provinces, which were to evolve into the Agricultural Bank (*Ziraat Bankası*) in 1888. These funds and later the bank aimed at providing producers with cheap credit.[42] The gradual liberalization of the landholding regime accompanied these developments in Ottoman agriculture. The Ottoman

Land Code of 1858 provided legal status for private property in land, thereby validating (if not initiating) the shift of the Ottoman economy towards a more market-oriented structure.[43] By legally recognizing the change from the state restrictions on the ownership and use of land to a system of private property and private entrepreneurship, the Land Code testified to the increasing decentralization of economic power in the empire.[44]

Regarding the industry, the conventional narratives of Ottoman economic history, starting with that of the Young Ottomans in the 1860s, have argued that the nineteenth century was the economic—as well as political—decline. According to this view, the opening to European industrial goods paved the way for the collapse of traditional Ottoman industries and to the foreign dominance in the Ottoman economy. However, the picture was much more complex than what the decline paradigm suggests.

> Broadly speaking, manufacturing in the Ottoman Empire and Europe often worked in intimately integrated and interwoven production networks. Manufacturers in both regions not only competed, borrowed and copied from one another, but they also provided the other with semi-processed materials for finishing. In this view, nineteenth-century Ottoman imports of European factory-made yarns and dyestuffs were a continuation of the long-standing relationship between the two manufacturing economies.[45]

As a result of the increasing integration in the nineteenth century, we observe a variety of outcomes in Ottoman industries, rather than a single ubiquitous trend.[46] Some traditional sectors declined significantly as a result of international competition, especially in the period of 1820–50. Yet, those which adapted to the demands of the international markets thrived,[47] especially after the 1870s.[48] It is important to note, however, that international competition struck many fatal blows to large-scale industrialization efforts in general. Efforts of establishing modern factories failed as a result of cut-throat competition with European rivals.[49] In addition to such external factors, many domestic prerequisites for industrialization were missing. Economic infrastructure was very weak, indigenous entrepreneurial and managerial skills (in modern industrial terms) were almost non-existent, and skilled labor was very limited. These adverse domestic conditions and a fierce international competition not only rendered industrialization efforts mostly fruitless, but also discouraged the state as well as Ottoman entrepreneurs from making large-scale investments in manufacturing sectors.[50] By the 1860s, Ottoman industrialization efforts had already begun to run out of steam.[51]

Regarding the development of the economy, a major concern that preoccupied the Ottomans and European investors alike was the lack of solid transportation network. According to many contemporary observers, the lack of roads was the primary reason for the economic underdevelopment of the Ottoman economy. In 1857, Ahmed Vefik Efendi (later Pasha), during a conversation with the well-known British economist of the mid-nineteenth century, Nassau Senior, complains about "the state of the country" as follows:

> What we most want are roads. We have nothing but tracks filled with stones in our towns, so that it takes you an hour to walk a mile, and, in the country, rocky, stony, or boggy, according to the ground. Except in the immediate neighbourhood of our towns, the land is not half cultivated, because the peasant cannot carry the produce to market. He produces, therefore, only for his own consumption. He is truly a proletaire; he contributes to the population of the country, but not to its wealth.[52]

Thirty years later, in 1886, we read similar observations about the reasons for the "commercial decline" of the Ottoman Empire in the pages of the *Levant Herald*:

> Any rational being who knows the main lines of trade questions could in a week draw up a report which would respond to the solicitude of the Sultan, whose earnest desire for the commercial development of the country is proved beyond all question. If we had had to prepare it, we would simply have said: "Your Majesty possesses territory rich in all that nature has to give; good soil, good climate, endless variety of commodities, a docile and industrious population. Bu in these modern days of competition, production goes for nothing, unless the produce has the means of conveyance at ready command. The producer produces, but his produce is worthless to him unless he can sell it at a profit, and to do so he must have the means of taking it to market. One thing, and one thing only, will animate native industry, and that one thing is means of transport such as other countries possess. If that means of is provided Ottoman trade will revive; until it is provided Ottoman trade must languish and if it is not provided Ottoman trade will die."[53]

The problem of transportation infrastructure as an aspect of economic development did not remain confined to newspaper pages and private discussions among intellectuals and statesmen. Almost every official memorandum about the economic conditions of the empire includes ideas similar to those that had appeared in the *Levant Herald*. For example, one of the advisers to the sultan, Müşir Şakir Pasha (1838–99), notes in a memorandum he submitted in 1890 that building roads would save the empire from the current economic crisis that "threatens both the public wealth (*servet-i umûmiye*) and [the central government's] budgetary balance (*muvazene-i mâliye*)."[54] Therefore, he adds, improving the transportation network was an issue of vital importance for the empire.[55]

Meanwhile the fiscal situation of the empire went from worse to worst. The comprehensive reform program, especially in the Tanzimat era, brought about major institutional rebuilding in the military and bureaucracy, and consumed huge amounts of resources. Meanwhile, wars (especially the Crimean War of 1853–56, and the Russo-Ottoman War of 1876–78), armed rebellions and independence movements stroke heavy blows to the fiscal situation of the empire. Besides, economic institutional reforms, and especially large-scale industrialization efforts also necessitated significant amounts of money. In time, the modernization process expanded to encompass all aspects of the political and social spheres—including visual dramatization of modernization such as the building of expensive palaces (like the Dolmabahçe Palace in Istanbul)—thereby requiring more and more financial resources every day. However the Ottoman state neither possessed these amounts in its treasury, nor did it have an effective governmental financial infrastructure to collect them.[56]

Starting in the early 1850s, Ottoman statesmen had no choice but to resort to debt. Although Ottoman statesmen did manage to find cash in the short-run through external borrowing, it was principally used for "covering [chronic] budget deficits, but not to improve the productive capacity of the country."[57] As a result, just as in other cases in the region (such as Tunisia and Egypt), and as the Young Ottomans had anticipated almost a decade before,[58] the Ottoman state could not escape from a debt spiral, losing its financial independence.[59] In 1875, the Ottoman government declared default, and in 1881, a new institution was established by its creditors to govern the Ottoman debt: the Ottoman Public Debt Administration (OPDA).[60] The *raison d'être* of this institution was the administration of the economic resources of the empire to secure payments to the creditors.[61] The administration channeled various revenues of the state directly to the coffers of the creditors as debt repayment. In addition to its economic implications, the existence of the OPDA signified loss of fiscal—and eventually political—independence and increasing foreign economic and financial control in the empire. The Tanzimat era (1839–76), thereby, left fiscal collapse, economic and political dependence, and a failed industrialization experience to the Hamidian era (1876–1909), and this legacy was to shape economic concerns and policies in the last decades of the empire.

Economics in the Ottoman Empire

The beginnings (c.1776–1850)

Economics as an independent field of social inquiry is a product of the nineteenth century, like other discipline of modern social sciences. The separation of economics from philosophy in this era is not a result only of the evolution of scientific inquiry. It is also an outcome of the separation of the economy from other social relations under free-market capitalism. As Karl Polanyi argues, the economic sphere in pre-capitalist societies had been embedded in the wider social sphere, whereas in the capitalist society, the market subordinates social and political relations.[62] With this analysis, Polanyi challenges Adam Smith's theses on capitalism and human history, which heavily influenced nineteenth-century political, social, as well as economic thought.[63] According to Polanyi, neither was a self-regulating market a ubiquitous reality in the pre-capitalist world, nor was capitalism a natural phase in the evolution of human societies. He asserts that both are rather anomalies in the evolution of human societies. Accordingly, he emphasizes the distinctive economy-centered characteristic of the new global capitalist system that emerged in the early nineteenth century.[64]

Adam Smith was not the first intellectual who wrote on economic affairs, but he was a "system builder."[65] In other words, he systematized the already-accumulated economic knowledge of his age and presented it as an independent field of study.[66] Moreover, unlike the Mercantilists and Physiocrats who preceded him,[67] Smith's economics was not a science of state administration which aimed at chiefly effective management of state finances. In the same vein, the revolutionary aspect of Smithian economics is that it considers the economy as an independent sphere of social relations with its own rules and dynamics governed by chaotic processes of individual human action. The unintended consequence of these dynamics is the self-regulating market and the invisible hand of the market mechanism. His followers, if not Smith himself, used these notions to claim that external interference (state intervention) disturbs the natural equilibrium of this system, and should thus be avoided at all costs.[68] This idea was to become the main subject of confrontation among economists and politicians of all countries from the early nineteenth century onward.

After Adam Smith's death in 1790, the influence of his magnum opus expanded in Europe through many translations into major languages of the region. The Ottoman Empire, in this case, was an exception. The four volume *Wealth of Nations* was never translated into any Ottoman languages before the empire came to an end in 1922. It first appeared in Greek in 1935, in Turkish in 1948, and in Arabic in 1959.[69] His influence, however, reached the empire through catechisms of his work in French, the *lingua franca* of the age. Ottomans visiting European countries, as well as Europeans living the empire also contributed to the cultural and intellectual exchange in this sense. Regarding the last point, it is important to note that tracing only the publications on economics would be misleading to understand the introduction of Smithian ideas into the Ottoman intellectual spheres.

Although not an impact of Adam Smith, concerns about financial and economic issues, separate from, but directly linked to, political problems, haunted the Ottoman elite, when economics was being shaped as a separate discipline, and economic thinking itself shaping the *Weltanschauung* of modernity at the dawn of the nineteenth century. In the last decade of the eighteenth century, the reformist sultan, Selim III (r. 1761–1808), asked several statesmen to pen advisory memoranda about the pressing problems of the empire. The proposals came in two main categories: "those advocating a return to the practices of the golden age of the Ottoman Empire, and those embracing reform through the emulation of contemporary Europe."[70] Some of these statesmen, such as Süleyman Penah Efendi, Tatarcık Abdullah Molla and Mehmed Şerif Efendi, put the emphasis on financial issues, and suggested a systematic and comprehensive reform in the financial and economic administration of the Ottoman state.[71]

These memoranda made such an important impact that even some sentences in these documents were copied in the new financial laws and statutes.[72] Moreover, having received these memoranda, Selim III issued numerous imperial decrees with a purely economic content, most of which reflected an implicit liberal approach.[73] All three statesmen, mentioned above, suggested a systematic reorganization of state finances and reforms in traditional economic institutions (e.g., *timar*), thereby introducing the notion—if not the concept—of economic development for the first time into the Ottoman state tradition.[74] Although their suggestions included the importance of learning from European successes, their works were not informed by any theoretical study of economics. This, however, would change soon as the Ottoman elite came to realize that the new Eurocentric world-order was an economy-centered one, and economics held the keys to understand its dynamics.

The first works drawing attention to the economic underpinnings of European advancement were the Ottoman diplomatic reports and travelogues in the late eighteenth and the early nineteenth centuries. During the reign of Selim III, permanent Ottoman missions were opened in London, Paris, and Berlin. The next generation of statesmen received their early training in these embassies.[75] Ottoman ambassadors submitted numerous reports to Istanbul including their observations on new economic and political institutions developing in European countries.[76] For example, Ebubekir Ratib Efendi, who was sent to Vienna in 1791, had an important responsibility in addition to his diplomatic duties: He was to examine Austrian institutions and submit reports about them directly to the sultan.[77] During the reign of Mahmud II (r. 1808–39), who followed Selim III's reform attempts, Sâdık Rıfat Pasha (1807–57) submitted more systematic treatises on Europe, again from Vienna. Sâdık Rıfat Pasha was the Ottoman ambassador to Austria during the second half of the 1830s and one of the most influent statesmen and intellectuals of the Tanzimat era. Especially his "Avrupa'nın Ahvâline Dâ'ir Risâle" (A Treatise on the Conditions in Europe, 1837) provided the Ottoman elite with a new perspective on Europe and the question of reform in the Ottoman Empire.[78] Moreover, economic matters held an important place in his analyses of European ascendancy in the modern age.[79] He was one of the early champions of the idea that in the modern age wealth and welfare of a nation rested on economic dynamism of a preferably large population, rather than military conquests and booty as in the old times. Therefore, he claimed, the government should provide agricultural, industrial, and commercial entrepreneurs with economic freedom and security as a prerequisite for a prosperous country and a powerful state.[80] Sâdık Rıfat Pasha was one of the early figures who emphasized the importance of economic development, based on liberal principles, within the broader question of reform. However, he was not alone. Ottoman political and intellectual atmosphere in the 1820s and especially 1830s was dominated by economic liberalism.

The first economic publications appeared in the Ottoman public sphere with the introduction of a new medium of mass communication in the empire: newspapers. In the 1820s, *Le Spectateur Oriental* (later *Le Smyrneen*), which was published in İzmir (Smyrna), included articles on economic matters. Especially after Alexander Blacque (Blacque Bey) took over the newspaper, it became an important channel of transmission for liberal economic ideas.[81] In 1831, Blacque Bey was assigned by the sultan to publish the French edition of the first Ottoman newspaper, *Takvîm-i Vekâyi'*, under the name *Le Moniteur Ottoman*.[82] *Takvîm-i*

Vekâyi' was the official gazette of the state, and it included documents and declarations issued by the government. The main difference between the Ottoman and French editions was the unofficial section of the latter, which became the main intellectual venue for economic liberalism in the Ottoman Empire.[83] Blacque, on these pages, defended liberalization of the Ottoman economy, writing against monopolies and political interventions at both the central and local levels. Considering that he filled this position under the auspices of the sultan, and that *Le Moniteur Ottoman* aimed primarily at foreign audience both in the empire and in Europe, it is safe to assume that Blacque's ideas reflected the central government's expression of willingness to embrace economic liberalism and to integrate the Ottoman economy with European markets.[84]

Blacque, in his efforts to promote economic liberalism in the Ottoman Empire, was followed by a Scottish diplomat and writer, David Urquhart (1805–77). Urquhart served at the British mission in Istanbul in the 1830s. During his term, he also wrote a book on the economic conditions and political organization of the empire, entitled *Turkey and Its Resources*.[85] In this book, along with his articles in *Le Moniteur Ottoman*, he suggested that the Ottoman Empire should undertake the role assigned to it by the international division of labor. In other words, the Ottoman economy would best be a supplier of raw materials and an importer of industrial goods. The idea was obviously based on the Ricardian theory of comparative advantage,[86] and the same policy was promoted by the British economists and policy-makers to all peripheral countries of the age. Moreover, from the early nineteenth century on, "Britain's agenda was to sign free-trade agreements with as many periphery countries as possible in order to gain foreign markets for their manufactures. The 1838 Anglo-Ottoman Commercial Convention was one such agreement."[87] Urquhart's theses, therefore, reflected the global concerns of British *laissez-faire* economic theory and policy-making, and aimed to provide a theoretical basis for economic liberalization in the Ottoman economy before the 1838 Convention.

In the early 1840s, William Churchill, the publisher of the newspaper *Ceride-i Havadis*, played an important role in promoting liberal theses about the Ottoman Empire. Churchill ignited the long-lasting discussion of "agriculture vs. industry" in Ottoman economic thought, regarding which one to specialize in for the Ottoman economy to develop under the international capitalist division of labor.[88] From then on, discussions on the strategy of economic development in the Ottoman Empire moved along two interconnected axes until the end of the empire: "agricultural vs. industrialization development" and "liberalism vs. protectionism." Churchill, until his death in 1846, published many articles to argue for Ottoman specialization in agricultural production and adoption of liberal trade policies in the empire, thereby contributing significantly to the development of economic liberalism in the empire.[89] In addition to contributing to intellectual discussions about these issues, a major motivation for Churchill seems to be influencing and encouraging Ottoman policy-makers to further liberalize the Ottoman economy.[90]

It is important to note that the liberal view which promoted Ottoman specialization in agriculture—as required by the theory of comparative advantages—

was not against industrialization per se. However, unlike protectionists, who believed in the urgency of industrialization and the necessity of state's active involvement and control to accelerate the process, liberals believed that interventionist and protectionist policies harmed the economy more in the long run.[91] This debate was not specific to Ottoman economic thought, but a reflection of the well-known controversy, which marked developmental strategies especially in the capitalist periphery in the nineteenth and twentieth centuries. As an example from Russia, during the same decades, Admiral N. S. Mordvinov (1754–1845), an influential economist in Russia and a long-term president (1823–40) of the President of the Free Economic Society,[92] criticized Russian overspecialization in agriculture as the primary obstacle to development. He suggested, instead, infant industry protection as the right strategy for development in the case of Russia.[93] Interestingly enough, Mordvinov was a liberal. He studied in England in the age of Adam Smith and Jeremy Bentham, and was influenced by both.[94] Nevertheless, his most influential work, *Some Considerations on Manufactures in Russia and of the Tariff* (1815),[95] preceded Friedrich List's *Das Nationale System* (1841) in its formulation of infant industry protection as an effective strategy of development in the capitalist periphery. This seemingly conflict in Mordvinov's economic views is a reflection of various dilemmas that intellectuals in the capitalist periphery had to face in the nineteenth century (and also the twentieth, for that matter) as they tried to apply European originated theories in their own countries. As we shall see later, similar ambivalences were observed in Ottoman economic thought as well, as the Ottoman followers of List, such as Ahmed Midhat and Akyiğitzade Musa, emphasized their belief in Adam Smith's *laissez-faire* approach in theory, but in practice, they added, the Ottoman economy needed a protectionist period until it attained enough competitive power vis-à-vis rivaling industrial economies.

New economic ideas penetrated the Ottoman intellectual sphere also through direct personal influence and contact, as we observe in the cases of David Urquhart and William Churchill. With increasing European interest in the "Orient," many European intellectuals as well as diplomats traveled in the Middle East and transmitted new ideas into the Ottoman intellectual atmosphere. The well-known British economist and the first professor of political economy at Oxford (1825–30), Nassau William Senior (1790–1864), was one of them.[96] Senior's published accounts of his travels and conversations include many interesting discussions about the economic policies of the empire with Ottoman statesmen such as Ahmed Vefik Efendi (1823–91)—who was to become a prominent figure in Ottoman modernization.[97] What is obvious in Senior's accounts is that there were Ottoman statesmen who were acquainted with modern economic theories and aware of debates on economic policies in Europe. These statesmen approached their country's problems using the methods and terminology of economics, and sometimes they even challenged an Oxford professor of economics on such matters. We read in Senior's accounts, for example, that the Minister of Commerce and Development [Hekim] İsmail Pasha (1807–60) opposed Senior's liberal arguments with references to successful protectionist trade policies in

France.[98] Similarly, Senior's notes about Ahmed Vefik Efendi's explanations on the main economic problems of the empire, ranging from inflation to monopolies, testify to his awareness of economic theory of his age.[99]

Until the 1850s, modern economic theories and ideas were transmitted to the Empire in a rather unsystematic way mostly through occasional newspaper articles. Nevertheless, it seems that Ottoman interest in economics began to produce some treatises in Turkish as early as in the 1830s. For example, an anonymous 86-page manuscript located in the National Library of Austria, entitled *Tedbir-i Ûmran-ı Mülkî* (Administration of Public Prosperity), is the earliest known Ottoman study on economics, with a content and style somewhat resembling European examples. The publication date is unknown, but İlber Ortaylı claims that it is *c.*1833.[100] Since the author cites a French source dated 1829,[101] and discusses the necessity of establishing a council of commerce (*Meclis-i Ticâret*) in the Ottoman Empire,[102] which was put into practice in *c.*1839,[103] it seems safe to assume that the manuscript belongs to the 1830s. A quick glance at the content (especially its comprising—almost exclusively—of domestic examples) and discursive properties of the text hints that the author penned an original work, referring to some European sources, rather than translating or adapting a specific text. Although the main objective of the work is introducing this new scientific discipline to the Ottoman elites, the main motivation of the author seems to be providing useful knowledge for state administration, with an eye on confronting the debilitating military challenge of the European powers. The author describes the importance of this discipline with a long discussion on the recent game-changing military technologies and skills that gave the Europeans an upper hand, and the central importance of financing these advances with the help of this new discipline.[104] Unfortunately we do not yet have any information about the impact of this work, but it surely constitutes a good example that reflects the initial motivation for the Ottomans for studying economics as a science of state administration.

The 1850s: first books on economics

Despite his indirect impact in the Ottoman intellectual sphere, Adam Smith's *The Wealth of Nations* was not translated into Turkish until 1948,[105] and even then it appeared as an abridged edition. The reason for not translating *The Wealth of Nations* in full was purely pragmatic and was simply caused by market conditions. Above all, the market for books was small due to very low literacy rate.[106] As Su'ad Bey argued in the introduction to his translation (1888) of Prosper Rambaud's *Précis élémentaire d'économie politique*, Ottoman readership was not interested in "long and detailed studies."[107] And Adam Smith's four-volume treatise was a good example of such studies. The urge for modernization led—both elite and middle class—Ottoman intellectuals to consult more readable and practical manuals, rather than delving into highly elaborate theoretical discussions.

The second treatise on economics in Turkish—following *Tedbîr-i ʿÜmran-i Mülkî*—is an adaptation by Serandi Arşizen (1809–1873) and Aleko Sucu (or

Suço) of a study by the Italian economist, Pellegrino Rossi (1787–1848).[108] It is entitled *Tasarrufat-ı Mülkiye* (*Political Economy*).[109] According to the introduction of the book, Serandi Arşizen, who was a physician and a former professor at the Mekteb-i Tıbbiye-i Adliye-i Şâhâne (The Imperial School of Medicine), used Rossi's work (probably the French translation of his *Curso de Economia Politica*, 1840) as a model for his own book.[110] Arşizen wrote the book in French, and then Aleko Sucu, a translator at the Ottoman Translation Bureau (*Tercüme Odası*),[111] translated it into Turkish.[112] Neither the French, nor the Turkish edition was published as a book, and both remained as manuscripts.[113] According to Fındıkoğlu, it is based on Arşizen's lectures at the Mekteb-i Tıbbiye-i Adliye-i Şâhâne.[114] The exact date of the publication is not known, but it seems to precede Sehak Abru's translation (*c.*1851) of Jean-Baptiste Say's (1767–1832) *Catéchisme d'économie politique*.[115]

Following Arşizen's adaptation, another official at the *Tercüme Odası*, Sehak Abru (1825–1900),[116] translated Say's economic best-seller, *Catéchisme d'économie politique* (1815). Shortly after its publication, Say's book achieved considerable success throughout the world and was translated into many languages, including Turkish. It became the classic compendium of Smithian political economy in the early nineteenth century. Say's popularity as an economist, starting with his *Traité d'économie politique* (1803), originated from his ability to put Smith's work in a more accessible form. His Ottoman translator Sehak Abru notes this feature of Say's book in his introduction by saying, "it is very rare to find an author, like Mr. Say, who can define the principles of aforementioned science [economics] with such an economy of words."[117] Rather than translating the book faithfully, Sehak Abru actually re-wrote it. First, he changed the format of the book. Instead of the original dialogical format, Sehak Abru used straight prose.[118] Second, the translator Ottomanized the examples. For instance, a French businessman in the original book became an Ottoman merchant who exports grain to Marseilles and imports coffee in exchange.[119] Third, Sehak Abru excluded some parts of the original text in his translation, most probably due to political concerns. For example he ignores some potentially sensitive and controversial Enlightenment-era principles like the power of humanity over nature and rejection of non-scientific (i.e., religious) thoughts and beliefs.[120]

It is essential to emphasize two conspicuous characteristics of early Ottoman economic literature: First, as the name of Say's book suggests, the Ottomans preferred translating compendia rather than magnum opuses such as Adam Smith's *The Wealth of Nations*. Second, the translators behaved very pragmatically, and they adapted the texts in terms of both format and content instead of remaining faithful to the original texts. Obviously, their sole aim was to provide a toolbox of a modern discipline to their fellow countrymen to be used on the path of salvation for the empire. Presenting exemplary behavior in terms of any sort of academic and intellectual ethics—in today's standards—was not high on their agenda; therefore they altered their sources without any hesitation. These two manifestations of Ottoman modernist pragmatism continued to mark the Ottoman intellectual sphere in the following decades.

Diffusion and popularization of economic knowledge (c.1860–76)

After some initial sporadic attempts, publication on economic matters gained momentum in the second half of the century. The 1860s came with significant developments in both the quality and quantity of publications on economics, along with some surprises. The first surprise in Ottoman economic literature was a book entitled *İlm Tedbiri Milk: "The Science of the Administration of a State," or an Essay on Political Economy*. The rest of the title page of this book reads, "in Turkish, being the first ever written in that language, by Charles Wells, Turkish Prizeman of King's College, London."[121] Although it was not the first book on economics written in Turkish, as the author claims, it was definitely one of the earliest examples of economic literature in this language. Wells' book is a study of economic history and thought, which was the dominant style of the era in the footsteps of Smith's *The Wealth of Nations*. It starts and ends with a general overview of the economic history of human civilization, while the rest of the book provides brief explanations about certain economic concepts such as barter, wealth, capital, paper money, taxation, and national debt.[122] We do not have any clues about the impact of this book yet, but we do know that Wells himself was in contact with the Ottoman elite, and he contributed to the study of the Ottoman Empire in many ways. He published articles on the empire in both English and Ottoman publications, and he was also the editor of the second edition of the well-known *Redhouse's Turkish Dictionary*. Thus, he was a recognized figure in the eyes of the Ottoman intellectuals of the era.[123] Based on this, we can safely assume that his work and economic ideas were known among the Ottoman elite.

The 1860s witnessed increasing efforts to popularize economic knowledge by a new generation of Ottoman intellectuals. Ottoman intellectuals and statesmen such as İbrahim Şinasi (1826–71), Münif Pasha (1830–1910), Mehmed Şerif Efendi, and Ohannes Efendi (1830–1912) wrote articles in various newspapers and journals throughout the 1860s about this new discipline.[124] Among them, Mehmed Şerif Efendi, Münif Pasha, and Ohannes Efendi, later taught political economy at the Mekteb-i Mülkiye (The Imperial School of Administration) and the Mekteb-i Hukuk-i Şâhâne (The Imperial School of Law), and their lecture notes were published as textbooks.[125]

As public intellectuals popularized this new discipline, it was also introduced in the curricula of the public schools. Economics was first taught at the Mekteb-i Mülkiye under the name "Ekonomi Politik" (*économie politique*), starting from its inauguration in 1859. Mekteb-i Mülkiye was followed by vocational schools and other higher education institutions such as İstanbul Sanayi Mektebi (School of Arts in Istanbul) in 1868, Kız Sanayi Mektebi (School of Arts for Girls) in 1870, and Hukuk Mektebi (School of Law) in 1874.[126] Later, schools of agriculture, veterinary medicine, and gradually high schools and even primary schools added economics courses to their curricula.[127]

In the 1860s and 70s, Smithian *laissez-faire* approach was dominant in both popular economic literature and economic education. However, objections to liberal theses about the Ottoman economy were not absent. Mehmed Şerif Efendi, for example, responded to the ongoing agriculture vs. industry debate with his articles and a book taking the former side.[128] In 1861, he wrote an article for the popular newspaper, *Tercüman-ı Ahval*, defending industrialization in the Ottoman Empire.[129] He argued that industry promoted sciences and technologies in addition to creating wealth and prosperity. Moreover, a developed industry, he maintained, would nurture agriculture by creating a growing demand for primary goods and through other spillover effects. Therefore, according to him, there was no need to focus on agriculture, even if the aim is the development of Ottoman agricultural sectors. Later he continued to defend this position in his articles in the first and very influential Ottoman popular science periodical, *Mecmua-i Fünûn*.[130] The publication of his *İlm-i Emvâl-i Milliye* (the Science of National Assets, 1863) followed his articles.[131] Before being printed in book format, the work was first serialized in *Tercüman-ı Ahval*, between November 1861 and May 1862. In his book, Mehmed Şerif developed his ideas on the necessity of industrializing the Ottoman economy and touched on major economic debates of the era, such as the alleged general indolence in Ottoman society and particularly the Muslims' indifference to economic life.[132] These two themes were to become main concerns for Ottoman reformists of the later decades.

As the Ottoman economic literature grew, the debates on the question of economic development began to find their way into political treatises and historical narratives penned by Ottoman statesmen as well. Although the lack of a reference system makes it difficult to document the impact of economic literature in Ottoman intellectual life, one can infer this impact through haphazard economic discussions reflecting traces of modern economic principles and notions. At times, even a general reference to the importance of economics hints at the author's acquaintance with this new discipline.

The prominent Ottoman statesman, jurist, intellectual, and historian Ahmed Cevdet Pasha (1822–95) referred to many economic phenomena in his writings, although he did not suggest any systematic economic analyses of events. According to him, economics was surely a science of state administration. His works included discussions on various economic issues, from debasement of coinage and taxation to even more technical issues, such as the "velocity of the circulation of money."[133] Although it is obvious that Cevdet Pasha was aware of classical economic theories, he referred to economic theories and concepts rather implicitly. For example, in his magnum opus, 12-volume *Tarih-i Cevdet* (1854–84),[134] he mentions the labor theory of value by stating that the most important "wealth of a nation" is the labor of its population, and not the precious metals in the state treasury.[135] Without labor, he adds, even the richest treasury would be exhausted. In another example, he refers to another central component of the classical political economy, that is, the free market. According to Cevdet Pasha, the idea of the free market and the rejection of state intervention are not the inventions of modern European economic thinking, but these notions were first suggested by the early *mujtahid*s of Islam,[136] based on the idea that only God's will regulates market relations.[137] As this example demonstrates, Cevdet

Pasha promoted Smithian economic principles by legitimizing them through Islamic sources, thereby providing an early example to the discussion on the tradition of Islamic economics.

A better example in this context is Tunuslu Hayreddin Pasha (Khayr al-Dîn al-Tunisî, *c.*1822–90). Hayreddin Pasha was a high-ranking official in Ottoman Tunis, and later in 1878–79 the grand vizier of Abdülhamid II. While he was serving still in Tunis, he was sent to France as a representative of Tunis, and had the chance to observe European institutions. Based on these observations, he wrote a political treatise about the necessity of modernization and how to achieve it in a book in 1867.[138] A distinct feature of his study is its conspicuous emphasis on the notion of economic development in a capitalist sense.[139] Hayreddin Pasha, throughout his book, tries to show that Islam does not oppose modern sciences and technologies. On the contrary, he argues, Islamic tradition has always encouraged scientific research and scientific management of worldly matters. According to him, the first duty of Muslims is to improve the living conditions of the entire Muslim nation (*ummah*), and the only way to achieve this is by adopting modern sciences, encouraging industry and commerce, and getting rid of laziness.[140] In this respect, Hayreddin Pasha's "ideas of economics appear quite close to the classical European economic theory."[141] Hayreddin Pasha suggests that the state should remove the barriers to economic activities, provide necessary rights as well as security for private property, and minimize taxes in order to promote economic enterprise.[142] However, he still attributes the pioneering role to the state, as expected from an Ottoman statesman of the era: the state must take measures to lead its people to entrepreneurship, hard work, and the use of modern sciences and technologies, which will pave the way for economic prosperity for the whole nation.[143]

The 1860s ended with an interesting translation phenomenon, which testifies to the increasing efforts to popularize economics as a reformist action. In 1869, two different editions of two best-sellers of economic literature were published: Benjamin Franklin's *The Way to Wealth* (1757)[144] and Otto Hübner's (1818–77) *Der kleine Volkswirth* (1852).[145] Both studies were written in everyday language with clear economic messages in order to teach basic economic principles and notions to the masses. They were both hugely successful, not only in their countries of origin—the United States and Germany respectively—but throughout the world, and were translated into many European and non-European languages. The multiple translations of these works in the Ottoman Empire marked a cornerstone in the history of Ottoman economic literature due to the changes they brought about in terms of both style and language. More importantly, these publications also demonstrate a substantial change in one of the important components of the Ottoman intellectual sphere: the target audience.

Reşad Bey's translation (or rather adaptation) of *The Way to Wealth*, entitled *Tarik-i Refah* (*The Way to Welfare*), was published as a lithographed manuscript in Paris in 1869. Interestingly, Franklin's protagonist, "poor Richard," becomes "virtuous Richard" ("*recûl-i salih Rişar*") in Reşad Bey's translation. This may be due to Reşad Bey's reluctance for presenting the way to wealth through the words of a "poor" Richard. Moreover, by making the protagonist "virtuous," Reşad Bey strengthened the religious emphasis in Franklin's work: "paradise is for the virtuous."[146] The translation, following the goal of the original book, obviously aims at promoting capitalist work ethic among Ottomans through very simple and practical messages, such as the vital importance of hard work,[147] knowledge and skills,[148] the significance of managing wealth as well as acquiring it,[149] the harmful effects of wasteful and conspicuous consumption,[150] and many others. More importantly, Reşad Bey uses everyday language in his translation instead of stilted Ottoman Turkish, which uneducated Ottomans could not understand.[151] The second translation of *The Way to Wealth* was made by Bedros Hocasaryan, and was entitled *Tarik-i Servet ez Hikmet-i Rikardos* (*The Way to Wealth by the Philosophy of Richard*, 1869).[152] This is a more faithful translation, but Hocasaryan uses a more sophisticated language than that of Reşad's.

As usual, translations were made from French editions, not from the English original, since French was the *lingua franca* of the era and a very few Ottomans knew English at the time. Unfortunately, we do not know much about the reception of these books in the empire, but it is easy to see the impact of Franklin in Ottoman economic thought and culture through other facts. First, in addition to these two different versions of his work, a second edition of Hocasaryan's translation published in 1908.[153] Moreover, two different biographies of Franklin appeared, one in 1882 (by Ebüzziya Tevfik) and another in 1890 (by Mehmed Hilmi).[154] Ebüzziya Tevfik especially worked hard for the popularization of Benjamin Franklin, through to his several translations from Franklin and biographical pieces on him in his *Mecuma-yı Ebüzziya* in the early 1880s.[155] Thanks primarily to these early efforts, Benjamin Franklin's economic ideas left visible marks on Ottoman-Turkish economic thinking, both at the elite and the popular levels.[156]

Otto Hübner's *Der kleine Volkswirth*—and its French translation *Petit manuel populaire d'économie politique* (1861), which was used by the Ottoman translators—had a more scholarly nature than *The Way to Wealth*, although its target audience was also the masses.[157] *Petit manuel* was written as a practical reference on the main themes of economics—such as work, capital, value, wealth, and poverty—written in dialogical style so that ordinary people can refer to it easily for economic issues that they encounter in their daily lives. In 1869 Ahmed Hilmi, another official from the Translation Bureau, rendered Hübner's book into Turkish with the title, *İlm-i Tedbir-i Servet* (*The Science of Management of Wealth*). Contrary to the main goal of Hübner, Ahmed Hilmi preferred a more sophisticated language rather than a more accessible colloquial Turkish. Also, unlike some examples mentioned above, Ahmed Hilmi did not alter the text to Ottomanize it, thereby providing a faithful translation.

By contrast, Mehmed Midhat's translation, *Ekonomi Tercümesi: Fenn-i İdare* (*Translation of Economics, The Science of Management*) was more faithful to the philosophy behind Hübner's book than to the text itself. It was first serialized anonymously in the newspaper *Terakki*, between February and April 1869. In his introduction, Mehmed Midhat stated that he preferred spoken (*kaba*) Turkish in order that "even an ordinary man who is barely literate can read the book and even teach it to an [illiterate] worker or a farm laborer."[158] Considering the importance of the subject and the scarcity of teachers who could instruct ordinary people in this subject, he presented his decision not as a preference, but a necessity.[159] In the same vein, in addition to using plain Turkish, he provided Turkish equivalents of some Arabic and Persian words that are mostly used in written language. Where this was not possible, he preferred to write these words as they are pronounced, and not in their original Arabic and Persian forms (e.g., he writes "*zenaat*" instead of "*san'at*" and "*tezgâh*" instead of "*destgâh*").[160] In this sense, Mehmed Midhat's translation marks another turning point in the popularization of economics: he added the barely literate and even illiterate workers among the audience of an intellectual product. Besides, his translation, like Reşad Bey's translation from Franklin, is a good example of the Turkification of the Ottoman-Turkish language, a movement that would gain impetus later on.

In addition to these developments in the economic literature, the late 1860s and early 1870s witnessed another important phenomenon in late Ottoman intellectual and political life: the rise of the Young Ottomans. Led by Ottoman intellectuals in voluntary exile in Europe, such as Ziya Pasha (1825–80) and Namık Kemal (1840–88), the Young Ottomans started an aggressive opposition movement against the Ottoman political and economic system that took shape during the Tanzimat era.[161] Their highly critical publications changed the Ottoman intellectual atmosphere as never before and challenged the status quo. The Young Ottoman economic criticism was directed towards the widely discussed problems of the Ottoman economic system, such as the traditional Ottoman economic mentality (i.e., laziness and Muslim indifference to economic enterprise), backward economic conditions (e.g., lack of modern industry), and unsuccessful Tanzimat-era economic measures that aimed to modernize the economy but instead caused even greater problems (e.g., an enormous public debt, corruption, and the loss of economic independence). The Young Ottomans attacked the *Tanzimat* statesmen for their inability to change these backward conditions into a modern socio-economic structure, and demanded a radical reform of the political system in order to overcome these fundamental problems.[162]

Moreover, the Young Ottomans' "politicization" of Westernization, as Şerif Mardin put it,[163] added another dimension to the problem of decentralization from the central government's perspective. The political reformist challenge in the Ottoman modernization process, which started with the Young Ottomans in the 1860s and continued with the Young Turks after 1890s, paved the way for Abdülhamid II's rather technocratic and centralist approach to modernization, which prioritized education and economic development rather than political change.

Conclusion

The long nineteenth century was the age of total transformation for the Ottoman Empire, as it was for the rest of the world. The rapid and partly devastating economic change caused by the impact of European industrial capitalism, in addition to the military and political challenge of the industrial powers, forced the Ottomans to reform or rebuild domestic institutions, from economic and fiscal policies to military and bureaucratic apparatuses. This willy-nilly and rather disruptive reform process accompanied an equally unsettling process of economic integration of the Ottoman economy into the international capitalist division of labor.

In such an age of turbulence, economics came to the Ottoman Empire first as an instrument to make sense of the rules of this new industrial and economy-centered age. Meanwhile, the state balances were under strenuous requirements because of the comprehensive institutional rebuilding process. Economics, in this context, was considered useful as it provided specific guidelines to improve state balances as well as to create prosperity in the country. Economics, therefore, was first taken as a science of state administration. Towards the end of the nineteenth century, however, economic modernization took on a new and more inclusive meaning. It began to include the aim of a total socio-economic transformation towards building a more economy-centered society. Education of the masses according to the modern principles of economics became an important concern for the Ottoman elite. As a result, by the 1870s, the meaning and importance of economics had changed from a science of state administration to an instrument of social change. In this respect, the Ottoman case showed a parallel development to the German case, in which the nineteenth century witnessed the shift from the cameralist *Staatswirtschaft* (state economy) to Smithian *Nationalökonomie* (national economy) and *Volkswirtschaft* (people's economy).[164]

The economic legacy of the Tanzimat period, in short, was a mostly failed industrialization process, a fiscally bankrupt state, and an increasingly externally-dependent economic and political system on the one hand, and a rapidly growing interest in economics as a scientific guideline to save and rebuild the empire, on the other.

Notes

1 "Düşmanlar kavî, tâli'ler zebûn, Hazîneler tehî, çok idi duyûn./İşte bu halde buldu devleti, Beyâna hacet var mı 'ayânı?... Bir çok mektebler te'sis olundu, Duyûn-ı devlet yoluna kondu./Hüsn-i himmet-i şahânesiyle, Emn ü asayiş oldu erzânî." Münif, *Destân-ı Âl-i Osman* (İstanbul: Mihran Matbaası, 1882), 7. (This is the part on Abdülhamid II in Münif Pasha's history of Ottoman dynasty in verse.) Münif Pasha's first verse is taken from the well-known Azerbaijani poet Fuzûli (*c.*1483–1556): "Dert çok, hemderd yok, düşman kavî, tâli' zebûn." (Fuzûlî, *Fuzûlî Divânı*, ed. Abdülbâki Gölpınarlı, Second Edition (İstanbul: İnkılâb Kitabevi, 1961), 119.) This verse was widely known and referred to by Ottoman intellectuals of the era.

2 Diane Wood, *Medieval Economic Thought* (Cambridge: Cambridge University Press, 2002), 1.

3 Maxime Rodinson, *Islam and capitalism*, trans. Brian Pearce (Austin: University of Texas Press, 1978), 35.

4 Abraham L. Udovitch, *Partnership and Profit in Medieval Islam* (Princeton: Princeton University Press, 1970), 11–12.

5 L. Baeck, *The Mediterranean Tradition in Economic Thought* (London, New York: Routledge, 1994), 99–105.

6 Ibid.
7 For introductory works on Islamic economics, see Shaikh M. Ghazanfar, ed., *Medieval Islamic Economic Thought: Filling the "Great Gap" in European Economics* (London: RoutledgeCurzon, 2003); Ahmed A.F. El-Ashker and Rodney Wilson, *Islamic Economics: A Short History* (Leiden: Brill, 2006).
8 For an overview of pre-modern Ottoman economic thought and especially its Islamic roots, see Fatih Ermiş, *A History of Ottoman Economic Thought: Developments Before the Nineteenth Century* (Routledge, 2014).
9 Halil İnalcık, "Ottoman Economic Mind and the Aspects of Ottoman Economy," in *Studies in the Economic History of the Middle East: From the Rise of Islam to the Present Day*, ed. Michael A. Cook (London: Oxford University Press, 1970), 207–18.
10 Ibid., 207.
11 Ibid., 208–9.
12 However, as one Ottoman economist, Süleyman Sûdi (1835–96) noted critically, confiscation was also often used as a political instrument by political elites to eliminate rivals. (Süleyman Sûdi, "Mebâhis El-Mâliye Fi'd-Devleti'l-Osmaniyye – XI," *Vakit*, 23 Zilkâde 1298, (October 17, 1881)).
13 For the history of and Islamic theoretical over the cash *waqf*s in the Ottoman Empire, see Jon E. Mandaville, "Usurious Piety: The Cash Waqf Controversy in the Ottoman Empire," *International Journal of Middle East Studies* 10, no. 3 (1979): 289–308; Murat Çizakça, *Islamic Capitalism and Finance: Origins, Evolution and the Future* (Cheltenham: Edward Elgar, 2011), 82–5.
14 Cemal Kafadar, "When Coins Turned into Drops of Dew and Bankers Became Robbers of Shadows: The Boundaries of Ottoman Economic Imagination at the End of the Sixteenth Century" (unpublished PhD dissertation, McGill University, 1986). For a more sweeping criticism of the thesis of Ottoman ignorance about economic realities, see M. Fuad Köprülü, "Osmanlı Müelliflerinde Ekonomik Düşünceler," *Ülkü*, July 1936, 339–44.
15 Suraiya Faroqhi, "Guildsmen Complain to the Sultan: Artisans' Disputes and the Ottoman Administration in the 18th Century," in *Legitimizing the Order: The Ottoman Rhetoric of State Power*, ed. Hakan T. Karateke and Maurus Reinkowski (Leiden: Brill, 2005), 177n2.
16 See I. Metin Kunt, "Dervis Mehmed Pasa, Vezir and Entrepreneur: A Study in Ottoman Political-Economic Theory and Practice," *Turcica* 9, no. 1 (1977): 197–214.
17 Ibid., 203.
18 Faroqhi, "Guildsmen Complain to the Sultan: Artisans' Disputes and the Ottoman Administration in the 18th Century," 177.
19 Mehmet Genç, *Osmanlı İmparatorluğu'nda Devlet ve Ekonomi* (İstanbul: Ötüken Neşriyat, 2000), 45.
20 Ibid., 45–8.
21 Ibid., 50–2.
22 Ibid., 48–50.
23 İnalcık, "Ottoman Economic Mind," 218.
24 Wood, *Medieval Economic Thought*, 153–4.
25 Shaikh M. Ghazanfar, "Medieval Islamic Socio-Economic Thought: Links with Greek and Latin-European Scholarship," in *Medieval Islamic Economic Thought: Filling the "Great Gap" in European Economics*, ed. Shaikh M. Ghazanfar (London: RoutledgeCurzon, 2003), 147.
26 Gabriel Baer, "The Administrative, Economic and Social Functions of Turkish Guilds," *International Journal of Middle East Studies* 1, no. 1 (January 1, 1970): 28–50.
27 Engin Deniz Akarlı, "Gedik: Implements, Mastership, Shop Usufruct, and Monopoly among Istanbul Artisans, 1750–1850," *Wissenschaftskolleg Jahrbuch* 1986 (1987): 223.

28 Onur Yıldırım, "Ottoman Guilds in the Early Modern Era," *International Review of Social History* 53, no. Supplement S16 (2008): 74.
29 Mehmet Genç, "Ottoman Industry in the Eighteenth Century: General Framework, Characteristics, and Main Trends," in *Manufacturing in the Ottoman Empire and Turkey, 1500–1900*, ed. Donald Quataert (Albany: State University of New York Press, 1994), 62.
30 Quataert, "The Age of Reforms, 1812–1914," 764.
31 For varied reactions of Egyptian artisans to the European capitalist expansion in the late eighteenth and early nineteenth centuries, see Nelly Hanna, *Artisan Entrepreneurs in Cairo and Early-Modern Capitalism (1600–1800)*, (Syracuse, NY: Syracuse University Press, 2011), 179–200.
32 "Tedbîr-i ʿÜmran-i Mülkî," n.d., Mxt. 1169, Österreichischen Nationalbibliothek.
33 Genç, *Devlet ve Ekonomi*, 92–5.
34 Ibid.
35 M. Şükrü Hanioğlu, *A Brief History of the Late Ottoman Empire* (Princeton: Princeton University Press, 2008), 24–25.
36 Tevfik Güran, *19. Yüzyıl Osmanlı Tarımı Üzerine Araştırmalar* (İstanbul: Eren Yayıncılık, 1998), 56–7.
37 Quataert, "The Age of Reforms, 1812–1914," 911–13.
38 Güran, *19. Yüzyıl Osmanlı Tarımı*, 57.
39 Engin D. Akarlı, ed., *Belgelerle Tanzimat: Osmanlı Sadrıazamlarından Âli ve Fuad Paşaların Siyasî Vasiyyetnâmeleri* (İstanbul: Boğaziçi Üniversitesi, 1978).
40 For the development of the Ottoman agricultural bureaucracy in the nineteenth century, see Donald Quataert, "Ottoman Reform and Agriculture in Anatolia, 1876–1908" (unpublished PhD Dissertation, University of California, 1973), 72–91.
41 Güran, *19. Yüzyıl Osmanlı Tarımı*, 45–54.
42 Ibid., 150–2.
43 Quataert, "The Age of Reforms, 1812–1914," 860.
44 For various arguments on the aims and practical results of the 1858 Land Code, see ibid., 856–61.
45 Donald Quataert, "Introduction," in *Manufacturing in the Ottoman Empire and Turkey, 1500–1900*, ed. Donald Quataert (Albany: State University of New York Press, 1994), 6.
46 For various aspects of economic transformation in Anatolia in the nineteenth century, see Mehmet Murat Baskıcı, *1800–1914 Yıllarında Anadolu'da İktisadi Değişim* (Ankara: Turhan Kitabevi, 2005).
47 For many concrete examples from Aintab, Aleppo, Diyarbekir, etc. see Donald Quataert, "Ottoman Manufacturing in the Nineteenth Century," in *Manufacturing in the Ottoman Empire and Turkey, 1500–1900*, ed. Donald Quataert (Albany: State University of New York Press, 1994), 87–121. Also see, Nelly Hanna's more recent study on the case of Egyptian guilds and individual entrepreneurs in this context: *Artisan Entrepreneurs*, 154–7.
48 For more details on particular industries, see Donald Quataert, *Ottoman Manufacturing in the Age of the Industrial Revolution* (Cambridge: Cambridge University Press, 1993). For a general evaluation of the impact of "incorporation into the European world-economy" on the Ottoman production structure, see also Suraiya Faroqhi, *Artisans of Empire: Crafts and Craftspeople under the Ottomans* (London: I.B. Tauris, 2009), 186–207.
49 Vedat Eldem, *Osmanlı İmparatorluğu'nun İktisadi Şartları Hakkında Bir Tetkik* (Ankara: Turk Tarih Kurumu, 1994), 65–6.
50 Ibid., 66.
51 For Ottoman industrialization efforts and many reasons of its failure with specific examples, see Ömer Celâl Sarc, "Tanzimat ve Sanayiimiz," in *Tanzimat: Yüzüncü Yıldönümü Münasebetile* (İstanbul: Maarif Matbaası, 1940), 423–40; Rıfat Önsoy,

Tanzimat Dönemi Osmanlı Sanayii ve Sanayileşme Politikası (Türkiye İş Bankası Kültür Yayınları, 1988).

52 Nassau W. Senior, *A Journal Kept in Turkey and Greece in the Autumn of 1857, and the Beginning of 1858* (London: Longman Brown Green Longmans and Roberts, 1859), 16–17.

53 "The Commercial Decline of Constantinople," *The Levant Herald and Eastern Express*, May 1, 1886, 2.

54 BOA, YEE 12/38/1, 29/Z/1307.

55 Ibid. For similar arguments in a memorandum by another important Hamidian era statesman, Kâmil Pasha (1832–1913), who served as Grand Vizier to Abdülhamid II three times, see Hilmi Kâmil Bayur, *Sadrazam Kâmil Paşa: Siyasî Hayatı* (Ankara: Sanat Basımevi, 1954), 92–3.

56 For the financial situation of the Ottoman state and the relevant reforms in the Tanzimat era, see Coşkun Çakır, *Tanzimat Dönemi Osmanlı Maliyesi* (İstanbul: Küre Yayınları, 2001).

57 Engin D. Akarlı, "Economic Policy and Budgets in Ottoman Turkey, 1876–1909," *Middle Eastern Studies* 28, no. 3 (1992): 443.

58 "İstikrâz-ı Cedîd Üzerine Yeni Osmanlılar Cemiyetinin Mütâlaʿatı," *Hürriyet* 22 (December 23, 1868), 1–6.

59 For a detailed study of the Ottoman debt and the consequent financial collapse, see İ. Hakkı Yeniay, *Yeni Osmanlı Borçları Tarihi* (İtanbul: İ.Ü. İktisat Fakültesi, 1964).

60 The classic study (in English) on the OPDA and the conditions that paved the way for its establishment is Donald C. Blaisdell, *European Financial Control in the Ottoman Empire: A Study of the Establishment, Activities, and Significance of the Administration of the Ottoman Public Debt* (New York: Columbia University Press, 1929). For a more recent study, see Murat Birdal, *The Political Economy of Ottoman Public Debt: Insolvency and European Financial Control in the Late Nineteenth Century* (London: Tauris Academic Studies, 2010).

61 Yeniay, *Yeni Osmanlı Borçları Tarihi*, 64–75.

62 Karl Polanyi, *The Great Transformation.* (Boston: Beacon Press, 1957), 46, et passim.

63 For a meticulous analysis of Adam Smith's intellectual impact on the political and economic thought, see Murray Milgate and Shannon C. Stimson, *After Adam Smith: A Century of Transformation in Politics and Political Economy* (Princeton: Princeton University Press, 2009).

64 Polanyi, *The Great Transformation.*, 56–76.

65 Robert B. Ekelund and Robert F. Hébert, *A History of Economic Theory and Method*, third edition (New York: McGraw-Hill, 1990), 100.

66 For a summary of pre-Smithian (or "pre-Adamite," as Blaug names it) economics see Mark Blaug, *Economic Theory in Retrospect*, Fifth Edition (Cambridge: Cambridge University Press, 1996), 10–32.

67 For a summary of the ideas of these schools of thought see Ekelund and Hébert, *A History of Economic Theory and Method*, 42–96.

68 For the explanation of the idea of invisible hand, see Mark Blaug, "invisible hand," *The New Palgrave Dictionary of Economics*, second edition, eds. Steven N. Durlauf and Lawrence E. Blume, vol. 4 (New York: Palgrave Macmillan, 2008), 564–6.

69 Keith Tribe and Hiroshi Mizuta, *A Critical Bibliography of Adam Smith* (London: Pickering & Chatto, 2002), 362–89.

70 Hanioğlu, *Late Ottoman Empire*, 42.

71 For a summary of these memoranda see Yavuz Cezar, *Osmanlı Maliyesinde Bunalım ve Değişim Dönemi: XVIII. Yy.'dan Tanzimat'a Mali Tarih* (Istanbul: Alan Yayıncılık, 1986), 142–148. Some of them were later published in *Tarih-i Osmani Encümeni Mecmuası* (*TOEM*) in the early twentieth century. For those by Tatarcık Abdullah Molla, see *TOEM*, 7/41, pp. 257–84; *TOEM* 7/42, pp. 321–46; and *TOEM*

8/43, pp. 15–34. For the memorandum of Mehmed Şerif, see *TOEM*, 7/38, pp. 74–88.

72 Cezar, *Osmanlı Maliyesinde Bunalım ve Değişim*, 148.

73 Ahmed Güner Sayar, *Osmanlı İktisat Düşüncesinin Çağdaşlaşması: (Klasik Dönem'den II. Abdülhamid'e)*, Second Edition (İstanbul: Ötüken Neşriyat, 2000), 182.

74 Cezar, *Osmanlı Maliyesinde Bunalım ve Değişim*, 142–6.

75 Malcolm Yapp, *The Making of the Modern Near East, 1792–1923* (London: Longman, 1990), 100.

76 For the economic content of such diplomatic reports, see Sayar, *Osmanlı İktisat Düşüncesi*, 172–5.

77 Ibid., 173.

78 Sâdık Rıfat Pasha, *Müntehâbât-ı Âsâr* (İstanbul: Ali Bey Matbaası, n.d.).

79 For an analysis of Sâdık Rıfat Pasha's economic ideas, see Sayar, *Osmanlı İktisat Düşüncesi*, 210–26.

80 Ibid., 213–15.

81 Ibid., 189. For a brief biography of Alexander Blacque and his intellectual and press activities in the Ottoman Empire, see Orhan Koloğlu, "Osmanlı Devleti'nde Liberal Ekonominin Savunucusu: Blacque (Blak) Bey (1792–1836)," *Tarih ve Toplum* 10, no. 57 (1988): 15–19.

82 Sayar, *Osmanlı İktisat Düşüncesi*, 190.

83 Ibid.

84 Koloğlu, "Blacque Bey," 18.

85 David Urquhart, *Turkey and Its Resources: Its Municipal Organization and Free Trade, the State and Prospects of English Commerce in the East, the New Administration of Greece, Its Revenue and National Possessions* (London: Saunders and Otley, 1833). For Urquhart's economic ideas and influence in the Ottoman Empire, see Sayar, *Osmanlı İktisat Düşüncesi*, 191–204.

86 For a short introduction to the Ricardian model, see Ronald Findlay, "Comparative advantage," *The New Palgrave Dictionary of Economics*, vol. 2, 28–9.

87 Şevket Pamuk and Jeffrey G. Williamson, "Ottoman De-Industrialization 1800–1913: Assessing the Shock, Its Impact and the Response," *NBER Working Papers*, no. 14763 (2009): 5. For a comparative study of the Ottoman and Chinese cases in this context, see Reşat Kasaba, "Treaties and Friendships: British Imperialism, the Ottoman Empire, and China in the Nineteenth Century," *Journal of World History* 4, no. 2 (1993): 215–41.

88 Sayar, *Osmanlı İktisat Düşüncesi*, 273–4. For a detailed analysis of the economic content of *Ceride-i Havadis*, see Tarık Özçelik, "Modern İktisadın Osmanlı'ya Girişi ve Ceride-i Havadis (1840–1856)" (Unpublished PhD Dissertation, Marmara University, 2003); Tarık Özçelik, "Ceride-i Havadis'de Ziraat, Ticaret ve Sanayi Tartışmaları," *İstanbul Üniversitesi Sosyal Siyaset Konferansları Dergisi*, no. 56 (2009): 469–518.

89 Özçelik, "Modern İktisadın Osmanlı'ya Girlişi ve Ceride-i Havadis (1840–1856)."

90 Ibid., 79.

91 For a detailed review of Ottoman economic literature between *c.*1860 and 1880 in the context of "*laissez-faire* vs. protectionism" debate, see Sayar, *Osmanlı İktisat Düşüncesi*, 279–393.

92 Vincent Barnett, *A History of Russian Economic Thought*, 1st ed. (New York: Routledge, 2009), 24.

93 Stanislav I. Smetanin, *Istorija Predprinimatel'stva v Rossii : Kurs Leksij* (Moskva: MTFER, 2008), 3.

94 Ibid.

95 Barnett, *A History of Russian Economic Thought*, 24.

96 For a biography and economic theories of Senior, see N. de Marchi, "Senior, Nassau William (1790–1864)," *The New Palgrave Dictionary of Economics*, vol. 7, 428–30.

97 Senior, *A Journal Kept in Turkey and Greece*. Senior's accounts have been an important source for the social and cultural life of the Ottomans, as well as the political and economic conditions of the empire. However, there is no scholarly work on his personal influence on the Ottoman economic thought, since an important fact about him has been ignored: at the time he came to Istanbul, he was a well-known economist who had already published his main works.

98 Ibid., 108–9.

99 See for example, Ibid., 134–6., for his discussions with Ahmed Vefik Efendi on the main economic problems of the empire, ranging from inflation to monopolies.

100 İlber Ortaylı, "Osmanlılarda İlk Telif İktisat Elyazması," *Yapıt*, no. October (1983): 37–44.

101 "Tedbîr-i ʿÜmran-i Mülkî," 71.

102 Ibid., 78.

103 Coşkun Çakır, "Tanzimat Dönemi'nde Ticaret Alanında Yapılan Kurumsal Düzenlemeler: Meclisler," *Sosyal Siyaset Konferansları Dergisi*, no. 43–44 (2000): 368.

104 "Tedbîr-i ʿÜmran-i Mülkî," 1–6.

105 Adam Smith, *Milletlerin Zenginliği*, trans. Haldun Derin, 2 vols. (İstanbul: Millî Eğitim Basımevi, 1948). *The Wealth of Nations* was translated into major world languages by the early twentieth century. For studies on translations and receptions of the book in various countries, see Cheng-chung Lai, ed., *Adam Smith Across Nations: Translations and Receptions of The Wealth of Nations* (Oxford: Oxford University Press, 2000).

106 For a concise analysis of the multilingual reading culture in the late Ottoman Empire, see Johann Strauss, "Who Read What in the Ottoman Empire (19th–20th Centuries)?," *Middle Eastern Literatures* 6, no. 1 (January 1, 2003): 39–76.

107 Suʿad, "Makale-i Mütercim," in Prosper Rambaud, *Telhis-i İlm-i Servet*, tr. Suʿad, (İstanbul: Mihran Matbaası, 1888), 13.

108 A transliterated (into modern Turkish) version of the book along with some biographical notes about the author can be found in Serandi Arşizen, *Tasarrufât-ı Mülkiye: Osmanlı İmparatorluğu'nda Bir Politik Iktisat Kitabı*, ed. Hamdi Genç and M. Erdem Özgür (İstanbul: Kitabevi, 2011).

109 For more information on Serandi Arşizen and his *Tasarrufât-ı Mülkiye*, see M. Erdem Özgür and Hamdi Genç, "An Ottoman Classical Political Economist: Sarantis Archigenes and His Tasarrufat-ı Mülkiye," *Middle Eastern Studies* 47, no. 2 (2011): 329–42.

110 Italian economist Pellegrino Rossi was the the successor to famous economist J.B. Say at the *Collège de France* as the professor of political economy. See Alain Béraud and Philippe Steiner, "France, economics in (before 1870)," *The New Palgrave Dictionary of Economics*, vol. 3, 479. According to Schumpeter, Rossi's work was "diluted Ricardianism plus a little Say." Joseph A. Schumpeter, *History of Economic Analysis* (New York: Oxford University Press, 1961), 511.

111 The Translation Bureau (established in 1832) was an important Ottoman governmental institution which provided a window to the outside (especially Western) world through its translations of numerous books on various subjects, from history to economics. It also served as an essential component of the Ottoman diplomatic bureaucracy as it undertook all the foreign correspondence.

112 Z. Fahri Fındıkoğlu, "İktisadi Tefekkür Tarihimizden Bir Parça," in *Ordinaryüs Profesör İbrahim Fazıl Pelin'in Hatırasına Armağan* (İstanbul: İstanbul Üniversitesi İktisat Fakültesi, 1948), 221.

113 Erdem Özgür and Genç, "An Ottoman Classical Political Economist," 331.

114 Z. Fahri Fındıkoğlu, "İktisadi Tefekkür Tarihimize Ait Yeni Bir Vesika," *Kongreye Sunulan Tebliğler, IV. Türk Tarih Kongresi* (Ankara: Türk Tarih Kurumu, 1952), 340.

115 Fındıkoğlu, "İktisadi Tefekkür Tarihimizden Bir Parça," 221.

116 For more information on Sehak Abru and his work, see Sezai Balcı, "Bir Osmanlı-Ermeni Aydın ve Bürokratı: Sahak Abro (1825–1900)," in *Osmanlı Siyasal ve Sosyal Hayatında Ermeniler*, ed. İbrahim Erdal and Ahmet Karaçavuş, vol. 304 (İstanbul: IQ Kültür Sanat Yayıncılık, 2009), 105–38.
117 "Mösyö Say gibi ilm-i mebhusun mesail-i esasiyesini az lakırdıyle ifade ve beyan etmiş olan müellifin nadir bulunur." Cited in Z. Fahri Fındıkoğlu, "Bizde Avrupavari İktisatçılığın Başlangıcı," *İş* 1 (1934), 47. Despite its problematic sounding in today's (particularly American) English, economics was a "science" in the scientific and academic paradigm of the age. Therefore, throughout this work, I translate the word " *'ilm*" as "science," also in the case of economics, as an effort to convey its original meaning and connotations in the late Ottoman context.
118 Ibid., 45.
119 Ibid., 47.
120 Ibid.
121 Charles Wells, *Ilm Tedbiri Milk: "The Science of the Administration of A State," or An Essay on Political Economy, in Turkish: Being the First ever Written in that Language* (London: Williams and Norgate, 1860), v. (Although Wells entitles his book *Ilm Tedbiri Milk* in Turkish, the proper Ottoman Turkish title would be "İlm-i Tedbir-i Mülk.") The book contains an introduction by the author in English; and the rest is in Turkish. The Turkish part is a lithographed manuscript, written with a rather clumsy handwriting most probably by Wells himself.
122 Wells, *Ilm Tedbiri Milk*, vii–viii.
123 His biography, some brief notes on his works, and some examples of his other publications in the Ottoman press can be found in Hüseyin Çelik, *Türk Dostu, İngiliz Türkolog Charles Wells: Hayatı, Eserleri ve Osmanlı Türkleri ile İlgili Düşünceleri* (Ankara: T.C. Kültür Bakanlığı, 1996).
124 Mehmed Şerif Efendi was the brother of Münif Pasha. (Ziyaeddin Fahri Fındıkoğlu, "Türk İktisadi Tefekkür Tarihi ve Mehmed Şerif," in *III. Türk Tarih Kongresi, Ankara 15–20 Kasım 1943, Kongreye Sunulan Tebliğler* (Ankara: Türk Tarih Kurumu, 1948), 260–8).
125 Mehmed Şerif, *İlm-i Emval-i Milliye* (İstanbul: Tab'hane-i Âmire Litoğrafya Destgâhı, 1863); Sakızlı Ohannes, *Mebadi-i İlm-i Servet-i Milel* (Dersaadet [İstanbul]: Mihran Matbaası, 1880). Münif Pasha's lectures were edited and published by one of his students: Mahmud Es'ad, *İlm-i Servet* (İstanbul: Mekteb-i Sanayi, 1885).
126 Rıfat Önsoy, "Tanzimat Döneminde İktisadi Düşüncenin Teşekkülü," in *Mustafa Reşid Paşa ve Dönemi Semineri, Bildiriler, Ankara, 13–14 Mart 1984* (Ankara: Türk Tarih Kurumu, 1994), 95.
127 Mehmed Cavid, *İlm-i İktisad: Mekteb-i İdadiye Mahsus* (Dersaadet [İstanbul]: Kanaat Matbaası, 1913), 14.
128 For a brief biography and summary of Mehmed Şerif's economic ideas, see Sayar, *Osmanlı İktisat Düşüncesi*, 306–14.
129 Mehmed Şerif Efendi, "Sanayi' ve Ziraatden Kangısının Hakkımızda Hayırlı Olduğuna Dairdir," *Tercüman-ı Ahval* 68 and 69 (1861).
130 *Mecmua-i Fünûn* was published by *Cemiyet-i İlmiye-i Osmaniye* (the Ottoman Scientific Society), between 1862 and 1867 (47 issues) and then another issue appeared many years later (1883) before it was closed down by the sultan indefinitely. It was the first Ottoman popular science journal, and it introduced some new fields of modern sciences such as geology and economics to the Ottoman public sphere.
131 In one of his earlier articles, Mehmed Şerif notes that he renders "*économie politique*" into Turkish as "*ilm-i emvâl-i milliye* (the science of national assets). He rationalizes his suggestion based on the title of the founding text of the discipline, Adam Smith's the *Wealth of Nations*. Therefore, his title is basically a rendition of Smith's work into Ottoman-Turkish. (Mehmed Şerif, "Ekonomi Politik 'İlminin

Tarîkiyle Hudûd-ı Tabî'iyesinin Tahdîdi Beyânındadır," *Tercüman-ı Ahval*, no. 75 (September 5, 1861): 2–3).

132 Mehmed Şerif, *İlm-i Emval-i Milliye*, passim.

133 Sabri F. Ülgener, "Ahmed Cevdet Paşa'nın Devlet ve İktisada Dair Düşünceleri," *İş*, no. 76 (1947): 19.

134 Ahmed Cevdet Pasha, *Tarih-i Cevdet*, 12 vols. (İstanbul: Matbaa-yı Amire and Matbaa-yi Osmaniye, 1854–1884).

135 Ülgener, "Ahmed Cevdet Paşa," 20.

136 A *mujtahid* is an authoritative interpreter of Islamic law.

137 "*narhı koyan ancak Allah'tır*..." (the price is only set by God). Ülgener, "Ahmed Cevdet Paşa," 22.

138 Khayr al-Dīn Tūnisī, *Kitāb Aqwām al-Masālik fī Ma'rifat Aḥwāl al-Mamālik* (Tūnis: Maṭba'at al-Dawlah, 1867). The book was translated into Turkish in 1879; Khayr al-Dīn Tūnisī, *Mukaddime-yi Akvam ül-Mesâlik Fi Marifet-i Ahval il-Memâlik Tercümesi*, trans. Abdurrahman Süreyya (İstanbul: Elcevaib Matbaası, 1879).

139 For a brief summary of his economic ideas, see Brown's illuminating introduction to Hayreddin's *work*; Leon Carl Brown, "An Appreciation of *The Surest Path*," in Khayr al-Dīn al-Tūnisī, *The Surest Path; the Political Treatise of a Nineteenth-Century Muslim Statesman*, ed. L. Carl Brown (Cambridge, MA: Harvard University Press, 1967), 53–6.

140 Tūnisī, *The Surest Path*, 77–8.

141 Brown, "An Appreciation," 55.

142 Ibid.

143 Ibid.

144 Benjamin Franklin, the American entrepreneur, inventor, philosopher, publisher and statesman, published a yearly almanac under the pseudonym "Poor Richard" or "Richard Saunders" from 1732 to 1757. *Poor Richard's Almanack* was a best seller in the American colonies, with its popular content of puzzles, poems, practical household hints, and other useful information for ordinary people. It also contained proverbs and aphorisms encouraging the principles of a capitalist work ethic, such as industriousness, thrift, saving, and investment. Later in 1757, Franklin gathered these maxims in a book entitled *The Way to Wealth*. As the title suggests, Franklin aimed to demonstrate the way to wealth to the ordinary people through simple changes in their economic thinking and behavior. This little book, which contained well-known phrases like "time is money," "have you somewhat to do tomorrow, do it today" and "there are no gains, without pains," was an even bigger success in America and also in England, and was translated into many other languages throughout the nineteenth century. For more information on *Poor Richard's Almanack*, see J.A. Leo Lemay, *The Life of Benjamin Franklin*, vol. 2 (Philadelphia: University of Pennsylvania Press, 2006), 170–91. For an analysis on Poor Richard's proverbs, see J.A. Leo Lemay, *The Life of Benjamin Franklin*, vol. 2, 192–213.

145 *Der kleine Vokswirth* was translated from German into French by the Belgian economist Charles Le Hardy de Beaulieu first in 1861. In the second (1862) edition, Le Hardy de Beaulieu modified his translation and adapted it to the French and Belgian context. This second edition gained international success and was translated into other languages. The Ottoman translators too used the 1862 edition for their rendering Hübner's work into Turkish.

146 Benjamin Franklin, *Tarik-i Refah*, translated by Reşad Bey (Paris, 1869) 10.

147 Ibid., 3–7; et passim.

148 Ibid., 9.

149 Ibid., 11–16.

150 Ibid., 14–20.

151 Reşad Bey later wrote a one-page article on "the science of wealth" to introduce this science to ordinary people. (Reşad, "Fenn-i Servet," *İbret* 10 (1872), 1).

152 Benjamin Franklin, *Tarîk-i Servet Ez Hikmet-i Rikardos*, trans. Bedros Hocasaryan (Dersaadet [İstanbul]: Mühendisoğlu Ohannes Matbaası, 1869).

153 Benjamin Franklin, *Tarîk-i Refah: Franklin'in Servet Hakkındaki Nesayihi ve Tercüme-i Hali*, (Saraybosna [Sarajevo]: Sultan Bayezid Sa'adet Kütübhanesi, 1908). Hocasaryan's second edition includes a short biography of Franklin by Ebüzziya Tevfik, who wrote a longer biography of Franklin between the first and second editions of Hocasaryan's translation: Ebüzziya Tevfik, *Benjamin Franklin* (Kostantiniye [İstanbul]: Matbaa-i Ebüzziya, 1882).

154 Mehmed Hilmi, *Benjamin Franklin* (Kostantiniye [İstanbul]: İstepan Matbaası, 1890).

155 See for example, *Mecmua-i Ebüzziya*, issues 1, 2, 5, 8 (1881).

156 Although he is not well-known in Turkey today, his many maxims still circulate in daily conversations of the Turkish people, such as "*vakit nakittir*" (time is money), and "bugünün işini yarına bırakma" (in Franklin's words, "have you somewhat to do tomorrow, do it today").

157 Otto Hübner, *Petit Manuel Populaire D'économie Politique, Imité de L'ouvrage Allemand Intitulé Der Kleine Economist*, trans. Ch. Le Hardy de Beaulieu, Second Edition (Bruxelles and Leipzig: A. Lacroix; Guillaumin, 1862), xi–xiv. Hübner notes in his preface that subversive ideas such as socialism and communism are the results of a significant gap in opportunities of education between different classes. Thus he aims to educate the less fortunate classes with this little book of "*économie politique morale*" in order to contribute to the efforts towards overcoming this major social problem. (Ibid., xi–xii).

158 Mehmed Midhat, "Mukaddime" [Introduction], in Otto Hübner, *Ekonomi Tercümesi: Fenn-i İdare*, trans. Mehmed Midhat (İstanbul: Cemiyet-i İlmiye Matbaası, 1869), 3. Another important detail about Mehmed Midhat's translation is that it was printed at *Cemiyet-i İlmiye Matbaası* (the printing house of the Ottoman Scientific Society), which was also publishing *Mecmua-i Fünûn.*

159 Ibid., 2–3.

160 Ibid., 3 et passim.

161 For a brief analysis of the Young Ottoman criticisms against the Tanzimat economy, see Christiane Czygan, "On the Wrong Way: Criticism of the *Tanzimat* Economy in the Young Ottoman Journal Hürriyet (1868/1870)," in *The Economy as an Issue in the Middle Eastern Press*, ed. Gisela Procházka-Eisl and Martin Strohmeier (Vienna: Lit Verlag, 2008), 41–54.

162 For the economic ideas and critiques of the two leading Young Ottomans, Ziya Pasha and Namık Kemal, see Sayar, *Osmanlı İktisat Düşüncesi*, 327–54; and Çakır, *Osmanlı Maliyesi*, 180–215. For an overall analysis of the Young Ottoman criticism regarding the financial crisis of the empire, see Nazan Çiçek, *The Young Ottomans: Turkish Critics of the Eastern Question in the Late Nineteenth Century* (London: Tauris Academic Studies, 2010), 173–236.

163 Şerif Mardin, *Jön Türklerin Siyasi Fikirleri, 1895–1908* (İstanbul: İletişim Yayınları, 2004), 222.

164 Erik Grimmer-Solem, "Germany: From Sciences of State to Modern Economics," in *Routledge Handbook of the History of Global Economic Thought*, ed. Vincent Barnett (New York: Routledge, 2015), 88–9.

2 Ottomanization of economics

> Every writer adapts political economy (just like in law, ethics, and other sciences) to his own country and society; and he writes according to the level of modernization and progress of his country. If we merely translate a work from an advanced country…, it would be an obvious mistake.[1]
>
> (Ahmed Midhat, 1879)

> We might have simply translated one of the books written in various countries on this discipline. This would definitely be easier. Yet, each of them is penned according to the current conditions and needs of its native country.[2]
>
> (Sakızlı Ohannes, 1880)

The 1880s witnessed the emergence of an Ottoman economic literature after a decades-long period of sporadic translations. It is the most productive, original, and socially influential decade of Ottoman economic thought. The major works of Sakızlı Ohannes (1830–1912), Portakal Mikael (1841–97), and Ahmed Midhat Efendi (1844–1912) were published between 1879 and 1889. These works not only inspired younger generations for writing economic texts, but also served as the standard references during the following decades, well into the early years of the Turkish Republic.

Meanwhile, following the global trend, protectionism was challenging the monopoly of the *laissez-faire* approach at both theory and policy levels in the empire. The dispute between liberals and protectionists intensified thorough various books as well as numerous articles in popular periodicals. Sakızlı Ohannes' *Mebadi-i İlm-i Servet-i Milel* (*Principles of the Science of the Wealth of Nations*, 1880) was the bible of Ottoman liberal economic tradition, whereas Ahmed Midhat Efendi wrote the first popular texts of the newly rising Ottoman protectionism. The following generation of Ottoman economists perpetuated both traditions with more elaborate studies.

This chapter provides an overview of the Ottoman economic literature in the late nineteenth and early twentieth centuries, with an eye on understanding how economics was "Ottomanized" by adapting its conceptual framework to Ottoman socio-economic context. After a brief discussion on the political and economic atmosphere of the age, it follows a chronological order in evaluating major discussions in the most prominent examples of late Ottoman economic literature. In addition to rather detailed discussions on relatively more original and influential works, it gives brief information about less influential works, to provide a more comprehensive view of the literature. Through an incisive and intertextual examination of Ottoman economic texts, from introductory textbooks to popular manuals, this chapter mainly deals with the cultural and linguistic dynamics of the transplantation of economic ideas from the Western European contexts to the—dominantly Muslim—Ottoman cultural and intellectual setting. In doing this, it demonstrates how modern economic principles were tailored by Ottoman intellectuals to analyze domestic socio-economic institutional setting, from the legal framework to the dominant work ethic, in search for the reasons of economic backwardness of the empire.

The political and economic atmosphere

The reign of Abdülhamid II (1876–1909) coincided with extraordinary socio-economic and political circumstances both at the domestic and global levels. Especially the first two decades of his rule coincided with the Long Depression of 1873–96, which was marked by several serious economic depressions accompanied by chronic financial crises in the European markets.[3] The Long Depression also marked the end of the golden age of economic liberalism, and a global rise of protectionism. In addition to economic and financial crises, the latecomer capitalist countries (the United States, Japan, and Germany) were challenging the monopoly of economic and political power of the core capitalist countries. In the early 1880s, the major Middle Eastern states (i.e., the Ottoman Empire, Egypt, and Iran) collapsed fiscally, mostly as a result of loans spent on rapid, inefficient, and wasteful modernization projects. This resulted in the loss of their economic and political independence.

The financial situation of the Ottoman Empire was at its worst. The industrialization efforts of the *Tanzimat* period had resulted in huge monetary losses. Other military, bureaucratic, and social reform projects as well as several debilitating wars had also consumed large amounts of financial resources. The visual aspects of modernization (e.g., the building of new European-style palaces such as Dolmabahçe) and the Westernization of the Ottoman elite's lifestyles also aggravated the financial problems of the state. Cevdet Pasha mentions that even sultan Abdülmecid I (r. 1839–61) complained about the extravagant lives of his family members and attempted to take measures to curb this trend.[4] The new ostentatious and wasteful lifestyles of the Ottoman elite, including the royal family, at a time when the state was collapsing financially haunted the minds of Ottoman reformists of the era. Chronic budget deficits as a result of all these multifaceted phenomena led the state into a debt spiral and consequently to a default in 1875.

Centrifugal political forces ranging from ethnic separatist movements to political reformist groups, such as the Young Ottomans, challenged the central government's power and authority. While using military means to stop nationalist movements, the Ottoman state responded to the radically liberal political demands of the latter by prosecution, censorship, and exile. In 1876, however, reformist politicians—such as the well-known Midhat Pasha (1822–84)—gained the upper hand in Ottoman politics and installed young Abdülhamid II as sultan.

> One of the first signs of a genuine change in the political atmosphere [in the earliest days of his reign] was the use by the new sultan in his first proclamation of words such as "fatherland" and "liberty." Both of these were Young Ottoman expressions par excellence.[5]

In such an atmosphere the first Ottoman Constitution was proclaimed in 1876, and this was followed by the convening of the first Ottoman parliament the next year. However, the new sultan would not live up to the Young Ottomans' expectations in the subsequent years. The debilitating defeat in the Russo-Ottoman War of 1877–78 gave the young sultan a pretext to end the first constitutional era (1876–78), thereby initiating his three-decade autocracy.[6]

As a result of pressing economic and financial problems as well as various political challenges to his authority, Abdülhamid II began to establish a centralized and autocratic political administration. The main pillars of his modernization project were education and economic development, opposing the radical political reformism of the Young Ottoman and later the Young Turk movements. As a result, economic education of Ottoman subjects became an essential component of Ottoman modernization, and a developing Ottoman economic literature in this era contributed to these efforts to a great extent.

Before delving into the economic literature in Turkish, it is worth noting that Turkish sources were not the only reference for Ottoman intellectuals. First, there were translations and adaptations (albeit smaller in number) in other languages of the empire too, such as Greek and Bulgarian.[7] Second, books and manuals in French were also being used by the educated elite. Some popular introductory works were serialized in French and English-language journals published in the empire. An example is, Philippe-Louis Bourdonné's *Simples Notions d'économie politique* (1869),[8] which appeared in *Le Journal de la Chambre de Commerce de Constantinople*, from November 19 to December 31, 1887. We even see, on the pages of these journals, articles on more specific issues, like the "new school" in economics, which actually includes "half-dozen other schools," such as the "historical school" and "chair socialists."[9] Therefore, the below examination of the Ottomanization of economics through translation of works and adaptation of ideas does not provide us with a complete picture of the formal economic toolbox in the hands of Ottoman intellectuals, but rather with an analysis of how this intellectual toolbox was assimilated into domestic institutional, linguistic (Turkish), intellectual, and cultural setting.

Sakızlı Ohannes and the birth of Ottoman economic liberalism

The pioneer of Ottoman economic liberalism was an Armenian economist, Sakızlı Ohannes (1830–1912).[10] After his studies in Paris, he returned to Istanbul in 1852, and was assigned to the Translation Bureau. He assumed important governmental positions, many of which were in economy-related institutions, such as the Ottoman Bank, the Ministry of Finance, and the Ministry of Commerce. In 1877 he was appointed to the Mekteb-i Mülkiye (The Imperial School of Administration) as the Professor of Economics and the Professor of Public Administration, and held this position until 1897 when he became the Minister of the Imperial Treasury (*Hazine-i Hassa Nazırı*).

Ohannes' early contributions to Ottoman economic literature were introductory articles about economics that came out in the early 1860s, when he was a clerk at the Translation Bureau. In these articles, such as "İlm-i Servet-i Milel" ("Science of the Wealth of Nations," 1863),[11] he presented a succinct summary of the Smithian view of human society, and introduced the Smithian principles of economics to the readers of the journal. These may not seem particularly novel, considering earlier Ottoman translations of (Smithian) economics. However, the importance of Ohannes' articles lies in the fact that they were published in popular periodicals, taking their place among the first works aiding in the popularization of economics in the empire. Moreover, Ohannes was not only a translator, but he was a trained economist. Therefore, Ohannes' article was the harbinger of the birth of a proper Ottoman economic literature, to which he made one of the most important contributions in 1880 with his book, *Mebadi-i İlm-i Servet-i Milel* (*Principles of the Science of the Wealth of Nations*).

Ohannes penned *Mebadi-i İlm-i Servet-i Milel* as the textbook of economics for the Mekteb-i Mülkiye. In the following decades, the book not only remained to be the textbook, from which the Ottoman elite learned economics, but also became a main reference and a source of inspiration for younger generation of economists. Almost all Ottoman intellectuals who wrote on economics and economic issues, whom we discuss below, were the graduates of this prestigious school and the students of Ohannes. Therefore, he was the towering figure of late Ottoman economic thought, especially for the liberals.

Mebadi-i İlm-i Servet-i Milel is an Ottoman example to numerous *Wealth of Nations* compendia of the age, as its title (*Principles of the Science of the Wealth of Nations*) also insinuates.[12] Yet it is not a translation or an adaptation of *The Wealth of Nations*. Ohannes notes in his introduction that he benefitted from the works of [Henri] Baudrillart (1821–92) and [Joseph] Garnier (1813–81), and that he also consulted some other prominent studies in the field without specifying any further names.[13] He explains why he preferred to write a book instead of translating a European best-seller by stating that every book published in European countries was written according to the conditions and needs of those countries, and most of them are either too short and simple, or too long and complicated. As a result, he notes, he decided to write a book for the Ottomans according to the conditions and the needs of their society.[14]

Throughout the book, Ohannes emphasizes the importance of encouraging individual entrepreneurship and supporting it with institutionalized property rights and economic freedom. He echoes Adam Smith in suggesting that there are two keys to wealth and economic modernization: labor and saving. He believes that since these and other modern economic principles must be followed by the members of all social strata, the science of economics should be read, understood, and used by every citizen of modern and modernizing societies.[15] Meanwhile, the state must refrain from interfering in market processes, especially with protectionist concerns aiming at protecting local manufacturers and "national interests." Ohannes states that this economic law is valid for developing as well as developed countries.[16] His reasons are as follows: First, industrially backward countries[17] need capital, and capital formation and inflow can only be promoted through providing (economic and political) safety and freedom of action to entrepreneurs. Second, the panacea for all economic problems is dynamism and hard work. Protectionism, however, encourages laziness and lethargy in national industries by impeding the provocative impact of foreign competition.[18] He gives the examples of Spain and Portugal, whose protectionist policies prevented success in industrialization despite their abundance of natural resources.[19] Ohannes mentions also that some protectionist economists argue that free trade brings about economic and political dependence for backward countries. He responds to such ideas by stating that interdependence among different countries is not a sign of backwardness for any party, but it is a sign of membership in an advanced civilization that is based on an international division of labor and cooperation. Thus, importing necessary goods from abroad is as beneficial as exporting national products. Accordingly, Ohannes concludes, every trade barrier, including restrictions and tariffs, constitutes an obstacle to economic development and modernization.[20]

In short, Ohannes' liberalism was an adaptation of Adam Smith's allegedly universal principles of economics to the Ottoman economy, something that would constitute the basis for Ottoman protectionists' criticisms against him and the liberal tradition he launched. As we shall see below, Ahmed Midhat, who was the standard-bearer of Hamidian-era Ottoman protectionism, criticized Ohannes and his followers for merely translating European knowledge and for suggesting nothing original. Regardless of such criticism, Ohannes' ideas made a strong impact in Ottoman economic thought principally due to the fact that several generations of Ottoman statesmen and intellectuals learned economics from him and his book at the Mekteb-i Mülkiye until the end of the empire. When his influence was at its peak, however, protectionism was on the rise in the Ottoman Empire, and it was intellectually pioneered by one of the most popular and influential Ottoman intellectuals of the late nineteenth century, Ahmed Midhat Efendi.

Ahmed Midhat and Ottoman economic protectionism

Adam Smith's economics was a child of the Scottish Enlightenment and a contemporary of the (British) Industrial Revolution. It is based on a firm belief in the idea of progress in terms of science and technology as well as social prosperity. Yet, although the capitalist system created an unprecedented mechanism for production of wealth, its distribution mechanism worked against the Smithian vision of a utopic industrial society. Abject poverty among the working classes and the Europe-wide wave of political and social upheavals in the early nineteenth century eventually brought about more pessimistic interpretations of his theories, such as those of Thomas Malthus and David Ricardo.[21]

In addition to the social havoc at the center of the capitalist world, modernization efforts in the periphery produced alternative economic models. Modernization projects induced the resurrection of economics as a science of state administration. This trend was reinforced as the continental economists observed the debilitating impact of the inflow of British manufactured goods (as a result mostly of *laissez-faire* policies) on national industries. In the late-comer capitalist economies (such as Germany and Italy), protectionist economic theories began to emerge as a response to economic liberalism enforced by the British Empire on the rest of the world. Within this critical trend, Friedrich List's (1789–1846) *National System* stood out as a powerful alternative for modernizing economies. List's model was based on economic nationalism and protection of national "infant industries"[22] from the destructive effects of foreign competition.[23] In the second half of the century, the slowing down of global economic growth, the collapse of grain prices, and financial crises contributed significantly to the rise of protectionism. Meanwhile, economic crises revealed discrepancies between the promises and the actual results of *laissez-faire* policies.[24] As a result, especially during the Long Depression of 1873–96, protectionism began to rise as a powerful alternative to the dominant economic liberalism throughout Europe, even in the standard-bearer of economic liberalism, Britain.[25] Although objections to *laissez-faire* universalism and protectionist arguments can be observed in Ottoman economic thought as early as in the 1850s, Ahmed Midhat Efendi turned protectionism into an influential line of thought in the late Ottoman intellectual sphere and in popular economic mentality.

Ahmed Midhat Efendi was among the most prominent and influential intellectuals of the late nineteenth century. He was a public intellectual and educator who authored and translated over 200 books and numerous articles.[26] He was also an active entrepreneur, who founded and ran the most influential daily of the era, *Tercüman-i Hakikat* (*The Interpreter of the Truth*, 1878–1922) and the printing press which published the newspaper and many popular educational books. Just as he taught to his readers, he remained a hard worker until his death as a teacher at the *Darüşşafaka Lisesi* (a high school for poor orphans) at the age of 68.[27]

Ahmed Midhat wrote four short books on economics and economy-related matters: *Sevda-yı Sa'y ü Amel* (*The Passion for Effort and Labor*,[28] 1879),

Teşrik-i Mesaʿî, Taksim-i Mesaʿî (*Cooperation, Division of Labor*, 1879), *Ekonomi Politik* (*Political Economy*, 1879), and *Hallü'l-ʿUkad* (*Untying the Knots*, 1890). These works were first serialized in newspapers before being made into books, except for the first one which was written based on a short newspaper article with the same title.[29] At the core of his economic thinking were his rejection of the liberal assumption for universal laws of economics, and his implicit Historical approach.[30]

The first two books, as their titles suggest, describe two essential principles of political economy that were the keys to economic development according to Ahmed Midhat. *Sevda-yı Saʿy ü Amel* (*The Passion for Effort and Labor*) is based on a basic capitalistic principle: labor is the sole source of success.[31] As Anson Rabinbach shows, late nineteenth-century European social thought was concerned with finding solutions to two powerful social challenges to an effective application of this principle: laziness and fatigue.[32] Following the discussions in France on *l'amour du travail* in this context, Ahmed Midhat's solution to this challenge was "passion for labor." After an introduction to the notions of "love" and "passion," and different forms of passion (such as that for a person, homeland, and freedom), he argues that the passion for labor paved the way for an unprecedented economic and social progress in European societies. He adds, however, that it is not peculiar to the Europeans, and in fact it exists in human nature. Therefore, Ottomans are not devoid of this basic instinct. According to him, what Europeans did was to unearth this inherent passion and process it through education in order to turn this potential power into a productive force, and the Ottomans should follow suit for economic development.[33]

In order to warm his readers to this new idea, Ahmed Midhat tells some imaginary stories in which some ideal characters of various occupations enjoy the pleasure of labor and its material and moral results. He gives the examples of a farmer, a worker, and a merchant, all of whom work hard, and at the end of the day enjoy the fruits of their toil with their beloved ones.[34] Then he gives a much more interesting and telling example by noting that sultan Abdülhamid II himself is among the "lovers of labor."[35] He relates stories he heard about the sultan and conveys the sultan's own words about the importance of hard work to his readers.[36] With this example, Ahmed Midhat emphasizes that the passion for labor is the greatest enjoyment in the world even for a sultan who does not need to work at all.[37] Although these ideas may seem like a typical eulogy for the sultan, praising a sultan for his labor (in the sense of productive work) clearly reflects a paradigm shift in Ottoman economic and political thought in the industrial age.

The principle of *Teşrik-i Mesaʿî, Taksim-i Mesaʿî* (*Cooperation and Division of Labor*) complements the passion for labor as an organizational prerequisite for development. Cooperation and division of labor were central themes in Smith's work, and they became staple topics of nineteenth-century classical economics as being the main organizing principles of an industrial economy.[38] By promoting these principles, which had been introduced earlier to Ottoman readership by Sakızlı Ohannes, Ahmed Midhat's message was simple and straightforward: in order to succeed in anything, we need to cooperate with others. He explains this principle by using the example of machines, a common reference in nineteenth-century social thought. Machines, he maintains, "comprise of ten to fifteen metal pieces" but produce miraculous results by simply obeying the laws of cooperation and division of labor. Then he asks his readers to imagine what millions of individuals can achieve by following the same principle.[39] In other words, his message to his readers is that the Ottomans can succeed in economic development. All they need is cooperation.[40] He then gives various concrete examples for interested individual readers, from starting a tannery business to founding a big paper factory, to inspire them to employ this principle in their own lives.[41]

In the introduction of *Teşrik-i Mesa'î, Taksim-i Mesa'î*, Ahmed Midhat states that despite earlier translations, there is still need for a popular political economy book written for the ordinary people in a simple language to help them understand and apply modern economic principles in everyday life.[42] He adds that the books which were translated earlier are mostly technical works, and they cannot be understood without help from a simpler introductory text.[43] The result of this concern is his *Ekonomi Politik* (*Political Economy* or *L'économie politique* in French, 1879). *Ekonomi Politik* is based on Belgian economist George de Brouckère's[44] *Principes généraux d'économie politique* (1850),[45] which was written as a popular manual of economics.[46] However, *Ekonomi Politik* is not a translation; it is even hardly an adaptation. Ahmed Midhat used the plan of Brouckère's book and ignored some parts that were not relevant to the current condition of the Ottoman economy.[47] Instead, he either added alternative explanations from other economists, or presented his own views about the Ottoman economy. This was an intended result of his approach to economics:

> Every writer adapts political economy (just like in law, ethics, and other sciences) to his own country and society, and he writes according to the level of modernization and progress of his country. For example, the intellectuals of Belgium, which has shown an outstanding progress, favor the idea that there should be no barriers to international commerce. Since their nation reached the highest stage of progress in commerce and industry, their ideas are justified. However, the intellectuals of backward countries, such as Italy, deemed protective measures necessary in order to protect internal wealth from being captured and swallowed by external trade [i.e., foreign merchants], and their ideas are equally justified. We are Ottomans, and our country is in a condition of decline. If we merely translate a work from an advanced country, such as the one we take as a model in this work, it would be an obvious mistake. Therefore, it is necessary to find the middle ground, and write political economy according to our conditions. This necessitates gathering the summaries of different authors [and alternative ideas] together. This short essay is based on this principle.[48]

As for the economists he referred to in his work, in addition to Brouckère, he names Sismondi, Droz, Say, and Rossi.[49] He mentions these names in passing while presenting different approaches to the name and scope of the discipline of political economy. His source, Brouckère's book, does not include these discussions. Yet, this does not automatically prove that Ahmed Midhat studied the works of these authors himself. On the contrary, his well-known fast working routine and his populist intellectual concerns would not let him study a single area (economics, in this context) so intensively. A more likely explanation is that he used a reference book that included all this information. This source might be Charles Coqueline's *Dictionnaire de l'économie politique*, which was a popular encyclopedic dictionary on economics in France in his age.[50] When we take a look at the entry "économie politique" in this dictionary, we can find the same names in it.[51] This may suggest that he used either this source or a similar reference for his book.

Ekonomi Politik reflects Ahmed Midhat's well-known *Hâce-i Evvel* (the first teacher) style.[52] Throughout the book he is in an imaginary dialogue with his students (i.e., his readers). He asks questions to them and responds to these questions, along with his other hypothetical questions that his readers might have. In some parts, he contradicts Brouckère's liberal theses. It is worth noting that Ahmed Midhat is definitely a liberal when it comes to issues like monopoly, private property, and private enterprise, and he also accepts the indispensable benefits of freedom of exchange and competition. He maintains that prohibitions on international trade are in fact not compatible with the fact that the God endowed different resources to different nations and countries.[53] In short, he is in accord with his source in suggesting that the monopolies and trade barriers are actually harmful, and they work against the interests of societies, whereas competition brings about wealth and progress.[54]

Nevertheless, he puts forward his reservations about *laissez-faire* policies in the short-run. In the chapter on freedom of external trade, he gives a summary of Brouckère's liberal theses, and then challenges each of them with the help of protectionist arguments taken from other "European economists," without specifying any names.[55] Reminiscent of Friedrich List's protectionism, Ahmed Midhat does not reject the validity of the *laissez-faire* approach in theory, but he asserts that these theories are only applicable and beneficial for the most developed countries. According to him, economically backward countries do not have developed industries that can compete with their European counterparts. Therefore any early attempt at competition will result in the total destruction of the existing domestic sectors.[56] He also maintains that even the developed countries do not always follow *laissez-faire* principles, and that they have recourse to protectionist policies whenever necessary.[57] In order to buttress his theses in the Ottoman context, he adds an analysis of Ottoman economic history, in which he examines the historical reasons of economic backwardness—focusing particularly on the European domination in the Ottoman economy—and suggests solutions from a protectionist perspective.[58]

After a decade-long break, Ahmed Midhat returned to political economy with another interesting book, *Hallü'l-'Ukad* (*Untying the Knots*, 1890). He developed his protectionist theses even further in this work. The book is a compilation of eight letters that are written to an unnamed dignitary in response to his questions concerning issues like classification of sciences and the place of economics within them, notions of wealth and money, and protectionism. According to him, answering these questions would "untie many knots" and educate the people about important economic matters.[59]

The first part of the book includes epistemological arguments on the *müsbet ilimler* (Ahmed Midhat refers to them as *sciences positives* in French), *sahih ilimler* (*sciences exactes* as he refers to them), and *zannî ilimler*[60] (which can be translated as "conjectural sciences," in which he includes economics).[61] Following the two letters on wealth[62] and money,[63] he repeats his protectionist ideas in his letter on trade.[64] Then he presents biographies of three famous mercantilist French statesmen/economists (*Maximilien de Béthune duc de Sully* [1560–1641], Jean-Baptiste Colbert [1619–83], and François Quesnay [1694–1774]), and he devotes the last letter to the life and ideas of Adam Smith.[65]

In *Hallü'l-'Ukad*, Ahmed Midhat complains about Ottoman liberals, who reject his protectionist arguments by claiming that "the time of Colbert has passed long ago."[66] He responds to such criticisms by suggesting that given the current level of development of the Ottoman economy, the time for Colbertian policies has not even come.[67] Then he launches a counter-attack against these liberals, some of whom, he notes, are teachers at imperial colleges. Although he does not mention any names here, he probably implies Sakızlı Ohannes and Mikael Portakal of the Mekteb-i Mülkiye. Ahmed Midhat argues that what these liberals understand from scientific inquiry is merely the knowledge of a foreign language, and thus what they do is nothing but translate European books.[68] Ahmed Midhat believes that in order to benefit from sciences for a country's problems, one must have a good grasp of the country's history and geography.[69] In other words, in economic context, the local conditions should be taken into account in economic policies, rather than simply following allegedly universal laws.

Ahmed Midhat does not specify any source for these ideas that clearly resemble those of the German Historical School. Scholars of Ahmed Midhat's economic thought have so far denied any relationship. Ahmed G. Sayar asserts that Ahmed Midhat was not influenced by the German Historical School, but derived his protectionist ideas from the mercantilists.[70] In a similar vein, François Georgeon notes that despite many parallels, a direct influence is very unlikely.[71] Although it is not easy to claim otherwise with undeniable direct evidences, this seems to be a weak argument especially concerning the strong resemblance of Ahmed Midhat's arguments and discourse to those of the Historical School. Besides, the theses of the German Historical School were so popular and influential in his time that they were summarized even in the works of liberal economists—at least to assert their inaccuracy. Therefore it seems plausible to assume that Ahmed Midhat came across the theses of the Historical School during his readings on political economy.

As for his mercantilism, it is true that in his *Hall'ül Ukad* he advises following the policies of mercantilist economists/finance ministers. Yet, his ideas reflect a more sophisticated knowledge base than those of the mercantilists of the eighteenth century. Besides, he uses the exact term, “protectionism” (*himâye usûlü*), in his discussions on economic policy.[72] Therefore, Sayar’s claim about the mercantilist influence being his only source for his protectionism is very unlikely. Ahmed Midhat seems to have chosen the mercantilists as the examples to follow not because of their theoretical approach, but due to their success in industrializing an agricultural economy thorough completely pragmatic—thus protectionist whenever necessary—policies. In any case, a quick review of the main argument of one of the most prominent forefathers of this school, Friedrich List, hints at the existence of an intellectual connection—direct or indirect—between two minds:

> It [the theory of free trade] seemed to me at first reasonable; but gradually I satisfied myself that the whole doctrine was applicable and sound only when adopted by all nations. Thus I was led to the idea of nationality; I found that the theorists kept always in view mankind and man, never separate nations. It became then obvious to me, that between two advanced countries, a free competition must necessarily be advantageous to both, if they were upon the same level of industrial progress; and that a nation, unhappily far behind as to industry, commerce and navigation, and which possessed all the material and moral resources for its development, must above every thing put forth all its strength to sustain a struggle with nations already in advance.[73]

Almost echoing Friedrich List, Ahmed Midhat, in his letter on Adam Smith, provides a summary of Smith’s ideas on economic liberalism, and concludes that “there is nothing to say to any of these, but one must be in England” to apply them.[74] He maintains that the British economy possesses extremely favorable conditions for the implementation of liberal policies, with its well-developed industry and powerful economic infrastructure.[75] However, the Ottoman economy has not reached such a high level of development; therefore international competition under free market rules would be disastrous for it. In this context, he reproaches Ottoman liberals who teach these policies at the imperial colleges, emphasizing the inappropriateness of this situation by stating that teaching liberal theories at Ottoman schools is just like teaching the Christian principle of “turning the other cheek.”[76] Moreover, he complains about the young liberal graduates of these schools who tend to criticize his ideas and efforts for the economic development of the country: “They even say, ‘you don’t know political economy!’ and try to teach it to me. Good God Almighty! [*Fesuphanallah*!]”[77]

Despite the protests of the liberals, he suggests, the Ottomans would better learn lessons from Sully, Colbert, and Quesnay. Ahmed Midhat was not the first Ottoman intellectual who introduced these names to the Ottoman intellectual sphere. In 1859, Münif Efendi (later Pasha) rendered Voltaire’s *Dialogue entre un philosophe et un controleur général des finances* (1751) into Turkish in his *Muhaverât-ı Hikemiye*. In this short piece, Voltaire’s *philosophe* discusses the importance of a successful comptroller-general of finance for increasing the wealth of a country, and he mentions Sully and Colbert as well-known examples.[78] Despite such early references, Ahmed Midhat was the first to suggest studying these examples in a systematic manner and following the pre-nineteenth century French example—if not necessarily the French mercantilist theory—for economic modernization in the Ottoman Empire.

Ahmed Midhat provides biographies of Sully, Colbert, and Quesnay, and he examines how they reinvigorated France by applying strict fiscal measures and protectionist policies that developed French industry and agriculture. Since the Ottoman economy of the late nineteenth century resembled more pre-Industrial-Revolution French economy than that of the post-Industrial-Revolution Britain, he finds these examples more relevant for his country.[79] He states: "Here are the biographies of three big economists, you will find the way to salvation no matter which one you choose to follow," and Adam Smith also developed his own theories based on the ideas and policies of these three economists.[80] Then, he emphasizes again that all of these economists wrote for the particular economic conditions that they lived in, and this is why the mercantilists emphasized agriculture, and Smith focused on industry.[81]

In short, contrary to prominent liberal Ottoman economists, Ahmed Midhat rejects allegedly universally valid *laissez-faire* policies. He instead aims at systematizing a historical and protectionist approach in Ottoman economics. However, despite his harsh criticisms of Ottoman liberals and his explicit protectionist arguments, he has a conspicuously liberal perspective on issues like private property, freedom of enterprise, competition, and the role of state in the domestic market. His strategy of economic development was built on cooperation and division of labor between hard-working and entrepreneurially-minded individuals, and not on state-led industrialization. In this respect, his protectionist ideas stood on obvious liberal principles. Where he disputed liberals most was in his belief in the protection of the domestic market—and particularly nascent industries—in the short run, and his rejection of universal laws in economics. All in all, he pioneered to develop an Ottomanized version of economics, which was a pragmatic mixture of liberalism and protectionism at the policy level and was inspired by the historical and institutional realities of the empire as well as the conceptual framework of classical political economy.

Following the first steps: the 1880s and early 1890s

In 1882, Nuri Bey, then an official at the Ottoman Customs Administration (*Cemiyyet-i Rüsûmiye âzâsı*), published his *Mebahis-i İlm-i Servet* (*Themes in the Science of Wealth*). Although there is no clear evidence in the book itself, the author is the well-known Young Ottoman leader Menâpirzade Mustafa Nuri Bey (1844–1906).[82] Several details in Mustafa Nuri Bey's biography support this identification. First, Mustafa Nuri Bey held the aforementioned position (*Cemiyyet-i Rüsûmiye âzâsı*) between June 30, 1880 and April 3, 1883.[83] Second, it is noted in his official records that "he has works on economics that are published and unpublished."[84] Third, a high-ranking official of the era, Tevfik Biren, states in his memoirs that "[Nuri Bey] studied economics, and such people were rare in those days. As far as I remember, he also wrote a book on economics."[85] Thus, it seems plausible to believe that *Mebahis-i İlm-i Servet* (1882) belongs to Menâpirzade Mustafa Nuri Bey. This adds to the importance of the book, since it constitutes the only proper economic treatise written by a leading member of the Young Ottoman movement.

In his introduction, Nuri Bey mentions two factors that motivated him to write the book. The first one is the importance of economics for "civilized societies." He argues that the coverage of this discipline expands with the progress of civilization, and its principles have become more and more relevant for a wider spectrum of human relations, both material and moral. Thus, it is impossible for any civilized society to ignore its principles. The second factor is his personal experiences. He states that although the importance of this discipline first inspired him to write a book on this subject, his experiences in the Ottoman Customs Administration expedited the process. After being assigned to the Administration, he realized that the transactions and the procedures in the Ottoman customs were a far cry from what the principles of modern economics would suggest. He witnessed a chaotic and arbitrary system, which made the Ottoman Customs Administration open to all kinds of abuse and corruption.[86]

Nuri Bey names only one Ottoman study on economics in his work: Ohannes' *Mebahis-i İlm-i Servet-i Milel*. Interestingly enough, despite Ahmed Midhat's immense popularity both as a public intellectual and an ardent supporter of protectionism, Nuri Bey openly ignores his writings. In any case, he argues that while Ohannes' book is a competent study, it lacks some important aspects that his own book aims to complete. He notes that a distinctive characteristic of his own work is the presentation of economic principles in a dialogical format to make them easier to understand. He also argues that Ohannes' book teaches, rather dryly, the principles of economics, but not its history. Nuri Bey's book, however, includes the history of economics and the biographies of prominent European economists. He also considers his own book an important study thanks to the inclusion of Arab contributions to economics.[87] Here, his reference to "Arab scholars" aims at proving the contributions of Muslims to this field; and by doing so, he traces an Islamic intellectual tradition of economics.

Although Nuri Bey was among the first Ottoman intellectuals who tried to unearth the tradition of Islamic economics, he was not the first one.[88] The Muslim reaction to the European claim for the invention of economics was older than Nuri Bey's book. As an example, we learn from a letter dated 1874 between two most prominent statesmen of the era, Midhat Pasha to Cevdet Pasha, that they discussed the issue, and the latter pointed out Ibn Khaldun's work as the proof of an Islamic economics tradition preceding modern European political economy.[89] It is worth noting that, in the same era, Ibn Khaldun's work was referred to by other Muslim intellectuals to prove the existence of an indigenous Islamic tradition of sociology in a similar manner.[90]

As a reflection of the two main factors that motivated him to undertake this study, Nuri Bey's book is organized in two parts: The first part provides a general introduction to the science of wealth (with its history, as well as the main principles); the second part deals with the question of the division of wealth, a great portion of which is devoted to the government's share in this division. In other words, the second part is mainly on public finance, and particularly on customs. Nuri Bey's book is a very interesting and important example in Ottoman economic literature, for various reasons. First, it is not a translation, although it is highly probable that he simply copied some parts from the works of European economists. For example, the first section (entitled *Tercüme-i Hal* [Biography]) of the first part is a conventional nineteenth-century narrative of the history of economics starting from ancient Greek philosophers and ending with the prominent economists of the nineteenth century like [Claude Frédéric] Bastiat (1801–50) and [Pellegrino] Rossi (1787–1848).[91]

The introduction stands out as a much more interesting text than the main body of the book thanks to Nuri Bey's narrative of the Arab-Muslim tradition of economic thought. As he acknowledges himself, this is an original contribution to not only Ottoman economic literature, but also to Islamic intellectual history in a broader sense. According to him, all students of modern sciences know that the contributions of medieval Arab scholars cannot be denied in the development of these sciences, and there should not be an exception for the science of wealth. "It is impossible," he states, "that the Arab scholars might have ignored this science which is directly related to the wealth and prosperity of society," especially considering the religious obligation on Muslim scholars to work for the well-being of the community.[92]

It is obvious in these statements that despite his strong belief in the existence of an early tradition of Islamic economics, the main ground of this belief is reasoning, rather than strong evidences. However, he tries to support his claim by tracing economic ideas—rather unsystematically—in the works of certain Arab-Muslim scholars. For example, he refers to Ibn Khaldun's arguments on *ilm-i tedbir-i menzil* (the science of household management) and *siyaset-i medeniye ilmi* (the science of urban management).[93] He concludes that since Ibn Khaldun based such arguments on politics, ethics, and wealth, which are the main components of economics, his writings should be considered within the science of wealth.[94] Then Nuri Bey uses examples from the words and deeds of two Rightly Guided Caliphs, Abu Bakr and Ali, to demonstrate the importance they ascribed to economic matters.[95]

He notes that his sources for these examples are the works of other Ottoman Muslim intellectuals of his age, such as Tunuslu Hayreddin Pasha and Subhi Pasha (*Evkaf-ı Hümayûn Nazırı* [the Minister of Imperial Pious Foundations], 1826–86), thereby revealing some earlier efforts to unearth the alleged Islamic tradition of economics. All in all, Nuri Bey's conclusion on the question is that that there was a strong economic awareness among scholars and statesmen of the early centuries of Islamic civilization, but this tradition was abandoned at some point in history. As a result, the Muslims of his age were unaware of the principles of this essential science, as well as its early Islamic roots.[96]

It was not only Muslim intellectuals who were interested in early Islamic economic ideas. In the nineteenth century, it was widely believed that "Political economy is in truth the creation of what has been called the European genius," as put by the Belgian jurist and author Ernest Nys (1851–1920).[97] However, it was known that the Islamic civilization was not devoid of ideas on economic issues. As Nys himself also stated in his chapter on the "Musulman and Byzantine Influences" on European economic thought,[98] "In their conquests the Arabs were by no means inspired by the mere spirit of destruction.... They were traders for ages before Mohammed."[99] Discussing the economic motivations behind the Islamic conquests, Nys provided examples of Islamic institutions for the management of the economy and public finance, from taxation to customs, with references to various works of Ibn Khaldun as well as to the works of European Orientalists such as Joseph von Hammer and Wilhelm von Heyd.[100] Therefore, Nuri Bey was not a romantic champion of a lost cause, but rather an investigator of possible connections between his own culture and Eurocentric capitalist modernity, through unearthing Muslim presence in pre-modern scientific and intellectual history.[101]

Following his introduction and the "biography" (i.e., history) of economics, Nuri Bey's book continues as a dialogue between an "objector" (*muʿteriz*) and a "respondent" (*mûcib*). His objector is not a mere uninformed student who asks questions, but rather a person who has studied the science of wealth and has some questions and confusion regarding his readings. The objector does not only ask questions, but sometimes literally objects to some widely accepted arguments, some of which were presented also by Ohannes. In some cases, both sides even blame each other for misunderstanding expressions and ideas in Ohannes' book.[102] In this sense, Nuri Bey stands in indirect dialogue with Ohannes' work along with some European economists.

The content of each chapter, except for the first chapter on the history of economics, reflects Nuri Bey's syntheses of ideas from European economists and various Ottoman sources. He does not mention any particular work that provided a basis for his book. However, in addition to some classic references like Smith, Rossi, and Say, he mentions the books, and even sometimes articles, of some prominent economists of his age such as Nicolas Villiaume, Michel Chevalier, Ferdinand Hervé-Bazin, Francis Lacombe, and many others. It is important to note that these names were not frequently referenced in Ottoman economic literature of the era. Moreover, he also refers to other more technical sources such as *Économie Annuaire*, which contains statistical information about the French economy.[103]

Another distinct characteristic of Nuri Bey's *Mebahis-i İlm-i Servet* is his general approach to economics, which can be defined by two keywords: normative and protectionist. Just like Ahmed Midhat, he does not believe that economics can be counted among the "positive sciences" with universal rules. Moreover, according to him, the science of wealth is not a science that merely explains the facts of acquisition of wealth without any concern for the source of wealth. In other words, notions such as ethics,[104] justice,[105] and concern for public prosperity[106] are and should be indispensable components of economics. However, he also strongly criticizes "unrealistic theories," such as socialism and communism, which propose radical changes in the social and economic system on the bases of equality and justice.[107]

Regarding economic freedom and state intervention, Nuri Bey does not hesitate to extend the borders of public interest into the boundaries of individual freedom, despite his objector's protests. According to him, the state should interfere whenever an individual's action clashes with the public interest. For example, if an agricultural producer insists on ignoring her/his social role by keeping her/his land uncultivated, the state can punish this producer or even confiscate the land.[108] In his response to the objector, who asks whether this is not against the notion of individual freedom, Nuri Bey reminds of a prerequisite of the idea of freedom: social responsibility. In other words, according to him, there are limits to individual freedom and there is no freedom without responsibility.[109] It is worth noting that these conventional arguments of nineteenth-century liberal political discourse match perfectly with the traditional land regime of the Ottoman Empire: although the land is distributed to the individual producers, the real owner of the land is always the state.

His protectionist perspective manifests itself especially in the section on external trade. Echoing Friedrich List—but without any direct reference to him, as in Ahmed Midhat's writings—Nuri Bey summarizes the arguments of the *laissez-faire* approach and maintains that they seem right in theory.[110] He states, however, that the applicability of these theories has a very important prerequisite, that is, similarity in the levels of industrialization of the trading countries. Otherwise, just as in the case of trade between European economies and the Ottoman Empire, the industry of the weaker party becomes incapacitated, and the country becomes economically dependent on foreign industrial powers.[111] Instead of *laissez-faire* policies, he argues for the infant industry protection in the short run. Nuri Bey emphasizes that this should only be a short- or medium-term policy, and as soon as a competitive national industry is built, the principles of free trade should be applied for further economic development. Otherwise, he believes, permanent protectionism is also harmful to economic development.[112]

Interestingly enough, the most prominent figure in Ottoman liberal economics, Mehmed Cavid Bey—whose work we shall discuss below—later praised Nuri Bey's work as an important contribution to Ottoman economic literature.[113] Nevertheless, concerning Nuri Bey's protectionist views and Cavid Bey's uncompromising liberal stance, Cavid Bey's words of sympathy cast some doubt on whether he actually read the work. Moreover, when Nuri Bey published his book, he was working under another prominent liberal economist: Portakal Mikael. Mikael was then the General Director of the Ottoman Customs Administration. Nuri Bey praises Mikael, and he includes a translation[114] of a memorandum written by Mikael, summarizing the conditions of the Ottoman customs regime.[115] Unfortunately, we do not have any hint regarding Mikael's response to Nuri Bey's work, nor do we have any information about the impact of this interesting work in the Ottoman intellectual sphere.

In 1885, three years after the publication of Nuri Bey's book, Mahmud Es'ad published a study entitled *İlm-i Servet* (*The Science of Wealth*).[116] According to the note on its first page, the book is based on Münif Pasha's (1830–1910) lectures at the Imperial School of Law.[117] However, Mahmud Es'ad later published his own multi-volume work on economics in 1909.[118]

Münif Pasha (1830–1910) was among the most prominent statesmen and intellectuals of the late Ottoman Empire. He received a traditional education in his early youth, but later studied modern philosophy and sciences during his diplomatic services as well as his stint at the Translation Bureau. In the early 1860s, he pioneered in the foundation of the *Cemiyyet-i İlmiye-i Osmaniye* (Ottoman Scientific Society), which published the first Ottoman popular science journal, *Mecmua-i Fünûn.* In addition to his numerous articles on education, grammar, history, and modern sciences, his early economic writings appeared in this influential periodical of the era. Later he became one of the key figures in the modernization of Ottoman education during the Hamidian era, as he served three terms as the Minister of Education (1877, 1878–80, and 1885–91).[119] Besides, according to some scholars, he taught political economy to Abdülhamid II.[120]

Münif Pasha's *İlm-i Servet* follows the typical outline of economics books of the era—production, distribution and consumption of wealth, and the population question in the conclusion. It is obvious from this outline that Münif Pasha referred to the works of European economists for his lectures, but unfortunately the book does not contain any information about its sources. The content and the tone of the book suggest that this is a narrative of political economic by an Ottoman intellectual rather than a translation of a particular work. Although the topics and the theoretical framework are taken from European—most probably French—sources, the examples and debates are mostly about the Ottoman Empire. The reader feels the didactic tone of an idealist teacher who aims at educating the youth, who are expected build a modern Ottoman country. According to him, not only every official of the Ottoman state, but all citizens must learn and follow the principles of this discipline for the country to achieve prosperity and development.[121]

Münif Pasha frequently refers to traditional Islamic sources (the Qur'an and *hadith*[122]) both explicitly and implicitly.[123] In addition to transmitting Western knowledge to his students through the filters of Islamic sources, he uses traditional ideas and references as the patterns in which he casts Western material. In other words, he employs the familiar to introduce the new. As an example, on the discussion of needs and economic value, he argues that there are both bodily and spiritual needs. Although the latter is more important than the former, according to him, the body should also be well-treated since it is the cover and the "mount" (*matiyya*) of the soul.[124] Here, Münif Pasha probably refers to a *hadith* (saying) of the Prophet: "your body is your mount (*matiyya*), treat it gently."[125] Thus, he casts the modern economic theory of value into a pattern derived from a *hadith*, and then uses this instrument to educate his Ottoman (not necessarily Muslim) students in modern economic principles. In order to transmit new ideas, he benefits from the references with which his students are well acquainted. In this sense, the traditional values play an essential pedagogical role even in modern education as they are used to explain or sanction new ideas. The book also includes important insights into a reformist Ottoman intellectual and statesman's envisioning for building a new society based on modern economic principles, which will be discussed in the next chapter.

In 1888, a graduate of the Mekteb-i Mülkiye, Suʿad, translated Prosper Rambaud's *Précis élémentaire d'économie politique: à l'usage des facultés de droit et des écoles* (1880), with the title *Telhis-i İlm-i Servet* (*A Summary of the Science of Wealth*, 1888).[126] This introductory book also follows the conventional plan (an introduction to economics, followed by parts on production, distribution and consumption of wealth), and the author adds a final chapter on additional relevant themes (the population question and Malthus, socialism and communism, and insurance). In his introduction, Suʿad provides a brief definition and the scope of the science of wealth. With references to European economists, he argues that just like other aspects of the physical world, economic phenomena are subject to certain natural laws. The science of wealth, as a branch of sociology, he adds, is the inquiry of such natural laws.[127] His main reason for choosing Rambaud's book for translation is that it is "short and useful" (*muhtasar ve müfid*).[128] He complains that Ottoman interest in "new" (European) studies is very limited and it is especially so if the works in question are long and detailed (*mufassal*).[129]

Rambaud's study is another example of not highly original introductory books, and Suʿad's translation is a faithful one. The only important detail about the work that is worth mentioning is Rambaud's approach to economics. In his introduction Rambaud argues that a person who writes on social issues must specify his approach in advance. Following this principle, Rambaud declares that he is not a materialist, and he believes that economics cannot be separated from ethics. He thereby expects his readers to use its principles not only for material but also spiritual prosperity.[130] Suʿad does not comment on this remark, so we do not know if this affected Suʿad's choice of this book, but Rambaud's moral concerns seem to suit to the Hamidian regime's emphasis on (Islamic) morality, particularly observed in the intellectual and educational spheres.[131]

Following Suʿad's translation, Ahmed İhsan (Tokgöz) (1868–1942) published his book, *İlm-i Servet* (*The Science of Wealth*), in 1892. Ahmed İhsan was another prominent figure in late-Ottoman and early-Turkish-Republican intellectual and press history. He graduated from the Mekteb-i Mülkiye (1886), where he was a student of Ohannes and Mikael. In 1891, he founded the well-known, *Servet-i Fünûn* (*The Wealth of Sciences*), which was first a popular science periodical, then turned into a literary journal and a very influential literary movement with the same name.

In his memoirs, Ahmed İhsan states that the lectures and books of these Ohannes and Mikael aroused his interest in economics.[132] However, his real inspirational figure was Ahmed Midhat, whom he followed in his career as a public intellectual, writer, publisher, and press entrepreneur.[133] After graduating from the Mekteb-i Mülkiye and a very brief stint of government service, Ahmed İhsan decided to become an entrepreneur instead of a civil servant, just as

Ahmed Midhat always suggested to the youth. He founded his own printing press (Servet-i Fünûn Matbaası) to the chagrin of his elders, who preferred him to be a respected official rather than a "shopkeeper," as his grandmother puts it in protest.[134] Such conflicts between established Ottoman families and their more bourgeois-spirited sons seem to be ubiquitous in the era. The well-known Egyptian intellectual of the era, Jurji Zaydan, also received a similarly adverse reaction from his family on his decision to become a journalist in 1887. His father "wanted his son to study something more 'decent,' such as medicine or law."[135] As both examples show, the economy-centered age, its bourgeois values and new economic ideas gripped the youth of Ottoman central and provincial elites, as the region was gradually integrated into the global capitalist system in intellectual, cultural, and political terms, as well as economic ones.

Ahmed İhsan first serialized *İlm-i Servet* (*The Science of Wealth*) in his *Servet-i Fünûn*, and then published it in book form. Although, he does not cite any sources in the book, it seems to be either an adaptation of a certain study or his summary based on some introductory political economy books. Ahmed İhsan, just like Ahmed Midhat and Nuri Bey, uses everyday language in a conversational tone, and follows the classic outline mentioned above. The book is organized in nine parts, and each part contains various questions about the principles of modern political economy, the last question serving as a brief conclusion.[136] In short, although Ahmed İhsan's *İlm-i Servet* does not include much original material, the author's story, particularly his interest in economics and his entrepreneurial spirit, tells us a great deal about the capitalist cultural transformation and the impact of economic education in social change in the late Ottoman Empire.

Books on public finance

Soon after Abdülhamid II ascended to the throne, a veteran Ottoman official advised him to employ a "Minister of Public Finance who knows political economy,"[137] for a successful reform in state finances. This pursuit of scientific administration of state affairs generated an increasing interest not only in economics, but also in public finance as a separate field.

In the same year that Sakızlı Ohannes published his book (1880), a graduate of the Mekteb-i Mülkiye and an intern at the Council of State[138] Hüseyin Kâzım translated Paul Leroy-Beaulieu's (1843–1916) influential book *Traité de la science de finances* (1877) with the title *İlm-i Usûl-i Mâliye*.[139] The translator notes in his introduction that the book does not include any information on Ottoman state finances, but he does not prefer to alter the original text to adapt it to the Ottoman economy. He believes that the same universal principles described in the book were also valid for the Ottoman Empire anyway. Nevertheless, he continues, "some honorable gentlemen" (*zevat-ı kiram*)[140] suggested him that the Ottoman case should be evaluated in a separate volume.[141] We do not know if Hüseyin Kâzım ever attempted to prepare another volume, as suggested by those "honorable gentlemen," but nine years after Hüseyin Kâzım's translation, we observe the publication of three books on public finance within the same year: Mehmed Rakım and Mustafa Nail's *Hayat-i Düvel* (*Life of the States*), Mikael Portakal's *Usûl-i Mâliye* (*Principles of Public Finance*) and Süleyman Sûdi's *Defter-i Muktesid* (*The Economist's Notebook*). Although they were all on the same topic, their approaches and target audiences were different.

Hayat-ı Düvel is a book by two of Mikael's former students from the Mekteb-i Mülkiye, Mehmed Rakım (d. 1937) and Mustafa Nail (1859–1919).[142] In the introduction, the authors state that it is the first book on public finance published in the Ottoman Empire.[143] This shows, first, they were not aware of Hüseyin Kâzım's translation, and second—since the publications year is the same as others—it appeared only months before Mikael's and Süleyman Sûdi's works. The authors state their reason to write the book as follows: "Unfortunately, this discipline has hitherto been taught only at the Mekteb-i Mülkiye by Mikael Efendi. Therefore, only the students of this school had the opportunity to benefit from it."[144] The authors note that they used the works of [Joseph] Garnier and [Paul] Leroy-Beaulieu in composing the book.[145] They also mention the lectures of Mikael at the Mekteb-i Mülkiye as another source for it.[146] In addition to theoretical explanations on various subjects, the authors use examples from the Ottoman Empire, and compare the Ottoman case with other cases from Europe.[147] Especially in this respect, Mehmed Rakım and Mustafa Nail's book was an important contribution to Ottoman economic literature, as it provided the readers with a comparative perspective to the empire's economic and fiscal conditions.

Shortly after his students' book, Mikael Portakal's (1841–97) influential work, *Usûl-i Mâliye* (*Principles of Public Finance*, 1889) appeared as a lithographed manuscript. *Usûl-i Mâliye* was published as the textbook for the fourth- and fifth-year students of the Mekteb-i Mülkiye, where Mikael was the Professor of Public Finance. The career path of this then famous Ottoman-Armenian economist resembles that of Sakızlı Ohannes—also an Armenian—as both assumed economy-related positions throughout their official careers. He was assigned first to the Translation Bureau (1861) and then became the Director of the Customs of Galata (1868). In 1878 he was appointed as the General Director of the Ottoman Customs and the Professor of Public Finance at the Mekteb-i Mülkiye. Later he became the undersecretary of the Ministry of Finance (1885). In 1888, he undertook the foundation of the Ottoman Agricultural Bank (*Ziraat Bankası*) and became its first General Director. Obviously, when he wrote the book, he was familiar with the Ottoman financial and administrative system as well as financial theory and policy in Europe. Later, in 1891, he was appointed as the Minister of the Sultan's Privy Purse (*Hazine-i Hassa Nazırı*), and remained in this position until his death in 1897.[148] As noted above, Sakızlı Ohannes took up the position after Mikael, which shows that the so-called pan-Islamist sultan, Abdülhamid II, entrusted his privy purse to Armenian economists.

The main body of Mikael Portakal's *Usûl-i Mâliye* is based on examples from leading European countries' public finance policies, along with liberal arguments about the Ottoman finances vis-à-vis those more advanced and ideal (i.e., European) cases. Although the author does not delve into any theoretical discussions, the theoretical backbone of the book is apparently liberal, and the main thesis of the book is that the Ottoman Empire should follow the universal (liberal) principles which proved to be successful from Prussia to England. Mikael also emphasizes that the science of public finance suggests general principles for managing the revenues and expenditures of the state, and does not deal with the creation of resources, the latter being the subject of economics (*ilm-i servet-i milel*).[149]

Mikael Portakal does not make any open suggestions for the economic strategy to follow in the empire. Nevertheless, in the secondary literature on Ottoman economic thought, his name has been mentioned among the leaders of Ottoman economic liberalism, without any direct reference to his ideas and work.[150] The main reason for this assumption about his importance in late Ottoman economic thought seems not to be any original ideas or arguments from him, but his impact on the students of the Mekteb-i Mülkiye. In any case, despite its importance as the textbook through which many Ottoman statesmen were educated in the science of public finance, Mikael's study does not contain much original content concerning the Ottoman fiscal and economic system.

In contrast to Mikael's work, Süleyman Sûdi's (1835–96) book, *Defter-i Muktesid* (*The Economist's Notebook*), was a highly original and important study of the Ottoman fiscal structure and practices, based on a meticulous study of Ottoman institutional framework and Islamic jurisprudence as well as modern theories of fiscal policy. His fame and influence, however, did not outlive him for long as in the case of Mikael. Similar to Ohannes and Mikael, Süleyman Sûdi's career followed a path in the Ottoman fiscal and economic bureaucracy. He began his career in 1859, when he was 15 years old, at the Imperial Revenues Office (*Gelirler Muhasebesi*), then worked at different positions in financial offices of the empire. He served as the head of the provincial treasury (*defterdar*) of important centers such as Salonica (1869) and the Province of Syria (1876), in addition to other higher level positions, such as the Director of the Ottoman Mint (1887).[151]

In addition to his practical experience in the Ottoman public financial system, we know that he studied public finance from European works. We have two sources to support this thesis: First, Ahmed İhsan, who personally knew him, notes that Süleyman Sûdi studied "economic sciences."[152] Second, a careful reading of the book reveals a strong theoretical underpinning.

Ahmed İhsan notes that Süleyman Sûdi was the first Ottoman intellectual who used the word *iktisad*,[153] which is still used in modern Turkish to denote both "economics" and "economy." Sayar takes up this claim and argues that Süleyman Sûdi put an end to the confusion and variation regarding the phrases used to render the meaning of the science of economics.[154] Despite Sayar's claim, however, Süleyman Sûdi did not suggest the term *ilm-i iktisad* (literally, the science of economics) for economics. On the contrary he makes a clear distinction between these two separate sciences, and uses *ilm-i tedbir-i servet* (the science of management of wealth) for "*économie politique*," and *ilm-i iktisad* for public finance. He notes also that he derived the word *muktesid* (literally, "economist") from the Arabic *iqtisād*, to denote a person who studies or practices *ilm-i iktisad*; in other words, a finance official.[155]

Süleyman Sûdi wrote *Defter-i Muktesid* for practical purposes. During his term as the chair of a selection committee for the employment of civil servants for the Ministry of Finance, he observed that candidates were able to answer all the questions based on basic knowledge of public finance principles, but they could not successfully respond to questions on the Ottoman fiscal system. This gave him the motivation to pen a comprehensive but practical manual for candidates as well as for active civil servants already working at the Ministry of Finance.[156] He realized that the rules and principles governing the Ottoman fiscal system were derived from Islamic jurisprudence (*fiqh*), and it was impossible for every finance official to master such a complicated field. Therefore he decided to write a compendium of public finance that includes Islamic principles of public finance and the basic features of the Ottoman system.[157]

In *Defter-i Muktesid*, Süleyman Sûdi explains each item in state finances on three grounds: a summarized history (*icmâlen tarîhi*), definition and assessment (*usûl-i tarhı*), and collection (*usûl-i tahsîli*). In this sense he discusses every item in its historical and practical context. Another important and original aspect of his work is that he provides etymological information for each major term, and such notes are longer especially if a French word has an Arabic or Persian (thus, so to speak, a Muslim) root.[158] As an example, he argues that the French word *douane* (customs) comes from Arabic *diwan*, which had been adopted from Persian. As an indicator of his synthetical (from Islamic and European sources) method, he refers to two sources for this argument: Ibn Khaldun and a "professor from the University of Bonn"—whom he does not name.[159] As another example, he suggests that the word *tarif* was derived from an Arabic word (*ta'rif*), and this time his source is a French dictionary of *économie politique*, which again he does not specify.[160]

In both its content and approach, *Defter-i Muktesid* offers a Muslim-Ottoman paradigm for the discipline of public finance, based on an Ottoman historical and institutional ground, supported by Islamic principles concerning public finance and economics. In addition many references to Qur'anic verses and *hadith* literature, Süleyman Sûdi narrates stories about Caliph 'Umar, who has been traditionally known for his justice, to give ideal Islamic examples of managing public finances.[161] However, it would be wrong to assume that these were his only sources. On the contrary, as Ahmed İhsan notes, Süleyman Sûdi was a "European-type" intellectual in terms of both his thoughts and lifestyle.[162] Thus, in every discussion, he refers to European studies and policy examples from major European countries (mostly France and Britain), placing the Ottoman fiscal and financial system in a comparative European context, similar to what some other Ottoman economists did before him. What is original in Süleyman Sûdi's approach, however, is that that he does not present European cases as ideals to be reached, but rather as comparative cases to study.

An interesting example that demonstrates his historical and comparative method in action is a discussion on the issue of cadaster and taxation. He starts with a short etymological explanation of the French word *cadaster*, then he discusses the French cadastral policies in the time of Colbert. Then, returning to the

Ottoman Empire, he argues that tax assessment based on cadastral surveys is a very old Ottoman state tradition, and it is even older in the history of Islamic civilization, going back to the age of Caliph ʿUmar.[163] This rather complex and informed synthesis of European theories and policies with Islamic principles and practices makes the work a unique example of "Ottoman economics" as such.

Süleyman Sûdi was a liberal. He believed in minimal state,[164] and argued for *laissez-faire* in international trade.[165] In his defense of free trade, for example, he argues that the Ottoman economy depends on imports, therefore free trade is a must for the Ottoman economy as well as it is for developed economies.[166] Nevertheless, his work received a very warm welcome also from the anti-*laissez-faire* intellectuals of the era. The reason for this was Süleyman Sûdi's building his theses on history and the actual functioning of domestic institutions, especially the Islamic law and Ottoman fiscal system—as much as on modern economic theories. Thus, his implicit Historical approach and the indigenous character of his work attracted the attention of Ottoman intellectuals who rejected the universal applicability and benefits of liberal policies. The introduction to his third volume includes praises on these grounds from three prominent Ottoman intellectuals and statesmen of the era: Fehim Efendi from the Board of Audit (*Divan-ı Muhasebat*), Ahmed Midhat Efendi, and (Mizancı) Mehmed Murad Bey (1854–1917).

Fehim Efendi suggests that Süleyman Sûdi's study is an extremely important and a long overdue contribution as a practical manual for the officials of the Finance Ministry.[167] Responding to the discussion on Islam and economics—and almost echoing Nuri Bey's words mentioned previously—Fehim Efendi asserts that the Islamic government tradition created a sophisticated fiscal administration system and a body of financial principles in its long history. However, he adds, due to the lack of a work that illuminates this history, these facts are not known in modern times, and as a result, some scholars claim that the science of public finance is a European invention. According to Fehim Efendi, Süleyman Sûdi's work successfully shows that many principles of the modern science of public finance existed in the Islamic tradition for centuries.[168]

According to Ahmed Midhat Efendi, *Defter-i Muktesid* is a wonderful summary of both Islamic financial principles and the latest European theories about the matter. In addition to praising the book, Ahmed Midhat uses the opportunity to attack *laissez-faire* economists through Süleyman Sûdi's work. He suggests that a summary of this book should be used as a textbook in Ottoman higher education, replacing existing textbooks—implying those of Ohannes and Mikael Portakal—which promote European theories that are in fact inapplicable in the Ottoman Empire.[169]

Mehmed Murad Bey, in his praise originally published in his own journal *Mizan* (*Balance*),[170] joins the other reviewers by stating that the book filled an important void by providing a history of the Ottoman financial system. Murad Bey, like Fehim Efendi, criticizes some European "ignoramuses" who claim that the Europeans invented the science of public finance and that there had been no such a discipline before Sully, Colbert, Turgot, and Adam Smith.[171] Süleyman

Sûdi, according to Murad Bey, proves the existence of a deeply rooted and sophisticated tradition of public finance in Islamic civilization much earlier than its appearance as a separate discipline in modern Europe.

All in all, Süleyman Sûdi's *Defter-i Muktesid* is a prime example of the Ottomanization of economics in terms of both content and approach. It is an original synthesis of insider knowledge on domestic institutions and a careful study of European sources. It explains the theory and practice of the Ottoman fiscal system in its historical and modern theoretical contexts with specific references to both modern European theories and practices and traditional Islamic principles. In this respect, despite its clearly liberal underpinnings, it can be considered a major contribution to Historical and institutional explorations in Ottoman economic thought, and perhaps the most original example of "Ottoman economics."

Protectionism vs. liberalism debate revisited: Akyiğitzade Musa and Mehmed Cavid

The dispute between protectionists and liberals grew stronger in the 1890s with a new generation of Ottoman economists. Meanwhile the ensuing rise of protectionism manifested itself also in the economic policies, and the 1890s witnessed a gradual departure from the decades-long adherence to liberalism in Ottoman economic policies. The discursive power as well as policy dominance of economic protectionism was to culminate in the post-1908 Young Turk era—paradoxically—under the Finance Minister Mehmed Cavid Bey, who had been one of the standard bearers of liberalism in late Ottoman economic thought starting from the late 1890s.[172]

In 1896, Akyiğitzade Musa (1865–1923) published his *İktisad yâhud İlm-i Servet: Âzâdegi-i Ticâret ve Usûl-i Himâye* (*Economics or the Science of Wealth: Freedom of Exchange and the System of Protectionism*).[173] As the title suggests, Akyiğitzade's book is not an introductory book about economics, but a treatise on a specific debate in it: *laissez faire* vs. protectionism. Akyiğitzade revived Ahmed Midhat's earlier cause against the dominant *laissez-faire* approach in Ottoman economic thought. However, his book differs from Ahmed Midhat's works by providing a more systematic and detailed response against the liberal theses. In his introduction, Akyiğitzade notes that he benefitted from the books on political economy that are studied in French higher education. More specifically, he mentions two names as his main sources of inspiration: (Friedrich) List and Paul Cauwès (1843–1917). By suggesting the names of these two economists of the Historical School of economics, Akyiğitzade openly declares his stance as a protectionist.[174] The book is not a translation of the work of any of these economists, but rather a free-style adaptation of their theses in the Ottoman context.

In the first part of the book, Akyiğitzade evaluates these two contending approaches separately by providing a detailed summary of the main theses of both sides.[175] Throughout the rest of the book, he provides comparisons between these two approaches and argues why a "moderate protectionism" (*himâye-i maʿkûle*) in the short-run is necessary for economic development. Akyiğitzade's main argument rests on List's hierarchical development model for human societies: "In reference to political economy, nations have to pass through the following stages of development:—The savage state, the pastoral state, the merely agricultural state, and the state at once agricultural, manufacturing and commercial."[176] According to the Listian model as presented by Akyiğitzade, nations go through four stages of economic development: hunting, animal husbandry, agriculture, and finally industry. Within the industrial phase, there are different stages in which the same nation produces different products. Therefore, the comparative advantage of a nation does not remain in the same sector.[177] Based on these "historical facts," Akyiğitzade claims, Ottoman liberals are simply wrong in asserting that the Ottoman Empire should remain as an agricultural producer because of its comparative advantage in agriculture.[178] He adds that agricultural prices are tied to the developments in external markets, and that this creates a continuous uncontrollable threat for local producers, thereby for the entire economy.[179] As another important reason for the necessity of industrialization, he notes that industry and consequent urbanization is at the heart of civilization, and that an advanced civilization cannot be found on a village economy. Therefore, the road to civilization passes through industrialization.[180]

Similar to what Ahmed Midhat and Nuri Bey suggested earlier, Akyiğitzade echoes List in acknowledging that Smith's theses hold in theory, yet there are some preconditions for their application. For example, there must be a balance of industrial power among the trading nations, otherwise the weaker state will simply destroy its own industry by allowing a complete freedom of exchange.[181] He supports this thesis by suggesting that all industrial nations currently promoting economic liberalism implemented protectionist policies in their early stages of development.[182] He maintains that these countries adopted economic liberalism only after reaching a certain stage of economic development.

Also similar to Ahmed Midhat, Akyiğitzade, in his defense of protectionism, clarifies that this idea is not against the principle of international division of labor, which constitutes the basis of free-trade arguments. He confirms that exchange between nations based on their comparative advantages is very beneficial. Because "God," he suggests, "endowed every country the ability to grow certain crops."[183] However, he adds, this should not lead to insisting—as liberals do—on remaining an agricultural producer and importer of industrial goods, thereby inhibiting industrial development.[184] In brief, the main argument in Ahyiğitzade's economic thinking is that industrialization is the unquestionable path to modern civilization (*medeniyet*), and in accordance with Listian thesis, this is only possible through protecting nascent industries until a higher stage of industrial development is achieved.

As a specific success story of protectionist policies that proves all of his points, Akyiğitzade refers to the United States. The United States, he argues, rose from an agricultural colony of England to an independent industrial power thanks to protectionist and *dirigiste* policies.[185] Akyiğitzade does not go back as far as to French mercantilism, as Ahmed Midhat did, but the main point of departure is similar in the sense that the American case—as a relative latecomer comer in industrialization—seems more relevant than the British case for the Ottoman economy. It is worth noting in passing that Akyiğitzade Musa Bey's interest in America is not unique in late-Ottoman reformist thought. Ottoman reformists turned their gaze to the United States especially in the 1880s and 1890s as a result of its rapid rise as a leading industrial power, in spite of its colonial and peripheral past. In the eyes of the Ottomans, America was the land of the miracles of civilization, thanks to industrial and technological innovations. Popular periodicals of the era, such as *Tercüman-ı Hakikat* and *Servet-i Fünûn*, are full of news about the latest "bizarre inventions" in this country; almost all such news items begin with sentences such as, "The Americans, who do everything to the extreme, including arts and sciences. . . ."[186] The extremes of "excess and deficiency" (*ifrâd ve tefrîd*), which is frequently referred to as an expression in describing America in such news items, was not tolerated in traditional Islamic thought. Nevertheless, in the 1890s modernist context, it implied more of a fascination along with a hint of reservation due to this traditional concern. It is also worth noting that the American example, along with the German case, enjoyed an exceptional status in late Ottoman economic as well as political thought. Unlike the British and French cases, the United States was not—yet—an imperialist power. On the contrary, it was perceived as an exemplary success by a former agricultural and colonial economy. In this respect, it invigorated Ottoman hopes to industrialize and take their place among the world's the so-called civilized nations.

Soon after Akyiğitzade's attack on *laissez-faire* economics, a student and a faithful follower of Sakızlı Ohannes, Mehmed Cavid Bey (1875–1926), came to the scene with his books, which became the new bibles of the Ottoman *laissez-faire* tradition. Moreover, Cavid Bey himself became the symbol of late Ottoman economic liberal thought and the legendary Minister of Finance of the empire after the 1908 Revolution.

Mehmed Cavid, like his mentor Ohannes, was both a finance official and an educator. Immediately after his graduation from the Mekteb-i Mülkiye, he began working at the Ziraat Bankası (the Agricultural Bank) and then at the Statistics Office of the Ministry of Education (*Maarif Nezareti Mektubî Kalemi İstatistik Şubesi Katibliği*). In 1898, in addition to his bureaucratic position, he was appointed as teacher of mathematics at Ayasofya Rüşdiyesi (Hagia Sofia High School) and instructor of economics (*ilm-i servet*) at *Darulmuallimîn-i Âliye* (Teacher Training College). But he played his main role in late Ottoman history after the 1908 Revolution. After the revolution, he was appointed as the professor of economics at his alma mater, Mekteb-i Mülkiye, in 1908. More importantly, as a member of the Committee of Union and Progress (*İttihat ve Terakkî Cemiyeti*) and a prominent economist, he became the Minister of Finance in 1909 for the first time. In the Young Turk period (1908–18), he held this position many times. Despite all critiques and controversies about him and his ideas, he became the super-star Finance Minister of this era. He was regarded—by many European financiers, as well as Ottoman statesmen—as the only person who had the sufficient knowledge and talent to discipline and administer the Ottoman financial administration.[187]

Mehmed Cavid published the first volume of *İlm-i İktisad* (*The Science of Economics*) in 1897. The book came out in four volumes, and he completed it with the publication of the last volume in 1899. Later, he published a more concise edition for high schools in 1908,[188] and then an even more easy-to-read edition in 1911 with the title *Ma'lumat-i İktisadiye* (*Knowledge of Economics*).[189] In 1901, he also published a book on statistics entitled *İhsaiyat* (Statistics).[190]

İlm-i İktisad is another typical example of introductory books on classical economics with some short extra parts on the Ottoman economy. The author's brief introduction is probably the first study on the history of Ottoman economic literature. Here, Cavid Bey provides a list of Ottoman economic publications, and he notes that although 20 years has passed since the publication of Ohannes's book, it is still the best work in the field. Cavid Bey also notes in his introduction that he benefitted from the works of [Pierre Émile] Le Vasseur (1828–1911), [Charles] Gide (1847–1932), [Henri] Baudrillart (1821–92), [Paul] Beauregard (1853–1919), and [Paul] Leroy-Beaulieu (1843–1916). The scholars of Ottoman economic thought as well as the editors of the new editions of Cavid Bey's works have taken this for granted, without checking its validity.[191] More interestingly, these scholars and editors have even ignored Cavid Bey's later words in the same introduction. He argues that his initial draft consisted of parts that are "taken" from the aforementioned four economists. For example, he states that in his early draft, "there were many pages taken especially from Beauregard."[192] He later decided to expand the text using Leroy-Beaulieu's massive work.[193] However, having seen the rich content of this latter study, he changed his draft of over 100 pages, and he mixed it with material from Leroy-Beaulieu's study.[194]

Looking at the text itself, it seems that the four-volume *İlm-i İktisad* is a selective summary of Paul Leroy-Beaulieu's *Traité théorique et pratique d'économie politique*, with some possible minor additions from other sources.[195] The plan of Cavid Bey's four volumes copies Leroy-Beaulieu's four-volume work. Yet Cavid Bey in some cases disregards parts in the original work and instead adds brief sections on the Ottoman economy.[196] He also changes the place of some parts, such as moving the population question from the fourth to the second volume. The chapter titles of Cavid Bey's work include the truncated versions of the titles of Leroy-Beaulieu's work. For example, "Les besoins humains et les richesses" becomes "İhtiyacat-i Beşeriye ve Servet—Besoins humains et richesse" (including the part in French).[197] His second and shorter *İlm-i İktisad* published in 1908 as a textbook for high schools is also an adaptation from Leroy-Beaulieu's *Précis d'économie politique* (1888).

In the footsteps of his two intellectual mentors, Ohannes and Leroy-Beaulieu, Cavid Bey became an ardent supporter of *laissez-faire* theses, even when he served as the Finance Minister of the increasingly protectionist and nationalist

Young Turk regime. His books, speeches, and articles in popular journals reflect his uncompromising belief in the universal laws of the science of economics.[198] According to him, the restrictions in traditional Ottoman economic administration on producers, such as the official guild regulations (*esnaf nizâmatı*) and the difficulty in obtaining permission (*gedik*) for artisanal production hindered the development of Ottoman economy.[199] He also believed that these restrictive measures even caused the collapse of the existing industries in the nineteenth century. Likewise, state monopolies and other obstacles impeding entrepreneurship, including the protective measures based on the infant industries argument, constituted similar obstacles to economic development.[200]

The solution, according to Cavid Bey, is full incorporation into the European economic system on the principle of comparative advantage. In this context, he maintains (or rather translates from Leroy-Beaulieu) that international trade agreements between different nations are indispensable means for establishing trade relations, thereby considering them beneficial for economic development.[201] Then he adds a short section on the trade agreements between the Ottoman Empire and European nations signed in the nineteenth century.[202] Although he does not explicitly declare his views about these specific agreements, the fact that he places this part just after the section on the benefits of international trade agreements hints that he is in favor of these agreements. Needless to say, these ideas were in direct contradiction with protectionist theses presented by Ahmed Midhat Efendi and Akyiğitzade Musa Bey.

In the same year that Mehmed Cavid published the last volume of his first *İlm-i İktisad* (1899) a certain Kahvecibaşızade Mahmud Hayri translated a book by one of Mehmed Cavid's main sources, Paul Beauregard.[203] This short work is actually an 88-page summary of the original book, which is over 330 pages. Mahmud Hayri's abbreviated translation was published with the same title as Ohannes' book, *Mebadi-i İlm-i Servet-i Milel* (*The Principles of the Science of Wealth*),[204] and it is another introductory book with a standard plan and a liberal approach. Mahmud Hayri, in his translation, includes original terms in French next to their Turkish equivalents or their transliterations in Perso-Arabic script. This short book in its entirety is not a distinct piece in Ottoman economic literature, but there are two details that are worth mentioning in the translator's introduction: First, Mahmud Hayri emphasizes the central role of labor in human society by giving references to the Qur'an and *hadith* literature.[205] Then, he adds that the science of wealth shows the ways to use this God-given power (i.e., labor) to produce wealth and prosperity through commerce and industry.[206] This is another example that testifies to the synthetical character of late Ottoman economic discourse that had begun to take shape in earlier works. Second, interestingly enough, the last paragraph of Mahmud Hayri strongly resembles the last paragraph of Sakızlı Ohannes' introduction to his own book. In this paragraph, Mahmud Hayri states that he used a clear and simple language without any compromise in the accuracy of its terminology, then he adds that although the work may have some mistakes, he hopes that it will be a pioneer to be followed by much better works.[207] This last sentence does not seem relevant for this rather late work as much as it was for Ohannes' book, which really was a trailblazer in Ottoman economic literature. Therefore, this resemblance is probably a result of Ohannes' impact on both ideas and styles in Ottoman economic writing.

Also in the same year, in 1899, Mustafa Nail's *Muhtasar İlm-i Servet* (*A Brief [Introduction to] Economics*) appeared as a textbook for high schools.[208] The book does not include any author's introduction. Thus, we do not have any information on his sources. In any case, the importance of the book is that it is a textbook which aims at introducing basic economic concepts and principles to high-school students. Although it is neither an interesting text, nor a significant contribution to Ottoman economic literature, its decent academic content gives us an idea about Ottoman economic education at the high-school level, or at least about its objectives.

Ottoman popular economics: Maurice Block and Ahmed Muhtar

As seen in the previous chapter, popularization of economics in the Ottoman Empire started as early as in the 1860s with short introductory articles in popular periodicals. As the Ottoman economic literature was enriched by new additions in the following decades, the impact of economics expanded in society. Considering the low literacy rate in the empire, which remained below 10 percent until the fall of the empire in the early 1920s,[209] this impact was of course still limited. It was, for example, cannot be compared even to the individual impact of Harriet Martineau (1802–1876)—whose books outsold J.S. Mill's work and printed in thousands of copies—in England in the 1830s.[210] Therefore, economics, in the Ottoman Empire, never gained the status of a "popular study" as Robert L. Heilbroner observed in the case of England in Martineau's age.[211]

Despite such limitations, the efforts for the popularization of economics continued thanks to the newly rising literate and reform-minded middle class, whose members adopted the objective of educating masses as a modernizing mission within the empire. In addition to the well-known members of this class—whose works are the subject of this work—there were many others all over the empire who volunteered to serve as a channel of new information from popular intellectuals to the masses. As one such example, in 1900 we see the author of a provincial journal published in İzmir (*Ahenk*) advising his rural audience to refer to books on economics to learn more about the realities of modern economic life:

> Look, I took these ideas from this book.[212] It shows you the way to wealth. It is called the book of wealth. If you read this book, you would know how to make money, how to take care of your farming implements, understand how capital is created, what a company is, and what trade and free trade mean.[213]

In such an economic-intellectual atmosphere, a very useful translation for such missionaries of economic modernization came out in 1906. It was a translation of a global economic best-seller, Maurice Block's *Petit manuel d'économie pratique* (1872), which had been translated into many languages in earlier decades.

Block's book is a manual of practical economic knowledge, and it consists of didactic short stories about a small French village. The young protagonists, Pierre, Paul, Louis, and Jerome, come across some practical as well as abstract economic problems and questions that they cannot resolve on their own. They seek help from their teacher (*l'instituteur*) who shows them how to apply the principles of modern political economy in their everyday lives. The stories introduce various principles of political economy and many economic institutions (from the importance of hard work to the use of banknotes), but as the author suggests in his preface, the book focuses on a single main message: "Work and thrift will facilitate the practice of many other virtues."[214]

Ahmed Muhtar, another graduate of the Mekteb-i Mülkiye, adapted the book into Ottoman cultural and economic context.[215] Ahmed Muhtar uses Ottoman characters and cities instead of French and other European ones. Ömer, Zeki, Fatin, Hasan, and Ali replace the French youngsters, and "*l'instituteur*" becomes *hâce* (the teacher). Other Ottomanized characters such as Mahmud Ağa (Mr Mahmud) and Veli Dayı (Uncle Veli) also appear along the stories. In the original book, cotton comes from America, India, and Egypt,[216] whereas in Ahmed Muhtar's translation India is replaced with Adana,[217] the famous cotton producing region in southern Anatolia. *La Banque de France* becomes *Osmanlı Bankası* (the Ottoman Bank) in the translation, and Ahmed Muhtar provides a brief summary of its history and functions.[218]

Ahmed Muhtar's introduction contains information about Maurice Block and his book, which had been translated into 13 other languages (including Bulgarian, Hungarian, and Japanese) by time of the publication of Ahmed Muhtar's translation.[219] Ahmed Muhtar also provides a very brief history of economics starting from ancient Greece, and he adds a brief note concerning the contributions of Muslim scholars. Unfortunately, just like Nuri Bey, Ahmed Muhtar does not provide any specific examples of such contributions, simply asserting their existence in passing. Moreover, this part reflects the increasingly Turkish-nationalist intellectual atmosphere of the period. Ahmed Muhtar mentions some contributions from the scholars of the "noble Turkish nation" (*Türk kavm-i necîbi*) in addition to those of early Muslim scholars.[220] Such contributions, according to him, can be found in the commentaries of the religious texts written by Turkish scholars.[221] He notes that economic ideas are scattered in these texts, but he does not give any further detail regarding the names of any of those scholars or their works. In this respect, Ahmed Muhtar's tone reflects the emergence of a Turkish nationalist discourse at the dawn of the Young Turk government in politics, along with the National Economy model of the following decade.

Conclusion

Economics brought about an epistemic shift in the Ottoman intellectual sphere in the second half of the nineteenth century. Ottoman intellectuals increasingly referred to tools of economic analysis to make sense of the new Eurocentric world order, and the place of the empire within it. In the same vein, economic analysis was employed to define the acute problems of the empire. The solutions, obviously, were developed by using the same toolbox that modern economics provided. In this respect, Ottoman reformists considered the "science" of economics an indispensable instrument for the salvation of the empire, first as a guide to strengthen state finances, later as an instrument for a comprehensive soft social engineering project through influencing popular economic mentality.

While economic knowledge was adopted and employed to understand and tackle domestic issues, its conceptual framework was adapted to the Ottoman cultural and institutional setting. Muslim Ottoman intellectuals referred frequently to the Islamic scripture in their teaching and writing in economics, and amalgamated economic jargon with Islamic lexicon to assimilate economic knowledge into the domestic Muslim culture. This was not only a pedagogical tool to help (particularly Muslim) students digest and embrace this new method of thinking and its conceptual framework, but also a way of justifying the idea that Islam was compatible with modern sciences and philosophies.

Besides, political economy became one of the fields in which Ottoman intellectuals responded to the late nineteenth-century debate about "Islam vs. modernity." Muslim-Ottoman intellectuals attempted to dig up (or rather invented) a modernity-compatible tradition of Islamic economic theory and policy. They emphasized that essential capitalist notions—like hard work, productivity, and private property—had already been accepted and encouraged in Islamic civilization. Besides, it was also suggested that Islamic political tradition had its own economic and fiscal administration systems and principles from its early history. Thus, these Muslim economists claimed, the disciplines of economics and public finance were not European inventions but had existed in the Islamic civilization long before the coming of the modern age. In short, this period witnessed the first steps toward an Islamic economics, which was to gain a much bigger importance especially after the rapid enrichment of some Muslim nations through oil in the twentieth century.[222]

The knowledge of modern economics led Ottomans reassess the political and economic institutional setup in the empire with a fresh perspective. Regardless of the adhered school of thought, intellectuals who analyzed the question of Ottoman economic backwardness reached at various deep-seated institutional issues as the reasons for underdevelopment and obstacles for economic development. While the most popular public intellectual, and a pioneering protectionist, Ahmed Midhat Efendi blamed the non-entrepreneurial mindset of (Muslim) Ottomans as well as foreign exploitation for economic underdevelopment, a prominent liberal economist Mehmed Cavid Bey held the traditional state intervention schemes (such as the guild system) accountable for the same result. Despite their diagonally opposite views about the economic policy, they both utilized the conceptual and theoretical framework provided by economics to suggest their institutional analyses regarding the economic condition of the empire.

All in all, Ottoman economic thought was not confined to domestic dynamics but mostly followed major global trends. This does not mean that the Ottoman intellectual sphere did not have its own internal dynamics—as in the case of the discussion of the Islamic roots of economics—or that it can only be understood through European patterns. However, it is obvious that at the end of the nineteenth century, Ottoman intellectuals were more in tune with modern European intellectuals of their age—in terms of discourse and ideas—than with their Ottoman predecessors of the early nineteenth century. In this context, economic thinking was an area in which the Ottoman integration into the European intellectual and sociocultural world-system—along with its integration into the Eurocentric capitalist world-economy—can be easily observed. The resultant Ottoman-Turkish modernization process was to culminate in the Young Turk nation-building project of the late Ottoman imperial and early Turkish Republican eras.

Notes

1 Ahmed Midhat, *Ekonomi Politik* (İstanbul: Kırkanbar Matbaası, 1879), 3–4.
2 Sakızlı Ohannes, *Mebadi-i İlm-i Servet-i Milel* (Dersaadet [İstanbul]: Mihran Matbaası, 1880), 11.
3 For an analysis of the effects of the Long Depression of 1873–96 on the Ottoman economy, see Şevket Pamuk, "The Ottoman Empire in the 'Great Depression' of 1873–1896," *The Journal of Economic History* 44, no. 1 (1984): 107–18.
4 Ahmet Cevdet Paşa, *Ma'rûzât*, ed. Yusuf Halaçoğlu (İstanbul: Çağrı Yayınları, 1980), 11–14. For Ahmed Cevdet Pasha's critique of the financial situation and the elite's extravagance in the Tanzimat era, see Ibid., 6–20.
5 Şerif Mardin, *The Genesis of Young Ottoman Thought: A Study in the Modernization of Turkish Political Ideas* (Princeton: Princeton University Press, 1962), 70.
6 For a concise analysis of the Hamidian regime, see M. Şükrü Hanioğlu, *A Brief History of the Late Ottoman Empire* (Princeton: Princeton University Press, 2008), 125–6.
7 Michalis M. Psalidopoulos and Nicholas J. Theocarakis, "The Dissemination of Economic Thought in South-Eastern Europe in the Nineteenth Century," in *The Dissemination of Economic Ideas* (Cheltenham, UK: Edward Elgar, 2011), 161–91. Although Greece gained its independence from the Ottoman Empire in 1830, thanks to a large population that did not emigrate, Greek continued to be one of the major languages of the empire.
8 Philippe-Louis Bourdonné, *Simples Notions d'économie politique* (Paris: E. Thorin, 1869).
9 "Économie politique–L'école nouvelle," *Le Journal de La Chambre De Commerce de Constantinople*, March 4, 1892. It is noted at the end of the article that it is a reprint from the journal *L'Économiste*.
10 A prominent Ottoman intellectual Ali Kemal, who studied economics at the Mekteb-i Mülkiye and also in Paris, notes in his memoirs that Ohannes was as good as the best political economy professors in Paris. (Ali Kemal, *Ömrüm*, ed. Zeki Kuneralp (İstanbul: İsis Yayımcılık, 1985), 67.) It is impossible to verify Ali Kemal's statement, but it at least testifies to Ohannes' influence on his students. For a short biography of Ohannes, and his students' descriptions of him, see Ali Çankaya, *Yeni Mülkiye Târihi ve Mülkiyeliler* (Ankara: Ankara Üniversitesi Siyasal Bilgiler Fakültesi, 1968), vol. 2: 1058–60.

11 The article was published in two installments in 1863, in *Mecmua-i Fünûn* issues 2 (pp. 86–92) and 6 (pp. 243–9).

12 The title of Ohannes' book is obviously inspired by the title of Adam Smith's magnum opus, *An Inquiry into the Nature and Causes of the Wealth of Nations*. Economics was first named as the "science of the wealth of nations" or "science of wealth" in the Ottoman Empire, as a result of Smithian dominance in this field.

13 Sakızlı Ohannes, *Mebadi-i İlm-i Servet-i Milel*, 12. Both of these economists have been almost totally forgotten today. Since Ohannes does not give exact references but only last names, we can only guess that the former work is Henri Baudrillart's *Manuel d'économie politique* (1857), and the latter must be one of many introductory books by the prominent liberal economist and later the editor of *Journal des Économistes, Joseph Garnier*. As Sayar notes, throughout the book Ohannes mentions the names of many economists such as A. Smith, J.B. Say, F. Bastiat, Took, and A. Young. (Ahmed Güner Sayar, *Osmanlı İktisat Düşüncesinin Çağdaşlaşması: (Klasik Dönem'den II. Abdülhamid'e)*, Second Edition (İstanbul: Ötüken Neşriyat, 2000), 357.) Nevertheless, contrary to what Sayar implies, this does not prove that Ohannes actually referred to the works of these economists. They were prominent economists of the era, and these names were mentioned in many introductory books on economics.

14 Sakızlı Ohannes, *Mebadi-i İlm-i Servet-i Milel*, 11.

15 Ibid., 4–5.

16 Ibid., 297.

17 "Sanayice geri kalmış memâlik".

18 Ibid., 298.

19 Ibid., 298.

20 Ibid., 299.

21 Both Malthus and Ricardo observed that wages in a capitalist economy naturally tend to decline, and this brings increasing poverty among the working class. For a summary of the "gloomy presentiments" of Malthus and Ricardo, see Robert L. Heilbroner, *The Worldly Philosophers: The Lives, Times, and Ideas of the Great Economic Thinkers*, Seventh Edition (New York: Touchstone Book, 1999), 75–104.

22 The "infant industry argument" was another popular protectionist argument of the nineteenth century. The argument is based on the idea that the newly emerging industries in a developing country have to be protected from the destructive effects of international competition with the developed foreign industries, until the infant industries achieve a certain maturity and strength to cope with its foreign rivals. (Douglas A. Irwin, "Infant-Industry Protection," in *The New Palgrave Dictionary of Economics*, vol. 4, 291–3).

23 For List's economic ideas, see K. Tribe, "List, Friedrich (1789–1846)," *The New Palgrave Dictionary of Economics*, vol. 5, 160–2.

24 Paul Bairoch, "European Trade Policy, 1815–1914," in *The Cambridge Economic History of Europe*, ed. Peter Mathias and Sidney. Pollard, vol. 8 (Cambridge: Cambridge University Press, 1989), 69.

25 For the economic factors that nurtured economic protectionism and national protectionist reactions in the central as well as peripheral Europe, see Bairoch, "European Trade Policy, 1815–1914."

26 The quality of Ahmed Midhat's works has always been an issue of debate among scholars. As an early example to such arguments, Abdurrahman Şeref notes that it is hard to find even a few sentences of Ahmed Midhat that are fit to be used as examples in a book on eloquence. (Abdurrahman Şeref, "Ahmed Midhat Efendi," *TOEM*, no. 18 (1913): 1116).

27 For a short biography of Ahmed Midhat, see M. Orhan Okay, "Ahmed Midhat Efendi (1844–1912)," *T.D.V. İslam Ansiklopedisi*, vol. 2 (İstanbul: Türkiye Diyanet Vakfı, 1989), 100–103. For a complete list of his books, see Hakkı Tarık Us, ed., *Bir*

Jübilenin İntiba'ları: Ahmed Midhat'ı Anıyoruz! (İstanbul: Vakit, 1955), 169–72. This list is in alphabetical order and does not contain publication dates and other bibliographic information. For a shorter list in chronological order and with such information, see M. Orhan Okay, *Batı Medeniyeti Karşısında Ahmed Midhat Efendi* (Ankara: Baylan Matbaası, 1975), 426–30.

28 The original term that Ahmed Midhat rendered into Turkish by this expression is "*L'amour du travail.*" See Ahmed Midhat, *Sevda-yı Sa'y ü Amel* (İstanbul: Kırkanbar Matbaası, 1879), 7.

29 Ahmed Midhat wrote a short article for *Vakit* newspaper on March 21, 1878 (March 9, 1294) entitled *Sevda-yı Sa'y ü Amel.* Two years later, when he decided to publish his serialized articles in book form, he also wanted to publish this work, but he realized that his ideas had changed since its publication two years earlier. Thus he used the article as a base and prepared a new text. (Ahmed Midhat, *Sevda-yı Sa'y ü Amel*, 2).

30 The Historical School of Economics was an influential school of economic thought in the late nineteenth century. Although it is generally referred to as the German Historical School, since it was most powerful in Germany, the Historical approach was also influential in other European countries, including the cradle of economic liberalism, Britain. The main points of divergence of the Historical School from the liberal approach were the rejection of the existence of universal laws, the emphasis on national differences (based on historical and geographical factors), and the tendency toward more protectionist policies. Unfortunately, Ahmed Midhat does not give any clue about the influence of the Historical School on his ideas. Therefore it is not possible to safely assert that he was "directly" influenced by these economists. However, it is important to note that the 1880s were the heyday of the Historical School throughout Europe. For more information on the Historical School, see Heath Pearson, "Historical School, German" *The New Palgrave Dictionary of Economics*, vol. 4, 5–48; and J. Maloney, "Historical Economics, British," *The New Palgrave Dictionary of Economics*, vol. 4, 42–5. For a broader analysis, see Geoffrey M. Hodgson, *How Economics Forgot History: The Problem of Historical Specificity in Social Science* (New York: Routledge, 2001), 43–134.

31 Şerif Mardin asserts that Ahmed Midhat was inspired by Samuel Smiles' *Self-Help* (1859), which was a global best-seller in the late nineteenth century. (Şerif Mardin, "Super Westernization in the Ottoman Empire in the Last Quarter of the Nineteenth Century," in *Turkey: Geographic and Social Perspectives*, ed. Peter Benedict, Erol Tümertekin, and Fatma Mansur (Leiden: Brill, 1974), 415.) According to Mardin, Ahmed Midhat selected Smiles's book "as one of the products of the West most suitable for propagation," and he gives reference to Ahmed Midhat's work for this information (*Sevda-yı Sa'y ü Amel*, p. 187). Later, Carter V. Findley stated, with a reference to Mardin's article, that Ahmed Midhat actually translated Smiles book. (Carter V. Findley, *Ottoman Civil Officialdom: A Social History* (Princeton, NJ: Princeton University Press, 1989), 12n22.) The problem, however, is that Ahmed Midhat never mentions Smiles' name in his book, nor can we find any such translation. Moreover, although Mardin's reference to Ahmed Midhat is page 187 of *Sevda-yı Sa'y ü Amel*, the book is only 78 pages. In the Turkish edition of the article, Mardin revises his earlier statement by arguing that *Sevda-yı Sa'y ü Amel* reflects the main themes of *Self-Help*; and this time he does not provide any page numbers in Ahmed Midhat's work. (Şerif Mardin, "Tanzimat'tan Sonra Aşırı Batılılaşma," in *Türk Modernleşmesi* (İstanbul: İletişim, 1991), 47.) Therefore, although Ahmed Midhat might have been inspired by Smiles, and there are in fact parallels between the two books in terms of themes, there is no concrete evidence for such a direct influence. It is also worth noting that *Self-Help* was translated into Arabic in 1880 in Cairo, and Smiles' ideas became very influential among the Egyptian reformists in the following years. (Timothy Mitchell, *Colonising Egypt* (Berkeley: University of

California Press, 1991), 108–11). Hence it is likely that Ottoman reformists in Istanbul, including Ahmed Midhat, were aware of Smiles' ideas in the 1880s. Later, Abdullah Cevdet, the well-known materialist intellectual of the early twentieth century, was to openly suggest adopting the ideas in *Self-Help*. (M. Şükrü Hanioğlu, *Bir Siyasal Düşünür Olarak Doktor Abdullah Cevdet ve Dönemi* (İstanbul: Üçdal Neşriyat, 1981, 199).

32 Anson Rabinbach, *The Human Motor: Energy, Fatigue, and the Origins of Modernity* (New York: Basic Books, 1990).

33 Ahmed Midhat, *Sevda-yı Sa'y ü Amel*, 7–12, et passim.

34 Ahmed Midhat, *Sevda-yı Sa'y ü Amel*, 41–4.

35 "Sevda-yı sa'y ü amel erbâbı".

36 Ibid., 49–53.

37 Ibid., 34.

38 "Adam Smith (1776) placed the division of labour at the forefront of his discussion of economic growth and progress. Neither in its social nor in its manufacturing forms did the idea originate with him. It retained a varying, but often very prominent, place in 19th-century writings (particularly those of Senior, Babbage, John Stuart Mill, Marx and Marshall)." Groenewegen, Peter, "Division of Labor," *The New Palgrave Dictionary of Economics*, vol. 2, 517.

39 Ahmed Midhat, *Teşrik-i Mesa'î, Taksim-i Mesa'î* (İstanbul: Kırkanbar Matbaası, 1879), 121.

40 Ibid., 111 et passim.

41 Ibid., 110–15.

42 Ibid., 88–91.

43 Ibid., 88.

44 Ahmed Midhat misspells this name, and since Brouckère is not a well-known economist today, many contemporary scholars have repeated his mistake. Thus in the existing literature on Ahmed Midhat's economic ideas, Brouckère is generally referred as "Brusker" or "Brosker" (based on Ahmed Midhat's writing "بروسكر")without any further information. (See for example, Sayar, *Osmanlı İktisat Düşüncesi*, 379, *et passim*.) Because of similar reasons, there is a confusion in the scholarship of Ottoman economic thought today concerning the names of European economists. Ottoman writers almost always wrote these names in Arabo-Persian script as they pronounce them (e.g., "Smith" is mostly written as Esmit–"اسميت"). Some scholars today cannot read these names properly and thus they give references to some European economists, who actually have never existed. For some other examples, see the note about the other works of Ahmed Midhat and the one on Mehmed Cavid's work below.

45 George de Brouckère (1796–1860) was a prominent liberal Belgian economist, businessman, and politician. (Guido Erreygers, "Economics in Belgium." *The New Palgrave Dictionary of Economics*, online edition, eds. Steven N. Durlauf and Lawrence E. Blume (Palgrave Macmillan, 2009), www.dictionaryofeconomics.com/article?id=pde2009_B000343 accessed on December 4, 2014) According to the title page of his book, he was a member of *La Chambre de représentants* and the burgomaster of Brussels. The first page of the book has a picture of the well-known liberal economist, J.B. Say; and this is a direct expression of the model that he follows. Brouckère's book was published by *Société pour l'émancipation intellectuelle, an organization for popular education, within the series of encyclopédie populaire.* (For more information about the society and the series, see Geert Vanpaemel and Brigitte van Tiggelen, "Science for the People: The Belgian *Encyclopédie populaire* and the Constitution of a National Science Movement," in *Popularizing Science and Technology in the European Periphery, 1800–2000*, ed. Faidra Papanelopoulou, Agustí Nieto-Galan and Enrique Perdriguero (Aldershot: Ashgate, 2009) 65–88).

46 "L'ateur n'a pas la prétention de présenter des théories novelles, ni de mieux exposer les principles de la science que ses devanciers; mais il a compris qu'une ency-

clopédie populaire réclamait un traité d'économie politique, et il a cédé à la demande de ses collaborateurs." Georges de Brouckère, *Principes généraux d'économie politique* (Bruxelles: Société pour l'émancipation intellectuelle, 1850), 5.

47 Such as the part on distribution of wealth, including chapters on industrial, financial and other revenues. (Brouckère, *Principes généraux d'économie politique*, 77–96) Ahmed Midhat complains about the lack of a developed Ottoman industry (and states the urgency of establishing it); and he ignores these parts that are no use for understanding the Ottoman economy at the time.

48 Ahmed Midhat, *Ekonomi Politik*, 3–4.

49 Ahmed Midhat, *Ekonomi Politik*, 6–14.

50 Charles Coqueline: *Dictionnaire de l'économie politique contenant l'exposition des principes de la science* (2 vols; Paris, Librairie de Guillaumin et Cie., 1852–53).

51 Many recent works on Ahmed Midhat misread and misspell these names. For example, Sayar mentions the names "Setrock" and "Derose" among Ahmed Midhat's sources (Sayar, *Osmanlı İktisat Düşüncesi*, 380). The correct names are (Henri-Frédérich) Storch (1766–1835) and (Joseph) Droz (1773–1850), respectively.

52 *Hâce-i Evvel* was the title of Ahmed Midhat's first popular educational work, published in 1870. Due to his popular educational style and his impact as a teacher on his readers, *Hâce-i Evvel* later became the title given by his readers to honor him.

53 Ahmed Midhat, *Ekonomi Politik*, 71.

54 Ibid., 72–6.

55 Ibid., 88–109.

56 Ibid., 128.

57 Ibid., 129.

58 Ibid., 110–35. Ahmed Midhat's analyses on the reasons of and solutions for Ottoman economic backwardness will be analyzed in more detail in Chapters 3 and 4.

59 Ahmed Midhat, *Hallü'l-'Ukad* (Dersaadet [İstanbul]: Kırkanbar Matbaası, 1890), 4.

60 He does not refer to any term in French for this last category.

61 Ibid., 4–34.

62 Ibid., 57–73.

63 Ibid., 74–91.

64 Ibid., 91–104.

65 Ibid., 182–96.

66 Jean-Baptiste Colbert (1619–83) was the well-known French minister of finance of King Louis XIV. He is among the pioneers of mercantilism, which is an earlier form of economic nationalism and protectionism.

67 Ibid., 53

68 Ibid., 55.

69 Ibid., 75.

70 Sayar, *Osmanlı İktisat Düşüncesi*, 390.

71 Georgeon, "Ahmed Midhat'a Göre Ekonomi Politik," 150.

72 Ahmed Midhat, *Hallü'l-'Ukad*, 127–8. Here, after discussing Sully's accomplishments in France, he states, "what led this man to success is protectionism." This shows that Ahmed Midhat used mercantilists as an example, but what he actually had in mind, in theoretical terms, was protectionist theories of his own age.

73 Friedrich List, *National System of Political Economy*, trans. G.A. Matile (Philadelphia: J.P. Lippincott & Co., 1856), v–vi.

74 "Bunların hiçbirisine diyecek olmaz, ama bunun için insan İngiltere'de bulunmalıdır." (Ahmed Midhat, *Hallü'l-ʿUkad*, 190).

75 Ibid., 191.

76 "Adam Smith'in ekonomisini mekteblerde tedris etmek, kiliselerde 'Size en büyük fenalık edenleri, ez dil ü can seviniz! Bir yanağınıza tokat vuranlara, diğer yanağınızı da çeviriniz!' diye verilen va'z ü nasihatlara benzer." (Ibid., 193).

77 Ibid., 196.

78 Münif, *Muhaverât-ı Hikemiye: Fransa Hükema-yı Benâmından Voltaire ve Fenelon ve Fontenelle'in Telifâtından* (Dersaadet [İstanbul]: Ceridehane Matbaası, 1859), 47–55.
79 Ahmed Midhat, *Hallü'l-'Ukad*, 192–3.
80 "İşte efendim! Size size üç büyük ekonomistin tercüme-i halleri ki bunların hangisine ittiba' edecek olsanız tarik-i refahı bulur çıkarırsınız. Hattâ Adam Smith'in bulduğu yol dahi, şu rehberler sayesinde keşf olunmuşdur." Ibid., 181.
81 Ibid., 184–5.
82 Sayar makes the same claim without providing any evidence, see Sayar, *Osmanlı İktisat Düşüncesi*, 40n25.
83 Mehmet Zeki Pakalın, *Sicill-i Osmanî Zeyli: Son Devir Osmanlı Meşhurları Ansiklopedisi*, vol. 13 (Ankara: Türk Tarih Kurumu, 2008), 108.
84 Ibid.
85 Yetimzade M. Tevfik Hamdi, *Bürokrat Tevfik Biren'in Sultan II. Abdülhamid, Meşrutiyet ve Mütareke Hatıraları*, ed. F. Rezan Hürmen, vol. 1 (İstanbul: Pınar Yayınları, 2006), 70.
86 Nuri, *Mebahis-i İlm-i Servet* (Istanbul: Mahmut Bey Matbaası, 1882), 3.
87 Ibid., 2.
88 I borrow this concept from Eric Hobsbawm and Terence Ranger (eds.), *The Invention of Tradition*, (Cambridge: Cambridge University Press, 1983).
89 BOA, YEE, 38/1, 15/Za/1291. For a recent study that claims that Islamic finance is not a recent phenomenon, but actually a tradition of "fifteen centuries old," and contemporary Islamic financial engineers are "not aware about the achievements of their forefathers," see Murat Çizakça, *Islamic Capitalism and Finance: Origins, Evolution and the Future* (Cheltenham: Edward Elgar, 2011).
90 Tripp, *Islam and the Moral Economy*, 19–20.
91 Nuri, *Mebahis-i İlm-i Servet*, part 1, 12–41.
92 Ibid., 4.
93 Ibid., 5.
94 Ibid., 6.
95 Ibid., 8–9.
96 Ibid., 10.
97 Ernest Nys, *Researches in the History of Economics*, trans. N.F Dryhurst and A.R. Dryhurst (London: Adam & Charles Black, 1899), x.
98 Ibid., 1–27.
99 Ibid., 9.
100 Ibid., 7–20.
101 The question was tackled more seriously almost a century later by various Muslim intellectuals and scholars, especially after the emergence of Islamic economic systems in countries such as Saudi Arabia and Pakistan. For a compilation of studies on the medieval Islamic economics, which aim at challenging the European hegemony in the history of economics, see Shaikh M. Ghazanfar, ed., *Medieval Islamic Economic Thought: Filling the "Great Gap" in European Economics* (London: RoutledgeCurzon, 2003).
102 Nuri, *Mebahis-i İlm-i Servet*, part 1, 54–6.
103 Ibid., 58–76.
104 Ibid., 51–8; et passim.
105 Ibid., 77–9.
106 Ibid., 80–8.
107 Ibid., 83–4.
108 Ibid., 80.
109 Ibid., 83.
110 Nuri, *Mebahis-i İlm-i Servet*, part 2, 32.
111 Ibid., 33.

112 Ibid., 37.

113 Mehmed Cavid, *İlm-i İktisad*, vol. 1 (İstanbul: Karabet Matbaası, 1897), ه. (Mehmed Cavid uses Arabic letters in his introduction as page numbers instead of numerals).

114 Nuri Bey notes that Mikael Pasha penned this memorandum in French. (Nuri, *Mebahis-i İlm-i Servet*, part 2, 39).

115 Ibid., 39–54.

116 İbn'ül-Emîn Mahmud Es'ad Seydişehrî (1855–1918) initially received a religious and later a modern education. With special permission from the Minister of the Imperial Military Academy, he became the only civilian student admitted to this school, but he did not graduate. In 1882 he passed a special exam and became a lawyer. After the establishment of the School of Law, he entered this school, where he took classes from Münif Pasha. He graduated in 1886. Mahmud Es'ad had a brilliant career and assumed very important high offices, in addition to receiving many important orders and titles from the sultan. Throughout his career he served in many teaching positions as a professor of economics and law. In 1897, for example, he replaced Ohannes Pasha to become the Professor of Science of Wealth at the Mekteb-i Mülkiye. Mahmud Es'ad wrote and translated many books in a wide range of topics from law (both Islamic and European) and legal history to economics and history of European civilization. For a detailed biography and a list of his works, see Çankaya, *Yeni Mülkiye Tarihi ve Mülkiyeliler*, vol. 2, 1021–32; also see *Büyük Türk Hukukçusu Seydişehirli İbn-ül-Emin Mahmut Esat Efendi* (İstanbul: Türk Hukuk Kurumu, 1943).

117 Mahmud Es'ad, *İlm-i Servet* (İstanbul: Mekteb-i Sanayi, 1885), 2.

118 Mahmud Es'ad, *İktisad*, 4 vols. (İstanbul: Matbaa-i Hayriye, 1909).

119 For a short biography of Münif Pasha, see İsmail Doğan, "Münif Mehmed Paşa," *T.D.V. İslam Ansiklopedisi* (İstanbul: Türkiye Diyanet Vakfı), 9–12. For more information on his role in Ottoman modernization, see Ali Budak, *Batılılaşma Sürecinde Çok Yönlü Bir Osmanlı Aydını: Münif Paşa* (İstanbul: Kitabevi, 2004); İsmail Doğan, *Tanzimatın İki Ucu: Münif Paşa ve Ali Suavi: Sosyo-Pedagojik Bir Karşılaştırma*, (İstanbul: İz Yayıncılık, 1991); and Adem Akın, *Münif Paşa ve Türk Kültür Tarihindeki Yeri* (Ankara: Atatürk Kültür Merkezi, 1999).

120 Sayar, *Osmanlı İktisat Düşüncesi*, 373.

121 Ibid.

122 *Hadith*, in very simple terms, is the normative tradition based on the words and deeds attributed to the prophet Muhammad.

123 He mentions, for example, the Islamic principles of "al-mahsūl lā yubeddul illā b'il-mahsūl" (crops are exchanged only with [other] crops) (Mahmud Es'ad, *İlm-i Servet*, 23), and "laysa li'l-insāni illā mā sa'ā" (that man will only have what he has worked towards [from the Surat al-Najm, 53:39]) (Ibid., 24).

124 Ibid., 5.

125 I reached this conclusion through Ferit Devellioğlu's Ottoman Turkish dictionary. (Ferit Devellioğlu, *Osmanlıca-Türkçe Ansiklopedik Lûgat* [Ankara: Doğuş Ltd. Şti. Matbaası, 1970]). Devellioğlu refers to this *hadith* in his definition of the word *matiyye*. The only reference to this particular *hadith* that I could track down is in Sultan Valad's (1226–1312) *Valadnameh*. See Sulṭān Valad. *Valadnāmah, az Sulṭān Valad*. eds. Jalāl al-Dīn Humāyī and Māhdukht Bānū Humāyī (Tehrān: Mu'assasah-i Nashr-i Humā, 1376 [1997]), 5. Sultan Valad was the eldest son of Mawlana Jalāl ad-Dīn Rūmī (1207–73) and one of the founders of the Mawlawiya order in Anatolia. Although his work does not carry any religious authority, it might be Münif Pasha's source for this *hadith*.

126 Su'ad, like many other Ottoman intellectuals, does not provide an exact reference to the work he translated. He only mentions that it is the work of a certain "M. Rambaud (docteur en droit)" (Prosper Rambaud, *Telhis-i İlm-i Servet*, trans. Su'ad (İstanbul: Mihran Matbaası, 1888)), 1. According to library catalogues, this is a

translation of a work by the well-known economist Joseph Rambaud. However, Su'ad translated Prosper Rambaud's *Précis élémentaire d'économie politique à l'usage des facultés de droit et des écoles* (Paris: Ernest Thorin, 1880). Comparison of the *avant propos* in Rambaud's book and the "*mukaddime-i mü'ellif*" (author's introduction) in Su'ad's translation proves it without any doubt. It is also worth noting that Joseph Rambaud published his books on economics after Su'ad's translation. Joseph Rambaud's books on economics are: *Sommaire détaillé du Cours d'économie politique professé à la Faculté catholique de droit de Lyon* (Lyon: impr. du "Nouvelliste, 1892); *Éléments d'économie politique* (Paris: L. Larose, 1895); *Histoire des doctrines économiques* (Paris: L. Larose, 1899); and *Cours d'économie politique* (Paris: Librairie de la Société du recueil Sirey, 1910–11).

127 Su'ad, "Makale-i Mütercim," in Prosper Rambaud, *Telhis-i İlm-i Servet*, tr. Su'ad (İstanbul: Mihran Matbaası, 1888), 5–6.

128 Ibid., 13.

129 Ibid.

130 Rambaud, *Telhis-i İlm-i Servet*, 15–16.

131 For the emphasis on Islamic morality in Hamidian education, see Benjamin Fortna, "Islamic Morality in Late Ottoman 'Secular' Schools," *IJMES*, vol. 32, No. 3 (Aug. 2000), 369–93.

132 Ahmed İhsan Tokgöz, *Matbuat Hatıralarım*, vol. 1 (İstanbul: Ahmed İhsan Matbaası, 1930), 29.

133 For a brief biography of Ahmed İhsan and a list of his numerous works, see Çankaya, *Yeni Mülkiye Tarihi ve Mülkiyeliler*, vol. 3, 232–44.

134 Tokgöz, *Matbuat Hatıralarım*, vol. 1, 26–7.

135 Ami Ayalon, *The Press in the Arab Middle East: A History* (New York: Oxford University Press, 1995), 221.

136 In the conclusion, Ahmed İhsan notes that the book is only a very brief introduction to this science, and the interested readers should refer to more detailed books in foreign languages for more information on any particular principle and for the application of these principles. (Ahmet İhsan Tokgöz, *İlm-i Servet* (Kostantiniye [İstanbul]: Âlem Matbaası, 1892), 119–20).

137 BOA YEE 10/36, 16/N/1293.

138 "Şura-yı Devlet mülazımlarından…"

139 Pierre-Paul Leroy-Beaulieu (1843–1916) was a prominent French economist of the French Liberal School. He was also a successful journalist, politician, and businessman. Being a follower of classical liberalism, he adopted Smithian optimistic *laissez-faire* approach instead of Malthusian–Ricardian pessimism. His *Traité de la science des finances* (1877) and *Traité théorique et pratique d'économie politique* (1896) were translated into many languages, including Turkish. For more information on Leroy-Beaulieu and his influence on the late nineteenth-century French economic and political life, see Dan Warshaw, *Paul Leroy-Beaulieu and Established Liberalism in France* (DeKalb: Northern Illinois University Press, 1991). For a more concise narrative of his life and economic thought, see R.F. Hébert, "Leroy-Beaulieu, Pierre-Paul (1843–1916)," *The New Palgrave Dictionary of Economics*, vol. 5, 92.

140 He does not mention any names.

141 Hüseyin Kâzım, "Mukaddime," in Paul Leroy-Beaulieu, *İlm-i Usûl-i Mâliye*, trans. Hüseyin Kazım (İstanbul: Mihran Matbaası, 1880), 1.

142 Both of the authors later assumed teaching and administrative positions at their alma mater. Mustafa Nail Bey later became the Professor of Public Finance at the Mekteb-i Mülkiye in 1894, and he held this position for 21 years. In 1899, he published a textbook of economics (*Muhtasar İlm-i Servet*) (For a brief biography of Mustafa Nail, see Çankaya, *Yeni Mülkiye Tarihi ve Mülkiyeliler*, vol. 3, 172–3). Mehmed Rakım (Açıkalın) also taught public finance at the Mekteb-i Mülkiye (1897–98). In

1909, he was appointed as the director of the school and worked in this capacity until 1911. (For a brief biography of Mehmed Rakım, see Çankaya, *Yeni Mülkiye Tarihi ve Mülkiyeliler*, vol. 2, 834–5).

143 Mehmed Rakım and Mustafa Nail, *Hayat-i Düvel* (İstanbul: A. Maviyan Şirket-i Mürettebiye Matbaası, 1889), 4–5.

144 Ibid., 5.

145 Ibid., 5–6.

146 Ibid., 6.

147 See for example, a comparison of annual state budgets of Britain, France, and the Ottoman Empire, Ibid., 17–21.

148 Upon his death, the sultan entrusted this position to Sakızlı Ohannes, another prominent Armenian economist of the era. For Mikael's biography, see Çankaya, *Yeni Mülkiye Tarihi ve Mülkiyeliler*, vol. 2, 1043–4.

149 Mikael Portakal, *Usûl-i Mâliye* (Istanbul: Mekteb-i Mülkiye-yi Şahane Litografya Destgâhı, 1889), 5–6, 8.

150 See, for example, Sayar, *Osmanlı İktisat Düşüncesi*, 260, 275, and 289.

151 For his biography, see Mehmet Ali Ünal, "Süleyman Sûdi Efendi" in Süleyman Sudi, *Osmanlı Vergi Düzeni (Defter-i Muktesid)*, ed. Mehmet Ali Ünal (Isparta, 1996), 3–4; and Salim Aydüz, "Süleyman Sudi Bey," in Süleyman Sudi, *Tabakat-ı Müneccimin* (İstanbul: Fatih Üniversitesi, 2005), 20–8.

152 Tokgöz, *Matbuat Hatıralarım*, vol. 1, 9–12. Ahmed İhsan also makes a note of Süleyman Sûdi's rich personal library, mostly consisting of books in French.

153 Tokgöz, *Matbuat Hatıralarım*, vol. 1, 9n1.

154 Sayar, *Osmanlı İktisat Düşüncesi*, 292. It was called *ilm-i tedbir-i menzil* (science of household management), *ilm-i tedbir-i servet* (the science of wealth management), *ilm-i servet* (the science of wealth), *ekonomi politik* (political economy or *économie politique*) and *ilm-i iktisad* (the science of economy or the science of economics) by different intellectuals.

155 Süleyman Sûdi, *Defter-i Muktesid*, (Dersaadet [İstanbul]: Mahmud Bey Matbaası, 1889), 10–11.

156 Ibid., 3–4.

157 Ibid., 6.

158 Using footnotes for such additional information is also another significant characteristic of the work. This reveals a direct European influence, since using footnotes was still not very common in the Ottoman writing of his time.

159 Süleyman Sûdi, *Defter-i Muktesid*, vol. 3, 20–1.

160 Ibid., 105.

161 Süleyman Sûdi, *Defter-i Muktesid*, vol. 1, 34, 37, 64, *et passim*.

162 Tokgöz, *Matbuat Hatıralarım*, vol. 1, 9.

163 Süleyman Sûdi, *Defter-i Muktesid*, vol. 2, 5–9.

164 See his ideas on the "limits of taxation" and the economic role of the state, Süleyman Sûdi, "Mebâhis El-Mâliye Fi'd-Devleti'l-Osmaniyye – VII," *Vakit*, September 5, 1881. For an analysis of this article and Süleyman Sûdi's liberal views regarding state and economy, see İsmail Özsoy, "Süleyman Sûdi'nin Osmanlı Mâliyesi ve Vergi Sistemi Ile İlgili Görüş ve Tesbitleri (1881)," *Akademik Araştırmalar Dergisi* 2, no. 4–5 (July 2000): 611–56.

165 For his ideas on the importance of free trade based on international division of labor, see Süleyman Sûdi, *Defter-i Muktesid*, vol. 3, 97–101.

166 Ibid., 117–19.

167 Ibid., 12.

168 Ibid., 13–14.

169 Ibid., 15–16.

170 [Mehmed Murad], "Defter-i Muktesid," *Mizan* 104 (1889), 999.

171 Süleyman Sûdi, *Defter-i Muktesid*, vol. 3, 17–19.

172 Akyiğitzade Musa, *İktisad Yâhud İlm-i Servet: Âzâdegi-i Ticâret ve Usûl-i Himâye* (İstanbul: Karabet Matbaası, 1896), 62.

173 Akyiğitzade Musa was a son of an elite Tatar family of Kazan. After finishing high school in Russia, he came to Istanbul and entered the Mekteb-i Mülkiye with a special permission from the sultan. After his graduation in 1891 he worked as a civil servant at various positions, and for a short time he published some journals and newspapers in the post-1908 period. In addition to his *İktisad yâhud İlm-i Servet*, he wrote *Avrupa Medeniyetinin Esâsına Bir Nazar* (*A Glance at the Essence of the European Civilization*, 1897), in which he evaluated and criticized European civilization, and compared it with Islamic civilization. Akyiğitzade's main thesis in this book is that the roots of European civilization stand on the scientific and philosophical contributions of Islamic civilization. Thus, he concludes that Islam is not incompatible with modernity; on the contrary, it actually is the source of modernity. He, just like many other Muslim intellectuals, uses examples from the Qur'an and *hadith* literature and suggests that the main principles and ideas of the Enlightenment and modernity have Muslim equivalents. For a short personal and intellectual biography of Akyiğitzade Musa, see Çankaya, *Yeni Mülkiye Tarihi ve Mülkiyeliler*, vol. 3, 468–71; also see Ülken, *Türkiye'de Çağdaş Düşünce Tarihi*, vol. 1, 343–52.

174 Akyiğitzade Musa, *İktisad*, 4.

175 For his overview of *laissez-faire* theses, see Ibid., 7–15; for protectionists' views, ibid., 15–21.

176 List, *National System*, 265.

177 Akyiğitzade Musa, *İktisad*, 21.

178 Ibid., 22.

179 Ibid., 30.

180 Akyiğitzade Musa, *İktisad*, 31–2.

181 Ibid., 33–8.

182 Ibid., 34.

183 Ibid., 37.

184 Ibid., 37–8.

185 Ibid., 61–2.

186 See, for example, "Amerika'da Gazete Revacı," *Servet-i Fünûn* 81 (September 29, 1892), 44. For an interesting example (an article on the Americans' excessive drinking habits), see "Amerika'da Sarhoşluk," *Servet-i Fünûn* 55 (March 31, 1892): 42.

187 Çankaya, *Yeni Mülkiye Tarihi ve Mülkiyeliler*, vol. 3, 683–5.

188 Mehmed Cavid, *İlm-i İktisad: Mekâtib-i İdâdîyeye Mahsus* (İstanbul: Matbaa-i Amire, 1908).

189 Mehmed Cavid, *Ma'lumat-ı İktisadiye: Mekâtib-i İdadiyenin En Son Programlarına Muvâfık Olarak Tertib Edilmişdir* (İstanbul: Kana'at Matbaası, 1911).

190 Mehmed Cavid, *İhsâiyat* (İstanbul, 1901).

191 See for example, the editor's introduction to the transcribed edition of Cavid Bey's book: Orhan Çakmak, "Takdim" in Mehmed Cavid Bey, *İktisat İlmi*, ed. Orhan Çakmak (İstanbul: Liberte Yayınları, 2001), ix. The problem of European names also appears in recent works on Cavid Bey as well as newly transliterated editions of his works. These studies contain names such as "Lauro Abulyo" (Leroy-Beaulieu), "Kene" (Quesnay), and "Emil du Velay" (Émile de Lavaye). See for example, Deniz Karaman, *Cavid Bey ve Ulûm-ı İktisâdiye ve İçtimaiye Mecmuası* (Ankara: Liberte Yayınları, 2001), 8; and Mehmed Cavid Bey, *İktisat İlmi*, *passim*.

192 Mehmed Cavid, *İlm-i İktisad*, vol. 1, و.

193 Paul Leroy-Beaulieu, *Traité théorique et pratique d'économie politique*, 4 vols. (Paris: Guillaumin et Cie, 1897).

194 "İlm-i İktisad namını vermeği daha münasib gördüğüm bu eser-i naçiz, ibtida 'LeVasseur', 'Baudrillart' ve 'Beauregard'in eserlerinden iktibas edilmiş idi. Yazdığım kağıdlarda saydığım kitablardan bilhassa 'Beauregard'dan alınmış pek

çok sahifeler vardır. Fakat bu tertibe riayet edecek olursam yine muhtasar bir kitab vücuda geleceğini düşündüm. Bununçün deha-yı iktisadisine bütün Avrupa'nın hayran olduğu 'Leroy-Beaulieu'nün üç bin sahifeye karib eser-i cesmine de müracaat eylemeğe lüzum gördüm. Halbuki bu eserdeki servet-i malûmat, vüs'at-i ihâta beni o derece meclub etti ki diğer eserlerden aldığım yüzü mütecaviz sahifeleri birer birer çizmeğe, bozmağa, bunlarla mezc etmeğe mecbur oldum." Cavid (1897, ز).

195 As an interesting side note, Dan Warshaw notes that Leroy-Beaulieu was one of the few economists who appeared in fiction, and his presence in Marcel Proust's *À la recherge du temps perdu* as a powerful political figure testifies to his formidable personality and his prominent place in French intellectual life of the era (Warshaw, *Leroy-Beaulieu*, 3). Likewise, Mehmed Cavid Bey and his mentor Sakızlı Ohannes are perhaps the only Ottoman economists who appeared in fiction. In Attila İlhan's *Dersaadet'te Sabah Ezanları*, Cavid Bey is mentioned in different conversations among the characters, (Attila İlhan, *Dersaadet'te Sabah Ezanları* [Ankara: Bilgi Yayınevi, 1988], 68, 175, 178), and in one of such conversations his economic ideas are criticized by two characters (Attila Ilhan, *Dersaadet'te Sabah Ezanları*, 313). Ohannes is also mentioned in the same conversation only in comparison to Cavid Bey.

196 See for example, Mehmed Cavid, *İlm-i İktisad*, vol. 1, 314–19, in which Cavid Bey excludes a part on Ricardo's theory of land rent and adds a section on the restrictions on industry in the Ottoman Empire ("Memalik-i Osmaniyede Serbesti-i İ'mal ve Sanayie Vuku' Bulan Tehdidat").

197 Compare Mehmed Cavid, *İlm-i İktisad*, vol. 1, 30, and Leroy-Beaulieu, *Traité théorique et pratique d'économie politique*, vol. 1, 98.

198 See Zafer Toprak, *Türkiye'de "Milli İktisat," 1908–1918* (Ankara: Yurt Yayınları, 1982), and Karaman, *Cavid Bey ve Ulum-ı İktisadiye ve İctimaiye Mecmuası*, 14–38.

199 Mehmed Cavid, *İlm-i İktisad*, vol. 1, 314–19.

200 Ibid.

201 Ibid., 317–22.

202 Ibid., 326–8.

203 Unfortunately Mahmud Hayri also does not provide any exact reference, but the original book must be one of the many editions of Beauregard's *Eléments d'économie politique*.

204 Fındıkoğlu claims that this might be due to Mahmud Hayri's being a graduate of the Mekteb-i Mülkiye, see Ziyaeddin Fahri Fındıkoğlu, *Türkiyede İktisat Tedrisatı Tarihçesi ve İktisat Fakültesi Teşkilâtı* (İstanbul: Akgün Matbaası, 1946), 40.

205 He quotes "laysa li'l-insāni illā mā sa'ā" from the Qur'an (Surat al-Najm; 53:39). See Mahmud Hayri, "İfade-i Meram" in Paul Beauregard, *Mebadi-i İlm-i Servet-i Milel*, trans. Mahmud Hayri (İstanbul: Mahmud Bey Matbaası, 1899), 2.

206 Ibid.

207 Mahmud Hayri, "İfade-i Meram," 3; also see Ohannes, *Mebadi-i İlm-i Servet-i Milel*, 12–13.

208 Mustafa Nail, *Muhtasar İlm-i Servet* (İstanbul: Matbaa-i Âmire, 1899).

209 Benjamin C. Fortna, *Learning to Read in the Late Ottoman Empire and the Early Turkish Republic* (New York: Palgrave Macmillan, 2011), 20.

210 Margaret G. O'Donnell, "Harriet Martineau: A Popular Early Economics Educator," *The Journal of Economic Education* 14, no. 4 (October 1, 1983): 59–64.

211 Robert L. Heilbroner, *The Making of Economic Society* (Englewood Cliffs, NJ: Prentice-Hall, 1968), ix.

212 Unfortunately, the author does not name a specific work but rather seem to encourage the peasants to refer to any book on economics.

213 Yazıcıoğlu Mustafa and Fahri, *Ahenk* 13 Teşrin-i Evvel 1316 (October 26, 1900); quoted in Zeki Arıkan, "İzmir'de İlk Kooperatifleşme Çabaları," *Tarih İncelemeleri Dergisi*, no. 4 (1989): 37–8.

214 "*Le travail et l'économie leur faciliteront l'exercice le beaucoup d'autres vertus.*" (Maurice Block, *Petit Manuel d'économie pratique*, cinquième édition [Paris: J. Hetzel, 1878], 6).
215 Ahmed Muhtar, "Mukaddime" [Introduction], Maurice Block, *Amelî İktisad Dersleri*, trans. Ahmed Muhtar (İstanbul: Mahmud Bey Matbaası, 1906), 11.
216 Maurice Block, *Petit Manuel d'économie pratique*, 19.
217 Maurice Block, *Ameli İktisad Dersleri*, 29.
218 Ibid., 58.
219 Ahmed Muhtar, "Mukaddime," 11.
220 Ibid., 7.
221 Ibid., 8.
222 For detailed analyses of Islamic economics, which emerged in the twentieth century, see Timur Kuran, *Islam and Mammon: The Economic Predicaments of Islamism* (Princeton: Princeton University Press, 2004).

3 The economic idea of society and social change for development

> Every man thus lives by exchanging, or becomes, in some measure, a merchant, and the society itself grows to be what is properly a commercial society.[1]
>
> (Adam Smith, 1776)

> When the people of a country get used to civilization, the [natural] human disposition and personal interests render those people capable and willing to improve their own living conditions.... Since the science of the wealth of nations studies the natural principles concerning the material interests of society, nobody from the ordinary people—as well as the elite—can be excused from studying this science.[2]
>
> (Sakızlı Ohannes, 1880)

Just as the Industrial Revolution in England brought about a far-reaching social change under the expanding hegemony of bourgeois social values, Ottoman efforts for economic modernization in the late nineteenth century was marked by a new understanding of society, which was informed by the classical political economy of the age. Society organized around a self-regulating market, the dynamics of which are determined by production and consumption decisions of individuals, was a revolutionary idea.

Economics not only redefined society, but it also categorized societies according to their modes of production—in Marxist terms—and put them in a hierarchical order, industrial economies usually being the most advanced form. Besides, in accordance with the Enlightenment idea of progress, which marked the social and economic thought of the age, economics retold the history of human civilization through stages of developmental patterns. From List's model to that of Marx, economists suggested their stage theories of socio-economic development evolving from the primitive to the advanced economies, thereby placing the existing countries and societies in a hierarchical order too. These novel ideas and methods caused an epistemological break in Ottoman social and economic thought, as it did in Western Europe. Economic narratives of world history and hierarchical interpretations of human civilization and societies—based on economic determinants—changed Ottoman understanding of the world and the Ottoman Empire's place in it, thereby shaping projections and plans for the future of Ottoman society.

This chapter examines the impact of capitalist modernity and its economics on late Ottoman understanding of society in economic and historical context. It focuses on the change in the Ottoman perception of the world and its history, the notion of civilization, and the assumptions about the socio-economic institutional reform that is necessary to be considered a civilized country—a major concern for the Ottoman elite of the era. The first section focuses on economic history and historicism in the early nineteenth century, and their implications in the Ottoman intellectual sphere. Then it examines some examples of Ottoman travelogues about Europe to see the self-perception of the Ottomans vis-à-vis industrial Europe under industrial capitalist paradigm of the age. The second section provides a survey of ideas on redesigning Ottoman society—starting from the citizens' economic mindset—according to these new parameters, including a brief part on how Ottoman women envisioned women's role in an economy-oriented Ottoman society.

World upside-down: the age of revolutions, economics and a new perception of the world

> The nineteenth century started with revolution.... The year 1789 introduced a new grammar of politics and formulated a new conception of society. The idea of a society of orders, where people were born into a particular class and stayed there, gave way to notions of mobility, where property, ownership, gender, and education defined a meritocracy of deserving citizens. These were bound up with the gradual and uneven emergence of a new grammar of economics, as it was formulated above all in Europe's "first industrial nation," Britain.[3]

Economics aims to explain society as a dynamic system of production and consumption relations. However, economics is not only about analyzing certain aspects of a pre-defined formation (i.e., society), it also suggests a specific definition of this formation, which was being reshaped by the economic and political revolutions of the late eighteenth and early nineteenth centuries.

As Karl Polanyi states, nineteenth-century economics arose on the discovery of "the existence of a society that was not subject to the laws of the state, but, on the contrary, subjected the state to its own laws."[4] This discovery itself, on the other hand, is not a sudden realization of an ever-existing mechanism, but a result of a peculiar nineteenth-century development: the self-regulating market and the consequent market society. According to Polanyi, the economic sphere is embedded in social relations in pre-capitalist societies. In the capitalist market economy, however, "Instead of economy being embedded in social relations, social relations are embedded in the economic system."[5] Moreover, the nation-state was rising as the new main political agency, ruling over on a closed "national" economy. In short, the market society, comprising the market economy and the nation-state, defined the modern notion of society, thereby causing a paradigm shift in early nineteenth-century social and economic theory.

Meanwhile, Newtonian physics perpetuated its unquestionable dominance over scientific and philosophical inquiries in Europe. And accordingly, economists were trying to reveal the natural laws that govern economic relations. In the same vein, machines were to become a perfect metaphor for social relations throughout the nineteenth century, as they are composed of individual metal pieces that obey the natural laws of division of labor and cooperation—as economics explained society since Adam Smith.[6] The human individual was likened to an interchangeable part of a machine, thereby becoming the starting point of all social engineering projects of the modern age. In the nineteenth-century economics, an essentialized and mostly misunderstood version of Adam Smith's *Homo economicus*—with its purely economically motivated behavior—determined the assessment of appropriate individual economic behavior. As human communities were being transformed into market societies, human individuals were expected to become economically-motivated atomic units in nineteenth-century social imagination. In the eyes of an economist, therefore, society is defined as a national organization of *Homines economici.*

With the emergence of self-regulating market and market society, the state lost its omnipotent role in analyses of socio-economic dynamics and historical change. In this respect, Adam Smith's economics suggested an alternative explanation of human history, that is, what we call today "economic history." From the perspective of economics, the history of human societies was the history of socio-economic organizations. In other words, the economic history of the nineteenth century suggested that the history of human civilization was one of production forces and production relations, in Marxist terms.

"Economic" history, historicism, and the Ottoman Empire

> Economic history is a sub-discipline within economics and, to a lesser degree, within history, whose main focus is the study of economic growth and development over time.... Although historians have practiced their craft at least since the time of Herodotus (the fifth century BC), economics emerged as a separate social science with the work of Adam Smith or, perhaps, as some have argued, that of the Mercantilists and the Physiocrats. Classical economists, with the notable exception of Ricardo, were almost all also historical economists. The reader of Smith, Mill, Marx, or even Marshall ploughs through thick volumes in which propositions in economic theory are embedded in often lengthy descriptions of historical events or the course of economic history. Throughout most of the 19th century, the divide between economists and economic historians was weak.[7]

Modern economics did not bring about only new principles that explain certain (i.e., economic) social relations, but also a new perception of the world. The new economic explanation of historical change suggested a self-regulating mechanism governed by its own laws, thereby excluding the state's and even God's role in explaining socio-economic dynamics. As a well-known example, Marx's historical materialism suggests a linear and hierarchical pattern of historical progress from primitive to advanced modes of production, that is, from primitive communism to capitalism—and eventually to socialism, according to Marx and Marxists.[8] Marx's economic historical perspective is not unique at all.[9] On the contrary, it resembles other similar hierarchical models of his age, such as Friedrich List's formulation of a progressive model of historical change from "the savage state" to the "manufacturing and commercial" state of nations.[10]

All in all, the economic historical paradigm of the age was shaped by optimistic industrial capitalism and self-assured Eurocentricism. Economic developments in late eighteenth-century Europe heralded a new phase in human history and inspired a new hierarchy of nations based on their levels of economic sophistication. In short,

> More work and inventiveness resulted in ever higher levels of social development and economic productivity, culminating in the scientifically oriented, industrialized nation states that had come to rule the globe. Work meant progress; industry produced prosperity; felt needs drove the Europeans to dominate the world.[11]

The world, thereby, began to be defined as "the West and the rest," which, in economic terms, corresponds to the separation of the industrialized world from the so-called primitive economies. To the chagrin of the proud Ottomans, their empire, with its non-industrial economy, took its place in the second category. This challenge had a deep impact on Ottoman modernization by both creating an anxiety and providing a set of rules for the modernization process: hard work, science, increasing productivity, inventiveness, and industrialization.

Moreover, the rise of economic history was accompanied by the emergence of historicism in the early nineteenth century. In fact, according to some scholars, it was Adam Smith's work of "historicization" and division of "mankind's social and economic development into periods or stages" paved the way for nineteenth-century historicism.[12] Beyond economic analyses, the unprecedented socio-economic and political change in the so-called Age of Revolutions created an overall interest in history.

> One important response to the rapid changes in French society since the Revolution of 1789 was a renewal of interest in history. If the events of the present seemed confused and disturbing, it was felt they might begin to make sense when seen in relation to events of the past. Napoleon and later governments encouraged the expansion of historical and philological studies by creating chairs of history in every university, and every field of endeavor was touched by the new historical sense.[13]

As the most well-known example to this new historical sense, G.W.F. Hegel's (1770–1831) philosophy of history explains social processes and institutions by their history. Hegel's notion of history, which unfolding into a certain direction under certain laws (or "Spirit"), was later adopted and reinterpreted by Karl Marx and other nineteenth-century philosophers in their progressive formulations of historical change. Meanwhile in the Ottoman Empire, chronic economic and political problems and the rapid change caused by the process of integration into the capitalist world-system aroused an interest in history among the elites who were influenced by such new interpretations of history and history's relevance to contemporary. Reformists hoped to reach the roots of the problems through examining the history of the political and economic institutional setting. As a result, the new historical sense of the early nineteenth century, which was informed by historicism and economic history, was to make a considerable impact on Ottoman economic and political thought in the later decades of the century.

Ottoman economic historiography and historicism

Until the mid-nineteenth century, Ottoman historiography was principally a tradition of chronicling military and political events from the state's perspective.[14] Although several Ottoman intellectuals before the nineteenth century included socio-economic analyses in their historical narratives and mirrors-for-princes, these analyses were predominantly based on the assumption of the state's omnipotence in shaping socio-economic life. The most well-known example of this phenomenon is the notion of "the circle of justice" formulated in Kınalızade Ali's *Ahlak-ı Alai* in the sixteenth century:

> There can be no government without men, no men without money, no money without prosperity, and no prosperity without justice and good administration." In other words, "On the ruler's justice and good administration depended the peasants' and merchants' ability to generate prosperity; from this wealth taxes flowed to pay the military, which supported the king and protected the realm.[15]

This traditional approach to economy regarded socio-economic factors that caused the rise and fall of a state as results of the rulers' decisions and actions. The deviation from this tradition came with the renowned statesman, intellectual, and historian Ahmed Cevdet Pasha (1822–95), who incorporated social, financial, and economic analyses into his narrative of the political history of the Ottoman Empire.[16] His new approach to Ottoman history was inspired by European intellectuals and historians such as Michelet, Taine, Hammer, Buckle, Macaulay, and Montesquieu.[17]

Ahmed Cevdet Pasha starts his 12-volume study of history with his conception of the progress of history,[18] inspired by Ibn Khaldun's evolutionary, cyclical, and organic conceptualization of history. According to this earliest institutional approach to history, states are born, grow and finally "die" due to various institutional factors. Ahmed Cevdet Pasha, following Ibn Khaldun, asserts that societies pass through certain hierarchical stages of development—

from nomadism to urbanism.[19] He maintains that in more advanced stages, societies possess more sophisticated social, economic, and political institutions.[20] According to this model, urban socio-economic organization constitutes the highest level of social development, with its most sophisticated production systems and highest standards of living.[21] The similarity of this fourteenth-century conceptualization of society and its history to nineteenth-century social theories explains why Ibn Khaldun's work struck a chord with the nineteenth-century European social thought as well as with Ottoman intellectuals.[22]

The aforementioned European economic historical paradigm gave the Ottoman elite a major impetus to catch up with the developed world within the parameters of the same paradigm. Ahmed Cevdet Pasha's approach to history, therefore, seems to be an early reflection of the impact of economic history and historiography in Ottoman reformism. Following Ahmed Cevdet Pasha, other Ottoman intellectuals adopted a historicist perspective, looking for the causes of their backwardness in the past. This Hegelian-type Ottoman historicism may explain the great interest in reading, and more importantly, writing history especially among Hamidian-era intellectuals. In this era, history-writing ceased to be under the monopoly of the court historian, and was undertaken by many intellectuals.[23]

Although Şerif Mardin attributes the first "economic interpretation of history" in the Turkish language to İsmail Gaspırah and his newspaper, *Tercüman* (1895),[24] we observe in the 1870s that Ottoman reformists had already begun using historical economic analyses to discuss problems in Ottoman society. Namık Kemal's historical analyses in the early 1870s, for example, help us to understand the impact of economic history and historicism on Ottoman intellectuals. Kemal attributes European progress to the economic, scientific, and technological developments of the eighteenth and nineteenth centuries, and he criticizes Ottoman failure to adapt to the times. He goes on to argue that the Ottoman inability to catch up with European industrialization paved the way for the destruction of the guilds in the Ottoman Empire, leaving Muslims out of the productive sectors of the Ottoman economy.[25] Along with foreign dominance, Kemal criticizes the traditional fatalistic and anti-entrepreneurial economic mentality of Muslim Ottomans as another major cause of backwardness.[26] As a solution, he recommends industrial and commercial education for Muslims in order for them to adapt to the new economy-centered age.[27] Similar ideas were to be repeated by many intellectuals following Kemal—as we shall see below. Likewise, the Hamidian government was to establish industrial and commercial schools, especially for Muslim students, as an essential component of its economic development efforts.

As Ottoman Muslim intellectuals made these analyses, similar arguments were put forward by intellectuals from other parts of the Muslim world. It is important to remember that nineteenth-century Middle East and North Africa was highly interconnected in intellectual and cultural terms—which waned gradually in the post-Ottoman era of nation-states—thanks to the circulation of publications as well as thinkers themselves, who were multilingual at various levels. In 1870, the internationally renowned, albeit highly controversial, Muslim intellectual of the era, Jamāl-al-Dīn al-Afghānī (1838–97), voiced similar concerns during his speech at the opening ceremony of the first modern Ottoman university, the Dâr ül-Fünûn (House of Sciences). Al-Afghānī urged Muslims to catch up with European economic progress in order to get rid of the yoke of European imperialism.[28] He asserted that Islamic civilization had been economically and scientifically advanced in the past, thanks to the diligence and industriousness of Muslims. He added, however, that in time, Muslim got used to comfort and indolence, and as a result, they lost their superiority and began to lag behind. In order to correct "the mistakes of the past," al-Afghānī suggested two remedies: hard work and education.[29]

Al-Afghānī was not the first Muslim intellectual to emphasize the past economic and technological superiority of the Islamic world. This was a common response of Muslim intellectuals to the challenge of Eurocentrism of the age. For example, as early as 1861, Mehmed Şerif Efendi argued that the Muslims had been advanced in science and industry in the past, and that this claim could be proved by a well-known anecdote that is found in history books:[30] the Abbasid Caliph Hārūn al-Rashīd (*c.*766–809 AD) sent an automated alarm clock to the King of France. The French regarded this gift as a "strange thing" due to their ignorance of automated machines. Nevertheless, Mehmed Şerif Efendi adds, the Europeans have advanced in science and technology since then, whereas the Ottomans have not shown the same enthusiasm in these fields.[31]

Ottoman economic historicism made its intellectual impact especially in the 1880s through the writings of Ottoman popular economists, and especially through Ahmed Midhat. His historical approach to economics was an assault on the economic liberalism taught at Ottoman institutions of higher education. As I discuss in more detail below, Ahmed Midhat asserted that the traditional militaristic and nomadic (thus anti-entrepreneurial) economic mentality of the Ottomans was the principal reason for economic backwardness. After him, Akyiğitzade Musa, suggested that the Ottomans should derive lessons from the history of European economic development and follow the same path—pursuing protectionist policies in the earlier stages of industrialization to reach the highest stage of development.[32] Meanwhile, on the opposite side of Ottoman economic thought, the well-known liberal economist Cavid Bey sought the reasons of backwardness of the Ottoman economy in history and suggested that the traditional practices of interference in the economy and limitations on economic enterprise were to be blamed.[33] In short, both sides of the "protectionism vs. liberalism" battle had recourse to historicism to support their arguments on the historical roots of economic backwardness.

In the early twentieth century, especially with the Young Turks, Ottoman historicism turned into harsh criticisms about the traditional Ottoman institutional framework, which allegedly kept the empire economically and socially backward. Presenting arguments similar to those of Ahmed Midhat, the famous Ottoman "philosopher" of the early twentieth century, Rıza Tevfik (1869–1949), argued for getting rid of some "traditional characteristics" of the Turks. According to him, nomadic and militaristic forms of societal organization had brought wealth and glory through conquests and plunder in the past. However, the intellectual setup it created became obsolete and even harmful in the modern age, as it led people to indifference and even abhorrence towards commerce.[34] He wrote, "[Our] laziness, immorality, and barbarity today are [the vestiges of] yesterday's pride, arrogance, nomadism, and Janissary fights."[35]

In short, the economic backwardness compared to Europe and the economic historical paradigm of the nineteenth century led Ottoman reformists to explore their history from an economic perspective to ascertain the reasons for failure. As the Ottoman thinkers began to identify the traditional institutional framework as the main culprit, proposals for a total institutional transformation in the empire overshadowed alternative proposals. As a result, in the late nineteenth and early twentieth centuries, Ottoman modernization efforts were shaped by the idea of building a modern society defined in economic terms. The second section below will discuss these proposals in more detail, but before that, it is important to see how Ottomans perceived themselves under the paradigm of Eurocentric capitalist modernity through a look at travelogues written by Ottoman observers of Europe.

The "Ottoman" vis-à-vis the "modern" in Ottoman travelogues

> I wandered in the lands of the infidel and observed cities and stately mansions. I traveled in the lands of Islam and saw nothing but waste land and ruins.[36]

Ziya Pasha's (1825–80) well-known verse is a neat summary of Ottoman self-perception vis-à-vis European capitalist modernity in the late nineteenth century. According to the dominant view among the modernist Ottomans of the age, Europe was the land of wealth and prosperity as well as industry and technology, which were the results of hard work, entrepreneurship, diligence, and thrift; and the Ottoman Empire was the land of poverty and ruin as a result of indolence and ignorance.

Every journey to a foreign land is also a journey into the labyrinths of one's own culture and identity. During these travels, our conception of the world widens and is enriched with new perspectives. In this respect, travelogues can be manifestations of such questionings of the "self" and the "other" during our endeavors to redefine our self in our new wider world; and the travelogues written by Ottomans are not exceptions. Ottoman travelers to Europe provide us with illuminating accounts reflecting the formation of a new Ottoman identity in a completely new Eurocentric world with its allegedly global civilization.[37] In economic sense, it is obvious that Ottoman self-perception was significantly influenced by the identity attributed to the Ottomans by Europeans.[38]

Ottomans, like other visitors from all over the world, were astonished by their observations of the industrial societies of Europe.[39] Later, these observations gradually intertwined with the idea of the backwardness of the home country, especially in terms of science, technology and economic structure. One of the common observations that Ottoman travelers made was that the driving force behind modern European civilization was the economy, and that the main inputs behind this new force was knowledge and hard work. This striking observation also changed Ottoman self-perception. From then on, Europe and the Ottoman Empire would be defined in terms of the dichotomy of industry and indolence.[40]

In one of the earliest examples of this literature, the *Resimli Seyahatname* (*Illustrated Travelogue*, a manuscript dating from 1838), the author compares two cultures (i.e., the Ottoman and European), particularly on the basis of labor. He concludes that the main sources of wealth and prosperity in Europe were hard work and great interest in new industrial skills and knowledge. The author complains about the relative indifference of Muslims to commerce and industry, although, according to him, the Muslims are much smarter than the "slow-witted infidels," meaning the Europeans.[41]

An important example from the mid-century is the *Seyahatname-i Londra* (*Travelogue of London*) of an anonymous Ottoman bureaucrat. It was first serialized in the newspaper *Ceride-i Havâdis* (May 1852–May 1853), and following its success, it was also published as a book by the same newspaper (1853).[42] The *Seyahatname-i Londra* is full of details reflecting the astonishment of a Tanzimat bureaucrat in the face of the progress of European science and technology, and the new patterns of economic and social organization accompanying these scientific and technological developments. The author informs his Ottoman readers of various examples of new socio-economic institutions, from shopping malls to the shopping habits of people, and from fishery, agriculture, and husbandry to the press industry.[43] He also discusses why observing Europe is essential for the economic and social development of the Ottoman Empire. The author's arguments on science and education boil down to the idea that, although the center of the "supreme sciences" (i.e., Islamic sciences) in the world is the Ottoman capital (Istanbul), the center of the new "strange" sciences and the new type of education is the European continent.[44]

The author of *Seyahatname-i Londra* emphasizes that Europeans never waste time, but continuously pursue useful, educational, and productive activities in their spare time. He also notes that the Europeans spend considerable amounts of money on such activities. As an example, he mentions how the people of London form many associations and clubs, wherein they spend their time reading and discussing with other people about their fields of interest.[45] He connects these examples to his observations on the British love for labor with an implicit comparison to his own society:

> The people of London take commerce so seriously that everybody rushes to work as if they are rushing to their beds.... Since there is no work on Sundays, they sit down and bemoan ... that they cannot work that day.... And just because the people here are so ambitious and avaricious for [and always busy with] commerce, other people who come to London cannot find anyone to chat with. Nevertheless, there are various amazing places like

> factories, where new and original goods are produced.... Thus they [the visitors] spend their time visiting these places, thereby appreciating these amazing industries and products which are the pride of humanity and civilization.[46]

Although the discourse as well as contents of the works describing Europe did change in time, similar observations and ideas regarding labor and technology were repeated by various authors. The prominent Young Ottoman intellectual, Namık Kemal, for instance, argued in an article published 20 years after the *Seyahatname-i Londra* that the sole source of wealth and prosperity in Europe was hard work.[47] He exaggerates this idea so much that his description of Europe comes to the conclusion that European civilization is a product and a symbol of labor,[48] and he praises London as the true miracle of this civilization.[49] It is worth noting that this remark does not only reflect Ottoman astonishment of these particular examples, but also the *Zeitgeist* of the era. In late nineteenth-century Europe,

> The language of labor power was more than a new way of representing work: it was a totalizing framework that subordinated all social activities to production, raising the human project of labor to a universal attribute of nature.[50]

Accordingly, neither the anonymous author of the *Seyahatname-i Londra* nor Namık Kemal were alone in their astonishment and admiration specifically for London. In their age,

> Journalists, artists, novelists, social reformers, clergymen, and other students of society were drawn to London as 'an epitome of the round world' where 'there is nothing one cannot study at first hand.' They came there to see where society was heading.[51]

Covering the entire travelogue literature is beyond the scope of this study, but one last example will provide us with insights into late Ottoman industrial romanticism—as opposed to pastoral romanticism of nineteenth-century Europe. Mehmed Enisî (Yalkı) visited some European coastal cities in 1895 and published his travelogue in 1911. He notes about Marseilles that this famous and beautiful coastline was "adorned with factories" as well as "other elegant buildings."[52] He adds that Marseilles, with its factories, high-rise buildings, and commercial offices was a product of the progress of human intelligence and civilization.[53] Reminiscent of Namık Kemal's words about London, Mehmed Enisî's romantic depiction of an industrial panorama reflects the late nineteenth-century fascination with industrialization.

What is to be done? Building a modern Ottoman society

The social reformist wing of the Ottoman modernist intellectuals, such as Münif Pasha and Ahmed Midhat Efendi, played critical roles in the Hamidian-era efforts for social reform based on modern economic principles. Before delving into social models, it is important to understand the separation between the "social" reformers and the "political" reformers of the age. Following the Young Ottomans' "politicization" of Westernization, two main wings emerged in the Ottoman modernization movement.[54] The first wing was the libertarians, like the Young Ottomans and then the Young Turks, who aimed at political liberalization and the establishment of a parliamentary system in the Ottoman Empire. The second wing focused on education and social change rather than immediate political change on the way to modernization. I loosely define these groups as the political reformers and social reformers respectively. However, it is worth noting that these categories are by no means exclusive. First, despite differences on the surface, both wings shared the same goal in essence, that is, modernization.[55] Second, many political reformers also suggested models for social change despite giving priority to political change. The following parts juxtapose the ideas of both social and political reformists on social change on the basis of modern economic principles, and show how the ideas of these opposing lines of reformism converged—under the influence of the industrial-capitalist paradigm of the age—when it came to developing plans to build a modern Ottoman society.

Münif Pasha and education: economic development as a social process

Mehmed Tahir Münif Pasha (1828–1910) was a leading reformist statesman of the latter half of the nineteenth century. He was also the pioneer of Ottoman *encyclopedism*, which began with the foundation of the Cemiyet-i İlmiyye-yi Osmâniye (Ottoman Society of Sciences, founded in 1861) and its journal, *Mecmua-i Fünûn* (*Journal of Sciences*). Münif Pasha was the founder and a leading figure of both the Society and the journal. *Mecmua-i Fünûn* constituted an example for the subsequent publications of the Ottoman *encyclopedist* movement, which later continued with Ahmed Midhat's *Tercüman-ı Hakikat*, Ahmed İhsan's *Servet-i Fünûn* and other similar popular periodicals. Almost all of Münif Pasha's writings on social, economic, and political matters were published before the Hamidian era. Nevertheless, thanks to his role as a prominent public intellectual, an important reformist statesman, and an educator, his ideas shaped the social and educational policies of the Hamidian regime in its early years. Moreover, he became Minister of Education three times between 1871 and 1891. He thereby contributed significantly to the shaping of the Hamidian education system and dedicated his life to the struggle for the formation of educated and industrious citizens.

As discussed in Chapter 2, Münif Pasha's lecture notes on economics were published as a book in 1885.[56] However his ideas on socio-economic matters had appeared in his earlier writings in *Mecmua-i Fünûn*. Münif Pasha's model for modern Ottoman society was based on cooperation among industrious and scientifically minded individuals who would understand and uphold the modernization project initiated by the state. In his speech at the opening ceremony of the Dâr ül-Fünûn, he states, "It is possible to obtain results from the modernization efforts [in the short run], but they would not last long without education."[57] In an article he wrote for *Mecmua-i Fünûn*, he summarizes his ideas through the example of ants, regarded as industrious and social animals:

> An ant, when it is alone, seems like a weak and insignificant insect. However, in its nest with its fellow creatures… it is considered a civilized individual of a society that is defined by mind, reason, labor, and effort.[58]

He goes on to explain how these "insignificant creatures" build magnificent structures and beat even lions as they act systematically and in cooperation.[59] Münif Pasha's message is clear: an individual has no significant power when alone, but if individuals work hard and cooperate with each other, following science and reason, they can overcome all sorts of difficulties and build a developed and civilized country. In this respect, his approach to scientific knowledge is purely pragmatic.[60] For him, education is necessary not only for civil servants, but for all citizens. He argues that in every occupation scientific education and know-how increase efficiency, and the lack thereof causes waste.[61] Accordingly, he concludes that if a government wants to increase social prosperity, it should establish institutions of education for every segment of society, from peasants to merchants.[62] This remark hints at his comprehensive approach to the question of economic development.

According to Münif Pasha, the most important criterion of economic development is the standard of living of ordinary people.[63] He argues that a country can be considered wealthy only if its people possess "valuable commodities," by which he means things that satisfy their needs—or in other words, consumer goods—in abundance and in good quality. He suggests a simple method for assessing economic development: when we wander the streets in a city, he argues, if we see that the things people eat and wear are of bad quality, we consider them poor, no matter how much gold the wealthier ones keep in their coffers.[64] As a result, since economic development is measured by the standards of living, the science of economics should be used as an instrument for public prosperity.[65] His instrumentalist approach to science in general and economics in particular is nothing but a manifestation of the distinct pragmatist nature of the nineteenth-century Ottoman reformism.

After providing a summary of the development of capitalism in Europe, Münif Pasha states that people who are not aware of the principles of economics cannot understand the fact that economic development is a comprehensive and long-term socio-economic process. He maintains that such people would assert that, although there are some successful Ottoman entrepreneurs, entrepreneurship is not appreciated and rewarded in the Ottoman Empire, and therefore economic development is not possible in this country. As a response to this sort of pessimism, he argues, "Those who know the truth [the principles of economics] would realize that summer does not come with a single blossom."[66] In other words, individual enterprise cannot produce any permanent results unless it is supported by broader reforms for economic development, such as the improvement and dissemination of general public education.

Münif Pasha believes that educated and industrious individuals constitute the backbone of Ottoman modernization. In this respect, time, labor, and knowledge are essential inputs of all production processes. Therefore, laziness, ignorance, and time-wasting stand as the main obstacles to economic development. In the first issue of *Mecmua-i Fünûn*, he argues,

> The ignorant spend their time doing nothing but smoking pipes, chattering with people like themselves, and doing similar trivial and *harmful* things. They waste a [beautiful] life with boredom. In contrast, wise people study the rise and fall of states..., the creation and working of all animate and inanimate beings, and minerals. In short, wise people would feel sorry for even a minute that was wasted idly.[67]

The scene at an ordinary Ottoman coffeehouse with its idle regulars appears in Münif Pasha's writings as an undesirable lifestyle that is the absolute opposite of the modern industrious lifestyle.

The coffeehouse as a center of idleness and waste of time and money rose to a serious concern for modernist intellectuals throughout the empire with the increasing influence of bourgeois work ethic in Ottoman (urban) social and intellectual life. Jurji Zaydan (1861–1914), a prominent Lebanese public intellectual complained later that,

> [S]taying in cafés for days on end is idleness and that this is particularly bad for the young given how difficult is has become to find work these days. After 35 you won't find a job. The chances for the youth are already diminishing after 15. Between 20 and 25 is the best time of life, so why waste it sitting in coffeehouses drinking beer and playing backgammon? It is then that we determine our future and the rest of our life depends on it. You lose time and money if you gamble.[68]

It is worth noting that such criticisms from Middle Eastern modernists about so-called "Oriental" work habits and perception of time has strong parallels with the Western critique of non-Westerners in the industrial age:

> [Western] essayists and colonial policymakers [of the nineteenth century] pointed to the supposedly inherent lack of punctuality exhibited by non-Western peoples, their improvidence and lethargic work habits, and their apparent indifference to time "lost" or "wasted" in gossip, meditation, or simply daydreaming.[69]

Although it is true that the above words from Middle Eastern intellectuals reflect self-Orientalism—influenced by European discourses about "the Orient"—it is equally true that these criticisms are also direct results of the impact of economic thinking. In the industrial age, "Time became a commodity that could be 'saved,' 'spent,' or 'wasted.' "[70] In this respect, this new perception of time in Ottoman intellectuals' works reflects the industrialist-capitalist understanding of the notion of time in the late nineteenth century.[71]

Returning to Münif Pasha, in addition to his place in late Ottoman economic thought, his ideas are the key to understanding the logic behind the transformation of the Ottoman education system in the Hamidian era. As Minister of Education in the early 1880s, he was one of the architects of the Hamidian education system, which was aimed principally at producing economically productive individuals.[72] Furthermore,

> It was felt that even though the state apparatus was in Muslim hands, the domestic and international economic and social developments were marginalizing the Muslim population and the Ottoman state. In correlation with such sentiments, there was a strong tendency in the early 1880s for the inclusion of a number of professional courses in the primary and secondary school curricula. These courses imparted practical knowledge and aimed at developing industry and trade particularly among Muslims.[73]

In other words, the Muslim ruling elite aimed to activate Muslim entrepreneurship in response to increasing non-Muslim dominance in the Ottoman economy. Children of Ottoman Christian communities, especially after the Tanzimat, were able to receive practical as well as theoretical education at church schools to develop commercial and industrial skills. The Hamidian administration established special schools with similar objectives (such as *sanayî mektebleri*—industrial schools) and introduced economy-related courses in the curricula of other schools to provide Muslims with similar opportunities.[74]

Although the goal of creating a Muslim-dominated economy could not be achieved to the fullest extent in the short run, such efforts had significant long-run effects. A network of modern high schools (*idâdî*) was established throughout the country. More importantly, the Mekteb-i Mülkiye of the 1880s and 1890s educated Ottoman youth with a new economic mentality. As Ahmed İhsan, a graduate of the school, notes in his memoirs, the professors at this school, especially Ohannes and Mikael Pashas, taught their students that "life is based on economy,"[75] and that the power of a nation depended on the strength of its financial and fiscal organization as well as on the people's effort.[76] Ahmed İhsan claims that these teachers, through these lessons, helped the Ottoman youth "get rid of the fatalistic medieval mentality."[77] In short, the main objective of Münif Pasha and other like-minded Ottoman bureaucrats of the late nineteenth century was the creation of a new Muslim middle class as a strategy of saving the empire.[78]

Münif Pasha's vision for a modern Ottoman society and his ideas on the relationship between education and modernization were echoed in the writings of later Ottoman intellectuals. Ahmed Midhat, for example, systematized such ideas with a much more specific and detailed blueprint to achieve the same goal. After Münif Pasha's concentrated efforts to further education at the formal and institutional level, Ahmed Midhat took over the baton to become the most prominent *encyclopedist* intellectual of the Hamidian regime.

Ahmed Midhat's Homo Ottomanicus *and building an economic society*

Historical roots of backwardness and the need for social transformation

Ahmed Midhat's historical approach to economics led him to emphasize the importance of taking historical and geographical conditions of a country into account in determining economic policies.[79] Accordingly, in his *Ekonomi Politik* (1879), he provides a brief economic history of the Ottoman Empire to illustrate the historical causes of economic backwardness: "We, the Ottomans, should take a look at the beginnings of our history to be able to assess our national wealth. Our history indicates that our first appearance [in history] was in the form of a military nation."[80] He then argues that the Ottomans also showed great success in industry, expanding their commercial enterprises along the Mediterranean coast. He adds that, although the vestiges of these great economic achievements are still evident, these achievements were mostly the works of the non-Muslims. Yet, "the Muslim-Turks," who are the "military element of the nation," constitute the majority in Ottoman population; he thus concludes that the Ottomans still count as a military nation.[81] Then, he connects this historical analysis to a characteristic nineteenth-century capitalistic idea about economy and economics: wars are the greatest obstacles to industrial and commercial development, therefore, economics promotes peace more than any other science.[82] He goes on to argue that the Ottomans' status as a military nation had not impeded its pursuit of wealth in the past thanks to the continuous flow of taxes and booty from newly conquered territories.[83] Wealth gathered through military power, however, is always prone to be wiped out by a more powerful enemy, and thus is not reliable from the perspective of economics, he argues.[84] The science of economics indicates, according to him, that the wealth of artisan and merchant nations is more likely to endure, even if their political and military power should wane.[85]

In the same context, in *Sevda-yı Sa'y ü Amel* (1879), Ahmed Midhat examines the traditional Ottoman mentality through an analysis of Ottoman material culture in its historical context. He notes that Ottoman rural and even urban lifestyles and mentalities still display some nomadic features.[86] Since nomads do not have time and means to invest in cultural and economic development, he believes, they cannot build a sophisticated civilization.[87] They lack notions like discipline, order, law, or even political notions such as "homeland."[88] In other words, according to Ahmed Midhat, nomads are the opposite of "civilized" (*medenî*). He maintains that until very recently Ottoman daily life (in many parts of the empire) was not very different from a nomadic lifestyle.[89] Some of his examples are meant to show that such lifestyles are not limited to distant corners of the empire, but are found in its capital, Istanbul. The Ottoman notion of "furniture" (or the lack thereof), according to him, is the most informative manifestation of the nomadic heritage.[90] For example, using chests instead of closets for clothes and other belongings is a remnant of a nomadic culture based on the practice of mounting horses at sunrise to move camp. Likewise, hanging spoons and bread on the wall is a residue of the tradition of hanging these on the saddles of animals while on the move. Using foldable mattresses (and folding and unfolding them before and after sleeping every day) is another good example of the nomadic lifestyle.[91] Thus, he concludes that the Ottomans' use of furniture resembles that of nomads who value mobility. He adds that even the marketplaces in Istanbul are not composed of permanent stores but of temporary stalls as yet another example to remnants of a nomadic culture.[92] Since permanent results cannot be obtained by temporary solutions, the first step in economic modernization, according to him, was to get rid of such vestiges of the nomadic lifestyle and establish a new economic mentality of building permanent structures through hard work, investment, and education.

Adhering to the classical labor theory of value, Ahmed Midhat argues that the only source of wealth is labor, and that even if wealth is somehow acquired, it does not create any value if it is not turned into capital. He asserts that in the Ottoman Empire the "old wealth"[93] has collapsed, but the means of creating "new wealth" (i.e., industrial and commercial capital) has not yet been established. This holds true not only for the Ottoman Empire but for the entire world of Islam.[94] Observing the Ottoman economy, he sees that every major economic sector is controlled by either foreigners or non-Muslim Ottomans.[95]

> In short, when we apply political economy to our country, its first conclusion would be that we possess neither capital, nor agriculture, nor industry, nor commerce, and not even skills. In order to make us a nation that is subject to political economy, the first step will be to create all of these things once again.[96]

According to Ahmed Midhat, the primary problem was not economic backwardness itself or the lack of economic and financial capital in this context. The primary problem was that Muslim Ottomans were totally out of the economic sphere because the commercial and industrial sectors were controlled by "the others," that is, the non-Muslim Ottomans and Europeans. Therefore the first problem to be solved was not the lack of capital, but the lack of indigenous (i.e., Muslim) skills to control and manage capital. As a result of this condition, the wealth created through local resources did not contribute to the wealth of the nation. Therefore, the solution was to establish a new society whose members were in control of directing and managing their own resources through their own labor. The management of resources to increase the wealth of society (i.e., economic development) would be the next step. From this arose a critical question:

how shall we transform Ottoman society in order for it to procure its own wealth and prosperity in the long run? In other words, what is the path to a radical bottom-up social transformation that would pave the way for industrialization and economic development? Ahmed Midhat's answer was the creation of a capitalist spirit (in Weberian terms) that would ignite a capitalistic social awakening.

The capitalist spirit according to Ahmed Midhat

Adam Smith asserts that the principles of economics are based on some natural instincts (namely, truck, barter, and exchange) of human beings. This assumption constitutes the backbone of his formulation of *Homo economicus*. Likewise, Ahmed Midhat formulated *Homo Ottomanicus*, who is also driven by economic instincts but differing significantly from *Homo economicus* with his cultural and moral concerns.[97] In addition to being industrious, thrifty, and self-disciplined—that may also define *Homo economicus* in a broad sense—*Homo Ottomanicus* is humbly obedient, cooperative and altruistic, instead of being a self-interested individualist person.[98]

Not only did Ahmed Midhat envision a new type of citizen, he also worked for the formation of this new type through his didactic works.[99] When we take a look at his bibliography, the range of topics—from economics and history to geography and French literature—gives us an idea about the kind of knowledge base he expected a modern Ottoman citizen to have.[100] But first and foremost, he wanted *Homo Ottomanicus* to be the embodiment of a new work ethic. Since labor is the only source of wealth, a modern Ottoman citizen should be industrious. Otherwise, he concludes, this "lazy man" is considered not only "useless," but also "harmful" to society due to his parasitic lifestyle, and "This lazy and harmful man should be kicked out of modern society."[101]

Interestingly enough, he fired his son-in-law, the well-known poet and writer Muallim Nâci (1850–93), from his *Tercüman-ı Hakikat*, on a similar ground:

> [A]s Ahmed Midhat stated it himself, dismissing his son-in-law had amounted in fact to the banishment of the themes of wine, love, and songs from his newspaper. Ahmed Midhat considered these themes immoral because they constituted a waste of national energy and were part of a contemplative hedonism which, he believed, had played an important part in the ruin of the Ottoman Empire.[102]

Although some people around him, like Mehmed Cevdet Bey and Şeyh Vasfi, tried to convince him to revise his decision about classical Ottoman poetry and Muallim Nâci, he dismissed them by saying, "Our doors are closed to the poetry of old times! No matter what you say!" Then, turning to the young author next to him, he added, "My son, light comes to us only from Europe.... Do not heed these garlic-headed poets!"[103] His interlocutor in this conversation was nobody other than Ahmed İhsan, one of the well-known followers of Ahmed Midhat's example as both a writer and a press entrepreneur.[104]

Ahmed Midhat's model for the new individual and the new society was based on two essential economic principles, elaborated in two separate books: *Sevda-yı Sa'y ü Amel* (*The Passion for Effort and Labor*, 1879) and *Teşrik-i Mesa'î, Taksim-i Mesa'î* (*Cooperation and Division of Labor*, 1879). *Sevda-yı Sa'y ü Amel* starts with Ahmed Midhat's arguments regarding the concept of *sevda*[105] and its various forms, such as *sevda-yı vatan* (passion for the homeland) and *sevda-yı hürriyet* (passion for freedom). According to him, *sevda-yı sa'y ü amel* is not inferior in importance to the other two.[106] Passion for the homeland and passion for freedom were the slogans of the Young Ottomans, and these were later taken up by the Young Turks. Ahmed Midhat, however, suggests an economic alternative to these rather politically oriented passions: the passion for labor. In order to show the power of this new idea, he compares this sort of passion with that for a person. He claims that "tasting" the passion for labor would change a person permanently, just as one may go mad as a result of his/her passionate love for his/her beloved.[107] Accordingly, he asserts, as soon as the Ottomans taste the joy of labor, they will work harder in order to have more of this unrivaled pleasure. He therefore considers passion for labor as a powerful force driving towards economic development.

This reminds us of a well-known idea in the social sciences which was formulated later by Max Weber in his *The Protestant Ethic and the Spirit of Capitalism* (1904–05).[108] Considering that neither could have influenced each other—unless we assume that Weber read Ahmed Midhat—the most likely general explanation for this similarity may be the *Zeitgeist*. Revealing Ahmed Midhat's sources for such ideas and establishing the connections between his and Weber's ideas require further studies. It is important to emphasize, however, that Ahmed Midhat's perception of labor differs from a purely ascetic work ethic as defined by Weber, since Ahmed Midhat encourages enjoying the material fruits of one's labor as well. As we read especially in his fiction, his ideal modern individual is someone who works hard, but who also lives a comfortable life thanks to his income.[109] In this respect, Ahmed Midhat's notion of labor more closely resembles the Saint-Simonian and Fourierian models, which reject degrading aspects of industrial labor and suggest a new society based on free and thus enjoyable forms of labor as well as on comfort and leisure. Nevertheless, as will be discussed in Chapter 5, Ahmed Midhat did create some fictional characters, such as Şinasi in his *Bahtiyarlık* (1885), who are closer to Weber's description of an ideal ascetic entrepreneur.[110]

Although Ahmed Midhat tried to introduce a new work ethic to his audience, he saw labeling it "new" as somewhat problematic, because it was not something foreign to be imported from Europe. In other words, Ahmed Midhat rejects the idea of an essential Oriental indolence vs. European industriousness, asserting that the passion for work exists in every human being. He maintains that the main driving force behind European success is labor, but this is not because they have an instinct others lack.[111] The European difference, according to him, derives from the fact that Europeans have processed and mobilized this instinct through education.[112] In a similar vein, his references for a new economic mentality were not necessarily European sources. He repeatedly emphasized that Islam also promotes such economic values and principles, giving examples from the Qur'an and *hadith* collections in addition to Ottoman proverbs that encourage hard work.[113] He thereby shows that the notion of passion for labor already exists in Muslim-Ottoman culture and that Islam prescribes industriousness. In short, Ahmed Midhat emphasizes that Ottomans possess the necessary spirit for economic development, but in a rather raw form. What remained was to process and mobilize this spirit for the construction of a new society.

For Ahmed Midhat, the critical matter is labor; to what end it is used is a secondary issue. He compares lazy and industrious people and concludes that an industrious person can work for work's sake—simply because it is pleasurable. Such a person works for charity even when he does not have to work for himself.[114] Nevertheless, he adds that there are certain professions that the Ottomans should pursue in order to help the empire on its way to economic development. For example, he notes that "even" the civil service might be a good profession for lovers of labor, and that it is definitely necessary for the country that hard-working people take up bureaucratic positions.[115] However, he adds, in the "developed and modern countries"[116] the lovers of labor prefer private entrepreneurship to civil service.[117] Such people can turn their diligence and creativity into the production of personal wealth, and this, in turn, brings about prosperity and wealth for the entire country. In order to support this Smithian idea with a visual example,[118] he compares the dynamism of the marketplace with the "well-known" sloth of civil servants.[119]

In short, according to Ahmed Midhat, although civil service could be considered an honorable duty, creative human labor should be channeled to productive sectors rather than the bureaucracy. In one of his famous novels, *Müşahedat* (*Observations*, 1891), his ideal entrepreneur Mehmed Seyyid Numan summarizes Ahmed Midhat's views: "My dear friend! One should not regard civil service as something to exploit [materially]. It is not [a source of] income and benefit. It is simply an honor."[120] Ahmed Midhat, appearing as a leading character in the novel, notes that these words "could constitute the most important part of a philosophy treatise."[121]

It is important to note in passing that this may not necessarily be a European-originated idea for Muslim Ottomans. We encounter similar opinions even in the earliest Islamic treatises on economic life. For example, in al-Shaybānī's (d. 805) *Kitāb al-Kasb* (*Book of Acquisition [Earning]*), there is a strong emphasis on the idea that

> money earned by commerce or crafts is more pleasing in God's eyes than money received from the government for civil or military service. The same point is argued by al-Jāhiz (d. 809) in an essay entitled 'In praise of merchants and in condemnation of officials' and is echoed by many later writers.[122]

Therefore, although Ahmed Midhat was apparently inspired by the *self-help* spirit of his age and *l'amour du travail* literature in French, he might have come across similar ideas in Islamic sources too. Yet, a satisfactory assessment of the influence of Islamic sources (other than the Qur'an, which he openly referred to) on Ahmed Midhat's economic thinking goes beyond the extent of this study.

It is also worth noting that the love of labor is not only an economic matter in Ahmed Midhat's thinking. According to him, labor is directly related to morality, self-discipline, and trustworthiness. Idleness, on the other hand, leads one to "evil thoughts" and to immorality. For example, in a 1887 piece about passing time (*Vakit Geçirmek*) he names various side effects of idleness and boredom, from hypochondria to depravity (particularly for women).[123] As a reflection of similar thinking from his age, Ali Bey, in his satirical dictionary, *Lehcet ül-Hakâyık*, defines boredom as the "devil's advocate" (*şeytanın da'vâ' vekili*), giving the term a more literal meaning.[124] In addition to his non-fictional writings, Ahmed Midhat illustrates this danger more explicitly in his fictional works.[125] In *Obur* (Glutton, 1885), for example, he asserts that since the root of all evil is idleness, Europeans fill their leisure times with useful and beneficial activities (like going to the theater) to avoid evil and immoral ideas.[126]

In short, Ahmed Midhat suggests that an industrious person is a not only a producer of wealth for himself and his country, but is also a self-disciplined and moral individual. In order to support his theory with religious principles, Ahmed Midhat has recourse to the then-popular quotation from the Qur'an: "We should never forget that God in His glorious book says, 'there is nothing for a human but his labor.'"[127] Here, he refers to a verse (Sūrat al-Najm, 53:39; *laysa li'l-insāni illā mā sa'ā* – "that man will only have what he has worked towards"),[128] which Ottoman intellectuals of his age frequently cited in the same context. Interestingly enough, the verse does not actually have any direct economic implication. The word *sa'ā* refers to "deeds," rather than "labor." More importantly, the verse is actually about divine judgment based on one's deeds, rather than material gains resulting from one's physical effort. In any case, as noted above, Ottoman modernists employed such divine rulings opportunistically so long as they served their cause of encouraging the Ottoman public to put more *sa'y* (effort) into economic development.

Consumption and waste

In addition to the theme of labor, the Europeanization of consumption patterns and social manners was another popular issue in late Ottoman intellectual life. "super Westernization," as Şerif Mardin defines it,[129] has generally been discussed under the rubric of "traditionalism vs. modernism" in the existing scholarship on Ottoman social change. However, the critique of super Westernization by Ahmed Midhat and other similar-minded intellectuals should be read in its economic context as well as in the cultural context of Westernization. According to many critical Ottoman intellectuals, super Westernization led to ridiculous quasi-Western appearances and mannerisms, along with an alienation from one's own culture.[130] More importantly, however, it caused the waste of huge resources on conspicuous consumption that could otherwise have been employed as capital. Ahmed Midhat, for example, was not against Westernization in the sense of adopting European scientific, intellectual, and even cultural patterns. On the contrary, he wrote a manual on European etiquette to educate his readers to adapt to social life in the "civilized world."[131] However, he opposed pseudo-Europeanization, which consists of mimicking the Europeans in dressing and talking (like sprinkling French words into everyday language), while ignoring their work ethic, which, according to Ahmed Midhat, was the real source of their economic and technological superiority. In short, he argued against a superficial and wasteful Europeanization, while definitely favoring a productive interpretation of Europeanization.

Ahmed Midhat's criticisms of wastefulness do not only concern material resources. His arguments on waste also include immaterial resources such as time. The industrial-age perception of time, that is, time as a commodity and as an input of production, is another idea promoted in his economic writings. In *Sevda-yı Sa'y ü Amel*, he provides comparisons between industrious and lazy behavior, and then contrasts a worker with a member of the leisure class (in Veblenian terms).[132] He contends that these two types have a natural mutual loathing for each other due to their completely opposite approaches to work.[133] He depicts an imaginary encounter early one morning. A worker is on the way to work, while a dandy is leaving a ball and heading to bed to spend the rest of the day asleep.[134] After describing their mutual abhorring gaze,[135] Ahmed Midhat analyzes the hatred towards work among the leisure class, and then argues that these people always pursue unproductive activities, such as playing cards, and if asked the reason for it, would simply say "*pour tuer le temps*" (to kill time).[136] He attacks this mentality by stating that although the British say "time is money,"[137] time is much more important than its potential monetary value. For him, "time is life itself; so when we kill time, we actually kill our lives."[138] Moreover, based on his earlier explanations of the passion for labor, he adds that life is not as enjoyable for the leisure class as it is for the lovers of labor, who get the pleasure of hard work every single day of their lives. He concludes that since the members of the leisure class do not experience the pleasure of work—thus that of life itself—they try to kill time in order to make it pass quickly. Yet, labor is the solution even to this problem: when we work, time "passes just as quickly as it does when two lovers are together."[139]

The comparison of European clubs and cafes with Ottoman coffeehouses in the context of leisure appears also in Ahmed Midhat's writings. He argues that even though some people "are burning with passion for labor,"[140] they do not know "how to declare their love to their beloved." In other words, such people do not know how and where to start working. His solution is pure and simple: Ottomans enjoy visiting their neighbors or going to coffeehouses in their leisure time, yet they could spend this time more productively reading or at least thinking about work and industry.[141] He once again turns to Europe for examples and states that although Europe is already advanced in science and technology, Europeans still organize conferences to find ways for further progress. He adds that in case it is not possible to act right away, even pondering these matters and developing ideas would be a good way to start.[142] For example, he says, if a person does not possess the capital to start a business, he can at least develop ideas about establishing a paper factory and put them on paper. Later, another person who possesses the necessary means to start a paper factory can find these ready-to-use ideas in the former's work and put them into practice.[143] Therefore, he concludes, even reading and thinking about labor, instead of spending time with neighbors talking about daily trivia, would lead to productive results.[144]

Ahmed Midhat and the state

Ahmed Midhat's economic thought cannot simply be regarded as the isolated ideas of an independent mind. On the contrary, he can be considered an important external component of the Hamidian education system, thanks to his vast popularity and the didactic character of his works.[145] His educational concerns and economic ideas were in perfect harmony with the goals of the Hamidian education system:

> An essential component of Ottoman education has been the function of 'social disciplining.' This term could be understood within the context of early-modern Absolutism and within the framework of the eighteenth-century European Enlightenment.... [Under Absolutism] people were expected to become obedient, pious, and hard-working subjects.[146]

Ahmed Midhat suggests that the sultan, Abdülhamid II, is a good example of "lovers of labor" (*sevda-yı sa'y ü amel erbâbı*), and he relates stories about the sultan's industriousness.[147] It is a well-known fact that Abdülhamid II was a skilled carpenter.[148] Supporting Ahmed Midhat's claim, Kemal Karpat argues that "He [Abdülhamid] was addicted to work. His regular day consisted of fourteen hours during which he personally read and answered much of the voluminous internal and external correspondence."[149] Abdülhamid II, in addition to encouraging labor and entrepreneurship through official (including religious) channels, presented himself as an example to his subjects:

> The root of all our problems is that the Ottoman man does not work to create material value. He is accustomed to play the master and make others work for him. For him, what is important is to live and to enjoy life to the full. Upon my request, the Sheikh ul-Islam declared that labor is praised by God and it is by no means degrading. This declaration will be read in schools as well. Our youth desire to become civil servants, soldiers or *'ulama*. Why does not even a single Ottoman want to become a big merchant, a skillful artisan, or a scientist? I am a good example to the people as I am engaged in carpentry. It is a shame that we are not used to this way of thinking. It is so hard to get rid of traditional ideas.[150]

The Nobel Prize laureate Scandinavian author Knut Hamsun testifies to the sultan's success in disseminating his image as an industrious figure. In his accounts

(1905) of his visit to Istanbul in 1899, Hamsun notes that Abdülhamid II is known as a very hard-working person who wakes up at dawn every day.[151] Hamsun also claims that Turkey has regained its dignity in the international arena thanks to the sultan's efforts for education, the development of commerce, the building of railways, and military reform.[152] Thus, Ahmed Midhat's ideas on industry and entrepreneurship reflect the Hamidian understanding of economic development, and his tales about the sultan's industriousness reflect the sultan's own concern to present himself as an example to promote such ideas as well as Ahmed Midhat's own intellectual objectives.[153]

Ahmed Midhat's impact on social change

Ahmed Midhat's work both reflected and influenced his age to a great extent. His articles on various subjects were carefully read and discussed among Ottomans of different generations. Moreover, his ideas had a significant impact on the intellectual development of intellectuals and statesmen of subsequent generations. As of the early 1880s Ahmed Midhat had been "busy with [writing and] publishing in arts and sciences for over fifteen years, and he was the teacher of everybody who came of age in this time period."[154] His popularity declined in the 1890s, never to be restored, due to both the increasing anti-Hamidian political reformism and the development of new literary styles and tastes, which his works could not keep up with in terms of quality. In other words, the literary tastes and political awareness of his students went beyond what Ahmed Midhat as an author could provide. However, his impact as the first teacher remained in the hearts and minds of the Young Turk generation who shaped the intellectual and political institutions in the twentieth-century Middle East.

One such example, Ali Kemal Bey, an influential liberal intellectual and Young Turk politician of the post-1908 period,[155] notes in his memoirs that when he was a student at the *Mekteb-i Mülkiye*, he and his friends followed Ahmed Midhat and his newspaper, *Tercüman-ı Hakikat*, so carefully that they almost memorized his every single word.[156] Ali Kemal Bey's remarks on the impact of Ahmed Midhat is not limited to his memoirs. Even as a more interesting example, which suggests Ahmed Midhat's influence on women, we see the female protagonist of Ali Kemal's novella, *Çölde Bir Sergüzeşt* (An Adventure in the Desert, 1898), Seher. Seher follows popular periodicals and writers, but she is a particularly keen follower of Ahmed Midhat's *Tercüman-ı Hakikat* and *Müntahabat-ı Tercüman-ı Hakikat*, just like Ali Kemal himself.[157]

The last official chronicler of the Ottoman Empire, Abdurrahman Şeref—who describes Ahmed Midhat as a "*publicist*" and a "*vulgarisateur*"—notes that his popular works on scientific issues were selling like hot cakes to those who "were thirsty for reading."[158] According to a well-known publisher of the age, Karabet Bey, Ahmed Midhat's immense popularity was primarily a result of his writing style. Karabet Bey stated in 1895 in a Spanish cultural review, that "[Ahmed Midhat's] prose, like that of the eighteenth-century French, has an incomparable clarity and simplicity."[159]

In *Hallü'l-'Ukad* (1890), Ahmed Midhat writes that the Ottoman dignitary to whom he dedicated the book wrote in a letter, "A book is one's best friend; and your *Tercüman* [Ahmed Midhat's newspaper] is such a great friend for fruitful conversations in these long nights."[160] In the same vein, Ahmed Hamdi Tanpınar notes that Ahmed Midhat changed Ottoman family life and gave a new meaning to nights at home. Tanpınar recounts that all members of the family gathered around the literate one to listen to Ahmed Midhat's works, and they then discussed new things that they had learned from him.[161] Another well-known Turkish intellectual of a later generation, Hüseyin Cahit Yalçın (1875–1957), also describes such family gatherings in his memoirs. He notes that his earliest memories of family life were mixed with these nightly reading and discussion hours. He wrote that novels, especially those of Ahmed Midhat, were read aloud during these gatherings, and Ahmed Midhat's long explanations on scientific and philosophical matters were also carefully listened to. Although Yalçın's mother found such parts long and boring, his father, an admirer of Ahmed Midhat, insisted that these parts should be read as well.[162]

The impact of Ahmed Midhat on children—therefore on the cultural and intellectual life in the following decades—was not limited to oral transmission of ideas in family gatherings. Many Ottoman children developed their literary taste and obtained their initial knowledge of the world by reading his works. For example, İbn'ül-Emîn Mahmud Es'ad Seydişehrî—a prominent intellectual, professor of the later decades, and the editor of Münif Pasha's book on economics—notes that his reading of Ahmed Midhat in his childhood made a great impact on his early intellectual development.[163] Moreover, many of Ahmed Midhat's young followers copied his style and themes in their own works. Hüseyin Cahid's first novel, *Nadide* (1892), includes praise of Ahmed Midhat praise on its first page. In this novel, he admits to copying Ahmed Midhat's style in terms of both the theme and the long explanations he provided for his readers.[164] We come across similar references to Ahmed Midhat's influence through stories of fictional characters as well. Yakup Kadri's novel *Hep O Şarkı* (1956) opens with the pratoganist's (Münire) attempt to write a novel, where she notes that Ahmed Midhat's novels were her favorites, especially in adolescence.[165]

The fact that his works were read aloud in family gatherings implies that Ahmed Midhat's popular influence was not limited to literate people. Everybody in the household was his student. Moreover, coffeehouses provided a similar service to the larger public.[166] The coffeehouse (as its Turkish name, *kıraathane*, literally "reading house," also denotes) was a place where newspapers and even books were read aloud, especially for the illiterate.[167] As a British observer put it in the 1830s:

> The publication of the news of the empire in this way soon became of universal attraction. The paper made its way to the coffeehouses, and the same Turk that I had noticed before dozing, half stupified with coffee and tobacco, I now saw actually awake, with the paper in his hand, eagerly spelling out the news. But the most usual mode of communicating it are news-rooms, and a place is taken where those who wish to hear it assemble. A stool is

> placed in the centre, on which the man who can read sits, and others form a circle round him and listen.[168]

This setting was simply a continuation of the ages-old storytelling tradition. Yet this time, the material was not "lousy old stories full of superstitions," as Ahmed Midhat would describe them,[169] but modern works, including scientific articles and news from all over the world.[170] Thus, his style as well as his themes were shaped by his awareness of a cultural context, wherein "Texts were written so as to be transmitted to an audience in the literal sense of the term—a listening, not reading, public."[171]

Finally, the verses (by Nigâr Hanım) inscribed on Ahmed Midhat's tombstone provides us with a very terse and neat summary of what has been discussed in this section on his impact in Ottoman society:

> It is your efforts that endeared the virtues of science to the *ummah.*
> It is your endeavors that introduced the love of labor to the nation.[172]

The Young Turks: sociocultural reform for a new polity and economy

Following earlier sporadic criticisms of the dominant tendency of young Muslim Ottomans to become civil servants rather than entrepreneurs, the Young Turks took a more definite stance against "*fonctionnarisme*" (*memuriyetperestlik*), as a well-known Young Turk leader, Abdullah Cevdet (1869–1932), put it.[173] The Young Turks, who are principally known for their radical political thought and action, gave priority to education and social change, especially before the 1902 Congress.[174] Even after 1902, some Young Turk leaders remained as the standard bearers of this approach to modernization. Among such intellectuals, Prince Sabahaddin (1877–1948) is one of the few in the Young Turk movement who continued to emphasize the importance of structural transformation in Ottoman society over top-level political change.[175]

Prince Sabahaddin Bey was a follower of Edmond Demolins (1852–1907), who suggested in his *A quoi tient la supériorité des Anglo-Saxons?* (1897) that the superiority of the Anglo-Saxons was a result of their individualistic education both in the family and at school. Demolins' distinction between communal and individualistic societies constitutes the backbone of Sabahaddin Bey's critique of "Oriental societies" in general and Ottoman social and political structure in particular. Demolins himself was the disciple of Pierre Guillaume Frédéric le Play (1806–82) who "campaigned for a social-science based reform program that would promote social peace in a new class-divided and individualistic industrial society."[176] As a follower of this approach, Sabahaddin Bey suggested that the only way to the salvation of the Ottoman Empire was a complete transformation of Ottoman society into a more Anglo-Saxon (i.e., individualistic and entrepreneurial) structure. He formulated his solution as "decentralization and private initiative" (*adem-i merkeziyet ve teşebbüs-i şahsî*). According to Şerif Mardin, his social thought includes four elements:

1 An ideal individual.
2 An educational model that would form the ideal individual.
3 A social model based on the ideal individual.
4 A method of social analysis that would be used to analyze existing societies.[177]

When we compare his social thought with that of Ahmed Midhat, we can easily see a basic agreement between the two. Nevertheless, the last element, that is, "a method for social analysis," gives Sabahaddin Bey a distinct place in late Ottoman social and economic thought. After the quasi-functionalist ideas of Münif Pasha and Ahmed Midhat,[178] their students (i.e., the Young Turks) continued Ottoman modernist social thought by openly adhering to the structural-functionalism of Émile Durkheim and Herbert Spencer. In this context, Sabahaddin Bey's systematic and methodological approach provided the Ottoman reformists with a well-defined model. His model created more controversy than unity among the Young Turks. Nevertheless, he launched the era of social models in Ottoman-Turkish modernization. After him, Ziya Gökalp was to introduce Durkheimian corporatism, which provided the Young Turks with a paradigmatic worldview and a social model to which they could resort during the Republican nation-building process.[179]

Regarding private initiative, Sabahaddin Bey also quotes the then-popular Qur'anic verse (53:39; *laysa li'l-insāni illā mā saʿā*), thereby concluding that private initiative is praised by God in the Qur'an.[180] He goes on to state that according to this Qur'anic principle, individuals should depend on their own labor and enterprise, not on their community and state, in order to earn their living.[181] Working hard and incessantly improving one's skills were the backbone of this principle. However, he notes, these ideas are still foreign to the Ottomans, who are accustomed to making a living by doing nothing but striving to get some sort of endowment from the state. In other words, according to him, Ottomans preferred civil service, not private enterprise, as the best career option.[182] Meanwhile, similar concerns are also voiced in the official governmental reports:

> [N]early all of the graduates of government schools enter into civil service, and since only a small minority decide to be engaged in productive branches such as agriculture, industry, and trade, the economic development of the empire cannot reach its desired level due to the lack of interest on the part of those sufficiently educated.[183]

Against this social backdrop, Sabahaddin Bey's formula for the salvation of the empire is the transformation of the bureaucratically and communally-minded Ottoman society into an individualistic society of entrepreneurially-minded citizens.[184] Sabahaddin Bey was not alone in this line of thought. As seen previously, earlier, Ahmed Midhat Efendi was the champion of a similar approach. Besides, the criticism of the general tendency to become civil servants in Ottoman society was a major theme in the publications of various Young Turk groups.[185] However, Sabahaddin Bey was the first intellectual who analyzed this phenomenon in detail within the context of a sociological model.[186] His ideas therefore made a significant impact on other prominent figures of the Young Turk movement. For example, another Young Turk leader, Abdullah Cevdet, followed Sabahaddin Bey's arguments and wrote extensively on the traditional mentality of *memuriyetperestlik* (literally, the love to become a civil servant) among the Ottomans.[187] According to him, *memuriyetperestlik* is among the most important reasons for underdevelopment;[188] he suggests adopting Samuel Smiles' ideas in *Self-Help* as a solution.[189]

In a related fashion, we frequently come across arguments on "Ottoman indolence vs. European industry," the joy of labor, and entrepreneurship in the writings of the Young Turks. For example, Sati' al-Husri (1882–1968), who was an Ottomanist Young Turk in his earlier political life and later became a prominent intellectual of Arab nationalism, states:

> When we compare ourselves with the Europeans, we say that they are hard-working and we are lazy. And we add that they do not indulge in [worldly] pleasures as much as we do. However when we talk about this with the Europeans who live in our country, they argue the exact opposite. They are surprised [to see] how we can live without such pleasures. The answer to this [paradox] is simple: The meaning of "pleasure" is different for us than it is for Europeans. We seek joy in idleness [and inactivity], but Europeans [find it] in activity. We regard movement and activity as "boring," but their greatest enjoyment is action.[190]

Al-Husri notes also that he was the first person to suggest that economics should be introduced into the curricula of the Ottoman schools to change this mentality.[191]

As another example, Akçuraoğlu Yusuf (1876–1935), in his early writings, emphasizes the importance of social change, rather than political intervention. In one of his articles in *Şura-yı Ümmet* (1902), he summarizes the main thesis of the social reformist approach within the Young Turk movement: "There is no need for a regime change to improve the [social and economic] conditions of the country. We need a total transformation of Ottoman society."[192] He goes on to argue that such a transformation entails changing the habits, sentiments, and beliefs that have shaped the Ottoman mentality for ages. Although this is a very difficult task, he adds, it is not altogether impossible.[193] Akçuraoğlu Yusuf was to become a very influential intellectual and political figure in the late imperial and early Republican eras. His ideas about social change, put forward in 1902, reflect a clear blueprint of the social engineering project of the Young Turks for the creation of a modern Turkish nation-state in subsequent decades.

Last but definitely not least, the ideas of another influential Young Turk leader, Ahmed Rıza (1859–1930), in this context, are especially important. Along with Sabahaddin Bey, and even before him, Ahmed Rıza was "seeking an evolutionary change and not a revolution … [as he] had consistently stressed since 1895."[194] Although his political ideas began to take on a more politically activist character towards the revolution in 1908,[195] his emphasis on social change through education attracted a significant following and made a deep impact on the complex and colorful pattern of Young-Turk ideology. Following Namık Kemal and other earlier modernists, he criticized fatalism, dependence on the state, and the anti-entrepreneurial mentality of Ottoman society as the impediments to progress:

> The people used to expect everything from destiny; they are completely unaware of the command, "make effort" (*sa'y ediniz*).[196] They have gotten used to expecting their rights from the government. All these hopes and expectations reflect laziness. A human should expect his well-being from his own effort and zeal.… One who earns his living through his own labor … would not be afraid of any government. Such feelings can be awakened among the people only through education.[197]

Therefore, for Ahmed Rıza, the principle of "effort and labor" (*sa'y ü amel*) is not only a key to individual—and consequently national—prosperity, but would also pave the way for political change. In other words, he suggests that reformists give priority to the education of the masses in order to make the principle of effort and labor prevail in Ottoman society. After this is achieved, he believes, the people will take their destinies into their own hands, realizing a revolution that will put an end to their misery.

Towards 1908, social reformism began to be overshadowed by more politically motivated activism within the Young Turk movement, thereby leading to the hegemony of the idea of a top-down political revolution followed by a dictatorship of the modernist elite. Despite all the aforementioned evolutionary and bottom-up arguments which put social reform before political revolution, the following decades of the Ottoman-Turkish history were to be shaped by the well-known principle of Young Turk modernization: "for the people, despite the people."

In short, from Namık Kemal and Ahmed Midhat to Sabahaddin Bey and Abdullah Cevdet, the critique of the lack of interest in entrepreneurship in Ottoman society constituted a major theme of Ottoman modernist thought. Accordingly, the objective of building an economically vibrant society composed of entrepreneurially-minded individuals, instead of traditional Ottoman *memuriyetperestlik*, was a common theme in the economic writings of various political groups and intellectuals. The most striking difference between the earlier models (e.g., those of Münif Pasha and Ahmed Midhat) and that of Sabahaddin Bey is that the latter represented the effort to transform Ottoman society from a *Gemeinschaft* into a *Gesellshaft*, in Ferdinand Tönnies' (1855–1936) conceptualization. In other words, earlier social models resemble a community-type societal organization, in which the individual is defined as a part of the whole and serves the community's interests more than his/her own. Sabahaddin Bey, however, suggested a societal organization based exclusively on individualism in the social sphere and decentralization in the political sphere. In any case, despite considerable differences in their political discourses, there existed a quasi-consensus on the necessity of building an economy-centered modern society based on entrepreneurially minded individuals. This idea was to be crystallized in the National Economy (*Millî İktisat*) program after the 1908 revolution.[198]

The Ottoman intellectual sphere was a predominantly all-male milieu. Besides, whenever Ottoman modernists mentioned an ideal modern Ottoman, they depicted a male character. This does not imply that women were excluded from modernization efforts, but they were usually assigned complementary roles in late Ottoman modernization strategies. Nonetheless, the Hamidian era witnessed the emergence of female intellectuals who joined reformist efforts for social change. In this respect, a semi-official publication of the Hamidian regime, *Hanımlara Mahsus Gazete* (The Newspaper Especially for Women), was aimed—as its title suggests—at a female audience, and it provides us with important insights into the Hamidian-era understanding of the place of women and their economic roles in an ideal Ottoman society.

Women of an economic society: the case of **Hanımlara Mahsus Gazete**

Ahmed Midhat Efendi and other Ottoman *encyclopedists* preferred to use "vulgar Turkish" (*kaba Türkçe*, or the language of the ordinary people) in their works in order to convey their messages and ideas to the masses more effectively. Ahmed Midhat states that it was essential to use simple language even in scientific studies in order to make these works more accessible "even to women."[199] Misogyny and disdain for women's mental capacities were indeed ubiquitous in the nineteenth century. Thus, one should not totally disregard this perspective in reading the texts of this age. However, the then-frequently used phrase, "even to women," in this context, does not necessarily connote a disdain for women. What Ahmed Midhat suggests is that if even the most complicated scientific arguments and theories are put in simple terms, they can be understood by uneducated people, and even by women, who had very limited opportunities to receive formal education.

For Ottoman modernists, not just intellectual women such as Fatma Aliye or Şair Nigâr Hanım, but also ordinary housewives, who had not actively participated in intellectual production processes, were expected to play a central role in the building of a new society. From a typical paternalistic perspective, women were considered the managers of the modern household and producers of the future citizens. Thus, they had to be educated in the latest scientific techniques of "household management" (or home economics, *ev idaresi*). This was essential for more efficiently managed households and consequently a more economy-driven society. Moreover, women had to be equipped to raise scientifically-minded individuals. It was therefore necessary that they become the consumers of popular works on modern sciences and technologies. This too is why Ottoman modernists preferred using a language that "even women" could understand.

Many elite Ottoman women were home-schooled by Ottoman and European instructors.[200] In the Hamidian era, these women began to transform the Ottoman intellectual sphere by their increasingly active involvement as consumers and even producers of intellectual products. In this respect, *Hanımlara Mahsus Gazete* (1895–1908) is an essential source for scrutinizing women's roles in the modernizing Ottoman Empire. *Hanımlara Mahsus Gazete* was the longest lasting and also the most influential women's periodical of the era.[201] It was written and edited by prominent women intellectuals, who were mostly the daughters and wives of leading intellectuals and bureaucrats of the era.[202] The main aim of the periodical was the education of women based on the latest scientific principles of household management as well as on Islamic morals.[203] In their statement of purpose, the editors argue that the education of women has a pivotal importance in the development of a country. Otherwise, only one part of the family (i.e., men) would be educated, and the other part (i.e., women) would remain ignorant. As a result, society would not be able to achieve complete and balanced development.[204] Moreover, since women were the primary educators of future generations, socio-economic development of the country depended on the children that they raised.[205] In addition to articles with practical information on household management—issues ranging from health care to children's clothes—the periodical includes articles on women's economic roles in a modern society.

Although the newspaper attributes equal importance to men's and women's education in the modernization process, its authors do not argue for equality. The traditional sexual division of labor, in which men were breadwinners and women were household managers, seems to define the discourse of the newspaper regarding the gender roles.[206] In a similar vein, we do not see any recommendations for increasing women's participation in the labor force. Yet, we observe that the general principles of capitalist work ethics are suggested as the indispensable guiding rules also in women's economic roles at home. For example, the granddaughter of Ahmed Cevdet Pasha, Zeyneb Hanım, argues that the responsibility of women in "developed" countries is to serve as the general managers of the household. Since effective time management should be a central concern for any manager, she criticizes women who waste their time gossiping and embroidering, arguing that this was no longer necessary given that manufactured goods had replaced handicrafts.[207] Women, she argues, should concern themselves with managing the household economy and with studying sciences in their leisure time.[208]

In another (anonymous) article, inspired and partly adapted from an article published in a British journal, the author suggests that women keep a ledger showing all allowances and expenses in order to manage the family budget more systematically.[209] Waste, in the context of the family budget, represented a serious issue for the newspaper. For example, Seniha Vicdan argues in her article entitled "*Moda-İsraf*" (Fashion-Waste) that, in addition to its "other irrational aspects" (such as wearing uncomfortable clothes just because they are fashionable), fashion leads to the waste of valuable resources.[210] She maintains that women's conspicuous consumption on the pretext of "following the latest fashions" can even drive a family into poverty in some cases.[211]

In yet another article with similar examples of the squandering of family wealth in order to follow the latest fashions, Nigâr Hanım promotes a principle to determine one's lifestyle and choices: effort and labor. In her "*Sa'y ü Amel*" ("Effort and Labor"),[212] she joins other Hamidian-era intellectuals who propose labor as the savior of humanity from all evil, which itself is primarily caused by laziness.[213] In line with Ahmed Midhat's arguments, Nigâr Hanım asks, "Is it possible to find anything more sacred than duty, anything better than working, [and] anything more honored [and sacred] than effort and labor?"[214] She argues that it is absurd to think that labor is reserved for males, and she adds that although it is not really necessary to remind readers of this obvious fact, it is imperative to emphasize the importance of labor in women's lives.[215] Then she gives examples of how women should not waste their time with trivia, but instead use their time wisely for both housework, and if possible, reading and writing.[216] In short, the principles of the capitalist work ethic, such as hard work and the economic management of resources, along with arguments against the waste of resources (including time), also appear in publications for women in order to educate them to be better household managers and educators of future generations.

Conclusion

The socio-economic dimension of Ottoman modernization in the Hamidian era rested on certain economic postulates of the nineteenth century. Modern economics engendered a new paradigm of history—that is, economic history—according to which societies and their histories were categorized by their dominant modes of production. Economic history, as presented by various nineteenth-century economists, thereby suggested a hierarchy among societies according to their relevant modes of production. Looking from this perspective, the Ottoman Empire was defined as a backward country due to its predominantly agricultural socio-economic structure in contrast to industrial—therefore "civilized"—European countries. As a result of this perspective, transforming the Ottoman economy into an industrial one through economic development became a priority for the Ottoman elite. At the same time, Ottoman reformists realized that the question of economic development was tightly connected to sociocultural reform. As Münif Pasha suggested, it was impossible to obtain permanent results in modernization unless it was complemented by building a modern society consisting of educated, industrious, and (economically) rational male and female citizens.

Münif Pasha's example of ants and Ahmed Midhat's examples of the small-business corporation both refer to a critical problem for Ottoman economic development: the lack of the accumulated capital. In other words, the lack of adequate capital for large-scale economic enterprises and the lack of a national bourgeoisie to undertake such investments led the Ottoman modernists to the idea of cooperation. Ottoman reformers expected that this practical economic principle will facilitate gathering larger amounts of capital through numerous modest contributions. Thus, thanks to its direct relevance to one of the biggest obstacles to economic development, the idea of cooperation became a central pillar of late Ottoman social and economic thought. In this respect, despite significant differences, we observe an obvious pattern of evolution from Münif Pasha and Ahmed Midhat's social visions (which were rather communitarian in essence) in the 1870s and 1880s to Sabahaddin Bey's model of private entrepreneurship and individualism in the 1900s. The same pattern in late Ottoman modernist social thought paved the way for the early twentieth-century Young Turk nation-building project that was to shape modern Turkey.

Notes

1 Adam Smith, *An Inquiry into the Nature and Causes of the Wealth of Nations* (Edinburgh: Thomas Nelson, 1843), 10.
2 Sakızlı Ohannes, *Mebadi-i İlm-i Servet-i Milel* (Dersaadet [İstanbul]: Mihran Matbaası, 1880), 4–5.
3 Stefan Berger, "Introduction," in *A Companion to Nineteenth-Century Europe: 1789–1914*, ed. Stefan Berger (Malden, MA: Wiley-Blackwell, 2009), xvii.
4 Karl Polanyi, *The Great Transformation.* (Boston: Beacon Press, 1957), 111.
5 Ibid., 57.
6 For the impact of the machinery question on the evolution of political economy in the early nineteenth century, see Maxine Berg, *The Machinery Question and the Making of Political Economy, 1815–1848* (Cambridge: Cambridge University Press, 1980).
7 Alexander J. Field, "Economic history," *The New Palgrave Dictionary of Economics*, vol. 2, 694–5.
8 For Marx's historical materialist model, see Karl Marx, *A Contribution to the Critique of Political Economy*, trans. N.I. Stone (Chicago: Charles H. Kerr & Company, 1904), 11–13.
9 Werner Sombart labels such classifications as "stage theories." He claims that "differentiating between periods or peoples according to dominant form of production" is the "oldest method" in historiography which is observed as early as in Aristotle's political theory. (Werner Sombart, "Economic Theory and Economic History," *The Economic History Review* 2, no. 1 (1929): 10.) Sombart further notes that these classifications are popular in social thought of the eighteenth and nineteenth centuries. (Ibid., 10–13).
10 "In reference to political economy, nations have to pass through the following stages of development: – The savage state, the pastoral state, the merely agricultural state, and the state at once agricultural, manufacturing and commercial." (Friedrich List, *National System of Political Economy*, trans. G.A. Matile (Philadelphia: J.P. Lippincott & Co., 1856), 265).
11 Michael Adas, *Machines as the Measure of Men: Science, Technology, and Ideologies of Western Dominance* (Ithaca: Cornell University Press, 1989), 256.
12 Mathew Jefferies, "The Age of Historism," in *A Companion to Nineteenth-Century Europe: 1789–1914*, ed. Stefan Berger (Malden, MA: Wiley-Blackwell, 2009), 317.
13 Anne Green, "The Nineteenth Century (1820–1880)," *Cassell Guide to Literature in French*, ed. Valerie Worth-Stylianou (London: Cassell, 1996), 134.
14 For a brief account of the Ottoman chronicling tradition, see B. Kütükoğlu, "Vekayinüvis," in *İslam Ansiklopedisi*, vol. 13 (İstanbul: Kültür ve Turizm Bakanlığı, 1986), 271–87.

15 Linda T. Darling, "Islamic Empires, the Ottoman Empire and the Circle of Justice," in *Constitutional Politics in the Middle East: With Special Reference to Turkey, Iraq, Iran and Afghanistan*, ed. Said Amir Arjomand (Oxford: Hart, 2008), 11.

16 For a summary and evaluation of Ahmed Cevdet Pasha's economic arguments in his works, see Sabri Ülgener, "Ahmed Cevdet Paşa'nın Devlet ve İktisada Dair Düşünceleri," *İş* 76 (1947): 5–23.

17 Tanpınar, *XIX. Asır Türk Edebiyatı Tarihi*, 164. It is important to note, however, that Ahmed Cevdet Pasha was not the first Ottoman historian who referred to European sources. Before Ahmed Cevdet Pasha, Vasıf Efendi (d. 1806), Kethüdazade Said Efendi, and Şanizade Ataullah Efendi (1771–1826) also used Western sources for their studies of history. (Mükrimin Halil Yinanç, "Tanzimattan Cumhuriyete Kadar Bizde Tarihçilik," in *Tanzimat: Yüzüncü Yıldönümü Münasebetile* [İstanbul: Maarif Matbaası, 1940], 574).

18 Ahmed Cevdet Pasha, *Tarih-i Cevdet*, 12 Vols. (İstanbul: Matbaa-yı Âmire, 1854–84).

19 Ülgener, "Ahmed Cevdet Paşa," 6.

20 Ibid.

21 Ibid.

22 For Ibn Khaldun's impact on nineteenth-century European historiography and social thought, see Mohammad Abdullah ʿInan, *Ibn Khaldun, His Life and Work* (Lahore: Sh. Muhammad Ashraf, 1944), 157–75.

23 Providing a complete list of popular history books published in this era is well beyond the scope of this study, yet it might be useful just to mention the most prominent ones in order to give an idea: Namık Kemal began writing history with his historical stories (e.g., Celaleddin Harzemşah), and later he wrote a multi-volume Ottoman history (1887–88). Ahmed Midhat wrote and published multi-volume world history books such as *Kâinat* (The Universe, 1871–81), *Tarih-i Umûmi* (General History, 1877–88), and *Mufassal Tarih-i Kurun-i Cedide* (Detailed History of the Recent Centuries, 1887–88). Just like many of his other works, these were first serialized in his *Tercüman-ı Hakikat* and then published as books. Ahmed Rasim wrote and adapted various books, such as *Terakkiyât-ı İlmiye ve Medeniye* (Scientific and Civilizational Progress, 1888) and *Resimli ve Haritalı Osmanlı Tarihi* (Ottoman History with Illustrations and Maps, 1908). Another prominent intellectual of the era, (Mizancı) Mehmed Murad Bey, was the Professor of History at the *Mekteb-i Mülkiye*, and penned the multi-volume *Tarih-i Umûmi* (World History, 1881–85) and *Muhtasar Tarih-i Umûmi* (A Brief History of the World, 1884). There are other similar works that could be added to the list, especially those on more specific topics like Ahmed Rasim's *Arabların Terakkiyât-ı Medeniyesi* (Civilizational Progress of the Arabs, 1884), and numerous articles on similar topics published in popular journals and newspapers such as *Mecmua-i Fünûn*, *Tercüman-ı Hakikat*, and *Servet-i Fünûn*.

24 Mardin, *Jön Türkler*, 46.

25 Namık Kemal, "Sanʿat ve Ticaretimiz", *İbret* 57 (1872), 1–2. It is important to note that guilds did not exclusively consist of Muslim producers. There were many guilds dominated by non-Muslim Ottoman producers as well. Nevertheless, in the late nineteenth century, the destruction of the Ottoman guilds—as a result of the influx of European commodities—was frequently associated with Muslim loss of dominance in the Ottoman economic sphere.

26 Namık Kemal, "İbret," *İbret* 3 (1872), 2.

27 Namık Kemal, "Sanʿat ve Ticaretimiz", 2.

28 For the full text of the speech, see *Takvîm-i Vekâyi*, 22 Zilkâde 1286 (23 February 1870).

29 Ibid. For the impact of al-Afghānī on the Young Turks, see Mardin, *Jön Türkler*, 65–6.

30 Mehmed Şerif Efendi, "Sanayi' ve Ziraatden Kangısının Hakkımızda Hayırlı Olduğuna Dairdir," *Tercüman-ı Ahval* 69 (1861), 3.
31 Ibid.
32 Akyiğitzade Musa, *İktisad yahud İlm-i Servet*, 20–2.
33 Mehmed Cavid, *İlm-i İktisad*, vol. 1, 314–19.
34 Rıza Tevfik, Felsefe Mecuması 1: 3; cited in Ülken, *Türkiye'de Çağdaş Düşünce*, vol. 1, 368.
35 Ibid.
36 "Diyar-ı küfrü gezdim beldeler kaşaneler gördüm. Dolaştım mülk-ü İslamı bütün viraneler gördüm." (English translation: Ahmet Evin, *Origins and Development of the Turkish Novel* (Minneapolis: Bibliotheca Islamica, 1983), 89.) For the full text of the original poem, see Önder Göçgün, *Ziya Paşa'nın Hayatı, Eserleri, Edebi Kişiliği ve Bütün Şiirleri* (Ankara: Kültür ve Turizm Bakanlığı, 1987), 281.
37 For overviews of this literature and its main themes, see Bâki Asiltürk, *Osmanlı Seyyahlarının Gözüyle Avrupa* (İstanbul: Kaknüs Yayınları, 2000). and İbrahim Şirin, *Osmanlı İmgeleminde Avrupa* (Ankara: Lotus, 2006). For economic observations of the Ottoman travelers, see Asiltürk, *Osmanlı Seyyahlarının Gözüyle Avrupa*, 445–75; and Şirin, *Osmanlı İmgeleminde Avrupa*, 311–22.
38 For a detailed analysis of various political aspects of the question of Ottoman identity vis-à-vis European Orientalism, see Selim Deringil, *The Well-Protected Domains: Ideology and the Legitimation of Power in the Ottoman Empire, 1876–1909* (London: I.B. Tauris, 1998). For the "Ottoman Orientalism" that emerged as a response to European Orientalism, see Ussama Makdisi, "Ottoman Orientalism," *The American Historical Review* 107, no. 3 (2002): 768–96.
39 For an illuminating analysis of the "turning point in Ottoman intellectual history" caused by the European challenge in the late eighteenth and early nineteenth centuries, and the emergence of the question of Westernization, see Hanioğlu, *Young Turks in Opposition*, 7–13.
40 Şirin, *Osmanlı İmgeleminde Avrupa*, 311.
41 "gabavet ü batâet-i tab' ile meşhur olan ehl-i küfr" (Şirin, *Osmanlı İmgeleminde Avrupa*, 312).
42 *Seyahatname-i Londra: Tanzimat Bürokratının Modern Sanayi Toplumuna Bakışı*, (ed.) Fikret Turan (İstanbul: Tarih Vakfı Yurt Yayınları, 2009), 1. The editor's choice for the subtitle is very appropriate: *Tanzimat Bürokratının Modern Sanayi Toplumuna Bakışı* (A Tanzimat Bureaucrat's View of Modern Industrial Society). It reflects the author's obvious emphasis on the social and cultural traits of industrial England, as well as its economic organization. This edition includes both the transcription of the original text and an adaptation to modern Turkish. The same travelogue had been adapted to modern Turkish and published by another editor, as *Bir Osmanlı Aydınının Londra Seyahatnamesi* (ed.) Erkan Serçe (İstanbul: İstiklal Kitabevi, 2007). In this study, I prefer to use the transcribed original text in the 2009 edition, instead of the adapted version of the 2007 edition.
43 *Seyahatname-i Londra*, 138, 144–5, 161–3, 170–1.
44 Ibid., 141.
45 Such an association was later founded in the Ottoman Empire in 1861 by Münif Pasha and his friends: *Cemiyet-i İlmiyye-i Osmâniye* (Ottoman Society of Sciences). The *Cemiyet-i İlmiyye* established the first modern research library and published the first popular science magazine (*Mecmua-i Fünûn*) in the Ottoman Empire. Ahmed Midhat Efendi (in 1887) also praises these European institutions on the same basis. He notes that such well-organized associations provide a venue for people to get involved in (socially and individually) beneficial activities. See Ahmed Midhat, *Müsâbahât-ı Leyliye, Birinci Müsâhabe: Vakit Geçirmek* (İstanbul, H. 1304 [1887]), 17–21.
46 *Seyahatname-i Londra*, 128.

47 Namık Kemal, "İbret," *İbret* 3 (1872), 1–2.
48 Şirin, *Osmanlı İmgeleminde Avrupa*, 317.
49 Namık Kemal, "İbret," 2.
50 Rabinbach, *The Human Motor*, 4.
51 Sylvia Nasar, *Grand Pursuit: The Story of Economic Genius* (New York: Simon & Schuster, 2011), 22.
52 Mehmed Enisi, *Avrupa Hatıratım*, vol. 1 (Kostantiniye [İstanbul]: Matbaa-yı Ebüzziya, R. 1327 [1911], 38.
53 Ibid.
54 Mardin, *Jön Türkler*, 222.
55 Mardin, *Jön Türkler*, 50.
56 Mahmud Es'ad, *İlm-i Servet* (İstanbul: Mekteb-i Sanayi, H. 1302 [1885]).
57 Münif Pasha, *Takvim-i Vekayi'*, 20 Zilkade 1286 [1870], 2.
58 Münif, "Karıncaların San'at ve Medeniyeti," *Mecmua-i Fünûn* 30 (1864), 230.
59 Ibid., 230–6.
60 İsmail Doğan, *Tanzimatın İki Ucu: Münif Paşa ve Ali Suavi: Sosyo-Pedagojik Bir Karşılaştırma* (İstanbul: İz Yayıncılık, 1991), 146.
61 "Mesela fenn-i ziraatde malumatlı, ehliyetli olan bir adamla olmayan beyninde külli fark vardır. Bir ekinci ziraat vaktini ve memleketin ahvalini bilür, arazisini ve tohumunu eyü intihab ider ve fenn-i ziraatde maharetli olur ise, bir kile yerine yirmi otuz kile alur. Lakin bunları bilmediği cihetle bir kusur iderse tahsil itmedikten başka sarf itdiği emeğini ve tohumunu bile itlaf itmiş olur." (Mahmud Es'ad, *İlm-i Servet*, 20).
62 Mahmud Es'ad, *İlm-i Servet*, 20–1.
63 Münif Pasha seems again to be inspired by the Smithian understanding of economics:

> The most important argument of *The Wealth of Nations* is that a market economy is best able to improve the standard of living of the vast majority of the populace—that it can lead to what Smith called "universal opulence". The book built on the Enlightenment assumption that worldly happiness was a good thing, and sought to show that material well-being need not be confined to "luxuries" available only to a thin stratum at the top. On the contrary, Smith made the purchasing power of consumers the measure of "wealth of the nation." The book also argued that under the right institutional conditions, the spread of "commercial society" would lead to greater individual liberty and more peaceful relations among nations.
>
> (Jerry Z. Muller, *The Mind and the Market: Capitalism in Modern European Thought* (New York: Alfred A. Knopf, 2002), 52–3)

64 Mahmud Es'ad, *İlm-i Servet*, 8.
65 Ibid.
66 "Bu ilmin mesailinden gâfil olanlar hakîkat-i hâli bilmezler, 'erbab-ı san'atın kadri bilinmiyor, filan kimse âlâ bir tefennün yaptı ama alan satan olmadı' diyerek ta'n iderler. Lakin hakîkat-i hâle vakıf olanlar bir çiçekle yaz gelmeyeceğini bilirler." (Mahmud Es'ad, *İlm-i Servet*, 23).
67 Münif, "Mukayese-i İlm ü Cehl," *Mecmua-i Fünûn* 1 (1862):30. (Emphasis added).
68 Al-Hilāl (October 15, 1897), 137–8; cited in Jens Hanssen, *Fin de Siècle Beirut: The Making of an Ottoman Provincial Capital* (Oxford: Clarendon Press ; Oxford University Press, 2005), 204.
69 Adas, *Machines as the Measure of Men*, 242.
70 Ibid.
71 For an incisive analysis of the industrialist-capitalist understanding of time and its alternatives, see E.P. Thompson's classic study, "Time, Work-Discipline, and Industrial Capitalism," *Past & Present* 38 (1967): 56–97. Similarly to Adas' example, Thompson shows how the English "leisured class" criticized "the leisure of the [English] masses" in the nineteenth century (Ibid., 90).

72 Selçuk Akşin Somel, *The Modernization of Public Education in the Ottoman Empire, 1839–1908: Islamization, Autocracy, and Discipline* (Leiden: Brill, 2001), 175.
73 Ibid., 174.
74 Osman Nuri Ergin, *İstanbul Mektepleri ve İlim, Terbiye, ve San'at Müesseseleri Dolayısiyle Türkiye Maarif Tarihi*, vol. 3 (İstanbul: Osmanbey Matbaası, 1941), 729.
75 Ahmed İhsan Tokgöz, *Matbuat Hatıralarım, 1888–1923*, vol. 1 (İstanbul: Ahmed İhsan Matbaası, 1930), 29.
76 Ibid.
77 Ibid.
78 Ergin, *Türkiye Maarif Tarihi*, 3: 715.
79 See Chapter 2 for an overall assessment of his economics thought.
80 Ahmed Midhat, *Ekonomi Politik* (İstanbul: Kırkanbar Matbaası, 1879), 110.
81 Ibid. What is obvious here is that although at first he writes about the "Ottomans," including both Muslim and non-Muslim subjects, his narrative of history boils down to a Muslim-Turkish economic nationalist discourse.
82 Ahmed Midhat, *Ekonomi Politik*, 111–12.
83 Ibid., 113–14.
84 Ibid., 114.
85 Ibid. His examples of these two categories of nations (i.e., militaristic and merchant) are the Romans and the Jews, respectively. (Ibid).
86 Ahmed Midhat, *Sevda-Yı Sa'y ü Amel* (İstanbul: Kırkanbar Matbaası, 1879), 14.
87 Ibid., 15.
88 Ibid., 15–16.
89 Ibid., 16. Compare with the words of Rıza Tevfik above.
90 For an illuminating analysis of Ottoman material culture in the late eighteenth century, see M. Şükrü Hanioğlu, *A Brief History of the Late Ottoman Empire* (Princeton: Princeton University Press, 2008), 27–33. For changes in material culture as a result of the European impact, see Hanioğlu, *Late Ottoman Empire*, 105–6.
91 Ahmed Midhat, *Sevda-yı Sa'y ü Amel*, 17.
92 Ibid., 17–18.
93 It seems that by "old wealth," he means traditional wealth-creating institutions from guilds to the military.
94 Ahmed Midhat, *Ekonomi Politik*, 115.
95 Ibid., 115–16. This argument reflects yet another frequent grievance of late nineteenth-century Muslim-Ottoman intellectuals. Starting with Namık Kemal, Ottoman Muslim modernists were complaining about the fact that the skilled labor in the empire consisted almost entirely of non-Muslims and that only "lowly" occupations (e.g., that of street porters) were left to the Muslims.
96 Ibid., 117–18.
97 Eyüp Özveren, "Ottoman Economic Thought and Economic Policy in Transition: Rethinking the Nineteenth Century," in *Economic Thought and Policy in Less Developed Europe: The Nineteenth Century*, ed. M. Psalidopoulos and Maria Eugénia Mata (London: Routledge, 2002), 139; Ahmed Güner Sayar, *Osmanlı İktisat Düşüncesinin Çağdaşlaşması: (Klasik Dönem'den II. Abdülhamid'e)*, Second Edition (İstanbul: Ötüken Neşriyat, 2000), 376–7.
98 Sayar, *Osmanlı İktisat Düşüncesi*, 376.
99 *Homo Ottomanicus* is definitely a male character. Ahmed Midhat frequently uses the word "*âdem*" ("man" or "guy") to give examples; and this is perfectly normal and ubiquitous in the nineteenth-century European social thought discourse. However, Ahmed Midhat encouraged the education of women and emphasized the importance of educated, rational, and hard-working women in his fiction and as well as his non-fiction works.

100 For a complete list of his books and treatises on topics ranging from political economy and history to religion and parenthood, see Us, *Bir Jübilenin İntiba'ları*, 169–72.

101 "O tenbel ve muzırr âdemi cem'iyet-i medeniyyeden def' itmelidir." Ahmed Midhat, *Ekonomi Politik*, 44.

102 Şerif Mardin, "The Mind of the Turkish Reformer 1700–1900," *Western Humanities Review*, no. 14 (1960): 433.

103 The word "garlic-headed" refers to the turban, a headdress worn mostly by traditionalists at the time, as Ahmed Midhat sees it as a symbol of traditional reactions against modernity.

104 Tokgöz, *Matbuat Hatıralarım*, vol. 1, 39.

105 *Sevda* can be translated as love or passion. In fact, "passionate love" gives a closer approximation to what Ahmed Midhat meant. However, in this study I prefer to use the word "passion" for the sake of simplicity.

106 Ahmed Midhat, *Sevda-yı Sa'y ü Amel*, 5–6.

107 Ibid., 24.

108 Max Weber, *The Protestant Ethic and the Spirit of Capitalism*, tr. Talcott Parsons (New York: Scribner's, 1950 [1904–5]).

109 See for example, Rakım Efendi in his *Felatun Bey ile Rakım Efendi* (1875).

110 See Chapter 5 an economics analysis of Şinasi's story.

111 Ahmed Midhat, *Sevda-yı Sa'y ü Amel*, 13.

112 Ibid., 12.

113 Ibid., 19. His examples to such proverbs are as follows: "*Meramın elinden hiçbir şey kurtulmaz*" (everything is possible through will); "*çiğnemeden yutulmaz*" (one cannot swallow without chewing); "*kime lazım ise ekmek, ona lazım ekmek*" (whoever needs bread should sow [wheat]).

114 Ibid., 27–8.

115 Ibid., 56–7.

116 "*Memalik-i müterakkiye ve mütemeddine.*"

117 Ibid., 57. In *Teşrik-i Mesa'î, Taksim-i Mesa'î*, he advises fathers to encourage their children to pursue entrepreneurial activities instead of civil service (pp. 115–16).

118 Cf. Adam Smith's words on private interest: "By pursuing his own interest he [an individual] frequently promotes that of the society more effectually than when he really intends to promote it." (Smith, *The Wealth of Nations*, 184).

119 Ahmed Midhat, *Sevda-yı Sa'y ü Amel*, 76–8.

120 Ahmed Midhat, *Müşahedat* (İstanbul, 1891), 132. In this novel, Ahmed Midhat presents his ideas on economic development through the words of a successful entrepreneur, Mehmed Seyyid Numan. Ahmed Midhat appears in the novel as himself, and during a long conversation, Seyyid Numan summarizes the main ideas of Ahmed Midhat's *Sevda-yü Sa'y ü Amel* and *Teşrik-i Mesa'î, Taksim-i Mesa'î*. (Ibid., 124–36). Ahmed Midhat then notes that the words and deeds of this exemplary Ottoman businessman inspired him to write these aforementioned books. (Ibid., 136) Therefore—unless this story is real and he really met such a person—he builds a reverse relation between this character and his books on economic issues.

121 Ahmed Midhat, *Müşahedat*, 132.

122 Bernard Lewis, *Islam in History: Ideas, People, and Events in the Middle East*, New Edition, Revised and Expanded [Chicago: Open Court, 1993], 97. For a detailed analysis of al-Shaybānī's *Kitāb al-Kasb*, see Michael Bonner, "The Kitāb Al-Kasb Attributed to Al-Shaybānī: Poverty, Surplus, and the Circulation of Wealth," *Journal of the American Oriental Society* 121, no. 3 (2001): 410–27.

123 Ahmed Midhat, *Müsâbahât-ı Leyliye, Birinci Müsâhabe: Vakit Geçirmek* (İstanbul, 1887), 9–10.

124 Ali Bey, *Lehçet Ül-Hakaik* (Mısır: Matbaa-yı Osmaniye, 1897), 14.

125 Rabinbach summarizes similar ideas of European intellectuals of the same age; see Rabinbach, *The Human Motor*, 8.

126 Ahmed Midhat, *Letaif-i Rivayat On Üçüncü Cüz'ü, (Obur) İsmiyle Bir Hikayeyi Havîdir*, İstanbul: Kırk Anbar Matbaası, H. 1302 [1885], 2–3.
127 Ahmed Midhat, *Teşrik-i Mesa'î, Taksim-i Mesa'î*, 133.
128 *The Qur'an*, tr. M.A.S. Abdelhaleem (Oxford: Oxford University Press, 2004), 348.
129 Şerif Mardin, "Super Westernization in the Ottoman Empire in the Last Quarter of the Nineteenth Century," in *Turkey: Geographic and Social Perspectives*, ed. Peter Benedict, Erol Tümertekin, and Fatma Mansur (Leiden: Brill, 1974), 403–46.
130 For satirical examples of such critiques, see Palmira Johnson Brummett, *Image and Imperialism in the Ottoman Revolutionary Press, 1908–1911* (Albany: State University of New York Press, 2000), 221–58.
131 Ahmed Midhat, *Avrupa Âdâb-ı Muaşereti yâhud Alafranga* (İstanbul: İkdam Matbaası, H. 1312 [1894]).
132 See Thorstein Veblen, *The Theory of the Leisure Class; an Economic Study in the Evolution of Institutions* (New York: The Macmillan Company; London: Macmillan & Co., Ltd., 1899).
133 Ahmed Midhat, *Sevda-yı Sa'y ü Amel*, 29–30.
134 Ibid., 30.
135 In this piece, the main issue of conflict is centered on the leisure-labor dichotomy, rather than reflecting a direct class conflict. Yet, in an earlier (1871) article, which Ahmed Midhat wrote during his "materialist" and dissident years before his exile, he develops a quasi-class-based analysis to compare lives of the poor and the rich. In the same article, he promotes ideas put forward by European socialists and the First International on social justice and equality. For Ahmed Midhat's earlier *socialisant* ideas, see Ahmed Midhat, "Fakr ü Gınâ," *Dağarcık*, no. 7 (1871): 194–9.
136 Ahmed Midhat, *Sevda-yı Sa'y ü Amel*, 34.
137 Ahmed Midhat frequently refers to this expression to propagate the idea of time as a commodity that could be "saved, spent or wasted." In *Vakit Geçirmek*, for example, he states, "The British who say 'time is money' … are aware of the fact that one should spend time economically, just as he should in spending money." (Ahmed Midhat, *Vakit Geçirmek*, 16). He even opposes spending time for just 'any amount' of money, meaning the money gained should match the time spent for that particular task (ibid.). This reflects his implicit concern for a time-money equation and a notion of value measured in labor-time.
138 Ahmed Midhat, *Sevda-yı Sa'y ü Amel*, 34. Eight years later, Ahmed Midhat expanded this subject into a pamphlet on boredom and killing time, and he gives the same example. See Ahmed Midhat, *Vakit Geçirmek*.
139 Ahmed Midhat, *Sevda-yı Sa'y ü Amel*, 35. Ahmed Midhat, thereby, accidentally enters into the field of relativity with an example very similar to the well-known quotation from Albert Einstein: "When a man sits with a pretty girl for an hour, it seems like a minute. But let him sit on a hot stove for a minute and it's longer than any hour. That's relativity." (Although this is one of the best-known quotations from Einstein, it does not exist in his books or well-known articles. It is from one of his least-known articles that appeared in the *Journal of Exothermic Science and Technology*, vol. 1, no. 9 [1938]).
140 Ahmed Midhat, *Teşrik-i Mesa'î, Taksim-i Mesa'î*, 128.
141 Ibid., 129–30.
142 Ibid., 130–1.
143 Ibid., 131. For an earlier real-life example of such an attempt to establish a factory by the merchants at the Uzunçarşı Bazaar of Istanbul in the early 1860s. See [Refik], "Esbâb-ı Servet," *Mir'at* 1 (1863), 11.
144 Ibid., 130.
145 For an analysis of Ahmed Midhat's rather complex relationship with the politial authority, see Abdulhamit Kırmızı, "Authoritarianism and Constitutionalism Combined: Ahmed Midhat Efendi Between the Sultan and the Kanun-i Esasi," in *The*

First Ottoman Experiment in Democracy, ed. Christoph Herzog and Malek Sharif (Ergon in Kommission, 2010), 53–65.

146 Somel, *The Modernization of Public Education*, 5.

147 Ahmed Midhat, *Sevda-yı Sa'y ü Amel*, 49–53.

148 Kemal Karpat notes that he simply followed "the long-established Ottoman imperial tradition of learning a practical trade." (Kemal Karpat, *The Politicization of Islam: Reconstructing Identity, State, Faith, and Community in the late Ottoman State* (Oxford: Oxford University Press, 2001), 160.)

149 Ibid.

150 Ali Vahbi Bey (ed.), *Avant la débâcle de la Turquie: Pensées et souvenirs de l'ex-sultan Abdul-Hamid, recueillis par Ali Vahbi Bey* (Neuchatel: Attinger Frères, *c.*1913), 205–6. (My translation).

151 K. Hamsun and H.C. Andersen, *İstanbul'da İki İskandinav Seyyah*, tr. B. Gürsaler-Syvertsen (İstanbul: Yapı Kredi Yayınları, 2009), 21.

152 Ibid.

153 Abdurrahman Şeref, argues that Abdülhamid II put Ahmed Midhat on the payroll under the pretext of "protection" (*himâye*) as part of his policy of silencing intellectuals through such pecuniary means. (Abdurrahman Şeref, "Ahmed Midhat Efendi," *TOEM*, no. 18 [1913]: 1115.) Although, Abdurrahman Şeref's overt accusation against the sultan reflects the anti-Abdülhamid II sentiments of the post-1908 political atmosphere, Ahmed Midhat had already been infamous for his cooperation with the Hamidian regime, especially among the revolutionaries. See for example, a very harsh response—with strong language—to an article of Ahmed Midhat by the official organ of the Committee of Union and Progress in 1897, "Ahmed Midhat Mel'ûnu," (The Cursed Ahmed Midhat) *Kânûn-ı Esâsî* 12 (1897), 8.

154 Fehmi, "Istılahat-ı Fenniye Vaz'ı," in *Müntehabât-ı Tercüman-ı Hakikat*, vol. 2 (İstanbul: Tercuman-i Hakıkat, 1884), 738.

155 He is also the paternal grandfather of the British politician and author Stanley Johnson, and therefore the great-grandfather of the Mayor of London, Boris Johnson.

156 Ali Kemal, *Ömrüm*, ed. Zeki Kuneralp (İstanbul: Isis Yayımcılık, 1985), 25, 31.

157 Ali Kemal, *Çölde Bir Sergüzeşt* (Kostantiniye [İstanbul]: Esseyid Mehmed Tahir, H. 1316 [1898]), 7. *Müntahabat-ı Tercüman-ı Hakikat* is a volumes of selections of articles from the newspaper *Tercüman-ı Hakikat.*

158 Abdurrahman Şeref, "Ahmed Midhat Efendi," 1117.

159 "Su prosa, como la del siglo XVIII francés, tiene una claridad y una sencillez incomparables." Garabed Bey, "El Movimiento Literario En Turquía," *La España Moderna* 77 (April 1895): 163.

160 Ahmed Midhat, *Hallü'l-'Ukad* (Dersaadet [İstanbul]: Kırkanbar Matbaası, 1890), 6.

161 Tanpınar, *XIX. Asır Türk Edebiyatı Tarihi*, 413.

162 Hüseyin Cahit Yalçın, *Edebi Hatıralar* (İstanbul: Akşam Kitaphanesi, 1935), 5–6.

163 *Büyük Türk Hukukçusu Seydişehirli İbn-il Emin Mahmut Esat Efendi* (İstanbul: Türk Hukuk Kurumu, 1943), 16.

164 Yalçın, *Edebi Hatıralar*, 19.

165 Yakup Kadri Karaosmanoğlu, *Hep O Şarkı* (İstanbul: İletişim Yayınları, 2004), 11.

166 For an illuminating analysis of "popular exposure to the press" in the Arab world—which is extremely relevant to the Turkish case—in this era, see Ami Ayalon, *The Press in the Arab Middle East: A History* (New York: Oxford University Press, 1995), 154–9.

167 Ibid.

168 R. Walsh, *A Residence at Constantinople, during a Period Including the Commencement, Progress, and Termination of the Greek and Turkish Revolutions* (London: F. Westley & A.H. Davis, 1836), 283.

169 Ülken, *Türkiye'de Çağdaş Düşünce*, vol. 1, 159.

170 This holds for the provinces as well as for Istanbul. Şerafeddin Mağmumi notes in his travelogue about Anatolia that although local people's interest in reading books and periodicals in Bursa was low (*c.*1892), he could find *Sabah* and *Tarîk* newspapers at coffeehouses. He also adds that, thanks to an exchange system, a local library brought newspapers and journals from all over the empire. (Şerafeddin Mağmumî, *Seyahat Hâtıraları* [Cairo, 1909], 40).

171 Ayalon, *The Press in the Arab Middle East*, 154. It is important to note also that the same applied to the reading culture of the West up to the late eighteenth century. Therefore, reading as an individual activity is a product of modern cultural and economic developments, such as the expansion of public education and advances in printing technologies (ibid.).

172 "Gayretindir sevdiren fazl-ı ulûmu ümmete,Verzeşindir anlatan sevda-yı sa'yı millete."

173 Hanioğlu, *Abdullah Cevdet*, 196. For a brief analysis of the Young Turks' arguments on bureaucracy, see Mardin, *Jön Türkler*, 292–3. Mardin notes that although Murad Bey and Ahmed Rıza also criticized corrupt Ottoman bureaucrats, Sabahaddin Bey was the first to attack bureaucracy itself as a harmful (i.e., unproductive) occupation.

174 Hanioğlu, *Young Turks in Opposition*, 207.

175 M. Şükrü Hanioğlu, *Bir Siyasal Düşünür Olarak Doktor Abdullah Cevdet ve Dönemi* (İstanbul: Üçdal Neşriyat, 1981), 195.

176 Andrew Wernick, "Le Play, Pierre Guillaume Frédéric, (1806–1882)," in *Cambridge Dictionary of Sociology*, ed. Bryan S. Turner (Cambridge: Cambridge University Press, 2006), 331.

177 Mardin, *Jön Türkler*, 290.

178 "Functionalists argue that society should be understood as a system of interdependent parts. The different parts of social life depend on each other and fulfill functions contributing to social order and its reproduction." (John Halmwood, "functionalism," in *Cambridge Dictionary of Sociology*, 218).

179 See Taha Parla, *Ziya Gökalp, Kemalizm ve Türkiye'de Korporatizm*, eds. F. Üstel and S. Yücesoy (İstanbul: İletişim Yayınları, 1989).

180 "Kur'an-ı Kerim'de '*aleyküm enfüseküm*' ve '*laysa li'l-insāni illā mā sa'ā*' ayât-ı fahiresiyle lüzum-u kat'isine işaret buyrulan teşebbüs-i şahsîye gelince…" (M. Sabahaddin, *Teşebbüs-i Şahsî ve Tevsi'-i Me'zuniyyet Hakkında Bir İzah* (Dersaadet [İstanbul]: Kütübhane-i Cihan, 1324 [1908]), 15).

181 Sabahaddin, *Teşebbüs-i Şahsî ve Tevsi-i Me'zuniyyet*, 15–16.

182 Ibid.

183 From a report by the Ministry of Public Education (1904): BOA IM 322 Ca 7–1–896 (649); quoted in Somel, *The Modernization of Public Education*, 179. (Somel's translation).

184 For his program for the "salvation of Turkey," see Sabahaddin, *Türkiye Nasıl Kurtarılabilir?Meslek-i İctimâ'î ve Programı*, İstanbul: Kader Matbaası, R. 1334 [1918]; especially pp. 53–79.

185 Hanioğlu, *Abdullah Cevdet*, 196.

186 Ibid.

187 "Memuriyetperestlik diye tercüme etmek istediğimiz *fonctionnarisme* hangi millette ifrad dereceye varmışsa o milletin istiklâli verem olmuş demektir. Zira milletler ferdlerin ictimaından hasıl olduğu gibi bir milletin kıymet-i hakikiyesi olan seciye-i milliyesi de kendisini teşkil eden ferdlerin temayül-ü tabiîlerinden, kuvvâ-i mahsûlesinden vücûdpezir olur." (Quoted in Hanioğlu, *Abdullah Cevdet*, 198).

188 Hanioğlu, *Abdullah Cevdet*, 199.

189 Ibid.

190 Quoted in Ülken, *Türkiye'de Çağdaş Düşünce*, vol. 1, 278.

191 Ibid.

192 Akçuraoğlu Yusuf, *Eski "Şura-yı Ümmet"de Çıkan Makâlelerimden* (İstanbul: Tanin Matbaası, R. 1329 [1913]), 41.

193 Ibid.
194 Hanioğlu, *Preparation for the Revolution*, 28.
195 Ibid., 29.
196 Ahmed Rıza seems to refer to a religious principle without giving any exact reference. As we have seen above, such references to the Qur'an and the *hadith* are ubiquitous in the publications of the era.
197 Ahmed Rıza, "Mukaddime," *Meşveret*, 13 Cemaziyüelevvel 1313 [1895], p. 1. (Quoted in Mardin, *Jön Türkler*, 190–1).
198 See Toprak, *Millî İktisat* for a detailed analysis of the post-1908 National Economy program of the Young Turks.
199 See, for example, Ahmed Midhat, *Fennî Bir Roman yahud Amerika Doktorları* (İstanbul, H. 1305 [1888]), 3.
200 For an interesting example, see Arminius Vambéry's (1832–1913) accounts of how he taught French to Sultan Abdülmecid I's daughter, Fatma Sultan, under the strict rules of the Harem: *The Story of My Struggles: The Memoirs of Arminius Vambéry*, Third Impression. (London: T. Fisher Unwin, 1905), 345–6.
201 For a short introduction to Ottoman women's intellectual activities and more information on *Hanımlara Mahsus Gazete* see Elizabeth Frierson, "Women in Late Ottoman Intellectual History," in *Late Ottoman Society: The Intellectual Legacy*, ed. Elisabeth Özdalga (London: RoutledgeCurzon, 2005), 135–61. For a more detailed study on the newspaper, see Frierson's dissertation, "Unimagined Communities: State, Press, and Gender in the Hamidian Era" (unpublished PhD Dissertation, Princeton University, 1996). A selection of articles from the newspaper has been transliterated and published by the Women's Library and Information Center in Istanbul: *Yeni Harflerle Hanımlara Mahsus Gazete (1895–1908) Seçki*, Fatih Andı and Mustafa Çiçekler (eds.) (İstanbul: Kadın Eserleri Kütüphanesi ve Bilgi Merkezi Vakfı, 2009).
202 Serpil Çakır, *Osmanlı Kadın Hareketi* (İstanbul: Metis Yayınları, 1994), 30.
203 As for "Hamidian Islamism," it is worth noting here that *Hanımlara Mahsus Gazete* does not represent a conservative or Islamist stance that situates itself against European values. Even a cursory glance at its pages will show this. For example, pictures of European-style dresses and dress patterns—for the women to sew similar examples at home—appeared on the pages of the newspaper. In short, the ideal Hamidian woman was definitely a European-looking, educated woman who at the same time preserved her Ottoman identity through her commitment to traditional Islamic morals.
204 "Tahdis-i Nimet–Ta'yin-i Meslek," *Hanımlara Mahsus Gazete* 1 (1895), 2–3.
205 Ibid. Also see "Kadınların Tahsili Hakkında Bir Mütala'a," *Hanımlara Mahsus Gazete* 20 (1895), 1–2.
206 See for example, an article by Ahmed Cevdet Pasha's granddaughter, Zeyneb Sünbül bint-i Sedad bin Ahmed Cevdet Paşa, about the education of women, *Hanımlara Mahsus Gazete* 7 (1895), 2–4; and see "Kızların Tahsili Hakkında Bir Mütala'a – 2," *Hanımlara Mahsus Gazete* 21 (1895), especially p. 2 for an anthropological explanation of gender differences.
207 Zeyneb Sünbül, *Hanımlara Mahsus Gazete* 7 (1895), 3–4.
208 Ibid., 4.
209 "Kadınların Para Kesesi," *Hanımlara Mahsus Gazete* 12 (1895), 3–4.
210 Seniha Vicdan, "Moda-İsraf," *Hanımlara Mahsus Gazete* 26 (1895), 2–3.
211 "Sırf nümayişten başka bir sebeb-i mâ'kule müstenit olmayan bu hâlin ne gibi avâkıb-ı vâhime vücuda getireceği şâyân-ı nazardır. İşte kendini böyle girdab-ı isrâf ve sefâhate kaptıran kadınların aileleri âkıbet-i hâlde bir sefalete düşmeleri bâid değildir." Ibid., 3. Seniha Vicdan, the author of the article, makes reference to a previously published article that provides examples of such family disasters: Fahrünnisa, "İki Aile Levhası," *Hanımlara Mahsus Gazete* 3 (1895), 1–3. (This is the title

that Seniha Vicdan gives to the article. Otherwise it does not have a title, but a long initial sentence that may be shortened as Seniha Vicdan does).

212 Nigâr bint-i Osman, "Sa'y ü Amel," *Hanımlara Mahsus Gazete* 61 (1896), 1–2

213 Ibid., 2.

214 Ibid., 1.

215 Ibid., 1.

216 Ibid., 2.

4 Imperialism, nationalism, and economic development

> [In our country] the benefits of commerce remain theoretical, since no one pursues it. In our age, being a merchant with small capital is almost synonymous with being a peddler. Nevertheless, since we still continue [pursuing business on a small scale], our sources of wealth are completely controlled by foreigners.[1]
>
> (*Hakayık el-Vaka'i*, 1872)

Although the past glories of a once-powerful empire were still alive in the minds of the Ottomans, the Ottoman Empire was simply the "Eastern Question" in the eyes of the nineteenth-century European intellectuals and statesmen. From this perspective, the Ottoman Empire was an obsolete political and economic entity, and Europeans had already begun discussing the political, diplomatic, and economic implications of its imminent collapse. As one British merchant who lived in Istanbul put it as early as the early 1850s: "'*Nullum remedium agit in cadaver.*' She is worse than a corpse; she is a corpse in a state of decomposition."[2] Of course, Ottoman statesmen and intellectuals were fully and painfully aware of such views. In the late 1850s, Ahmed Vefik Efendi, for example, criticized the literature on the Ottoman Empire by arguing:

> To know this country, you must do four things. First, you must learn the language; secondly, you must unlearn all your previous notions; thirdly, you must seek the truth, not facts in support of preformed conclusions; and lastly, you must stay among us for three or four years. Slade's [studies] ... are among the best works on Turkey, and Urquhart's, favorable as he is to us, are among the worst; he is an advocate, not a critic. But you must trust none of them.[3]

Ottoman periodicals of the later decades, especially those of the Young Ottoman and Young Turk line of thought, published numerous articles complaining about the ignorance or superficial knowledge of European intellectuals about the Ottoman Empire, and the consequent contempt they express regarding the socio-economic and political situation of the empire.[4] As Ahmed Vefik Efendi also stated, there were European observers who challenged widely accepted opinions about the empire, such as Sir Adolphus Slade (1802–77).[5] However, alternative views, such as Slade's, were largely neglected due to their being "thoroughly out of accord with the commonly accepted opinions of nineteenth-century Europe."[6]

According to the dominant economic paradigm in the second half of the nineteenth century, civilization meant industrialization (and vice versa). Under this paradigm, the Ottoman economic system seemed unquestionably archaic, thereby its society was thought to be living in barbaric conditions compared to the European industrial societies. Moreover, the same paradigm stigmatized the so-called Oriental nations as a whole with economic and social backwardness, laziness, and hatred of organization and order.[7] Since the same paradigm gradually dominate the economic thinking also of the Ottoman elite of the age, many Ottoman reformists connected the question of the the salvation of the empire directly to industrialization. The same idea, by the way, shaped modernization processes in other major non-European empires, such as Russia and China.[8]

The discussions of the Ottoman reformists on economic development revolved around two main aspects of the problem: social-cultural and material-economic. The social-cultural aspects included the traditional economic mentality (e.g., lack of interest in entrepreneurship) and the dearth of human capital (e.g., an unskilled and uneducated population). The material-economic aspects consisted of the scarcity of financial resources and of the obstacles to controlling the domestic wealth-creating resources (e.g., the capitulations and foreign dominance). The previous chapter analyzed the suggestions and models of the Ottoman modernists for overcoming the obstacles in the first category, and the current chapter focuses on the latter.

This chapter is a multifaceted analysis of the question of economic development in late nineteenth-century Ottoman economic thought, and the emergence of Muslim-Turkish economic proto-nationalism in this context. The chapter begins with a historical discussion of the question of economic development in the Ottoman Empire. The second section sheds light on the early roots of Muslim-Turkish economic nationalism through a historical and contextual examination of the Young Ottomans' economic writings in their popular periodicals. The following two sections reveal the intellectual and conceptual connections between the economic discourse of the Young Ottomans of the 1870s and the Young Turks of the twentieth century, thereby providing insights into the evolution of Muslim-Turkish nationalism in the late Ottoman Empire. The third section contextualizes (Young Ottoman and later) Muslim-Ottoman economic proto-nationalism through a discussion about the rise of nations and nationalisms in the Ottoman Empire, and Muslims' reactions to it. Then the fourth section focuses on the discussions about foreign exploitation and capitulations as obstacles to economic development in the post-Young-Ottoman decades. The final section is a historical and contextual analysis of the sultan Abdülhamid II's views about the economic conditions of the empire and his ideas on the question of economic development. In addition to being the first attempt to understand the economic thinking of an Ottoman sultan, this section reveals interesting connections between economic thought and policy-making in the late Ottoman Empire.

The question of economic development and the early industrialization attempts

In 1888, Friedrich Engels wrote a preface to the English edition of a speech by Karl Marx on the issue of free trade.[9] Engel's preface provides us with important insights into the economic paradigm of the late nineteenth century. After presenting an overview of the emergence of the theory of free trade as a product of British economic interests, he especially emphasizes the hypocrisy of British economic theory:

> England thus supplemented the protection she practiced at home, by the Free Trade she forced upon her possible customers abroad; and thanks to this happy mixture of both systems, at the end of the wars, in 1815, she found herself, with regard to all important branches of industry, in possession of the virtual monopoly of the trade of the world.[10]

Then he goes on to argue that English economic interests were buttressed by intellectual and academic support through *laissez-faire* economics:

> [T]he free trade doctrines of classical political economy—of the French physiocrats and their English successors, Adam Smith and Ricardo—became popular in the land of the John Bull. Protection at home was needless to manufacturers who beat all their foreign rivals, and whose very existence was staked on the expansion of their exports.[11]

As a result,

> Free trade became the watchword of the day. To convert all other countries to the gospel of Free Trade, and thus create a world in which England was the great manufacturing centre, with all countries for its dependent agricultural districts, that was the next task before the English manufacturers and their mouth pieces, the political economists.[12]

Nevertheless, as Engels notes, England's European rivals, primarily France, resisted this trend by keeping their economies behind the high walls of protection until they could gain competitive power vis-à-vis British industries.

The economic paradigm of the age suggested that only industrial countries were to be regarded as civilized. A short anecdote from Engels' accounts reflects this undisputed assumption of the age: during a train trip in the late 1860s or early 1870s, Engels met a Glasgow merchant and the two men began to talk about the protectionist policies of the United States. The Glasgow merchant, a supporter of free trade, complained about the fact that "sharp businessmen" like the Americans allowed their government to pursue such an "obviously harmful path," i.e., protectionism. Engels reminded him of the other side of the story:

> You know that in coal, water-power, iron and other ores, cheap food, home grown cotton and other raw materials, America has resources and advantages

> unequalled by any European country; and that these resources cannot be fully developed except by America becoming a manufacturing country. You will admit, too, that nowadays a great nation like the Americans cannot exist on agriculture alone; that would be tantamount to a condemnation to permanent barbarism and inferiority; no great nation can live, in our age, without manufacturers of her own.[13]

Engels closed his words by saying that if protectionist policies will provide the Americans with a shorter and safer path to industrialization and thus civilization, it is unquestionably more rational for them to follow this path.[14]

As this anecdote demonstrates, in the second half of the nineteenth century, industrialization was considered an indispensable aspect of becoming a civilized nation. The alternative—that is, remaining an agricultural economy—simply meant remaining in the barbaric stage in the eyes of the civilized nations. Ottoman intellectuals who followed European intellectual circles were fully aware of this perception. Moreover, in time many Ottoman intellectuals came to think along the same lines in their efforts to save the empire from the primitive conditions which, according to the same paradigm, had paved the way for an imminent collapse of the Ottoman socio-economic and political system.

According to some European observers, the Ottoman economy had the potential to thrive. As a friend of Nassau Senior put it, "Turkey once opened to European enterprise, industry, and capital, will be a new America, with a better climate and a better soil."[15] Nevertheless, the British plan for the integration of the Ottoman economy into its global economic system was different: it was to become an agricultural producer providing the British manufacturing industry with cheap primary goods and a vast market for British industrial products.[16] In other words, the interests of the global superpower of the age were at odds with the idea of Ottoman industrialization, especially if this would lead to protectionism, as in the case of the United States.

The Ottomans were not as late in their industrialization efforts as it has generally been assumed in scholarship. The first industrialization projects were put into practice as early as in the reign of Selim III (r. 1789–1807); these were mostly military industries.[17] However, "in the 1840s Ottoman recognition of disadvantages inherent in Ottoman dependence on foreign manufactures, and of the necessity for a more ambitious form of 'defensive modernization'—economic if not social—apparently reached a peak."[18] The state invested in many industrial projects, and encouraged private Ottoman entrepreneurs with highly profitable concessions and subsidies. Meanwhile, many councils and offices such as the *Meclis-i Ziraat ve Sanayi* (Council of Agriculture and Industry, 1838; it later adopted the name *Meclis-i Umûr-u Nafia*, Council of Public Works), and the Ministry of Commerce (1839), which aimed to support industrial and agricultural modernization as well as to promote commerce, were founded for the central planning of economic development.[19] In 1866, the *Islah-ı Sanâyî Encümeni* (Industrial Reform Commission) was founded. One of its earliest decisions was that traditional guild production had long been an obsolete form of manufacture;

thus a rapid transition to the modern factory system was necessary.[20] Despite Ottoman optimism about the attainment of civilization through industrialization, the economic conditions and the results of some earlier efforts were not very encouraging:

> The timing of this far-flung industrial program is peculiar. Already in 1838 the Ottoman government had abandoned most state monopolies and other import-export controls by terms of the Anglo-Turkish Commercial Convention of Balta Liman. By 1841 the European powers were able to force this convention on Muhammad Ali, the Porte's nominal vassal in Egypt, and the ensuing foreign competition quickly brought rust and ruin to his factories on the Nile. Thus, any cause for optimism concerning additional investments in factories seemingly already had been eliminated at the beginning of the Tanzimat. Paradoxically this foreboding example did not deter Sultan Abdülmecid and his advisers. Almost simultaneously they initiated the supreme Ottoman effort to industrialize the shores of the Bosporus and the Marmara.[21]

It is important to note that although these gloomy conditions could easily have led Ottoman statesmen to monopolistic tendencies and state capitalism, they did not incline to such policies. On the contrary, the two leading statesmen of the Tanzimat era, namely Âlî Pasha (1815–71) and Keçecizade Fuad Pasha (1814–69), were ardent supporters of economic liberalism, as their political testaments presented to Sultan Abdülaziz clearly demonstrate.[22] For example, Âlî Pasha suggests that the state should not be an entrepreneur itself, and instead it should encourage and support the private sector as much as possible. He maintains that his government avoided state monopoly in many cases, and he and his colleagues at times preferred foreign investors over the Ottoman subjects for practical economic reasons.[23] He explains this choice by stating that the Ottoman Empire did not have qualified engineers and skilled managers to undertake these projects efficiently.[24] Nevertheless, he recommends a long-term economic development perspective based on domestic resources (including human capital). He argues that the state should encourage Muslims to engage in commerce, industry, and agriculture, just as the Christians do, because, he notes, "The only permanent capital is labor. Salvation is only possible with toil."[25]

Âlî Pasha and his colleagues' efforts to develop a market economy in the Ottoman Empire were not confined to government policies and investments. They were actively involved in business and even introduced some modern business methods and ideas into the Ottoman economy. An important enterprise in late Ottoman economic history, the *Şirket-i Hayriye* (the Bosporus Ferry Company), was founded in 1851 by the two comrades of Âlî Pasha, namely Ahmed Cevdet and Fuad Pashas.[26] In addition to these leading statesmen, some members of the royal family—including the sultan himself—and high-ranking officials were among the shareholders of the company.[27] As stated earlier, the Ottoman elite had always invested in profitable business ventures.

> [T]he Ottoman government hardly was ignorant of or irrational in economic matters in the nineteenth century. On the personal level, political positions were intertwined with economic interests; a grand vizier, a palace chamberlain, and state ministers invested in mining enterprises that sought to drive out the European companies while other Ottoman officials placed their trust and money in the foreign corporations. On the official level, Ottoman administrators also were economic planners with visions of the future and of the economically possible.[28]

What makes *Şirket-i Hayriye* a turning point in Ottoman economic history, however, is that it the was founded on the basis of a new idea: the joint-stock company. Cevdet Pasha's daughter, Fatma Âliye Hanım, notes that her father and Fuad Pasha founded the *Şirket-i Hayriye* to serve as a model for prospective modern Ottoman companies.[29]

Despite all these efforts and some successful cases such as the *Şirket-i Hayriye*, Tanzimat-era state-led industrialization efforts mostly failed to meet its goals by the 1860s. There were many reasons for failure, from mismanagement and inexperience, to the lack of skilled labor and the impact of foreign competition, and it is beyond the scope of this work to discuss these reasons in detail.[30] A discussion on how Ottoman intellectuals perceived the reasons for failure and what they suggested for future success, however, is essential to understand the nineteenth-century roots of economic nationalism and discussions on economic development, which were to shape economic thought and policies in the twentieth century.

The roots of Ottoman-Turkish economic nationalism: the Young Ottomans

The Young Ottomans was a secret network of reformist intellectuals and statesmen who criticized Tanzimat-era reforms and Ottoman governments from a more (politically) liberal and radical perspective. In the late 1860s and the 1870s, they became the standard-bearers of Ottoman reformism. Despite their emphasis on political liberties and freedom in general, their economic worldview was shaped profoundly by the contemporary Muslim reaction against foreign domination in the Ottoman economy. Yet, they did not suggest any coherent economic strategy, but a curious mixture of economic liberalism (regarding the domestic market) with proto-nationalist and protectionist arguments against foreign dominance.[31] All in all, Young Ottoman political discourse and its symbols deeply impacted the earlier phase of Young Turk ideology,[32] which shaped the late Ottoman Empire and the early Turkish Republic.

The economic writings of prominent Young Ottomans such as Ziya Pasha (1825–80), Ali Suâvi (1838–78), and Namık Kemal (1840–88) constituted the basis for economic proto-nationalism and protectionism in the Ottoman Empire. The prominent figures of this line of economic reasoning in the later decades, including Ahmed Midhat and especially the Young Turks, adopted the Young

Ottoman ideas and discourses regarding the question of development and foreign domination in the Ottoman economy.[33] Moreover, as Akçuraoğlu Yusuf (1876–1935), a prominent Young Turk and an early champion of Turkish nationalism, asserted, even though Abdülhamid II himself was the Young Ottomans' arch-enemy, he was actually their student with regard to the outlines of his political and economic thinking.[34] Therefore, in order to understand the emergence of economic nationalism in the late Ottoman Empire, we must begin by tracing its roots to Young Ottoman ideology.

A significant issue in the Young Ottomans' harsh economic criticisms regarding the Tanzimat era was the financial crisis of the empire. The culprits, according to them, were primarily the political elite of the era (excluding the sultan, as a result of their intrinsic Ottoman paternalism), not only because of their mismanagement of state finances, but also their extravagant Westernized lifestyles, when ordinary people suffered from poverty and an overall economic decline in the empire.[35] Financial issues, however, were not the only reasons of economic backwardness, according to them. Perhaps more importantly, they suggested that foreign dominance in the Ottoman economy along with a ubiquitous Muslim indifference to industry and commerce lied at the roots of the economic backwardness of the empire.

An unsigned article in *Hürriyet* provides a succinct summary of the situation of the post-1838 Ottoman economy from the Young Ottoman perspective.[36] After noting the increasing European economic power resulting from the concessions given to European merchants, the anonymous author suggests reasons for economic underdevelopment and dependence:

> The first reason is the external interference.... Upon [receiving] the concessions, the European merchants saw that the commerce in Turkestan [i.e., Ottoman territory] was much more profitable and easier than other places. Besides, they enjoyed the low cost of water and air [i.e., low cost of living] in the country. As a result, they loaded the ships with cheap rubbish produced in European factories and came and settled in Istanbul with their families. Since our people have an interest in such cheap and flashy things, they preferred [shoddy European cloth to that of Damascus].... The rugs of Uşak and Gördes, and the clothes from Salonica and Bursa began to seem coarse to us; meanwhile the Europeans developed an interest in [our goods]. In return [for our rugs], we purchased their flowery French rugs and towels that are made of grass, assuming that they were both cheap and good in quality. Yet, since they were made of poor quality materials and thus wore out in a short time, we had to change them frequently. As a result, we wasted our money thinking that we were saving it. This situation was not limited to printed cloth and rugs. Due to our ignorance, we preferred the products of European factories to our own products of all sorts of clothes and upholstery. Moreover, as our government supported this trend as it increased and expanded such concessions, our industries collapsed. Our merchants went bankrupt, and manufacturers who had lived on their industries became

> miserable and wretched. Our money began to flow abroad, and our state finances went into crisis. The government had to print more money and issue bonds with interest. Nevertheless, since the real reason for all these ills continued to exist, such measures proved to be ineffective and the situation worsened every day. Finally, we ended up with today's much-feared situation.[37]

At first sight, this Young Ottoman reaction to the opening of the Ottoman market to the flood of British manufactures and the consequent collapse of traditional industries may resemble the ideas of some early modern European conservative critics of capitalism. The social consequences of industrialization (e.g., urbanization, poverty, the collapse of the guild system) were an important concern for many early nineteenth-century European economists and social thinkers.[38] In Germany, for example, Justus Möser (1720–94) openly defended the traditional guild manufacture system against the socially disruptive effects of capitalism. He accused peddlers of polluting peasants' minds—with a consumer culture—by providing them with goods they did not really need.[39] Möser also blamed capitalism for destroying local cultures and social institutions which had been organized around the traditional guild structure, by altering the production structure.[40]

Although a similar socially conservative critique could very well be relevant to the Ottoman case, and the Young Ottomans also complained about the collapse of traditional industries, Ottoman protectionism never took on a predominantly anti-industrial or anti-capitalist character.[41] Unlike Möser and other similar conservative economists, the Young Ottomans and their followers did not favor traditional industries or the social structure that went with them, but they supported a native path to industrialization and a parallel modernization of social life. In other words, Ottoman-Muslim modernists of the age did not resist capitalism per se, but they strove to maintain control of the economy against the increasing power of foreign capitalists. In many respects, Ottoman economic protectionism, from its earliest stages in Young Ottoman thought to the Young Turks' post-1908 National Economy (*Millî İktisat*) program, had strong parallels with Friedrich List's national economy approach.[42]

Since the "industrialized=civilized" equation occupied a central place in late nineteenth-century European social and economic thought, anti-capitalism was usually not an alternative for the reformists of any non-industrialized country at the time. In this regard, Namık Kemal complains that although the Ottomans were a clever and talented people, they imported even their clothes from Europe, since they did not have their own industries. As a result, he states, "some European intellectuals assume that the Ottomans lack competence for industry."[43] He joins other Young Ottomans in arguing that, despite all unfavorable historical conditions (e.g., continuous wars), the Ottomans possessed a self-sufficient economy with its own industries; yet with the trade agreements that were made with the Europeans, Ottoman traditional industries collapsed in the Tanzimat era.[44] Thus, as echoed in the writings of the later generation of Ottoman protectionists, he maintained that although the *laissez-faire* approach is right in theory, one should be careful in applying it to the Ottoman case because of its potential dangers.[45] He emphasizes that he is not against free trade or free trade agreements, and he does not suggest that "the Ottomans ... imprison themselves instead of joining the world [market]."[46] Yet the government should have taken the necessary steps to benefit from these agreements instead of letting them ruin the empire's industries.[47] This indicates that Young Ottoman economic protectionism was not at its core mercantilist or autarkist. On the contrary, they argued for the incorporation of the Ottoman economy into the world market. Yet they also suggested that the Ottoman Empire should join the game as a major industrial player, not merely as a peripheral agricultural supplier.

Another prominent Young Ottoman, Ali Suâvi, reveals yet another dimension of the question of "foreign" dominance. Although, according to the Tanzimat-era legal reforms and the ideology of Ottomanism in general, the non-Muslims of the empire were considered Ottomans as subjects of the Ottoman Empire, their economic partnerships as well as their cultural and political ties to European countries gradually led the Muslim Ottomans to regard them as "others." Ali Suâvi's words on the non-Muslims of the empire reflect such thinking:

> They [non-Muslims] have privileges that the Muslims also demand but cannot obtain. For example, a Christian is not conscripted if he pays a fee. The Muslims have to provide [the state with] soldiers, but [the Christians] do not. As for the equality in terms of laws and treatment, the Christians are not equal to the Muslims. They have a superior position, because the Christians have their local notables, their representatives in the parliament, and their own national assembly under the Patriarch. They have patrons in Europe. Whenever a Christian is harassed by a district governor, he complains to a local notable, and the Patriarchate is also informed immediately. The Patriarch appeals to the Sublime Porte. Meanwhile, the embassies also adopt the case, and finally they have the district governor [who had mistreated this Christian] dismissed.[48]

In addition to the criticism of the privileged position of the non-Muslims, there was also a strong self-critical aspect to Young Ottoman writings on the socio-economic conditions of the Tanzimat. The idea of Muslim indifference to entrepreneurship, for example, has its roots in Young-Ottoman thought. Ali Suâvi, in this context, complains that Muslims "bury" their money in land-ownership whereas Christians invest it in commerce. He argues that commerce can be very profitable even with small amounts of capital but that only Christians pursue these trades. Therefore, Christians get wealthier, whereas Muslims' capital remains idle.[49] Moreover, Ali Suâvi makes an interesting economy-based cultural analysis: he asserts that since Muslims mostly invest in land, they became more attached to the land, and their feelings of patriotism were more powerful than those of Christians and Jews, who mostly possess movable property.[50] In a similar vein, in an article in Namık Kemal's periodical, *İbret*, the author (most probably Namık Kemal himself) argues that foreigners get rich by exploiting the empire's resources.[51] Yet, he concludes that it is the Muslims who should be blamed for this result, since they surrendered their own natural wealth to foreigners because of their laziness and imprudence.[52]

In the following decades, numerous articles with similar arguments appeared on the pages of reformist publications. An interesting example from 1891 shows that sometimes even the non-Muslim reformists criticized the disadvantaged situation of Muslims in the Ottoman Empire. Demetrius Georgioades, in the journal *La Turquie Contemporaine*, which bore "*Organe de la Jeune Turquie*" under its title, stated that the Turkish peasantry was the most unfortunate in the world since it did not enjoy the backing of embassies and foreign powers like the Christians.[53] After 1897, the Young Turks frequently aired similar grievances about the situation of "Turkish" peasants through their influential periodicals, such as *Osmanlı* (Ottoman).[54] In short, the economically as well as politically disadvantageous position of the Muslim Turks and the importance of encouraging and educating them for commerce and industry became staple topics of economic writings especially by reformists in the late nineteenth century.[55] More importantly, similar ideas were echoed in the official correspondence at the highest governmental level, and influenced the modernization efforts of the Hamidian regime.[56] Encouraging Muslim students for commerce and industry, for example, became a major concern that influenced educational policies in the 1880s and 1890s.[57]

The rise of nations and nationalisms

There is an important detail in Ali Suâvi's words that gives away an underlying reason for the Muslim-Turkish proto-nationalist reaction to socio-economic change in the empire throughout the nineteenth century. He complains that "the Christians get wealthier." It is understandable that he encourages the Muslims to do the same, but this expression itself reflects the Muslims' anxiety about the rise of non-Muslim bourgeoisie at the expense of Muslims' social and economic status.

The traditional Ottoman economic policy towards non-Muslim merchants and artisans was a tried and true method for securing the economic prosperity of the empire. The non-Muslim communities were "protected" in return for their essential roles in the economic sphere and their virtual non-existence in the central political sphere. Yet, by the nineteenth century, times had changed. The modern age assigned economic power, and therefore business skills—in which non-Muslims had a traditional superiority in the Ottoman Empire—a decisive role in social and political power relations.[58] As Gellner states,

> The situation changes radically and profoundly with the coming of mobile, anonymous, centralized mass society. This is particularly true for minorities specializing in financial, commercial, and generally urban specialist occupations.... Their urban style of life, habits of rational calculation, commercial probity, higher rates of literacy and possibly a scriptural religion, all fit them

> better than either the members of the old ruling class, or of the old peasantry, for the new life-style.[59]

As a result, the nineteenth century witnessed a continuous and multidimensional rise of the non-Muslims in the Ottoman Empire. In addition to economic factors, non-Muslims improved their social and political power in the Ottoman system with the introduction of the notion of citizenship regardless of religion and ethnicity, and other Tanzimat reforms on similar grounds. As the well-known traveler and orientalist of the age, Arminius Vambéry (1832–1913), puts it in rather dramatic terms:

> The Christian element, as compared with the Moslem, has increased enormously; the European quarter of the city is full of life and animation, and the Turk, always wont to walk with bowed head, now bends it quite low on his breast as he loiters among the busy crowds of the Christian populace. He is buried in thought, but whether he will be able to pull himself together and recover himself is as yet an open question.[60]

Meanwhile, the increasing social and political importance of economic power merged with the idea of nationalism, giving rise to a new possibility for major ethnic communities, that is, the creation of states of their own. As a result, independence movements, especially in the Balkans, began to challenge the traditional Ottoman central state structure based on Muslim rule. As an important side effect of these trends, the tension between the "main constituent" (*millet-i hâkime*, i.e., the Muslims) and other constituents of the Ottoman population increased. It is worth reminding that these tensions were not peculiar to the Ottoman Empire. In Europe, hostility towards minorities, especially the Jews who allegedly control financial and economic resources, intensified throughout the nineteenth century and culminated in Eastern Europe in the pogroms and genocides of the late nineteenth and especially the early twentieth centuries.

European capital diffused rapidly into the Ottoman economy by taking over existing economic networks in addition to providing local merchants with new international opportunities.[61] Non-Muslim commercial networks and merchants were perfect partners for European capitalists thanks to non-Muslim businessmen's commercial skills (including literacy) and knowledge of local markets as well as their cultural links to European societies through their shared religious background. This naturally developed partnership did not escape the notice of Muslims. When Muslim reformists complained about the increasing European dominance in Ottoman economy, they also turned their gaze towards the local partners of Europeans, and it constituted another reason for the Muslims to regard non-Muslims as "foreigners," especially in economic contexts.

Furthermore, the discourse of the Eastern Question led the Muslim elite to defensive modernization based on Muslim proto-nationalism, as can be observed in the Young Ottoman ideology. Later, the Young Turks formed their Muslim-Turkish nationalist modernization program on this ideological legacy of the

Young Ottomans. In the writings of late nineteenth-century Muslim modernists, one can easily observe efforts to prove that the Muslims can be "modern" too and that Islam is in fact compatible with modernity. Interestingly enough, although the anti-imperialist theories of the age (like socialism) would have perfectly suited the concerns of the Young Turks, we do not see any systematic interest in such ideas.[62] Nevertheless, as Mardin puts it, "It is possible to come across the reflections of some unidentifiable versions of these theories" in their publications.[63] As an example of the impact of the Eastern Question on Ottoman economic thinking, the popular Young Turk newspaper *Osmanlı* includes paragraphs such as the following:

> The reason for touching upon an economic issue is that we know that the reprise of "Muslim fatalism" in the Eastern Question is simply a mask of the Europeans that hides their efforts to destroy the East (Ottomans, Turks, Armenians, and Greeks).[64]

In this particular example, the apparent Ottomanist discourse still seems to be in place (in 1898) to defend all ethnic and religious communities of the Ottoman Empire against the assault of the European imperialists.[65] However, the turn of the century witnessed the emergence of "reformers who equated nationalism with modernity,"[66] and the economic ideology of industrialization began to be complemented by the political ideology of (Turkish) nationalism in the modernization process.

It is worth noting at this point that the idea of Turkism, and even the emphasis on the Anatolian Turks, and the conceptualization of Anatolia as the heartland of the Turks have their roots in the early decades of the Hamidian era.[67] By the early 1890s, the emphasis on Turkishness began to supplant Muslim-Ottoman proto-nationalism in the eyes of Muslim intellectuals and even the sultan. Şemseddin Sami (1850–1904) had planted the seeds of Turkish nationalism on a linguistic basis, suggesting that the language of the main constituent of Ottoman society was Turkish. He claimed that this name, which had been applied to the ignorant Anatolian peasants, was in fact the name of a "great nation."[68]

At first, this language-based Turkish nationalism did not attract the attention of the Ottoman intelligentsia. Nevertheless the failure of the Ottomanist ideology in keeping the supposed Ottoman nation together brought about a slow transition from Ottoman-Muslim proto-nationalism to Turkish nationalism. Mardin notes that the well-known Young Turk leader Mizancı Murad Bey, for example, emphasizes the word "Turk" to voice his proto-nationalist ideas, but uses it without distinguishing it clearly from the notion of "Ottoman."[69] Although this holds for most of his early political writings—just like those of other prominent intellectuals of the era—an earlier version of Anatolian-Turkish nationalism is apparent in his novel, *Turfanda mı, Turfa mı?* (1890).[70] An another important example in fiction, Ahmed Midhat's novel *Ahmed Metin ve Şirzad* (1891), which he calls "a novel based on historical facts,"[71] includes an account of the pre-Ottoman history of the "Turkish nation." Ahmed Midhat presented a copy of the novel to Abdülhamid II along with a petition. In his petition, he emphasizes that his novel sings the praises of the "noble Turkish nation" (*Türk kavm-i necîbi*) and their services to Islam in Seljuk and Ottoman times.[72]

Ahmed Midhat remained rather ambivalent in his attitude towards Turkish nationalism until the end of his intellectual career.[73] However, his note to the sultan hints at his awareness of the sultan's appreciation of such ideas. Arminius Vambéry, who personally knew Abdülhamid II rather well, testifies to the "Turkist" ideas of the sultan and to the change in the Ottoman attitude towards Turkishness during his reign. He notes that when Abdülhamid II heard about Vambéry's study of the pre-Islamic Turkish monuments in the Uighur language, "the Sultan smiled, quite pleased, thinking that with these monuments he could prove the unadulterated Turkish national character of the Osmanli dynasty."[74] Vambéry goes on to write that, "This vanity surprised me greatly, as a while ago the Turks were rather ashamed of their Turkish antecedents, and now their monarch actually boasted of them."[75] As these examples also demonstrate, the idea of a primordial "great Turkish nation" began to supplant the emphasis on Ottoman identity in the Ottoman intellectual and political spheres (including the higher echelons) as early as the 1890s.

The questions of foreign exploitation and the capitulations

In the late nineteenth and early twentieth centuries (including the post-Ottoman decades), Muslim intellectuals' nationalist economic thinking and discourse followed the Young Ottoman path. In this respect, Ahmed Midhat seems to play an important role. His early connections with the movement caused him exile between 1873 and 1876. Although he later denounced this rather radical period of his intellectual career, his economic thought and discourse continued to resemble those of the Young Ottomans.

In *Ekonomi Politik* (1879), Ahmed Midhat asserts that liberal policies paved the way for the collapse of traditional Ottoman industries, and trade, industry, and agriculture remained in a pitiful state. As a result, Ottomans had to import everything from their fezzes to matches. Besides, in the same process Muslims were barred from industrial and commercial sectors and confined to unskilled jobs, as a result of increasing foreign dominance in the economy.[76]

> [O]ur commercial sectors have been invaded by the foreigners. They control not only external trade, but also internal trade. If we argue that one of the reasons for the collapse of our old wealth (*servet-i kadîme*) is foreigners, would it be an exaggeration? Many people remember their initial status. These people were [merely] European tramps when they first came to Istanbul; today they are millionaires. Did they bring money from abroad? No, they found it here and stole it. They have even burdened the state budget with two-hundred million [of debt]. This means that in addition to pocketing the old wealth of the nation, they robbed everybody of ten lira through loans.[77]

These words remind us of the Young Ottomans both in tone and content. But it also reflects a shared feeling—and discourse—among Muslim intellectuals as a result of actual economic conditions in the broader Middle East. Similar grievances were common in other intellectual centers of the region as well. In a satirical piece on Egyptian economy, published in a popular periodical published in Egypt (*al-Ustādh*) in 1892, we read:

> [A]l-Muʿallim Hanafi (Master Hanafi) approaches Nadim and begins to complain about the worsening economic conditions, whereupon Nadim angrily responds, "What can the people do, now that all goods are imported? Cooked canned meat, dried milk, tailored garments, even cotton and woolen textiles used to make turbans and caftans are manufactured and imported from Europe. . . ." [Then Nadim asks Hanafi], "So, we don't have any craftsman?" To this Hanafi sarcastically responds, "Oh, not at all. Thank God we still have plenty of garbage men, donkey drivers, porters, servants, shoe shiners, doormen [*bawwābīn*], falafel and bean [*ful*] sellers, etc."[78]

Against a similar economic backdrop, Ahmed Midhat complains about the fact that although the first duty of a government is the protection of its subjects and their economic interests, the Ottoman government does not undertake any action to fulfill this duty. European governments, he maintains, take this duty seriously by assigning consuls to important foreign port cities to secure the economic interests of their businessmen abroad. In the Ottoman case, by contrast, not only did the government fail to protect its commercial interests abroad, it could not even provide any protection for its own subjects within the empire. In the context, he also complains about the privileged status of foreign merchants and businessmen, the capitulations, and the interference of the embassies, pointing out the reasons of Ottoman officials' lack of power in protecting Ottoman interests.[79] Moreover, he adds, the government continued to grant concessions to foreign entrepreneurs to take advantage of the empire's forests and mines.[80]

Regarding the natural resources and economic potentials of the Ottoman Empire, numerous articles were published in the 1880s and 1890s, in the journals particularly aimed at foreign and domestic businessmen, such as the *Levant Herald* and *Le Journal de la Chambre de Commerce de Constantinople*. An eminent Young Turk intellectual, Hüseyin Cahit Yalçın (1875–1957), argues in his memoirs that these periodicals—in addition European ones—were the most important sources for Turkish-language periodicals of the era. Ottoman periodicals continuously translated and adapted articles from these publications.[81] *Journal de la Chambre de Commerce de Constantinople* was an especially important source for those who were interested in general and sector-specific conditions and market opportunities in the empire.

The Istanbul Chamber of Commerce (Dersaadet Ticaret Odası) was founded in 1882, and began to publish *Le Journal de la Chambre de Commerce de Constantinople* in 1885 along with its Turkish edition, *Dersaadet Ticaret Odası Gazetesi*. The *Journal* was published regularly (with some breaks) in the subsequent decades well into the Republican era. In addition to current information on various markets in the empire, it published articles on economic institutions, ranging from private banks and insurance companies to local customs offices and other economic administrative units. Several issues also include charts and data on various sectors and geographical regions of the Ottoman economy, including the Anatolian and Arab provinces, as well as the overall trade statistics of the Ottoman economy. Moreover,

> Articles from commercial and financial periodicals of Paris, Cologne, Odessa, or Alexandria were occasionally reproduced, indicating a wide acquaintance by the Journal's staff with economic news and events abroad. The topics included recent enterprises undertaken by other chambers of comers, whether in Lyons or Blackburn; unusual commercial or judicial questions; the opening of new markets; and novel uses for agricultural and industrial products.[82]

In addition to providing valuable market information, the *Journal* and the *Levant Herald* were significant venues for liberal economists and businessmen to express their opinions on the Ottoman economy. The dominant view in these journals about the economic potential of the empire was that it was extremely rich in resources, but poor in capital and entrepreneurial skills. This led to an underdeveloped economy sitting on a great potential; a problem that could easily be solved by easing the conditions for concession grants to European investors:

> Its impoverishment is plain to the most causal observer. The only remedy is to develop the national resources and this cannot be done without capital. That capital proffered Turkey on fair terms. Why she does not accept it without further hesitation remains a mystery.[83]

These words were printed in 1886. However, similar arguments had been voiced by liberal economists and businessmen for decades. And the protectionist and proto-nationalist response was not absent. However, for protectionists, the question was not purely a matter of economic theory. Protectionists more often than not sensed imperialism, self-interest (at the expense of public ones), and profit-seeking behavior lying behind such liberal claims. Ahmed Midhat, for example, openly blamed the liberal camp for putting their personal economic interests before the empire's interests, and his words succinctly summarize the protectionist take on the issue of natural resources and foreign capital:

> I know that the advocates of freedom of exchange and liberty of exports and imports, and especially those foreigners who are accustomed to enrich themselves in our country will get angry and criticize these words harshly. Because when they say, 'the Ottoman Empire is in its natural condition [i.e., it is not an industrial country], and its mines, forests and other natural resources are sufficient to enrich this state, therefore [the state] should

exploit these sources,' they simply mean that their own companies should undertake [such projects].[84]

Ahmed Midhat—and other protectionists for that matter—was obviously aware of the lack of domestic capital and entrepreneurial skills and experience that are capable of undertaking large-scale economic enterprises. He nevertheless suggested that the government could at least save domestic resources until its own subjects have gained the necessary skills, instead of opening them unconditionally to foreign exploitation.[85] Even if foreign capitalists were granted concessions, he thought, there should be strict regulations and conditions to protect imperial interests.[86] In this context, he suggested the examples of Peter the Great of Russia (1672–1725) and Mehmed Ali of Egypt (1769–1849), as implementers of this path who had succeeded to lead their countries to a successful development pattern. According to him, these were what the "science of economics"—obviously a protectionist interpretation of it—showed the Ottomans as examples to follow suit.[87]

From the perspective of Muslim proto-nationalists, there was even a bigger problem than the danger of foreign capitalists exploiting the empire's natural resources, and it was the capitulations. The capitulations, in the Ottoman context, were originally bilateral agreements—between the Ottoman Empire and a foreign government—that provided the subjects of both parties with commercial, legal, fiscal, and political privileges and exemptions. The idea behind such agreements was promoting commerce, as well as being a symbol of reciprocal political goodwill and alliance. As the Ottoman Empire weakened, however, they began to acquire the character of unilateral concessions given to (particularly European) foreign citizens. As a result, "In the second half of the nineteenth century the capitulations came to be perceived as the symbol of Ottoman inferiority vis-à-vis Europe."[88] Capitulations, thereby, became a main concern for the Muslim elite, in both intellectual and administrative spheres. Moreover, since capitulations provided the citizens of the relevant countries with legal, fiscal, and political exemptions and immunizations, especially non-Muslim subjects increasingly sought acquiring European nationalities to benefit from these privileges. The capitulations, therefore, became a significant source of tension between the bourgeoning Muslim bourgeoisie, who were devoid of any such specific privileges, and the non-Muslim Ottoman bourgeoisie and Europeans. This increasing tension contributed to the rise of an exclusive Muslim-Turkish nationalism in the last decades of the empire.

As emphasized earlier, in the Hamidian era, economic development was at the center of Ottoman modernization efforts. In the same vein, in this era, "the Ottoman attitude towards the capitulations changed drastically: they came to be seen not merely a violation of sovereignty but as a major barrier to economic reform and progress."[89] The capitulations undeniably restricted the state's control over the empire's resources, and thereby its planning capacity.[90] For example, the legal immunity of foreign subjects and the power of embassies constrained the ability of local and central branches of the government to regulate the market, thereby restricting its powers to enforce economic regulations and enact measures to promote economic development. As one foreign observer stated later:

> Economically, the capitulations meant much in the way of privilege. Foreigners were exempt from every tax levied by the Ottoman Government except the ad valorem export and import duties whose maxima were fixed by the capitulations. Almost no internal tax could be levied on foreign goods. It should be stated that the powers have abused their economic privileges in many instances to the extent of preventing Turkey from developing their own industries while inferior European goods have been unloaded upon the country in great quantities. On the other hand, Turkey has been assisted through foreign countries providing markets for native raw products.[91]

Modernization involved an extensive and intensive transformation process that covered all aspects of life and was minutely controlled by a modern bureaucracy. By rendering such a process impossible, a "capitulated system" would simply be the opposite of a modernizing system.

The renowned press entrepreneur, intellectual, and occasional statesman, Ahmed İhsan Tokgöz (1868–1942), provides us with different dimensions of the problem as he personally experienced it in various capacities. An interesting and illuminating anecdote from his memoirs shows how the capitulations created unforeseeable problems for Muslim businessmen as well as for the state. The well-known periodical that he published, *Servet-i Fünûn*, was an illustrated journal; and this was rare in the Ottoman press of the time. In 1892, Ahmed İhsan invited an engraver from Paris, Mr Napier, to improve the quality and increase the quantity of the pictures published in the journal.[92] As soon as Napier arrived in Istanbul, he became aware of the extent of the rights and privileges conferred upon him by the capitulations, and he began to spend his time enjoying the various pleasures of Istanbul instead of working.[93] Ahmed İhsan tried to dismiss him, but he could not, because Mr Napier was a French citizen and therefore protected by the capitulations. After a while, Napier began to participate in politics, exploiting his privileges in the empire. Upon hearing of his political activities, Sultan Abdülhamid II intervened. Napier was "persuaded" to leave Istanbul with a decree of the sultan and the payment of a significant amount of money from the government.[94]

After the 1908 Young Turk Revolution, Ahmed İhsan faced the problem of the capitulations again in the capacity of a local administrator. In 1912, he was appointed as the mayor of the Beyoğlu district, which was mostly inhabited by foreigners and non-Muslims. He noted that there was then no systematic knowledge about municipal services in the Ottoman Empire, and no relevant skills, so he decided to implement improvements based upon his observations in Geneva and Vienna.[95] He tried to collect statistics and developed a method for the systematic collection of taxes and the organization of municipal services (like collecting garbage and building pavements). However, serving as the mayor of a district inhabited predominantly by "*levantine*s who claimed to be foreigners" was difficult, because it was almost impossible to make them obey the rules and regulations.[96] Thanks to their legal immunity and support of their embassies, foreign residents and their business enterprises refused to pay taxes. Moreover, they also resisted municipal policies and projects regarding health issues and the spatial reorganization of the streets.[97] The officials of the municipality could not enforce any rules, nor could they fine these people and businesses for breaking the laws.[98] Whenever Ahmed İhsan tried to enforce such plans, he found representatives from the embassies filling his office to protect their citizens' interests.[99]

He also notes, in his memoirs, that corruption was ubiquitous and that foreigners were frequently using it as an instrument to obtain whatever they demanded from municipal officials.[100] One interesting example was a story involving the well-known food products manufacturer, Nestlé. The doctors of the municipality laboratory published a report on Nestlé-brand milk, concluding that this milk did not contain the necessary nutrition for infants. Upon the publication of the report, the Swiss manager of the company complained to the inspector of the municipality—who was also of Swiss nationality—that the doctors who prepared the report demanded 200 gold coins for the "revision and correction" of their findings. Ahmed İhsan intervened and exposed the plot, but while the doctors were sent to prison, he received the "corrected" second report they had prepared before getting caught. The report reads,

> We realized that the word **Nestele** [*sic*] in the report, which was published last week, was misread. There are two dots, not one, on the first letter of this word. In other words, the milk that has insufficient nutritious value does not belong to **Nestele** [نستله], but to **Testele** [تستله]. The Nestele-brand milks are excellent in terms of nutritional content.[101]

Another Young Turk bureaucrat who related similar anecdotes in his memoirs is Tahsin Uzer (1878–1939).[102] Uzer was also appointed as a local administrator (*mutasarrıf*) in the Beyoğlu district (1913), and his accounts of the problems he faced due to the capitulations bear a strong resemblance to those of Ahmed İhsan. Uzer states that this post "showed him what [kind of a problem] the capitulations were and how the [Ottoman] has been reduced [as a result] to nothing but a specter."[103] He confirms Ahmed İhsan's accounts with his own examples of foreign nationals' resistance to official policies as well as taxes, and their de facto immunity because of the capitulations and the intervention of the embassies.[104] "As a result," he states,

> it was impossible for us to achieve success in any of our enterprises. I almost went crazy at times.... I was the governor of Van when the capitulations were abolished [in 1914]. I cannot express the ecstasy that I felt that day.[105]

Yet another prominent Young Turk intellectual, Yakup Kadri Karaosmanoğlu, later depicted the everyday frustration that the capitulations created among Muslim Ottomans in *Bir Sürgün* (An Exile, 1937), a novel in which he tells a story of a self-exiled Young Turk in the Hamidian era.

> The Shadow of God [the Caliph; Abdülhamid II] has to secure his reign with "tightrope politics." I say "secure," but Turkey is a commodity which belongs to the caliph of the Prophet but whose usage rights belong to others. Because Turkey is a country with capitulations. I mean—how shall I put this?—imagine a house. Its title belongs to you or me. But everybody can come and dwell in it and use its furniture as if he/she owns them. However, the owner of the house cannot even complain. He does not have this right, because ... he is capitulated.[106]

Ahmed İhsan argued that although the main reason for economic underdevelopment was the lack of interest, skills, and knowledge for economic enterprise, the capitulations destroyed any attempt to change these conditions. Was it impossible to alter the situation? According to Mizancı Murad Bey, a Young Turk leader of the early 1890s, the Ottomans were persistently told so. Murad Bey maintained that, although everything was constantly changing in nature, society, and politics, European politicians were talking as if this universal rule did not apply to the case of the Ottoman capitulations. Murad Bey, like Ahmed Midhat, complained about the hypocritical behavior of European governments, especially with respect to economic policies.[107] He noted that although Europeans insisted that it was impossible to alter the Ottoman capitulations, they would change similar agreements at will—as France rejected capitulations after losing the Franco-Prussian War.[108] He also argued that other European countries would make necessary changes in their customs regulations and other economic policies according to their fiscal and economic needs, and that everybody regarded such changes as normal. Then he asked why the Ottoman case was considered differently and why the Ottomans were denied the most basic right to determine their own economic policies according to their own interests.[109] He also complained that allegedly "immature ideas" about the inalterability of the capitulations system had been "tiring the ears of the Ottomans" since the beginning of the Tanzimat;[110] and he asserted that the powerful Sultan (i.e., Abdülhamid II) would eventually change this gloomy picture.[111] Nevertheless, neither the sultan nor the post-Hamidian Young Turk governments would live up to his hopes. Even as he expected the solution from the sultan, Abdülhamid II himself was despairingly complaining about the same situation:

> If we had the power, we could abolish the capitulations gradually, and we could change the customs agreements. We could use this power to temper the harmful privileges granted to the foreigners to the extent that their existence could not be felt. The reputation of the country would be improved;

> and they [the foreigners] could not interfere in our internal and external affairs. The state could act more easily.
>
> However, today if a Muslim and an Armenian fight on the street, a translator [of an embassy] will interfere right away. When we ask, "These are both subjects of [this] state, what right do you have to interfere?" They respond by saying, "*el-hükmü li-men gâlebe*" (might is right).[112]

In short, the capitulations rendered the modernization efforts rather fruitless in its economic as well as political and legal aspects. From Muslim entrepreneurs to local and central statesmen, Muslim Ottomans experienced the capitulations as impeding many efforts at modernization, thereby eroding hopes for change. Although late Ottoman economic thought was never dominated by autarkist and mercantilist views, the existence of the capitulations and other privileges for foreigners paved the way for a defensive economic nationalism, which tended towards more protectionist policies if not total isolation from the world market.

It would be ideal to complement the above discussion of economic development with an analysis of the actual economic policies of the era. But, we still lack a comprehensive study on the economic development policies of the Hamidian regime,[113] and an attempt to fill this void would exceed the scope of the current study. We do know, however, that the Hamidian government—following the global trend resulting partly from the chronic financial and economic crises of the Long Depression (1873–96)—tended to pursue more protectionist policies starting in the 1890s.[114] Moreover, we have access to Abdülhamid II's personal views on the Ottoman economy within the context of his modernization efforts.

The economy according to the sultan

Abdülhamid II studied political economy with Münif Pasha and was interested in global as well as domestic economic and financial issues.[115] In addition to following Ottoman and European periodicals, he requested numerous memoranda from his retinue on a wide variety of topics.[116] As for his own views on economic matters, the best sources are the notes and memoranda he dictated about social, political, and economic issues.[117] The majority of these memoranda pertain to political matters, from diplomatic relations with European countries to internal problems such as independence movements within the empire. Nevertheless, in these documents we can also see references to the economic aspects of these problems or passing references to the economic and financial difficulties of the empire. Moreover, in addition to his memoranda on general financial and economic matters, we find interesting references to specific issues, such as improving horse and cattle breeding in the empire.[118] A close reading of such memoranda shows Abdülhamid II's rather systematic concern with the question of economic development and the main obstacles to development of the Ottoman economy.

Corruption, bureaucracy, morality, and economic development

Abdülhamid II was aware that he was a ruler in an economy-centered age. Domestic social and political stability, and the international status of the empire were determined by economic factors.

> To the Sultan, the development of the economy meant, above all, the availability of greater financial resources with which to conduct the government's business, but he also viewed it as a means of assuring the loyalty of the population to the state. He believed that an economically prosperous nation (*memleket*) kept in peace and order by an effective, efficient and benevolent government would certainly improve the international position and prestige of the Ottoman state.[119]

He was also fully aware that the situation was far from an ideal one in this context. In a memorandum written in 1888,[120] Abdülhamid II complains about "the difficult situation, and the material and spiritual problems of the state and country, which have been known to everybody for years."[121] He summarizes the economic and financial hardships that the empire had long been suffering and the consequences of the attempts to solve these problems:

> As a natural result of large amounts of borrowing, and consequently, the allocation of state revenues to the capital and interest payments of these debts, the state has gone through a serious financial crisis. This situation has created the most disheartening consequences by rendering the payment of civil servants' paychecks and the procurement of the most basic needs of the state impossible. In order to ameliorate these conditions with the means at hand and to compensate for the lost revenues [due to the loss of territories] by other means, many concessions were given on the wealth resources of the country such as forests and mines, roads, and other agricultural and commercial resources. The government has repeatedly warned [those who received concessions], reminding them of the necessity of watching over the financial interests and the prestige of the government and the Ministry of Finance when using these resources. Nevertheless, for some reason, either due to the unskillfulness and incompetence of the concession holders or the inability of these resources to guarantee the expected profits, these concessions did not provide the expected beneficial results. There have been complaints about the financial crisis, but no one could provide any satisfactory and practical solutions to the causes of these shortages and crises.[122]

Abdülhamid II goes on to put forth his own explanations of economic problems with references to conditions in some former territories of the empire. He argues that the Ottoman state had showed no success even in maintaining order and stability in regions such as Bulgaria, Bosnia and Herzegovina, and Crete, yet the same territories showed obvious signs of progress and affluence after gaining their autonomy. Not only did these regions—under the Ottoman rule—had failed to contribute any taxes to the central government, they had been sucking up large sums from the central budget for security reasons as well as for local public services. In other words, these territories had become a burden on the state budget despite their rich natural resources. As newly independent governments, however, they used the same resources not only to procure order and stability but also for economic development and increasing military power.[123]

> Upon seeing these achievements of diligence and progress in these aforementioned provinces and considering that we could have achieved the same progress easily with some effort and labor, it is impossible not to feel deeply sad and not to deplore the reasons for this situation.[124]

Although he does not openly suggest any specific reasons, his long conclusion about the behavior of Ottoman officials implies a well-known culprit: the inefficiency and corruption of the Ottoman bureaucracy.

He complains about civil servants who do not fulfill their responsibilities towards their sultan, state, and religion. He argues that this is because some of these people have lost their belief in imperial institutions and expect solutions to arrive from the foreign powers.[125] In another note, he puts the question of "the loss of belief in the empire" and its consequences more explicitly:

> Another distressing situation is that many high level Ottoman officials ... have lost their belief in the eternity of the Ottoman Empire. Therefore, they do not concern themselves with the future of the empire any more, and instead waste their time with enjoying themselves [instead of working]. As a result of their [idleness], they become prone to various sorts of corruption and embezzlement. This situation impoverishes not only the state's finances, but also the people and the country.[126]

The sultan notes that such people are particularly prevalent in the Christian communities, and that they try to tie their interests to those of the European powers. He maintains that this leads both to foreign interventions that weaken state authority and to independence movements that could eventually dissolve the empire.[127] According to Abdülhamid II, loyal and honest citizens must follow two principles: first, to give priority to the territorial integrity of the empire; and second, to channel efforts towards the empire-wide endeavor to increase wealth and prosperity.[128] Otherwise, he concludes, the state could lose its independence and perish under foreign domination:

> Conditions in the country are pressing. Its financial affairs are complicated. State revenues are insufficient; and we cannot benefit fully from our sources of wealth. The only important source at hand is the customs dues; but when they are allocated to the repayment of debts, the state loses all of its [financial] resources. The foreign powers are seeking opportunities for intervention in

> our internal affairs by using all sorts of means. Besides, they might demand (God forbid) the establishment of an international commission, just as they did in Egypt, by asserting that since they have control over the resources of state revenues, they want a more efficient management of these resources. They might thereby achieve their goals by taking over the [political] administration of the country. The huge dangers and disasters that such a situation might cause are obvious to everyone.[129]

Complaining, once again, about how the Ottomans could not take advantage of their rich natural resources, whereas "the foreigners can exploit the benefits even of dry stones,"[130] he finally comes to the core of the matter:

> Foreigners are accusing [our] civil servants of corruption. Such unpleasant remarks circulate among government officials and the [ordinary] people, and finally they reach the foreigners and are published in their newspapers and travelogues.... Recently, an anecdote has attracted attention from among many other claims and accusations in the travelogues of French travelers that were published during the term of the French Ambassador Marquis de Noailles. According to this anecdote, [certain] travelers request the Ambassador to intervene in order to keep their luggage immune from Ottoman customs control when they are leaving the country. The response of the Ambassador is as follows: "You need neither any [official] permission and privilege nor any favor from me to do it. Here, things work with bribes. Just give the customs officers a little tip, and they will not touch your luggage."[131]

Abdülhamid II complains that the ubiquitous corruption of the Ottoman bureaucracy paves the way for serious threats to the security and wealth of the empire. He argues that some people can take gems and other valuables out of the empire and smuggle weapons and other sorts of dangerous items into the country. Therefore, he concludes, corruption and irresponsibility due to low morale among the Ottoman government officials cause serious material losses, thereby constituting the main obstacle to the wealth of the country.[132]

According to the sultan's adviser Müşir Şakir Pasha, (1838–99), the main reason for corruption was inadequate and irregular paychecks to civil servants due to cash shortages. He adds that Ottoman officials abused their positions and powers simply to make ends meet. Şakir Pasha concludes that solving the payroll problem was an issue of vital significance in both political and economic terms.[133]

In his search for solutions to these problems in bureaucracy, Abdülhamid II turns again to education. He gives the example of schools and other public services provided within the Christian communities, especially focusing on the wealth they create out of limited resources through strong community cooperation.[134] To put these arguments in a context, we can refer to specific examples—which testify to the sultan's complaints—in Şerafeddin Mağmumi's

(1869–1927) travel notes about the villages of Bursa (*c.*1892). Şerafeddin Mağmumi compares public schools with those founded independently by Christian communities. He observes that Muslim villages had some run-down buildings, which were ("allegedly") schools bearing the name of the sultan,[135] whereas Christian villages possessed well-established modern schools wherein competent teachers taught in well-organized classrooms.[136]

As a response to these circumstances, Abdülhamid II suggests an overall education reform. His words in this context demonstrates obvious economic concerns behind Hamidian-era education policies:

> The curricula of our schools are not effective in sowing the seeds of love for religion, sultan, and motherland in the minds of our students. The evil tricks of our enemies prevent them from distinguishing good from evil. The state spends huge amounts on [existing] schools and for extending universal education throughout the country. Yet [students graduate with] inadequate and impractical knowledge and skills. Moreover, [despite all efforts and investments] the number of honest, upright, and knowledgeable graduates from our [state] schools is still lower than that of the graduates of the Christian schools.
>
> The government needs a strong system that will secure improvements in the living standards of civil servants. By designing and building such a system, we should get rid of the insolence of some civil servants—a result of immoral character and a tendency to treason—that evil-minded and malicious foreigners have observed. Such a system will bring about an efficient administration of the judicial, security, fiscal, and political establishment. It will also help us to prevent corruption and benefit from industry and the wealth of the country to the utmost extent, thereby improving the reputation, prestige, and honor of the government and regaining its financial credibility. It would also pave the way for a total reform of the bureaucracy by [following the principle of] assigning officials to specific tasks, rather than creating [futile] tasks for [redundant] personnel. We should also make sure that only qualified, patriotic, and meritorious people are employed, and that ranks and orders are bestowed upon only those who truly deserve them.[137]

Obviously, the sultan suggests that Muslims should be well-educated in moral and patriotic values as well as professional skills. Therefore, as this document clearly suggests, Abdülhamid II considered the issue of morality not only as a matter of religious and spiritual values, but more importantly as a central pillar of economic development. By the promotion of (religious) morality, he aimed at eliminating corruption and inefficiency in the state administration, thereby preventing the waste of domestic resources. In other words, according to the sultan, the education of moral, faithful, educated, and skillful bureaucrats and citizens was the prerequisite for economic development. This shows us that the emphasis on morality in the Hamidian education system was not merely a result of the sultan's so-called Islamist ideology.[138] Morality was an essential component of

Hamidian efforts for modernization, with its political, social, and especially economic implications.

Regarding the question of patriotism in the context of development, it is important to note in passing that as Abdülhamid II presented himself to his subjects as an example for industriousness and hard work,[139] he also pioneered in nationalistic consumer behavior. Ahmed Midhat Efendi praises the sultan's (economic) patriotism which manifested itself in his personal life as well. He argues that "the principle reason for the decline of the national wealth was the demand for foreign goods," and that the sultan was aware of this obvious fact. As a result, he adds, the sultan ordered his clothes to be made of locally produced cloth (at the *Feshane-i Âmire*), and he encouraged his retinue to do the same.[140]

Reasons of underdevelopment: mistakes of the past governments, and foreign intervention

Another important document dating from 1895 was written directly to Münif Pasha after an interesting conversation between the pasha and the sultan.[141] According to the document, Münif Pasha criticizes the sultan for ignoring advice from the "doctors" (Ottoman statesmen) for curing the economic and social ills of the "patient" (the Ottoman Empire). The pasha maintains that in recent decades, Russia, Germany, and Austria have made great progress and joined the great powers of Europe, despite having once been "insignificant" countries, while the Ottoman Empire has remained backward, especially in terms of industry and agriculture. The sultan, in his written response to these arguments, analyzes the situation like an economic historian and deals with the issues in detail with their multiple dimensions. First, he criticizes the unsuccessful economic policies of the Tanzimat-era governments (including those of Âlî, Fuad, and Midhat Pashas) and the resulting financial and economic failure. He asserts that his uncle, Sultan Abdülaziz, had listened to these "doctors" without questioning their abilities and judgments, just as Münif Pasha recommends to him.[142] However, he notes, the result was nothing but bankruptcy, corruption, and the failure in economic development.[143]

This criticism, but more interestingly, the "doctors" analogy is another striking reminder of Akçuraoğlu Yusuf's note about Abdülhamid II being a student of the Young Ottoman ideology. In 1872, when Abdülhamid II was still a relatively liberal-minded prince and in good terms with the Young Ottomans, the well-known Young-Ottoman periodical of the era, *İbret*, published an article on the empire's debt problem. The author, Reşad Bey, criticizes the late Fuad Pasha's words, "this state cannot live without debt," using the "doctors" analogy in the same manner as Abdülhamid II would do later. Reşad Bey argues that even if this "prescription" were correct, considering that the state had actually lived without debt for centuries before the coming of this doctor (Fuad Pasha), it seems that the sickness was caused by the very doctor who prescribed it.[144]

Returning to Abdülhamid II's views, he further argues that as a result of excessive borrowing under these "doctors," the state plunged into debt to the extent that it became handicapped and its revenues were all funneled directly to the repayment of loans and interest. Interestingly enough, having suggested that the aforementioned statesmen embezzled huge amounts of money, he criticizes them not for this malpractice itself but rather for not being able to keep their wealth—acquired through misappropriation—within their families. More specifically, he criticizes them for entrusting their money to non-Muslim bankers, thereby giving these bankers the chance to deny the existence of these sums of money upon the death of these pashas, which they did. He goes on to state that if this wealth had remained within these families, they could have used the money to establish financial institutions to give credit to local merchants and farmers. In other words, the sultan overlooks corruption, but he does not forgive the imprudence that caused the outflow of domestic resources that could have been used for economic development.[145]

Regarding the question of industrialization, Abdülhamid II notes the imperialist strategies adopted by the European powers against Ottoman industry in order to make sure that they maintain their monopoly over the empire's industry and trade.[146] He mentions a domestic industrial enterprise, a glass factory, which was dragged into bankruptcy by an Austrian plot. He argues that although the factory managed to produce and sell glass panels at a very low price, the Austrians sold the same product at even a lower price and at a loss until the Ottoman factory fell victim to this cut-throat competition.[147] He adds that as long as the existing obstacles to economic development (such as low customs duties and privileges for foreign companies) continue to haunt domestic producers, it is not possible to avoid continuing failure.[148] He then summarizes his efforts at economic development, such as the construction of roads and railroad, which provide farmers with the means to put their produce on the market. He concludes that the accusations of the pasha are quite unfair, considering the change in the economic situation of the empire and in the state administration during his rule.

Finally, it is possible to bring out a few distinct features of Abdülhamid II's economic thinking to have a general sense of the official economic mindset that shaped the final decades of the Ottoman Empire. First, he was fully aware of the history of the Tanzimat-era Ottoman economy and its problems in detail. Second, he adopted an anti-imperialist and Muslim-Ottoman nationalist perspective to economic matters. The tone of his arguments reflects a sense of realism in acknowledging the problems of the empire, from bureaucratic corruption to economic underdevelopment. Moreover, he suggested critical analyses and practical solutions for these issues rather than simply brushing them over. Third, he followed external developments, seeking to derive lessons from other countries' experiences for his own country (e.g., his above-mentioned note on the international commission in Egypt and a similar danger for the Ottoman Empire). Fourth, having inherited burdensome financial and economic difficulties from his uncle Sultan Abdülaziz and his brother Murad, he gave priority to economic development, while assessing other (e.g., educational, political, and diplomatic) issues from this perspective. As an example, he would frequently refer to "the wealth and prosperity of the country and the people" in his memoranda, the topics of which range from diplomacy with European countries to internal security. Finally, it is also worth noting that if we compare his economic discourse with that of the Young Turks, who struggled against Hamidian rule, the two actually seem almost identical except in some details. The economic policy of the Young Turks after the 1908 Revolution also followed the general program that their arch-enemy had already started. This is perhaps not a very surprising conclusion, since the political and economic mindsets of both parties were products of the same age and same economic conditions and concerns.

Conclusion

The question of economic development in the late nineteenth century was tightly connected to the question of civilization. In this context, Ottoman protectionists in particular—from the Young Ottomans to the Young Turks—warned policymakers of the danger of remaining a "barbaric" (non-industrialized) nation. This emphasis on the urgency of industrialization stood in contrast to liberals' emphasis on accepting the role assigned to the Ottoman economy as an agricultural economy within the international division of labor. It is worth noting, however, that the protectionists defended neither autarky nor isolation. Seeking to join the so-called "civilized" nations of the age, they too promoted integration into the global market, but with a more protectionist and proto-nationalist strategy in the short-run.

Economic protectionism went hand-in-hand with the emergence of Muslim-Turkish nationalism in the late nineteenth century. Muslim intellectuals in particular reacted negatively to the increasing dominance of European capital in the Ottoman economy. As the non-Muslim subjects of the Ottoman Empire became the local partners and representatives of European capital, Muslim-Ottoman economic nationalism began to rise at the expense of a more inclusive Ottoman identity. The dominant European discourse on the incompatibility of Islam and civilization also contributed to the dissolution of the bonds of Ottomanism, as this discourse led Muslims to develop a defensive modernization project that sought to prove the feasibility of a modern Muslim nation. In short, the intellectual pillars of Muslim-Turkish economic nationalism in the late Ottoman context were based on concerns regarding civilization, economic development and the avoidance of peripheralization.

Hamidian-era economic policies still await detailed analysis. Nevertheless, we do know that the sultan himself entertained protectionist ideas and supported the promotion of such ideas in the Ottoman public sphere. His protectionist attitude was not merely a theoretical inference. His government's efforts (at both the local and central levels) for economic development were rendered fruitless by the continuous foreign intervention in economic and political matters as well as the aggressive strategies of European companies. Nevertheless, despite his active involvement in supporting protectionist ideas, the capitulations and foreign dominance in the economic and political spheres limited his control over the economy at the policy level. As a result, he simply waited—or rather hoped—for the coming of the right time and conditions for abolishing all such external obstacles. Interestingly enough, it would be his arch-enemies, the Young Turks, who would find the opportunity to launch effective assaults on these obstacles through their National Economy program in the post-1908 era.

Notes

1 *Hakayık el-Vaka'i* (614), 7 Cemaziyelevvel 1289 [July 13, 1872]; quoted in Galib Haldun, "Tanzimat Devrinde Neşriyat-ı İktisadiye," *İktisadiyat Mecmuası* 37 (1916), 4.
2 Nassau W. Senior, *A Journal Kept in Turkey and Greece in the Autumn of 1857, and the Beginning of 1858* (London: Longman Brown Green Longmans and Roberts, 1859), 87.
3 Ibid., 138.
4 See, for example, Namık Kemal, "Avrupa Şarkı Bilmez," *İbret* 7 (1872), 2; and following Kemal (in terms of the title, as well as the main idea), Ebüzziya [Tevfik], "Avrupa Şarkı Bilmez," *Mecmua-i Ebüzziya* 49 (1886), 1551–52. Ebüzziya Tevfik added the translation of a short essay from a French newspaper to provide an example of European ignorance of the Orient (Ibid., 1552–3).
5 For Slade's views about the Ottoman Empire, see Bernard Lewis, "Slade on Turkey," in *Islam in History: Ideas, People, and Events in the Middle East*, New Edition, Revised and Expanded. (Chicago: Open Court, 1993), 67–83.
6 Ibid., 69.
7 Such ideas can be observed in almost every memoir or travelogue written by nineteenth-century Europeans. Senior's accounts are a good example as they convey both his personal views and the arguments of other Europeans whom he met during his time in the Ottoman Empire. See for example, Senior, *A Journal*, 28–32, *et passim*.
8 Wayne Dowler, "The Intelligentsia and Capitalism," in *A History of Russian Thought*, ed. William Leatherbarrow and Derek Offord (Cambridge University Press, 2010), 268–9; Margherita Zanasi, *Saving the Nation: Economic Modernity in Republican China* (Chicago: University Of Chicago Press, 2006).
9 Friedrich Engels, "Preface," in Karl Marx, *Free Trade: A Speech Delivered before the Democratic Club, Brussels, Belgium, Jan 9, 1848*, translated by F.K. Wishnewetsky (Boston: Lee and Shephard Publishers, 1888), 3–24.
10 Ibid., 4. In the Ottoman case, the Anglo-Ottoman Commercial Convention of 1838 opened Ottoman markets to British capital and manufactures.
11 Friedrich Engels, "Preface," 5.
12 Ibid., 6.
13 Ibid., 9.
14 Ibid.
15 Senior, *A Journal*, 44. For other similar accounts, see M.A. Ubicini, *Letters on Turkey: An Account of the Religious, Political, Social, and Commercial Condition of the Ottoman Empire, the Reformed Institutions, Army, Navy, Etc., Etc*, trans. Lady Easthope (London: John Murray, 1856), and David Urquhart, *Turkey and Its Resources: Its Municipal Organization and Free Trade, the State and Prospects of English Commerce in the East, the New Administration of Greece, Its Revenue and National Possessions* (London: Saunders and Otley, 1833).
16 See Urquhart, *Turkey and Its Resources*, as the best formulation of this view. For an analysis of British efforts to open the Ottoman and Chinese economies to free trade, see Reşat Kasaba, "Treaties and Friendships: British Imperialism, the Ottoman Empire, and China in the Nineteenth Century," *Journal of World History* 4, no. 2 (1993), 215–41.

17 Stanford J. Shaw, *Between Old and New: the Ottoman Empire under Sultan Selim III, 1789–1807* (Cambridge, Harvard University Press, 1971), 138–44.
18 Clark, "The Ottoman Industrial Revolution," 67.
19 Tevfik Güran, *19. Yüzyıl Osmanlı Tarımı Üzerine Araştırmalar* (İstanbul: Eren, 1998), 45.
20 For more information on the Commission, see Onur Yıldırım, "The Industrial Reform Commission as an Institutional Innovation During the Tanzimat," *Arab Historical Review for Ottoman Studies* 17–18 (1998), 117–26. Also see Vedat Eldem, *Osmanlı İmparatorluğu'nun İktisadi Şartları Hakkında Bir Tetkik* (Ankara: Türk Tarih Kurumu, 1994), 58–66.
21 Edward C. Clark, "The Ottoman Industrial Revolution," *IJMES* vol. 5, no. 1 (1974), 71–2. Namık Kemal suggests another dimension of the matter by stating that the Tanzimat governments pursued *laissez faire*-style policies at a time when traditional Ottoman industries were in decline and thus incapable of coping with international competition (Kemal, [untitled article] *Hürriyet* 7 [1868], 2).
22 For the full texts of these documents in modern Turkish, see Engin D. Akarlı, *Belgelerle Tanzimat: Osmanlı Sadrıazamlarından Âli ve Fuad Paşaların Siyasî Vasiyyetnâmeleri* (İstanbul: Boğaziçi Üniversitesi, 1978). For an economic analysis of the testaments, see Tevfık Çavdar, *Türkiye'de Liberalizmin Doğuşu* (İstanbul: Uygarlık Yayınları, 1982), 47–62.
23 Akarlı, *Belgelerle Tanzimat*, 25.
24 Ibid., 25.
25 Ibid., 31.
26 For more information on the company, see Eser Tütel, *Şirket-i Hayriye* (Istanbul: İletişim Yayınları, 1994).
27 Tevfik Çavdar, *Türkiye Ekonomisinin Tarihi, 1900–1960* (Ankara: İmge Kitabevi, 2003), 21.
28 Donald Quataert, *Social Disintegration and Popular Resistance in the Ottoman Empire, 1881–1908: Reactions to European Economic Penetration* (New York: New York University Press, 1983), 150.
29 Fatma Aliye, *Ahmed Cevdet Paşa ve Zamanı* (Dersaadet [İstanbul]: Kana'at Matbaası, R. 1332 [1914]), 57–8.
30 For specific examples as well as overall analyses of the failure of Ottoman industrialization efforts in the Tanzimat era, see Ömer Celâl Sarc, "Tanzimat ve Sanayiimiz," in *Tanzimat: Yüzüncü Yıldönümü Münasebetile* (İstanbul: Maarif Matbaası, 1940), 423–40; Rıfat Önsoy, *Tanzimat Dönemi Osmanlı Sanayii ve Sanayileşme Politikası* (Türkiye İş Bankası Kültür Yayınları, 1988).
31 Ahmet İnsel, "Milliyetçilik ve Kalkınmacılık," in *Modern Türkiye'de Siyasi Düşünce 4 – Milliyetçilik*, ed. Tanıl Bora, vol. 4 (İstanbul: İletişim, 2002), 763.
32 Şerif Mardin, *Jön Türklerin Siyasi Fikirleri, 1895–1908* (İstanbul: İletişim Yayınları, 2004), 31.
33 As an example to this continuation, a prominent Young Turk, Ebüzziya Tevfik published the works of Namık Kemal in his *Mecmua-i Ebüzziya*, including his "Sa'y" (*Mecmua-i Ebüzziya* 9 [1880], 267–72) and other economic writings. Meanwhile, Ebüzziya Tevfik was also serializing a translation of Benjamin Franklin's *The Way to Wealth*. At the end of Kemal's article, "Sa'y," Ebüzziya Tevfik inserted an addendum wherein he compared both works. He maintains that Kemal's work is a combination of imagination, which is generally attributed to the East, and philosophy, which is attributed to the West. Yet he defines Franklin's work as resembling Eastern thinking, i.e., dominated by imagination. (Ibid., 276).
34 Akçuraoğlu Yusuf, *Üç Tarz-ı Siyaset* (İstanbul: Kader Matbaası, 1911), 8.
35 Nazan Çiçek, *The Young Ottomans: Turkish Critics of the Eastern Question in the Late Nineteenth Century* (London: Tauris Academic Studies, 2010), 173–236.
36 Coşkun Çakır attributes this article to Ziya Pasha, see Çakır, *Osmanlı Maliyesi*, 183.

37 (Untitled), *Hürriyet* 42 (April 12, 1869), 7–8. This is a long article which was serialized in *Hürriyet* starting from number 25 (December 14, 1868). The journal presents the article as the memoirs of "a person from among the Young Ottomans" (*"Yeni Osmanlılar'dan bir zât*").
38 For various examples, see Elisabeth Jay and Richard Jay, eds., *Critics of Capitalism: Victorian Criticism of "Political Economy"* (Cambridge: Cambridge University Press, 1986).
39 In this respect, he was one of the earliest anti-consumerist critics of capitalism. For Möser's biography and criticism of industrialization, see Jerry Z. Muller, *The Mind and the Market: Capitalism in Modern European Thought* (New York: Alfred A. Knopf, 2002), 83–103.
40 Muller, *The Mind and the Market*, 97. For Möser's critique of the market economy's destructive impact on local cultures, see ibid., 95–8.
41 We observe the emergence of anti-capitalism as an offshoot of economic nationalism in some other peripheral countries. For the Rumanian case, for example, see Michalis M. Psalidopoulos and Nicholas J. Theocarakis, "The Dissemination of Economic Thought in South-Eastern Europe in the Nineteenth Century," in *The Dissemination of Economic Ideas* (Cheltenham, UK: Edward Elgar, 2011), 170–1.
42 List too complains about the British imports that ruined his country's (Germany's) industry. (W.O. Henderson, *Friedrich List, Economist and Visionary, 1789–1846* (London: F. Cass, 1983), 144.). Nonetheless, his answer was never anti-capitalist, nor does he promote a perpetually closed economic system.
43 [Namık] Kemal, (untitled article) *Hürriyet* 7 (1868), 1. Before Namık Kemal, Mehmed Şerif Efendi protested the same assumption in his article in *Tercüman-ı Ahval*, which he wrote to defend the industrialization of the Ottoman Empire; see his "Sanayi' ve Ziraatden Kangısının Hakkımızda Hayırlı Olduğuna Dairdir," *Tercüman-ı Ahval* 68 and 69 (1861).
44 Kemal, (untitled article) *Hürriyet* 7 (1868), 2.
45 Ibid.
46 Ibid., 3.
47 Ibid.
48 Ali Suâvi, *Le Mukhbir* 2 (1867): 2–3, 8; quoted in Çakır, *Tanzimat Dönemi Osmanlı Maliyesi*, 185.
49 Suâvi, "Memalik-i Osmaniye'de Ticaret," *Ulûm* 12 (1869), 735; quoted in İsmail Doğan, *Tanzimatın İki Ucu: Münif Paşa ve Ali Suavi: Sosyo-Pedagojik Bir Karşılaştırma* (İstanbul: İz Yayıncılık, 1991), 295.
50 Doğan, *Tanzimatın İki Ucu*, 296.
51 Cf. Ahmed Midhat's arguments below.
52 "Ticaret," *İbret* 22 (1872), 1.
53 Mardin, *Jön Türkler*, 36.
54 Ibid., 149–50.
55 For echoes of these ideas in the Turkish-Cypriot press of the era, see Martin Strohmeier, "Economic Issues in the Turkish-Cypriot Press (1891–1931)," in *The Economy as an Issue in the Middle Eastern Press*, ed. Gisela Procházka-Eisl and Martin Strohmeier (Vienna: Lit Verlag, 2008), 171–85.
56 Hilmi Kâmil Bayur, *Sadrazam Kâmil Paşa: Siyasî Hayatı* (Ankara: Sanat Basımevi, 1954), 58, 79–80.
57 Selçuk Akşin Somel, *The Modernization of Public Education in the Ottoman Empire, 1839–1908: Islamization, Autocracy, and Discipline* (Leiden: Brill, 2001), 174–5.
58 For the reversal of the relationship between economic and political power in the modern age, see Polanyi, *The Great Transformation*, 46, et passim. For the relevance of Polanyi's argument in the case of the Tanzimat reforms as they "reversed the relationship between the political and economic domains of power," see Özveren, "Economic Agents," 13.

59 Gellner, *Nations and Nationalism* (Ithaca: Cornell University Press, 1983), 103. Timur Kuran provides a brief overview of the rise of Ottoman non-Muslims' economic power in the nineteenth century and the corresponding resentment of the Muslim elite; see Timur Kuran, *The Long Divergence: How Islamic Law Held Back the Middle East* (Princeton: Princeton University Press, 2011), 189–208.
60 Arminius Vambéry, *The Story of My Struggles: The Memoirs of Arminius Vambéry*, Third Impression. (London: T. Fisher Unwin, 1905), 385.
61 For the earlier phases of this process, see Bruce Masters, *The Origins of Western Economic Dominance in the Middle East: Mercantilism and the Islamic Economy in Aleppo, 1600–1750* (New York: New York University Press, 1988).
62 Mardin, *Jön Türkler*, 154.
63 Ibid.
64 *Osmanli, Supplément Français*, March 10, 1898; quoted in Mardin, *Jön Türkler*, 155.
65 For examples of "Ottomanist" economic patriotism in the Arab press in the late nineteenth century, see Strohmeier, "Economic Issues."
66 A. Holly Shissler, *Between Two Empires: Ahmet Ağaoğlu and the New Turkey* (London: I.B. Tauris, 2003), 7.
67 For political historical analyses of the Hamidian-era roots of Turkish nationalism, see David Kushner, *The Rise of Turkish Nationalism, 1876–1908* (London: Frank Cass, 1977); M. Şükrü Hanioğlu, "Turkish Nationalism and the Young Turks,1889–1908," in *Social Constructions of Nationalism in the Middle East*, ed. F.M. Göçek (Albany, NY: State University of New York Press, 2002), 85–97.
68 Mardin, *Jön Türkler*, 114.
69 Ibid.
70 Mehmed Murad, *Turfanda mı, Turfa mı?* (İstanbul: Mahmud Bey Matbaası, 1890).
71 Ahmed Midhat, *Ahmed Metin ve Şirzad* (Istanbul: Tercüman-ı Hakikat Matbaası, 1892), 1.
72 Başbakanlık Osmanlı Arşivi, Y. MTV., 28/ZA/1311 (March 6, 1894), 96/98. (For a transliterated copy of the petition see Şahmurad Arık, "'*Ahmed Metin ve Şirzad'* Romanının Sultan II. Abdülhamid'e Takdimi ve Bir Maruzat," *Atatürk Üniversitesi Türkiyat Araştırmaları Enstitüsü Dergisi* (35), 2007, 161–2.
73 Jale Parla, "Rakım Efendi'den Nurullah Bey'e Cemaatçi Osmanlılıktan Cemiyetçi Türk. Milliyetçiliğine Ahmet Mithat'ın Romancılığı," in *Merhaba Ey Muharrir!: Ahmet Mithat Üzerine Eleştirel Yazılar*, ed. Nüket Esen and Erol Köroğlu (İstanbul: Boğaziçi Üniversitesi Yayınevi, 2006), 17–51.
74 Vambéry, *The Story of My Struggles*, 353.
75 Ibid.
76 Ahmed Midhat, *Ekonomi Politik* (İstanbul: Kırkanbar Matbaası, 1879), 116.
77 Ibid., 117.
78 Ziad Fahmy, *Ordinary Egyptians: Creating the Modern Nation through Popular Culture* (Stanford: Stanford University Press, 2011), 78.
79 Ahmed Midhat, *Ekonomi Politik*, 120–2.
80 Ibid., 119.
81 Hüseyin Cahid Yalçın, *Edebî Hatıralar* (İstanbul: Akşam Kitabhanesi, 1935), 100.
82 Margaret Stevens Hoell, "The Ticaret Odasi: Origins, Functions, and Activities of the Chamber of Commerce of Istanbul, 1885–1899" (Ohio State University, 1974), 69.
83 N. N. "Turkey's Opportunity," *The Levant Herald*, August 23, 1886.
84 Ahmed Midhat, *Ekonomi Politik*, 119.
85 Ibid., 119.
86 Ibid., 134.
87 Ibid., 134–5.
88 Feroz Ahmad, "Ottoman Perceptions of the Capitulations 1800–1914," *Journal of Islamic Studies* 11, no. 1 (2000): 6.

89 Ibid., 9.
90 See Engin D. Akarlı, "Economic Policy and Budgets in Ottoman Turkey, 1876–1909," *Middle Eastern Studies*, vol. 28, no. 3 (1992), 455–6.
91 G. Bie Ravndal, "Capitulations," in *The Modern Turkey: A Politico-Economic Interpretation, 1908–1923 inclusive, with Selected Chapters by Representative Authorities*, ed. E.G. Mears (New York: The Macmillan Company, 1924), 433.
92 Ahmed İhsan, *Matbuat Hatıralarım*, vol. 1: 76.
93 Ibid., 77.
94 Ibid.
95 Ahmed İhsan, *Matbuat Hatıralarım*, vol. 2: 134.
96 Ibid., 134. *Levanten* (originally *Levantine*) is the name given to the non-Muslims especially of the Ottoman port cities who were involved in international business. The term began to be used frequently during the Tanzimat era.
97 Ibid.
98 Ibid., 141.
99 Ibid.
100 Ibid., 143. See the sultan's similar arguments below.
101 Ibid., 150 (Emphasis in the original).
102 Tahsin Uzer, *Makedonya Eşkiyalık Tarihi ve Son Osmanlı Yönetimi* (Ankara: Türk Tarih Kurumu Yayınları, 1979).
103 Ibid., 325.
104 Ibid., 325–9.
105 Ibid., 328–9. Also see Ahmed Cevdet Pasha's similar complaints about the capitulations and the power of the embassies in his accounts, based on his experiences as a central as well as a provincial administrator: Ahmed Cevdet Paşa, *Ma'rûzât*, ed. Yusuf Halaçoğlu (İstanbul: Çağrı Yayınları, 1980), 194–6.
106 Yakup Kadri Karaosmanoğlu, *Bir Sürgün* (İstanbul: İletişim Yayınları, 1987), 200–1.
107 "İmtiyazat-ı Ecnebiye" (Privileges of the Foreigners), *Mizan* 48 (1888): 425.
108 Ibid.
109 Ibid.
110 Ibid., 424.
111 "Müdahelat-ı Ecnebiyeyi Men' İçün En Kısa Tarik," *Mizan* 34 (1887): 279.
112 Abdülhamid II, *Devlet ve Memleket Görüşlerim*, ed. A. Alâaddin Çetin and Ramazan Yıldız (İstanbul: Çığır Yayınları, 1976), 297–8.
113 For a broad-brush examination of Hamidian era economic policies and Abdülhamid II's personal influence on them, see Mehmet Aslanoğlu, "II. Abdülhamid'in İktisadi ve Mali Politikalar Üzerindeki Etkisi," *Toplumsal Tarih*, no. 63 (1999): 25–32. For an analysis of Hamidian economic policies focusing on the problem of budget deficits, see Engin D. Akarlı, "Economic Policy and Budgets in Ottoman Turkey, 1876–1909," *Middle Eastern Studies* 28, no. 3 (1992): 443–76. Akarlı's PhD dissertation provides us with a richer analysis in this context, see Engin Deniz Akarlı, "The Problems of External Pressures, Power Struggle and Budgetary Deficits in Ottoman Politics under Abdulhamid II (1876–1909): Origins and Solutions" (unpublished PhD Dissertation, Princeton University, 1976). For a study on Ottoman fiscal policies during the Hamidian era, see Ö. Faruk Bölükbaşı, *Tezyid-i Varidat ve Tenkih-i Masarifat: II. Abdülhamid Döneminde Mali İdare* (İstanbul: Osmanlı Bankası Arşiv ve Araştırma Merkezi, 2005).
114 Akyiğitzade Musa Bey, in his 1896 book, applauds the Ottoman policy-makers for turning to protectionist measures in the 1890s (Akyiğitzade Musa, *İktisad yahud İlm-i Servet*, 62).
115 Sayar, *Osmanlı İktisat Düşüncesi*, 373.
116 For a review of memoranda presented to Abdülhamid II, see Mustafa Oğuz, "II. Abdülhamid'e Sunulan Lâyihalar" (Unpublished PhD Dissertation, Ankara University,

2007). For specifically Ottoman economy-related ones, see Mustafa Durusoy, "Sultan II. Abdülhamid'e Sunulan Layihalar Işığında Dönemin İktisadi Özellikleri" (Unpublished MA Thesis, Marmara University, 1995).

117 The sultan's memoranda have been transliterated and published in two separate books, which have almost the same content with different editorial and language preferences (e.g., direct transliteration vs. edited into present-day Turkish): Sultan II. Abdülhamid Han, *Devlet ve Memleket Görüşlerim*, ed. A. Alâaddin Çetin and Ramazan Yıldız (Istanbul: Çığır Yayınları, 1976); and Sultan II. Abdülhamid Han, *Abdülhamit Han'ın Muhtıraları (Belgeler)*, ed. Mehmet Hocaoğlu (Istanbul: Oymak Yayınları: 1975). The quotations that I provide in this section are all my translations. I corrected occasional mistakes in meaning (due to typos as well as inaccurate reading) and in some European names.

118 Abdülhamid, *Devlet ve Memleket Görüşlerim*, 265–79.

119 Akarlı, "The Problems of External Pressures," 214.

120 Abdülhamid, *Devlet ve Memleket Görüşlerim*, 17–30 (Original document: BOA YEE, 9/2008/72/4).

121 Ibid., 17.

122 Ibid., 17–18.

123 Ibid., 18–19.

124 Ibid., 19.

125 Ibid.

126 Ibid., 36–7 (Original document: BOA YEE, 9/820/72/4).

127 Ibid., 21–4.

128 Ibid., 24.

129 Ibid., 25.

130 Ibid.

131 Ibid., 26.

132 Ibid., 28–9.

133 BOA, YEE, 10/2287.

134 Abdülhamid II, *Devlet ve Memleket Görüşlerim*, 29.

135 Such as *Feyz-i Hamidî* and *Avn-i Hamidî*.

136 Şerafeddin Mağmumî, *Seyahat Hâtıraları* (Cairo, 1908), 95–6.

137 Abdülhamid, *Devlet ve Memleket Görüşlerim*, 29.

138 For an analysis of the emphasis on Islamic morality in the Hamidian education system, see Benjamin Fortna, "Islamic Morality in Late Ottoman 'Secular' Schools."

139 See the section above.

140 Ahmed Midhat, *Üss-i İnkılâb, Kısm-ı Sâni: Cülûs-ı Hümayûndan Bir Seneye Kadar* (İstanbul: Takvim-i Vakâyi Matbaası, 1878), 33.

141 Abdülhamid, *Devlet ve Memleket Görüşlerim*, 289–300 (Original document: BOA YEE 1/156/XXV/3).

142 Akçuraoğlu Yusuf, *Üç Tarz-ı Siyaset*, 8.

143 Abdülhamid, *Devlet ve Memleket Görüşlerim*, 292–3.

144 Reşad, "İstikraz," *İbret* 19 (1872, [3 Cemaziyülevvel 1289]), 1.

145 Abdülhamid II, *Devlet ve Memleket Görüşlerim*, 293.

146 Ibid., 291.

147 Ibid. The fact that the sultan gives exact figures about this case hints at his interest in the matter as well as his concern about the question of industrialization. He notes that the factory was producing "50 cm × 70 cm glass panels for 2 *kuruş*;" but the Austrians supplied the market with the same product for only 40 *paras* (1 *kuruş* = 40 *paras*). For similar examples and some industrial statistics from the Hamidian era, see Vedat Eldem, *Osmanlı İmparatorluğu'nun İktisadi Şartları Hakkında Bir Tetkik* (Ankara: Türk Tarih Kurumu, 1994), 65–6.

148 Abdülhamid, *Devlet ve Memleket Görüşlerim*, 291.

5 Changing hearts and minds

Economic thought in late Ottoman fiction

> In poetry's gallery of diverse ways of thinking, diverse aspirations, and diverse desires, we come to know periods and nations far more intimately than we can through the misleading and pathetic method of studying their political and military history. From this latter kind of history, we rarely learn more about a people than how it was ruled and how it was wiped out. From its poetry, we learn about its way of thinking, its desires and wants, the ways it rejoiced, and the ways it was guided either by its principles or its inclinations.[1]
>
> (von Herder, 1993)

> The novels … gave political economy something it ordinarily lacked: a sustained encounter with the states of vitality and sensation it invented but failed to explore fully. Reading political economy through … novels while also reading the novels through political economy will … defamiliarize not only those two modes of writing but also the very notion of life and feeling on which they relied.[2]
>
> (Gallagher, 2006)

Humans are the only species that have recourse to fiction to make sense of the world around them. From the earliest traditions of mythology to organized religions, human beings created and passed on to following generations many stories that are supposed to unravel the complexities of the natural and social life and the best ways to act in it. Muslims have referred to traditional narratives about the lives of archetypical figures (such as the *hadith* literature about the Prophet Muhammad) to inspire in tackling problems in their own lives. In the increasingly secular and Eurocentric nineteenth century, Ottoman intellectuals discovered new (European) fictional forms—such as the novel and short story—and used them in reaching the hearts and minds of the masses for social change. In this respect, the Ottoman social novel of the late nineteenth century not only provides us with detailed pictures of Ottoman social and economic life of the era, but also reflects Ottoman reformists' projections for an ideal future for the empire in the age of capitalist modernity.[3]

The oppressive political regime of the Hamidian era and its heavy censorship directed many Ottoman reformists to less dangerous fields of social criticism. One such field was economics;[4] another was fiction. This chapter looks examines the intersection of these two fields. It suggests close textual analyses of some of the popular literary works of the era in order to reveal and contextualize their economic content. The main aim of the chapter is to demonstrate how some Ottoman reformists used fiction as an instrument of soft social engineering through inoculating Ottoman readers with a new economic value-set. It also shows how bourgeois sensibilities already permeated into all aspects of the late Ottoman sociocultural life as a result of popular economic literature, which was discussed in the earlier chapters.

The chapter focuses on the works of two popular intellectuals of the late nineteenth century, Ahmed Midhat Efendi (1844–1912) and (Mizancı) Mehmed Murad Bey (1854–1917). The main reason for choosing these two figures are the obvious economic elements in some of their fictional works, whose plot, moral, and the characters reflect specific economic principles and notions. Besides, the existence of their non-fictional economic writings on similar issues presents us an opportunity to make intertextual analyses between fiction and non-fiction. It is also worth noting that these two authors had significant cultural and intellectual influence in their age and on subsequent generations, which makes their works particularly important in gaining insights into the impact of fiction in social change.

The first section below discusses the connection between the novel as a literary form and the question of modernization in late Ottoman history. The second section focuses on the fictional works of Ahmed Midhat Efendi in order to investigate how he used fiction to promote his ideas regarding economic development. The third section provides an analytical re-reading of Mehmed Murad Bey's novel, *Turfanda mı, Turfa mı?*, to reveal how the idea of modernization through bottom-up economic development is hidden behind the story of an Ottoman romantic hero. With frequent references to the case of Ahmed Midhat, this last section also aims at revealing the patterns of the use of fiction in late Ottoman intellectual history for social change with economic motives.

Modernization and the Ottoman novel

Ottoman modernists such as Şinasi (1826–71), Namık Kemal (1840–88), Şemseddin Sami (1850–1904), and Ahmed Midhat considered literature as both an indicator of the level of civilization and an essential instrument for modernization.[5] They believed that traditional Ottoman literature was full of pre-modern styles and themes that should be jettisoned on the way to a sophisticated literature of a modern society. Unscientific, irrational, and unrealistic themes in folk tales (such as the love story "Kerem ile Aslı" or the heroic Battal Gâzi stories) and traditional poetry, which promoted melancholy and drunkenness (as opposed to the modern emphasis on labor), were regarded as inimical to modernization efforts. Şemseddin Sami, for example, criticized the vastly popular Middle Eastern folk tale "Leyla ve Mecnun" from a rationalist and positivist perspective. He argued that the story includes many unrealistic and irrational scenes: Leyla talks to a candle and Mecnun gathers wolves, lambs, lions, and gazelles around himself and chats with them. Şemseddin Sami labeled such stories "childish" and maintained that an educated person, even a child, could not enjoy such stories in the modern age.[6]

The first attempts to modernize Ottoman literature came from Young Ottomans like Şemseddin Sami and Namık Kemal, who introduced new forms (such as the novel and short story) as well as new ideas (such as liberty and motherland—*vatan*). Early Ottoman novelists were almost exclusively moralist and didactic, telling allegorical stories about some culturally conservative ideal types for pedagogical—rather than purely literary—purposes.[7] Later Ahmed Midhat took this reformist-pedagogical approach to fiction to another level by using fiction as a school for ordinary people. In addition to his non-fiction books and articles, he wrote and adapted hundreds of short stories and novels full of encyclopedic knowledge. Young Ottomans dismissed traditional folk tales as obsolete. Ahmed Midhat, however, employed many stylistic and moral elements from traditional storytelling to reach a wider audience and to popularize new forms by mixing them with more familiar ones.[8] The quality of his writings was not high in literary terms, but this was least of his concerns. Ahmed Midhat knew that he was the *Hâce-i evvel*, the first teacher, a pioneer who would be followed by more knowledgeable, sophisticated, and specialized ones.[9] Therefore, his main objective was to familiarize his fellow Ottomans with modern European forms of literature and especially with modern sciences. He professes this strategy in a foreword he wrote for the book of a young author:

> My son! One should study only one thing, but one should do it perfectly. Or one should study everything, but of course only superficially! Regarding the conditions that we, the Ottomans, live in today, the latter is more preferable. And I advise you [to do] that. However, in the future the former will be more preferable. So, you will advise it to your son![10]

The novel was not only an artistic form in nineteenth-century Europe either. For many novelists, it was a means of critique of capitalist society. Starting with the French realists, such as Stendhal (1783–1842) and Honoré de Balzac (1799–1850), many novelists told stories of ordinary people who constantly struggled for survival under cruel working and living conditions under capitalism. Through these stories such authors criticized or even presented alternatives to capitalist social relations, as we see in the works of Émile Zola (1840–1902). The novels of Charles Dickens (1812–70) constitute the most notable examples of this genre. As Stefan Zweig puts it,

> His novels should be the instrument for helping the poor, forsaken, and forgotten children who, like himself of old, were suffering injustice at the hands of teachers, badly conducted schools, indifferent parents; who were pining away because of the slothfulness, the lack of affection, the selfishness of their natural protectors and guardians.[11]

Especially towards the end of the century, some writers, such as the American author Horatio Alger, Jr. (1832–99), went beyond social criticism and turned the novel into a survival manual in a capitalist society.[12] In this genre, the main goal of the writer was not merely to criticize poverty and inequality, but to show ways to succeed under these conditions. These popular dime novels were rags-to-riches stories that displayed the "ways to wealth" to the poor masses. This particular use of the novel matched the social and political concerns of Ottoman modernists.[13]

The introduction of *roman feuilletons* (serialized novels) in early nineteenth-century France not only accelerated the popularization of the novel as a genre by making it more affordable for the greater masses, but also increased newspaper sales, thereby nurturing the press industry.[14] Ahmed Midhat and other Ottoman press entrepreneurs did not fail to realize the importance of this powerful instrument for popularizing this new genre and for increasing profits. Not only novels, but also books on history and other subjects were serialized in their periodicals both to increase the circulation of the papers and to educate the public. Meanwhile, Hamidian educational reforms and the rise of an Ottoman middle class in the late nineteenth century created a market for the novel as well as for newspapers and other forms of intellectual production. In addition, the government provided subsidies and other forms of financial support to the developing independent Ottoman press. The growth of the literate population and the development of the press industry accelerated the bourgeois transformation of the Ottoman public sphere in the late nineteenth century.

In terms of its historical development and its socio-political roles, the Ottoman novel follows European examples. It is worth noting, however, that I do not adopt the conventional "imitation" discourse that would assume that the Ottoman novel was merely a primitive imitation of the French novel. The problem of this discourse is not that it is completely wrong, but rather that it is tautological. Since every successor follows—and to some extent imitates—its predecessor, Ottoman novelists imitated European examples. Nevertheless, European novelists of the same age were also perpetuating the stylistic and thematic patterns of their predecessors. Since the latter are considered a part of the same national or "civilizational" (i.e., European) pedigree, inter-European influence is usually regarded as simply evolution or development, not imitation. In the Ottoman case, however, Muslims have historically been considered outsiders to European civilization. Thus, their efforts to adopt modern forms and institutions have often been regarded as "aping the West." In short, this chapter, in rejecting such a simplistic view, assesses the Ottoman novel as a natural branch of a modern literary genre (i.e., the novel), instead of treating it as an unnatural and odd mutation in the "Oriental" literary and intellectual tradition.

Hâce-i Evvel and storytelling as an instrument of development

Ahmed Midhat, as a modern storyteller and a pioneer of the idea of bottom-up economic development through education, used fiction to alter the Ottoman economic mindset.[15] Not only did he introduce a new work ethic through his writings, he also embodied this ethic in his working habits and business enterprises.[16]

A recurring theme in his fictional works is a dialectical story of an ideal Ottoman hero, who achieves economic and social success through diligence, and a "super-Westernized" anti-hero, whose laziness and mannerisms result in failure and impoverishment.[17] These two characters obviously stand as metaphorical equivalents of industriousness and entrepreneurship on the one hand, and laziness and *fonctionnarisme* (tendency to become civil servant) on the other.

Before analyzing Ahmed Midhat's way-to-wealth stories, it is worth noting that the outstanding example of an ideal Ottoman entrepreneur in his fiction was Seyyid Mehmed Numan, the main character in his novel *Müşahedât* (Observations, 1891). Mehmed Numan is an old Egyptian businessman who comes to Istanbul as a young and sharp clerk. He builds a very successful international trade network stretching from Egypt and the Aegean islands to Marseilles and London.[18] Ahmed Midhat presents this old businessman to his readers as a model to emulate and makes an open call for future generations of Ottoman writers to create similar characters in order to promote entrepreneurship in Ottoman society.[19] Although Mehmed Numan exemplifies the ideal Muslim-Ottoman entrepreneur, I have preferred not to deal with this story in this chapter for two main reasons: first, in the novel, Ahmed Midhat summarizes his reflections about economic development and the roles of the elite in this process through the words and actions of Mehmed Numan. However, Mehmed Numan does not say anything original but simply reiterates Ahmed Midhat's main theses in his *Sevda-yı Sa'y ü Amel* and *Teşrik-i Mesaî, Taksim-i Mesaî.*[20] Second, and more importantly, Ahmed Midhat does not share the details about how Mehmed Numan achieved success. In other words, Ahmed Midhat simply gives the example of a businessman who is already rich, thanks to his earlier successful business ventures and hard work, but does not turn Mehmed Numan's story into a practical manual for achieving success.

The stories that will be discussed in the section provided young and enthusiastic Ottoman readers with a detailed step-by-step approach to economic and social success.[21] It is obvious that Ahmed Midhat outlined these stories not only as enjoyable tales, but also as ready-to-apply patterns to put these new ideas in practice. In the introduction to one of his earliest stories of the same type—in which some young and idealistic characters establish a small firm—Ahmed Midhat states his motivation very clearly: "Although this association is nothing but fiction, I want to describe it in such a way that if someone would like to put it into practice, it should be possible."[22]

Alafranga ***and the leisure class in Ahmed Midhat's stories***

The *alafranga* (*alla Franca*) is probably the most well-known type in the Ottoman-Turkish novel. Felatun Bey in Ahmed Midhat's novella, *Felatun Bey il Rakım Efendi* (1875) has been considered the prototype for this character.[23] Following Ahmed Midhat, other Ottoman novelists also depicted the *alafranga* character in similar stories. Hüseyin Rahmi Gürpınar (1864–1944)—a follower of Ahmed Midhat in intellectual and literary terms—wrote *Şık* (Chic), which was published by Ahmed Midhat in *Tercüman-ı Hakikat* in 1884.[24] In 1896, Recaizade Mahmud Ekrem wrote *Araba Sevdası* (*The Carriage Affair*), which has been considered one of the most important and influential novels of late Ottoman literature in terms of its characters, plot, and style.[25] The main theme of both stories is the ludicrous situations that superficial Europeanization gives rise to. Bihruz Bey in *Araba Sevdası* wastes his money on ostentation, just like Ahmed Midhat's anti-heroes as we shall see below.

Felatun symbolizes an inappropriate form of Westernization through merely aping French manners and consumption patterns and living an ostentatious life in Beyoğlu (Pera), the Europeanized district of Istanbul.[26] This type usually hates everything Ottoman and Oriental and associates being European with being sophisticated and civilized. However, despite his rather extreme interest in European civilization, he has only superficial knowledge of it, and his knowledge of his own culture is even narrower. He does not speak French well, but he uses French words and expressions in his everyday language.

It is worth noting in passing that using French in everyday language was a typical upper-class behavior in the late nineteenth century, not only in the Ottoman Empire but also in other countries that were under French cultural influence. In the Russian case, for instance, Tolstoy's *Anna Karenina* (1877) includes many depictions of such behavior among the Russian elite of the age. As an interesting example from the Ottoman Empire, Arminius Vambéry notes about the sultan Abdülhamid II that "without knowing French he would often interlard his Turkish conversation with French words and sayings, to impress ambassadors and other exalted guests."[27] Speaking—or at least using—French in everyday language was basically an attempt of presenting oneself as an elite, educated, and intellectually sophisticated person.

Alafranga type usually appears as an ignoramus with the crude veneer of a European gentleman. According to some scholars of the Ottoman novel, this character represents the contempt of Ottoman intellectuals towards the super-Westernized Tanzimat generation of the Ottoman elite.[28] As a reaction to this tendency, Ottoman modernists, like Ahmed Midhat, make a distinction between appropriate and inappropriate forms of Westernization by condemning the uncritical adoption of European styles and manners at the expense of one's own cultural values. These critical intellectuals, instead, promote a synthesis of Western material and intellectual culture with Muslim-Ottoman religious and cultural values to construct a native modern Ottoman lifestyle. More importantly, however, the late-Ottoman modernist vision of such a lifestyle was inspired by obvious economic concerns in addition to cultural ones. For example, several of Ahmed Midhat's stories not only show proper Westernization in social and cultural terms, but also reflect the author's suggestions for a bottom-up economic development strategy for the salvation of the empire. Ahmed Midhat's three novellas, *Felatun Bey il Rakım Efendi* (1875), *Bahtiyarlık* (*Bliss*, 1885), and *Para!* (*Money!*, 1887) stand out as the most important works to be discussed in this context.

As Felatun Bey was the prototype of the *alafranga* character in later Ottoman fiction, his story also became the prototype of a genre in the Ottoman-Turkish literature of the late nineteenth and early twentieth centuries.[29] Felatun Bey is a Westernized fop, a cocky, extravagant, and lazy man from a wealthy family. On paper, he works as a civil servant; however, instead of going to the office, he prefers frequenting the chic cafes and hotels of Beyoğlu with his mistress, Polini. The hero of the story, Rakım Efendi, on the other hand, is a modest, well-educated, moral, thrifty, and industrious gentleman. He is morally and culturally more traditional and conservative, but he is also Westernized in his manners and with a vast knowledge of modern European sciences and philosophy. In this respect, Rakım represents the ideal modern Ottoman citizen who benefits from advanced European knowledge while preserving Muslim-Ottoman values in the private sphere.

In terms of economic behavior and work ethic, these characters remind us of two key concepts in social and economic theory: Thorstein Veblen's (1857–1929) "conspicuous consumption"[30] (Felatun) and Max Weber's (1864–1920) "capitalist spirit and Protestant ethic" (Rakım).[31] Interestingly enough, Ahmed Midhat wrote these stories long before both concepts were introduced into economic literature. Moreover, not only does Ahmed Midhat introduce these two notions, he also juxtaposes them in the same stories and treats them as two opposite poles of economic behavior that lead to either success or failure.[32]

Felatun Bey does not represent only inappropriate Westernization and consequent cultural alienation. He is also the embodiment of the conspicuous and wasteful consumption of the Tanzimat-era Ottoman leisure class (in the Veblenian sense).[33] In addition to the conspicuous consumption of the elite, wasteful governmental spending on the visual aspects of modernization—such as new palaces—was also an important characteristic of the pre-Hamidian era. As a result, the lack of adequate resources for economic development, huge amounts of wasteful consumption, and failed economic enterprises became serious concerns for Ottoman intellectuals and influenced the literature of the era.

Felatun Bey, as a member of the Ottoman leisure class, is a wasteful character. Although his father works hard to provide him with a good education, he is not interested in knowledge and learning, but nevertheless presents himself as a wise gentleman. In order to put more emphasis on this paradox of the *alafranga* elite, Ahmed Midhat chose a special name for him: Felatun, the Ottomanized version of the name of the ancient Greek philosopher Plato. Felatun's family moves from Üsküdar (a conservative Muslim district) to Beyoğlu (the Westernized district of Istanbul) as they climb up the ladder of economic and social status.

Felatun lives an extravagant life with his French mistress Polini in an expensive hotel in Beyoğlu.[34] Their appetite for ostentation is endless. One night, Felatun loses a huge amount at poker as a result of her forcing him to continue playing despite his poor record. Polini's motivation, according to Ahmed Midhat, is to show that she is with a rich gentleman who can afford such losses. In other words, Felatun's great loss in monetary terms has a direct positive correlation with Polini's social standing in Beyoğlu.[35] The next day, Felatun, seriously depressed over his loss, organizes an ostentatious excursion to the countryside with two luxury horse carriages and two large music bands.

Although he spends a lot of money to cure his depression resulting from a large monetary loss, the reaction of observers proves that it is worth the cost in terms of the social status this excursion provides: "Bravo! He spends a lot of money, but he is enjoying himself like a Prince."[36]

Ahmed Midhat associates such irrational behavior with the basic human instinct for ostentation:

> It is due to human nature that a person is not satisfied with his happiness, but also wants to show it to everybody. Even if he is not happy, he lies to others to make them believe that he is happy. This behavior is so common that it does not usually attract our attention. However some exaggerated behaviors like using a twenty-five lira cord, or even more expensively, using a cord with diamonds, for a five-lira watch are examples of this attitude. Obviously, a watch is a necessary device for us. But why do we need a watch chain? If it is needed for the protection of the watch, a cotton cord could also be used. But no, that is not the case. Every human being wants others see that he has such a large fortune that he uses a cord worth twenty-five golden pieces just to protect his watch.[37]

For Ahmed Midhat, this is not merely an innocuous instinct. On the contrary, it usually have destructive consequences. Felatun wastes all his family wealth and takes on a considerable amount of debt to perpetuate his lifestyle. In the end, he finds a job in Alexandria and moves there as a penniless junior civil servant. However his last words to his friend Rakım show that he has not learned anything from his mistakes: "If I can live long enough to save some money after repaying my debts, I can still have some time for self-indulgence in my nineties."[38] This note hints at Ahmed Midhat's giving priority to instincts over experience in shaping economic behavior.

Senâi in *Bahtiyarlık* (*Bliss*) is another *alafranga* character and shares many features with Felatun. The son of the landlord of an estate called "Berrak Pınar" (Pristine Spring), Senâi emulates the French nobility and signs his letters "Senâi de Berrak Pınar."[39] He knows from books that French aristocrats get loans in their youth to be paid off when they inherit the family fortune, and he does the same. His wasteful and expensive lifestyle leads him into a spiral of debt that consumes his family's entire wealth. As a last resort, he borrows some money to present himself as a good and wealthy marriage prospect for the daughters of rich families. Ahmed Midhat notes,

> He began to live so gently with the rest of his money that he proved his suitability for this marriage. Everybody congratulated Abdülcabbar Bey [the head of a rich family and Senâi's father-in-law] for having such a generous son-in-law.[40]

Thus conspicuous consumption proves to be useful for Senâi to indicate high social standing, just as Veblen defined it, and to hoodwink a wealthy family.

However, this does not solve Senâi's problem for good, but rather leads to the bankruptcy of his wife's family. In the end, Senâi escapes to Switzerland with the money he borrowed in the name of his father-in-law, leaving behind a huge amount of debt in both his own and his father-in-law's names.[41]

Sulhi of *Para!* (*Money!*) is another offshoot of the Felatun prototype. Sulhi believes that the most important thing in life is money, and that money is the only source of high social status. According to him, "Money is a general measure. When one asks about a person, one does not ask whether he is a physician or a surgeon, but asks how much money that he possesses."[42] Sulhi attends the medical school, but he gets dismissed due to his laziness. Yet, this does not cause him any sorrow since he thinks that wealth, and not a profession, is the source of reputation and happiness. He says, "Thanks to my aunt's fortune, I do not have to work at all. If I want to be richer someday, I can engage in trade."[43] At some point, he understands that his aunt's wealth will not last long if he continues to lead his ostentatious life and marries the daughter of a very rich man—reminding us of Senâi in *Bahtiyarlık*.

When Sulhi meets the girl, he proves his social status by emphasizing his leisure class identity. He introduces himself by saying, "My name is Mehmed Sulhi. I live in Aksaray! I have lots of real estate. I do not work at all, and I live on the returns of these properties."[44] The classic moral ending of Ahmed Midhat's stories awaits Sulhi too: he wastes his aunt's and then his father-in-law's wealth, which had once been considered "endless." The successful character of the story, Vahdeti, who becomes rich through hard work despite his modest background, offers a small loan to Sulhi to be used as initial capital for a business. Sulhi's response reflects Ahmed Midhat's belief in the hopelessness of the *alafranga* character: "I am confident that I would spend that money in a very short period, but I doubt that I can make money by using it as capital."[45]

Sulhi's description of the social importance of money remind us of the works of Honoré de Balzac (1799–1850), who had a considerable influence on the Ottoman novelist of the era:

> [Balzac] investigated money values and introduced them into his novels. Ever since the days when aristocratic privileges was abolished, ever since the vast differences of status were reduced to a general level of equality, money has come more and more to be the blood and the driving force of social life. Money value gradually came to determine all things; the worth of every passions was estimated in terms of the material sacrifices entailed; every human being was judged by what his income happened to be in hard cash. Money circulates in these novels. Balzac allows his heroes to accumulate vast fortunes, only to lose all in the end [...].[46]

French literary romanticism made a formative impact on the development of Ottoman novel, and Balzac as one of its leading figures was of course well-known among the Ottoman literary elite. Therefore the idea of "Money is a general measure" in *Para!*, or in more general terms "the circulation of money" (from accumulation to bankruptcy) as a theme in Ahmed Midhat's fiction may be an inspiration from Balzac. However, we should also remember that Balzac's fiction reflected not only his imagination, but more importantly the social reality he witnessed. According to many contemporary observers (including Balzac), the radical social transformation brought about by capitalism situated money at the center of social relations. After all, the capitalist transformation and the *Zeitgeist* it created led Georg Simmel—a contemporary of Ahmed Midhat—to write *The Philosophy of Money* (1900) to explain how money and the act of calculation shaped social relations in modern age. In this respect, Ahmed Midhat's putting the circulation of money in his fiction seems to reflect his observations on the social change in European capitalist societies as well as his literary and economic readings. Considering the role he assumed in Ottoman intellectual life—the conveyor of European knowledge to his society and the teacher of the masses on this basis—it is not surprising to see the same social and intellectual trends shaped his work with that of Georg Simmel or Max Weber.

Returning to his *alafranga* characters, the common characteristics of Ahmed Midhat's anti-heroes are that they come from wealthy families, but they are lazy, extravagant, immoral, and careless by nature. They usually attend the best schools of the empire, but they are either expelled or they can barely finish their schooling. They never work, and they are not interested in any sort of productive activity, including using their wealth for investment. *Alafranga* types waste all their family wealth—and in some cases the wealth of other families—in conspicuous and wasteful consumption. Hence, a financial tragedy always awaits them and their families at the end of the story. By including their families in the story, Ahmed Midhat emphasizes that a lazy and unproductive individual is harmful not only to himself but to his society too. As he puts in his introductory economics book, *Ekonomi Politik* (1879), Ahmed Midhat believes that such a "lazy and harmful man should be kicked out of modern society."[47] Now that we have seen the reasons for economic—and thereby social—failure as presented in Ahmed Midhat's fiction, it is essential to take a look at the opposite side of the story to see how he fictionalized his economic ideas on individual success and economic development that we discussed in earlier chapters.

Ahmed Midhat's ideal entrepreneurs

Rakım Efendi of *Felatun Bey il Rakım Efendi*, Şinasi in *Bahtiyarlık*, and Vahdeti in *Para!* are examples of ideal Ottomans in Ahmed Midhat's stories. As indicated previously for Rakım, they are all modest, well-educated, thrifty, moral, and industrious. They start with modest means, as the sons of middle class families, but thanks to the modern education they receive in imperial colleges and their hard work, thrift, and systematic thinking, they succeed in accumulating significant amounts of wealth in the end. Besides, they marry ideal Ottoman women, who are also moral, modest, and educated; they thereby achieve happiness in private life in addition to material comfort.

In his own life, Ahmed Midhat was loyal to the principles that he promoted to the readers of his economic writings. He was a "lover of labor" himself, with his entrepreneurial spirit and devotion to hard work and self-discipline. It is also known that there is a strong connection between his biography and fiction.[48] The heroes in his stories simply represent and propagate the social and economic values which he put forward in his economic writings and pursued in his own life. While Rakım and Vahdeti are also good examples of such a type with an obvious "love of labor" spirit, Şinasi in *Bahtiyarlık* stands out as a self-made man and an ideal Muslim-Ottoman capitalist entrepreneur in Ahmed Midhat's mind, thereby deserving special attention.[49]

Şinasi's story begins when he is a student at the Mekteb-i Sultâni (The Imperial High School), an elite educational institution of the era. Although the graduates of this school are expected to become high-ranking officials and diplomats of the empire, Şinasi plans to follow a completely different career path. While at school, he is interested in modern agricultural techniques and rural life, and he plans to become a "peasant."[50] According to one interpretation of the story, Şinasi's preference to settle in a village reflects the influence of nineteenth-century pastoral romanticism—more specifically of Rousseau—on Ottoman literature.[51] However, the real reason is his decision to live a productive life, instead of a non-productive but comfortable life in Istanbul thanks to his diploma. Moreover, pastoral romanticism was a reaction to rapid industrialization and the consequent social problems of urbanization in the nineteenth century. As we shall see more clearly below, Şinasi's main objective actually opposes the ideals of pastoral romanticism as he works toward transforming traditional rural life into a modern capitalistic form.

After graduation, Şinasi decides to settle in a village in Anatolia to live his dreams, and his initial capital is the pocket money that his father gives him. In a letter to his father, he explains his plan:

> Please keep sending me the money for two more years. Let me go to Anatolia and experience peasant life.... Even if I waste all of it, we lose nothing, because I would have probably wasted that money in Istanbul anyway. Whatever I can save from that money will be my initial capital, and with the help of God, I will expand my capital.[52]

It is worth noting that Şinasi, with such naive ideas, was not unrealistic as a character for a novel. On the contrary, he reflects a growing interest among Ottoman reformists in the possibilities for an agrarian-based socio-economic transformation. For instance, the renowned Young Turk leader, Ahmed Rıza Bey (1859–1930), was a real-life example of the Şinasi character, at least in his intentions. After observing conditions in Anatolia in his youth, Ahmed Rıza decided to study agriculture. Having completed his studies at the *École d'agriculture de Grignon* in France (1884) and returned to Istanbul, he looked for Ottoman financiers who would invest in his project for a modern farm, where he could apply modern agricultural techniques.[53] Much to his dismay, he could neither realize this project, nor find a suitable job for his education (even in the Ministry of Agriculture) due to capital shortages, insecure conditions in rural Anatolia, and general indifference to modern farming in the Ottoman Empire. Finally, he gave up his dreams to follow the classic path to reviving the country: education.[54]

Unlike Ahmed Rıza Bey, Şinasi is able to secure some capital (from his father), and after buying a small piece of land and settling in a village, he starts work immediately. Although his father sends him a sufficient amount of money for a comfortable life, he has a hand-to-mouth existence. The reason for this is his dedication to his enterprise. He uses all his money to buy land, animals, and modern tools, such as the pickaxe, shovel, and wheelbarrow. It is worth noting in passing that these simple metal tools, in the context of late nineteenth century Ottoman agriculture, were considered products of advanced industrial technology compared to the wooden implements that the villagers were using at the time.

At this point, we can refer to Weber's definition of an ideal capitalist entrepreneur for a rather theoretical explanation of Şinasi's seemingly irrational obsession with his business at the expense of his personal comfort and his indifference to the question of social status:

> [The capitalist entrepreneur] has no relation to such more or less refined climbers. He avoids ostentation and unnecessary expenditure, as well as conscious enjoyment of his power, and is embarrassed by the outward signs of the social recognition which he receives.... He gets nothing out of his wealth for himself, except the irrational sense of having done his job well.[55]

Apparently, Ahmed Midhat and Max Weber thought along similar lines regarding the worldview and lifestyle of an entrepreneurially-minded capitalist.

In Şinasi's village, new tools, machines, and techniques at first seem strange to the peasants; they therefore watch him with suspicion. However, in the end they cannot resist the protagonist's modernizing and therefore rationalizing (in the Weberian sense) capitalistic venture. They begin to work with Şinasi and learn new techniques from him.[56] As Şinasi introduces modern production methods gleaned from books and even builds primitive machines such as a simple incubator,[57] another autobiographical detail about the author manifests itself: Ahmed Midhat built a model farm in Beykoz, on which he applied modern agricultural techniques. He shared his experiences with his readers in the pages of *Tercüman-ı Hakikat*.[58] Besides, as an admirer of industrial capitalism, his many fictional and non-fictional works are full of expressions reflecting his admiration for machines as a symbol of the progress of human civilization.[59]

In addition to the author himself, we find other real-life examples of Ottomans with entrepreneurial spirit from the era—which helps us contextualize these stories. In Şerafeddin Mağmumî's (1869–1927) accounts of his travels in Anatolia (*c.* 1894–95), we read the story of a certain Hüsnü Bey who establishes a modern farm in Ahvat, a village of Bursa. Hüsnü Bey, as a man of the nineteenth century, has a keen interest in machines and modern agricultural technologies. To establish his modern farm, he brings tools from Istanbul. At first, just as in Şinasi's case, his neighbors derides him saying, "farming cannot be done *alafranga*-style!"[60] Yet he never gives up his project and eventually becomes successful. One of the factors behind his success is his perseverance in getting his fellow villagers accustomed to modern farming, just like Şinasi.[61] Thus, Ahmed Midhat's stories were not only inspiring quasi-utopian narratives, but they were also reflections of a capitalist spirit that had already captivated modern-minded entrepreneurs like himself and Hüsnü Bey.

Şinasi presents a brief report about his investments and the results of his enterprise in another letter to his father. His meticulous calculations and detailed input-output analyses in the letter testify to his rational and systematic thinking in capitalist terms. According to the Şinasi's calculations, the total amount of money received from his father is 24,000 *kuruş* over a six-year period. Yet, the value of his lands already exceeds 20,000 *kuruş*, and he owns 37,000 *kuruş* worth of animals and tools. More importantly, at the end of these six years, he starts to employ workers and begins production for the market.[62] This letter stands as a proof of Şinasi's success thanks to his diligence, industriousness, entrepreneurial mentality, dedication to work, thrift, and systematic thinking, or in Weberian terms, his capitalist spirit. Şinasi, in short, exemplifies an ideal entrepreneur not only in Ahmed Midhat's thinking, but also in Max Weber's understanding of capitalism—which indicates the impact of the same *Zeitgeist* on these two intellectuals of completely different social and economic settings:

> The question of motive forces in the expansion of modern capitalism is not in the first instance a question of the capital sums which were available for capitalistic uses, but above all, of the development of the spirit of capitalism. Where it appears and is able to work itself out, it produces its own capital and monetary supplies as the means to its ends, but the reverse is not true.[63]

An analysis of economic thought in Ahmed Midhat's fiction

The ideas of a native Ottoman modernity and modernization through economic development constitute the subtext of Ahmed Midhat's *romans à thèse*.[64] The heroes of his stories are culturally and morally conservative Ottoman Muslims who never compromise their traditional identities for any economic and social gain. Yet, they also equip themselves with the latest ideas, techniques, and skills from Europe. In this sense, Ahmed Midhat's idealized modern Ottomans are Ottoman in their cultural and religious values, and European in their work ethic and rationalist approach to problems. As a result, for Ahmed Midhat's heroes there is not an essential clash between modern European and traditional Muslim-Ottoman values. The problem arises whenever Ottomans try to ape Europeans at the expense of their own culture. The question of "what to take and what not to take from the West" was the main question of Ottoman-Turkish modernization of the late nineteenth and early twentieth centuries. For Ahmed Midhat's characters, however, it was not an issue.

An obvious characteristic of Ahmed Midhat's heroes, in terms of their economic thinking and behavior, is that they prefer private entrepreneurship to state employment. Even if they work as civil servants, they regard it as a service to their country, not a source of income. This is not simply an anti-bureaucratic stance. This is rather a reflection of Ahmed Midhat's bottom-up approach to economic development. The Smithian idea of a nexus between private and public interests marked the late Ottoman approach to economic development, and it is apparent in Ahmed Midhat's thinking too. The open challenge to the traditional (militaristic-bureaucratic) Ottoman economic mentality reveals itself clearly in Ahmed Midhat's advice to his readers. However, he does not totally discourage his audience from the civil service. He believes that if it is done properly, civil service too can contribute to the country's wealth.[65] It is also worth noting that the character of the young and lazy Tanzimat bureaucrat, who is generally depicted as a spoiled son of a high-ranking official, is another subject that frequently appears in the Ottoman novel.[66] Ahmed Midhat's stories include these types as they represent his criticism of the wasteful and unproductive lifestyles of the Tanzimat-era Ottoman leisure class.

A chronological analysis of Ahmed Midhat's stories about economic success shows us that his emphasis shifted from hard work to capitalist entrepreneurship between the early 1870s and the late 1880s. Yet the traditional militaristic-bureaucratic economic mentality, and especially laziness and fatalism, remained at the focus of his criticisms. As early as 1870, for example, he voiced his criticism of the bureaucratic economic mentality through his adaptation of an Aesop's fable about a diligent donkey and some lazy dogs.[67] The story begins with the dogs complaining that no one feeds them even with leftovers. Hearing this, the donkey criticizes the dogs for doing nothing but jumping up and down to entertain and flatter their owners. In contrast, the donkey works all day and earns its living by carrying water and wood; the farmers, in return, feed it hay every night. The donkey says it is unwise to complain about one's fate if one is not making any effort to change it. In the end, the donkey concludes that the way to earn one's living should be service, not fawning. It is important to note once more that the moral of this story is to earn one's living through effort and service, although Ahmed Midhat's later stories emphasize entrepreneurship in addition to effort.

As the donkey's story also shows, the classical labor theory of value not only shapes Ahmed Midhat's economic thought, it also makes its way into the essence of his stories. Ahmed Midhat's successful characters show how value—and consequently wealth—is created by labor alone. It is neither the initial capital nor any form of rent, but labor (directed by a capitalist work ethic) that constitutes the way to wealth. His anti-heroes, on the other hand, prove a belief frequently repeated in the economic literature of the era: the wealth at hand, however large, is doomed to perish unless it is turned into capital and processed and augmented through labor.

Ahmed Midhat's way-to-wealth stories remind us of the genre of rags-to-riches stories, which was immensely popular in Europe and especially in the

United States during the same era. However, it is essential to note that Ahmed Midhat's characters do not start from "rags."[68] His successful characters generally hail from the newly rising middle classes, just like himself. Thus his target audience is not the desperately poor, but middle-class youth. Moreover, it is also possible to read his stories as a metaphorical development strategy—through hard work and education—for a country of modest means. In this sense, his stories imply that the non-industrialized and underdeveloped Ottoman Empire could achieve industrialization and development if its citizens received a good education, worked hard, and created wealth through entrepreneurship despite the country's relative lack of wealth. In short, Ahmed Midhat's stories provide a dramatic presentation of the dominant approach to economic development in the Ottoman economic thinking in the era.[69]

In addition to Ahmed Midhat's inspiration from economic theory, economic ideas found in French novels of the age also influenced his fiction. Ahmed Midhat admitted that he was influenced by Émile Zola, despite his criticism of Zola's pessimistic naturalism.[70] One of Zola's most popular works of the same era provides us with important insights into Ahmed Midhat's possible sources of inspiration for his own stories:

> [In *Au Bonheur des Dames* (1883)] Vallagnosc has no ambition, despite a brilliant school career…; life, he feels, is pointless. Octave starts from the bottom of the ladder and works his way up, by charm, drive and effort, to become director of his mighty emporium, while Vallagnosc is stuck in a tedious, if respectable, bureaucratic post. Where Vallagnosc represents decaying upper class, so exhausted that it has lost faith even in itself, Mouret is the force of the new age, open to every kind of change and driven by an irresistible lust for life and power.[71]

Similarly, as we have seen previously, Ahmed Midhat tells stories of lonely idealist characters who represent a new work ethic in a society still dominated by the laziness and lack of entrepreneurial spirit of the old elite. In a sense, he tells us stories of a Weberian clash of rationalization-versus-tradition in a burgeoning capitalism.

Despite his emphasis on cooperation and division of labor in his economic writings, we do not see these principles very frequently in action in Ahmed Midhat's fiction. He puts the emphasis on the loneliness of his ideal characters. The only exception to this is the sexual division of labor among male and female protagonists. He created ideal wives for his heroes based on the same criteria (e.g., diligence and resourcefulness).[72] These ideal wives appear as the chief assistants of their husbands by virtue of being competent managers of the household economy. The wives of Rakım and Şinasi, for example, work hard and use limited resources economically, thus contributing significantly to their husbands' efforts. It is important to note, however, that Ahmed Midhat's ideal family operates within the rules of the traditional patriarchal system, and that his female characters do not actively individually participate in the labor force.[73]

Ahmed Midhat's heroes are obvious reflections of his own life story, lifestyle, and economic worldview.[74] He came from a modest family and achieved success simply by educating himself and working harder than others. He earned his living through his labor (mostly by writing and publishing) and his business enterprises. His family worked together at his printing press, exemplifying a household type of cooperation and division of labor.[75] In short, Ahmed Midhat himself exemplified the ideal modern Ottoman—in bourgeois-capitalist standards—in his own life as a hard-working writer, editor, and entrepreneur, and used fiction to present himself, as well as his economic ideas, to his audience, with an eye to influencing their economic mentality and behavior.[76]

An early Young Turk manifesto-novel: *Turfanda mı, Turfa mı?*

(Mizancı) Mehmed Murad (1854–1917) was an important figure in late Ottoman intellectual and political life.[77] After some years of service as a junior civil servant, he became professor of history at the Mekteb-i Mülkiye (The Imperial School of Administration) in 1876 and assumed other high posts in the state in the first two decades of the Hamidian regime.[78] In 1886, he began to publish his popular newspaper *Mizan*, which earned him the moniker Mizancı Murad (Murad of Mizan). In his early career, he appeared to be a successful but sometimes refractory bureaucrat, intellectual, and educator in the Hamidian regime. In the early 1890s, however, he began to be more critical of the regime and joined the secret organization of the Committee of Union and Progress (CUP), rising to the position of committee leader by 1896.[79] In 1891, he was appointed to the Duyûn-ı Umûmiye (The Ottoman Public Debt Authority) as an inspector,[80] and he retained this position until his self-exile in 1895. As an intellectual, teacher, and also as a Young Turk leader, he was very influential, particularly on the Hamidian-era youth.

Murad Bey wrote *Turfanda mı, Turfa mı?* while he was still following the line of social reformism but slowly drifting towards Young Turk radicalism.[81] The novel includes very significant details about the social, economic, and political problems of the era, and it also provides us with important insights into the reformist thinking of the era. Moreover, it depicts interesting examples of ideal modern Ottomans and a blueprint for a comprehensive socio-economic development project in the mind of a reformer of the era. Murad Bey's messages and lessons for his readers start with the title of the book. In his introduction, he states that he presents some characters that are "products of recent times,"[82] and then asks his readers: "are they avant-gardes (early fruits) of a new society or are they simply strange outcasts?"[83] The question is actually rhetorical. It is obvious that Murad Bey presents his protagonists as models for his Ottoman male and female readers to emulate. The novel also includes harsh criticisms about the Ottoman political and financial system, and proposes a new social and political order. In this respect, the novel goes beyond being a *roman à thèse* and takes the form of a manifesto-novel. Therefore, a careful reading of *Turfanda mı, Turfa mı?*—keeping the discussions about economic development in Ottoman economic thought of the era in mind—will reveal how major economic ideas of the age permeated the Ottoman novel as a result of reformists' pedagogical purposes, with an eye on social change.

Mansur as the idealist civil servant

The protagonist of *Turfanda mı, Turfa mı?*, Mansur, is a typical romantic hero of the nineteenth-century novel.[84] He is an idealized Ottoman type in terms of his moral and intellectual attributes as well as his work ethic. Just as in the case of Ahmed Midhat's heroes, Mansur represents the author's own worldview transposed into fiction. It is easy to see that Mansur's biography has a strong resemblance to that of Murad Bey, and many details in the story have strong parallels in Murad Bey's memoirs that he published later.[85]

Murad Bey's Mansur is a young and idealist man from an elite Algerian family. His belief in Islamism and Ottomanism leads him to move to Istanbul instead of Europe, contrary to what many like-minded young people did at the time.[86] However, from the moment he arrives, the European impact on the "capital of the Caliphate" causes a great disappointment for him. He observes, for instance, that French francs are preferred to Ottoman *kuruş* in everyday life,[87] and that the Beyoğlu district is dominated by signs and advertisements in French rather than Turkish.[88] In addition to its obvious Ottomanist, Islamist, and anti-imperialist tone, the novel carries the seeds of Turkish nationalism, which was to dominate the early twentieth-century Ottoman-Turkish political sphere through the Young Turk ideology. Although Mansur is mostly referring to "Ottomans" when he says "Turk," at several places in the novel he and his friend Doctor Mehmed praise the virtues of the "pure Turks" of Ankara, Konya, Kastamonu, Çankırı, and Yozgat.[89] This is one of the earliest traces of an Anatolian-Turkish nationalist discourse in the Ottoman intellectual sphere.[90]

At several junctures in the novel, we read long tirades of Mansur that provide us with detailed blueprints of Murad Bey's own socio-economic reform program for the empire.[91] His program operates at two separate but internally connected levels: governmental and individual. According to Murad Bey's narrative, at the governmental level the problems of the Ottoman Empire could be analyzed under two main categories: first, the ineffective organization of the Ottoman bureaucracy and the problematic work ethic of Ottoman civil servants; and second, the chaotic and inefficient financial and economic administration of the country. At the individual level, lack of education, laziness, and an anti-entrepreneurial popular economic mentality constitute the main obstacles to economic development. All in all, economic messages given in the novel through Mansur's words and deeds seem to reflect major discussions and suggestions in late Ottoman economic thought regarding the question of economic development—which we discussed in the previous chapters.

Mansur begins to observe the ineffective and wasteful administration of the Ottoman bureaucratic system on his first day at the office. As a young physician, he decides to pursue two parallel career paths: he earns his living through practicing his profession—working as a teacher as well as a medical doctor at the

Imperial School of Medicine—and he joins the civil service out of patriotic feeling in order to serve his country.[92] He decides to work at the Ministry of Foreign Affairs, and like many educated young people who knew foreign languages in the era, he is appointed to the Translation Bureau.[93] However, on his very first day on the job, he realizes that there is actually no work to do at the office. He witnesses many senior officials spending their days doing nothing but "sitting on their chairs and eating rice pudding (*sütlaç*)..., having their meals, drinking fruit juice (*şerbet*) or coffee, smoking, and yawning, and sometimes leaving the office for a promenade [arm-in-arm with other fellows] in the corridor."[94] He understands that all this eating and drinking is not because of hunger or appetite, but only to pass the time.

> [Mansur] was terribly dismayed. He understood that it is impossible to improve one's intellectual capacity under these conditions. On the contrary, he thought, one can lose everything that one knows. Mansur investigated the reasons for this situation ... [and] he realized that the office did not need so many people. Just a redactor, a translator, and a recording clerk would suffice. The rest [of the staff] was simply redundant.[95]

Later, Mansur learns also that these redundant personnel are not even educated, and they lack the skills and talents for any sort of civil service. Most of them hold these posts because of their personal connections with senior officials, reflecting the institutionalized favoritism of Ottoman bureaucratic mechanisms. While observing undeserved appointments and promotions, he learns that he and another junior official are being considered for promotion. This becomes the last straw for Mansur.[96] He rejects this promotion saying that he did not do anything to earn it, and that in fact he hardly worked at all since there was no work for him to do at the office. This open rebellious attitude to the established system annoys his superiors.[97] However, his protests against wrongdoing in the office continue with increasing intensity, culminating in his refusal to go to work.[98]

One day, he is introduced to the Minister of Public Works, Emin Pasha. During his conversation with the pasha, Mansur's idealism and ideas for reform erupt into a quasi-manifesto—in the form of a dialogue between the old and the new—for a comprehensive reform in the Ottoman Empire:[99]

> Mansur told the pasha that he had studied in Europe and wanted to see everything [in the Ottoman Empire] as orderly and organized as it is in Europe, and that he could not bear the situation at the office. He even mentioned the promotion incident. Upon hearing this, Emin Pasha said:
>
> – My dear son, not everything can be [as] orderly and perfect [as we wish]. One should let it be. The order that you saw in Europe is unattainable in our country.[100]

Mansur immediately rejects this idea and suggests that if every Ottoman official took his job seriously and worked hard and faithfully, everything would be as perfect as in Europe.[101] He adds that the Ottoman Empire has more faithful and moral subjects than Europe does. However, in his view, there are two great obstacles: a general ignorance in society and the irresponsibility of civil servants. He maintains that the sultan is aware of all these problems and has even issued a decree to fight them.[102] Emin Pasha, in response, reminds Mansur of the fact that reform is always easier said than done, and he adds that people who try to fight for such causes always give up eventually. Therefore, Emin Pasha confidently concludes, Mansur will sooner or later understand this reality and simply surrender to the status quo.[103] Mansur rejects these pessimistic and conformist ideas by arguing that although it is true that fighting is hard for junior officials, it should not be so for the senior ones who hold political power. He thinks that the power one holds should also go with certain responsibilities.[104] In response, the pasha complains about the many obstacles, such as inadequate financial sources, the lack of educated personnel, and especially the youth whom the state sends to Europe:

> We send many young people to Paris to study. However, none of them returns as we expect. They lose their good manners and morals and become useless [for the state]. All they learn is to dress elegantly, to waste money on self-indulgence, and to become French by losing their moral and religious values.[105]

Mansur agrees with the pasha on this matter, but as a solution he suggests sending talented and meritorious youth instead of the spoiled sons of the Ottoman elite.[106] The pasha responds to this by saying that the state by itself cannot afford to provide a comfortable life to those who go to Europe; therefore, sending the sons of the rich is the only practical solution.[107] At this point the discussion concentrates around three main problems: the uneducated and unskilled bureaucracy, the lack of an educational system that could solve the human capital problem, and the inadequacy of financial resources that lies at the heart of everything. Mansur tells the pasha that government offices are overstaffed with useless personnel, and that this puts a huge burden on the government's budget.[108] He then suggests a comprehensive educational reform, including opening up new schools to train officials. The pasha, once again, puts forward the obstacle of inadequate financial resources and complains that only a small fraction of the state's budget is allocated for education; he then adds that the Ministry of Finance is unable to pay even this small amount.[109] This time, Mansur's response comes in the form of a long tirade about an overall economic development project for the whole country:

> Sir, you are the one who will make them pay! Make them pay it! ...
>
> You say that there are financial difficulties. If we take a look at the [amount of] waste, it is not possible to believe in the existence of such difficulties. Let's assume that they exist; we still do not see any attempts to solve this problem. Isn't it your responsibility? The reform in fiscal affairs

> and the expansion of state revenues are both tied to public works. In Anatolia, surplus production goes bad due to the lack of roads for freight and transportation. As a result, people cannot benefit from surplus.
>
> Other nations make all kinds of sacrifices to build railways in order to increase their revenues and augment their power and [productive] capacity. Attracting foreign investors to our country—even it takes begging them—is a necessity for the sacred interests of the state. However, [in our country] even those [foreign investors] who come voluntarily lose all hope and return [to their countries] because of never-ending negotiations and meetings with irresponsible, unskilled, and uneducated bureaucrats.[110]

Mansur goes on to say that the Ministry of Public Works should make a plan and give concessions to deserving investors. He complains that neither such a plan exists, nor does the Ministry send engineers to Anatolia.[111] After his harsh criticisms against the Ministry of Public Works, he openly blames the pasha for not taking any action for the construction of land routes, and he asks: "Now, if there is financial difficulty, who is to blame?"[112] The pasha tries to defend himself and the system by telling Mansur a secret that proves the impossibility of the situation:

> The government budget constantly runs a deficit. In order for you to comprehend our financial situation, I will tell you a secret that should stay between us: In the last few years, we have had to turn to external borrowing even to pay off the interest on our existing foreign loans.[113]

Upon being informed of this scandalous secret, Mansur shows how this method is economically irrational and has potentially disastrous consequences by making a simple but educated economic analysis:

> Mansur – So, sir, the Treasury is hoping to receive a large sum of revenue in the near future?
>
> Emin Pasha – What does this mean?
>
> Mansur – Sir, this means that last year and the year before the Treasury had recourse to foreign loans to achieve budgetary balance and to pay off the interest on the foreign loans. As your excellency has also stated, [when the borrowed money is used to pay interest] the money obtained under very heavy conditions of foreign borrowing goes directly [into the coffers of the financiers] abroad, instead of being used for works that could augment the state's revenues. Under these conditions, borrowing will not give any results other than further expanding the amount of interest payments in the following year's budget.[114]

Emin Pasha understands Mansur's point and responds to his initial question by saying that there is no such "miraculous revenue" that could solve the problem. Upon Mansur's insistence on getting an explanation for such a dangerous policy, the pasha finally admits that he has been ordered to find solutions simply to stave off bankruptcy.[115] Mansur understands that the pasha implies an order from the top, that is, from the sultan. However, as a manifestation of his adherence to traditional Ottoman paternalism, he dismisses any possibility that the sultan would force his men to ruin his own country, and accuses the pasha of treason; but the pasha responds in cold blood: "[The state's] master demands this. We cannot do anything."[116] Mansur, filled with feelings of patriotism and loyalty to the sultan, puts an abrupt end to the discussion as he storms off repeating his accusation of treason.[117] Meanwhile, the pasha understands that Mansur belongs to "the harmful group" and blacklists him in order that he be taken care of later.[118] This brief note hints at both what will happen to Mansur at the end of the story and what happens to anyone who questions the status quo in the Hamidian regime. In writing this, Murad Bey seems to be pondering the possibilities for his own future too.

Mansur as the vanguard of the rationalization process

After resigning from his post, Mansur dedicates himself to his patients, his studies, and more importantly to his bottom-up reform project for the empire. He presents a reform proposal to the Ministry of Education.[119] However, having seen that the state is incapable of a comprehensive educational reform such as he has envisioned, he decides to start his own project. Meanwhile, he observes that foreign powers, through the interference of the embassies, have their proposals for new missionary schools passed through the same commissions.[120] Mansur thereby witnesses once again the power and influence of the embassies over the Ottoman government. Upon the uprising in Herzegovina against Ottoman rule, Mansur writes articles for a newspaper criticizing the interference of the European powers. In response, the embassies force the Ministry of Foreign Affairs and the Directorate General of the Press to take action against him. Eventually, the same newspaper is left no choice but to publish another article rejecting Mansur's claims, labeling him a traitor, and calling him non-Ottoman and non-Turkish.[121] Mansur appeals directly to the Sublime Porte to protest these claims, but to no avail. Then, having lost all his faith in a top-down change in the Ottoman Empire, Mansur decides to move to Anatolia in order to start a bottom-up transformation: "They say that reforms should begin at the bottom. This is obviously true. In Europe, efforts at development appeared in the provinces earlier than the capitals."[122]

As another biographical connection between the author and his protagonist, we know that the author, Murad Bey, later presented a memorandum of reform upon the request of the sultan just before he went into exile in 1895. He also had a chance to receive an audience of the sultan to explain his ideas.[123] However, just as with Mansur, these last efforts to find legitimate ways for change did not produce any results, and Murad Bey left the country to join the Young Turks in exile in 1895.

Similar to the story of Şinasi in Ahmed Midhat's *Bahtiyarlık*, which was discussed previously, Mansur goes to Anatolia and settles on a farm in Western

Anatolia that he inherited from his late uncle. He uses his estate to launch a small-scale modernization project, yet a much more comprehensive one than that of Şinasi. In addition to running his farm, he becomes the main agent of modernization with his various roles: a physician who treats poor peasants for free, a warm-hearted creditor who provides interest-free loans to the peasants, an altruistic employer, and the founder of modern schools.[124]

At the end of the book, we find Mansur's letters written to his friends about the hardships and successes of his project. In one of these letters, we can clearly see Murad Bey's criticisms of the Ottoman tax system as one of the biggest obstacles to development.[125] Mansur appoints a literate person as the headman of his village and centralizes the tax collection system under the headman's management. Under this new system, the collection process, which caused resentment and even fights before Mansur's arrival, begins to be handled relatively smoothly, the taxes being paid even before the deadline.[126] However, one day a revenue officer comes to the village and demands money from the peasants, even though the peasants have paid their taxes already. Upon hearing this, Mansur intervenes in the situation and then realizes that this is not a simple misunderstanding, but an unpleasant remnant of the old inefficient system. The revenue officer requests that Mansur abolish the new system and says that the livelihood of his family depends on it. He then explains the situation:

> We make money every time we come to the village. It is not our salary, but these [small] payments allow us to make ends meet. The less we collect [on each visit] and the more we come to collect the remaining parts, the more profitable it is for us. Especially the late payments are our [source of] main income. We come here at the worst time for the peasant. We harass him and threaten him with selling his ox in return for his debt. Finally, we make a deal and get some money for ourselves in return for postponing the collection for three months. We do not come three months later, because then he would have the money. We wait until he is poor again, and we come at such a time so that we can get twice as much as we got the last time.[127]

Upon hearing this scheme that "even the Devil could not think of,"[128] Mansur dismisses him from the village and informs the district governor of the situation. However, the district governor responds to him resentfully, saying that it is not right to bother those "poor revenue officers."[129] Moreover, Mansur observes that the provincial administration is in a worse situation than the central administration in Istanbul, and that irresponsibility and corruption are both more overt and more widespread in the rural parts of the empire. In addition, all channels for the people to voice their problems and communicate with the central government are closed because of the oppression of the provincial officials.[130] Once more, Mansur realizes the hopeless situation of the Ottoman bureaucratic system at both the central and provincial levels. This last incident also shows him the roots of the financial crisis of the state that Emin Pasha was complaining about: "Now I begin to understand the mystery of our revenues not being in proportion to our natural resources and territorial expansion."[131] In other words, Mansur realizes that although the Ottoman Empire has vast and rich territories, the revenue is lost during the collection and transmission process. This causes chronic fiscal shortages, which in turn impedes economic development.

As mentioned earlier, Mansur acts as the vanguard of a modernization process in the village. Not only does he bring modern education, he also introduces new economic institutions that would constitute the backbone of a prospective capitalist system. For example, his provision of interest-free credit to the peasants is by no means a simple act of philanthropy, but rather a deliberate economic development scheme in a capitalist sense. In other words, Mansur advances these loans not to help the poor, but to encourage peasants to invest in their property to expand their productive capacities.[132] More importantly, he puts the idea of cooperation into action—just as Ahmed Midhat also suggests—to establish a yarn factory by gathering small contributions from the peasants.[133] For him, this enterprise is important not only for its imminent economic results, but also for the change in mentality that it would lead to:

> At first, I considered founding it at my own expense and profit. But later I decided to familiarize our rural uncles [peasants], who cannot think beyond the limits of tradition, with the idea of profit-seeking.[134] First, I had ten *kuruş* [piasters] of donation collected from each household of the nearby villages by using their trust in me. Then, their neighbors also wanted to contribute.... Finally, I added the same amount as the sum collected from the peasants, and I founded a company based on fifty-fifty shares. Things have gone well so far. The cost of our product is one hundred *paras*,[135] whereas the same quality European yarn costs five *kuruş*es. I am trying to bring it down to sixty *para*s.[136]

In short, Mansur, just as Ahmed Midhat suggested earlier, establishes a successful factory that can compete with European producers simply by gathering modest amounts of capital. He thereby solves the ubiquitous problem of financial capital. By dragging the peasants into shareholding, he aims to transform the mentality in the village into a capitalistic one. In this respect, Mansur's capitalist rationalization process includes both short- and long-term projections for economic development. However, Mansur does not live to see the final results of his project, since, like many other nineteenth-century romantic heroes, he dies prematurely as a result of an unfortunate accident.

Mansur's story gives us important insights into the emergence, in Ottoman economic thinking, of the idea of the salvation of the empire through bottom-up economic modernization instead of a political power struggle at the top. Mansur is a patriotic Ottoman who believes in the sacredness of the Ottoman state and of its sultan, who is also the caliph of the Muslims. However, Mansur witnesses the incapacity of the bureaucracy to govern the country effectively. Institutionalized corruption, favoritism, ignorance, irresponsibility, and indifference to the Ottoman central and provincial bureaucracy kill all hopes for a better future.

Furthermore, the same political and administrative system chokes any idealistic attempt to carry out reforms and punishes the idealists. Upon understanding both the inability of the central government to solve the problems of the empire and the danger facing the reformists, Mansur has to turn to a bottom-up approach to economic development, taking up the endeavor to build a new society based on new economic principles. In this respect, Mansur's story provides us insights into why both Ahmed Midhat and Murad Bey adopted social reformism upon their return from exile (1873–76 and 1895–97, respectively), which was caused by their earlier political reformist stance.

As another connection of the story to real life, it is worth noting that cooperatives, like that of Mansur, did not appear only in such quasi-utopian literary works of the era. On the contrary, some reformist Ottoman statesmen actually established such institutions to encourage economic development at the local level.[137] The best-known example is the *Memleket Sandıkları* (District Funds) founded by Midhat Pasha in the Danube province in the early 1860s.[138] The main objective of these funds was to provide the peasantry with cheap credit.[139] In another example, Kâmil Pasha (1832–1913) initiated the *köy bakkalları* (village grocers) project in the province of Aydın in 1900 to replace exploitative local merchants with a kind of consumer cooperative. With this project, Kâmil Pasha aimed at relieving the peasants of the heavy exploitation of local merchants and usurers, thereby improving economic conditions in rural areas.[140] Turning back to the realm of fiction, Kâmil Pasha's project provided the well-known Ottoman satirist Şair Eşref (*c.*1847–1912) with inspiration for his poem, *Köy Bakkalları* (village grocers, *c.*1900).[141] In this poem, Eşref advises Ottoman Muslim peasantry to put some capital together in order to establish a grocery shop in the village to take over the business of the Greek merchant (whom he calls "Yani"). According to him, exploiters such as Yani—thanks to their limited literacy that Muslims lack—establish businesses and get rich simply by cheating poor peasants. Eşref accuses Muslim peasants of laziness, ignorance, and traditionalism, which provide these shrewd shopkeepers with the opportunity to exploit them.[142] In short, Eşref's poem is the equivalent of Ahmed Midhat's and Murad Bey's novels in poetry, as it promotes a new capitalistic economic mentality to the Muslim peasantry. Moreover, it also reflects the emerging Muslim-Turkish economic proto-nationalist discourse of the era.

Murad Bey's marks the end of the idealist era of the Ottoman novel.[143] *Turfanda mı, Turfa mı?* is the most radical example of the Ottoman *roman à thèse* because of its bold social and political criticisms.[144] After the publication of *Turfanda mı, Turfa mı?*, Ottoman novelists had to change their course due to the increasing pressure of the Hamidian censors.[145] The novels of the 1890s and 1900s, therefore, focused more on social and cultural problems such as slavery, the education of girls, and marriage, instead of issues with direct political implications.[146] Hüseyin Cahid Yalçın (1875–1957) used the metaphor of "tightrope walking" to describe the dangers and hardships of being a writer under the paranoia of the Hamidian regime.[147] However, it is also important to note also that although many books and periodicals were banned in those years, the government was never able to prevent their illegal circulation completely.[148] As a result, the idealist examples of early-Hamidian-era fiction made a deep impact on the Young Turks in their formative years.

Conclusion

The quasi-utopian fiction of Ahmed Midhat and Mizancı Murad Bey provide us with insights into the mindset of late nineteenth-century reformers. These works also demonstrate how economic discussions of the age had already permeated into the social and cultural sphere, and bourgeois-capitalist values began to have a role in social change in Ottoman society. The fictional communities in these narratives, which can be regarded as the authors' simulations for the future of Ottoman society, are imagined to be built with a capitalist spirit and are organized according to the principles of cooperation and division of labor. It is not hard to see that through these stories, both authors not only make a criticism of the existing social and economic order, but they also present an alternative that can be built with the help of modern economic principles and a capitalistic approach.

Ahmed Midhat and Mizancı Murad used fictional stories about some idealized Ottoman vanguards of modernization as a practical guide to put bourgeois economic values and some economic principles in action for a prospective modern Ottoman society. The ideas of cooperation and division of labor, a capitalist work ethic, and the importance of science, technology, and education were presented to readers in easy-to-digest stories about success and failure. The authors showed the ways to wealth and social reputation through hard work, thrift, diligence, moderation, and rational thinking, and they hoped that their readers would emulate the protagonists. At the same time, they also warned their audience against the destructive consequences of ignorance, laziness, indifference, irresponsibility, and irrational behavior. In fictionalizing such an apparently capitalist-bourgeois value set, both Ahmed Midhat and Mizancı Murad hoped to influence popular economic mentality and behavior, with an eye on a bottom-up social change towards an advanced industrial capitalist society.

It is also important to note that the existence of some real-life examples of the characters of Ahmed Midhat and Murad Bey indicates that these stories also reflect an already started change in Ottoman society. The propagated the social and economic values, from entrepreneurial spirit and hard work to meritocracy and moral integrity, had already started to make an impact in the empire thanks to a newly rising Ottoman bourgeoisie. This new class and its economic values were in clash with the economic mentality and behavior of the old elites. In such a social and economic atmosphere, both authors criticize the parasitic *alafranga*-type old Ottoman elite and promote an alternative upper-class behavior reminiscent of a Weberian-type entrepreneurial bourgeoisie. In other words, Ahmed Midhat and Murad Bey, through their novels, not only reflected the rise of bourgeoisie in Ottoman society, but also promoted the emergence of a "national bourgeoisie" —with its entrepreneurial as well as patriotic mindset—which was expected to supplant the Ottoman leisure class of the Tanzimat. In the following decades, this idea was to shape the main economic objective of Young Turk governments, starting from the 1908 Revolution well into the first decades of the Republican era.

Notes

1 Johann Gottfried von Herder, *Against Pure Reason: Writings on Religion, Language, and History*, translated, edited, and with an introduction by Marcia Bunge (Minneapolis: Fortress Press, 1993), p. 143, quoted in Catherine Gallagher and Stephen Greenblatt, *Practicing New Historicism* (Chicago: University of Chicago Press, 2000), 6–7.

2 Catherine Gallagher, *The Body Economic: Life, Death, and Sensation in Political Economy and the Victorian Novel* (Princeton: Princeton University Press, 2006), 6.

3 Many scholars have pointed to this fact, see for example, Şerif Mardin, "Super Westernization in the Ottoman Empire in the Last Quarter of the Nineteenth Century," in *Turkey: Geographic and Social Perspectives*, ed. Peter Benedict, Erol Tümertekin, and Fatma Mansur (Leiden: Brill, 1974), 403; Kemal Karpat, "Traditionalist Elite Philosophy and the Modern Mass Media," in *Political Modernization in Japan and Turkey*, ed. Robert E. Ward and Dankwart A. Rustow (Princeton: Princeton University Press, 1964), 266. More recently, Carter Findley noted, without much elaboration, that conservative Ottoman writers used the novel as an instrument of social engineering. See his "Competing Autobiographical Novels, His and Hers," in *Many Ways of Speaking about the Self: Middle Eastern Ego-Documents in Arabic, Persian, and Turkish (14th–20th Century)*, ed. Ralf Elger and Yavuz Köse (Otto Harrassowitz Verlag, 2010), 133–40.

4 Şerif Mardin, "Tanzimat'tan Cumhuriyete İktisadî Düşüncenin Gelişimi (1838–1918)," in *Tanzimat'tan Cumhuriyet'e Türkiye Ansiklopedisi*, vol. 3 (İstanbul: İletişim Yayınları, 1985), 629.

5 Ahmet Evin, *Origins and Development of the Turkish Novel* (Minneapolis: Bibliotheca Islamica, 1983), 15. For more information on the Ottoman novel and the question of modernization and Westernization, see Ibid., 10–19; Güzin Dino, *Türk Romanının Doğuşu* (İstanbul: Cem Yayınevi, 1978), 18–22; and Berna Moran, *Türk Romanına Eleştirel Bir Bakış*, vol. 1 (İstanbul: İletişim Yayınları, 1983), 9–22.

6 Moran, *Türk Romanı*, 1:10; see a similar example from Namık Kemal in Evin, *Origins and Development of the Turkish Novel*, 19. Ahmed Midhat Efendi also regarded such traditional works as "lousy old stories that are full of superstitions," although he benefitted from this genre in forming his own popular style. (Hilmi Ziya Ülken, *Türkiye'de Çagdaş Düşünce Tarihi*, vol. 1 (Konya: Selçuk Yayınları, 1966), 159).

7 Jale Parla, *Babalar ve Oğullar: Tanzimat Romanının Epistemolojik Temelleri* (İstanbul: İletişim Yayınları, 1990), 18–19, 52.

8 For Ahmed Midhat's understanding of fiction and its social roles, see Fazıl Gökçek, *Küllerinden Doğan Anka: Ahmet Mithat Efendi Üzerine Yazılar* (İstanbul: Dergah Yayınları, 2012), 43–78.

9 For critical studies on Ahmed Midhat's literary style, themes, and characters, see Nüket Esen and Erol Köroğlu, eds., *Merhaba Ey Muharrir!: Ahmet Mithat Üzerine Eleştirel Yazılar* (İstanbul: Boğaziçi Üniversitesi Yayınevi, 2006); Gökçek, *Küllerinden Doğan Anka*; Nüket Esen, *Hikâye Anlatan Adam: Ahmet Mithat* (İstanbul: İletişim Yayınları, 2014).

10 Quoted in M. Orhan Okay, *Batı Medeniyeti Karşısında Ahmed Midhat Efendi* (Ankara: Baylan Matbaası, 1975), xv.

11 Stefan Zweig, *Master Builders: A Typology of the Spirit* (New York: Viking Press, 1939), 64.
12 For an analysis of Alger's novels as "guidebooks for survival in an industrializing economy," see Carol Nackenoff, *The Fictional Republic: Horatio Alger and American Political Discourse* (New York: Oxford University Press, 1994), 52–77.
13 Using fiction to teach economic ideas is not exclusively a nineteenth-century phenomenon. In the twentieth and early twenty-first centuries, fiction continued to be an instrument to teach the principles of the "dismal science." Two well-known authors who devoted their literary works to teaching economics are Russell Roberts (a professor of economics at George Mason University) and Marshall Jevons (a fictitious writer created by two economists, William L. Breit and Kenneth G. Elzinga, and named after two well-known economists, Alfred Marshall and William Stanley Jevons).
14 Anne Green, "The Nineteenth Century (1820–1880)," in *Cassell Guide to Literature in French*, ed. Valerie Worth-Stylianou (London: Cassell, 1996), 128.
15 Scholars of the Turkish novel have presented various analyses of Ahmed Midhat's economic ideas as reflected in his fiction. See for example Okay, *Batı Medeniyeti Karşısında*, 114–21; Evin, *Origins and Development of the Turkish Novel*, 83–93; Ahmed Hamdi Tanpınar, *XIX. Asır Türk Edebiyatı Tarihi*, ed. Ahmet Kuyaş (İstanbul: Yapı Kredi Yayınları, 2006), 411–12. However, all of these studies, except for Okay's, focus only on his most popular novel, *Felatun Bey il Rakım Efendi* (1875).
16 For a biography of Ahmed Midhat with a special emphasis on his industriousness and entrepreneurship, see M. Orhan Okay, "Teşebbüse Sarfedilmiş Bir Hayatın Hikayesi," *Kitap-lık*, no. 54 (2002): 130–6.
17 I borrow the term super Westernization from Mardin, "Super Westernization."
18 Ahmed Midhat, *Müşahedat* (İstanbul, 1891), 127–9.
19 Ibid., 129.
20 Interestingly enough, Ahmed Midhat notes in the novel—in which he appears as a character as himself—that Seyyid Mehmed Numan inspired him to write these books (Ibid., 137).
21 Evin presents a concise analysis of Mehmed Numan's character and the economic ideas he represents for the interested reader (Evin, *Origins and Development of the Turkish Novel*, 108–13).
22 Ahmed Midhat, "Te'âvün ve Tenâsür," *Dağarcık*, no. 2 (1871): 57.
23 Abdullah Uçman, "Türk Romanında İlk Alafranga Tip: Felatun Bey," *Kitap-Lık*, no. 54 (2002): 140–7.
24 Hüseyin Rahmi tells the story of *Şık*'s publication in his introduction to the second edition of his book (1919). See Hüseyin Rahmi Gürpınar, "Muharririn Önsözü," in *Şık* (İstanbul: Pınar Yayınevi, 1964), 5–6.
25 For summaries and literary analyses of the novel, see Robert P. Finn, *Türk Romanı, İlk Dönem: 1872–1900* (Ankara: Bilgi Yayınevi, 1984), 87–99.; and Evin, *Origins and Development of the Turkish Novel*, 158–72.
26 For an analysis of the political and cultural roots of the late Ottoman suspicion of the *alafranga* type and his "conspicuous consumption," see Mardin, "Super Westernization."
27 Arminius Vambéry, *The Story of My Struggles: The Memoirs of Arminius Vambéry*, Third Impression. [London: T. Fisher Unwin, 1905], 371.
28 Moran, *Türk Romanı*, 1:38–9; Evin, *Origins and Development of the Turkish Novel*, 80–1.
29 For an analysis of this genre in the Turkish novel, see Moran, *Türk Romanı*, 1: 219–26.
30 "Conspicuous consumption means the use of consumer goods in such a way as to create a display for the purpose of impressing others rather than for the satisfaction

of normal consumer demand. It is consumption intended chiefly as an ostentatious display of wealth. The concept of conspicuous consumption was introduced into economic theory by Thorstein Veblen (1899) in the context of his analysis of the latent functions of 'conspicuous consumption' and 'conspicuous waste' as symbols of upper-class status and as competitive methods of enhancing individual prestige." (F. Stanković, "Conspicuous Consumption," ed. Steven N. Durlauf and Lawrence E. Blume, *The New Palgrave Dictionary of Economics* (New York: Palgrave Macmillan, 2008), 118).

31 According to Weber, a particular work ethic (or a capitalist spirit) is more responsible for the capitalist development than material reasons. He traces the source of this spirit to "the 'worldly asceticism' of reformed Christianity, with its twin imperatives to methodical work as the chief duty of life and to the limited enjoyment of its product. The unintended consequence of this ethic … was the accumulation of capital for investment." (David Beetham, "Max Weber," ed. Steven N. Durlauf and Lawrence E. Blume, *The New Palgrave Dictionary of Economics* (New York: Palgrave Macmillan, 2008), 716.) As Ahmed Midhat suggests in his stories, the work ethic of a capitalist entrepreneur is diametrically opposed to leisure-class behavior.

32 These stories are analyzed in detail in the context of the dialectics of the notions of conspicuous consumption and capitalist spirit in another study. See Deniz T. Kılınçoğlu, "Weber, Veblen ve Ahmed Midhat Efendi'nin Kahramanları," in *Kurumsal İktisat*, ed. Eyüp Özveren (Ankara: İmge Yayınevi, 2007), 441–72.

33 Thorstein Veblen, *The Theory of the Leisure Class: An Economic Study in the Evolution of Institutions* (New York: The Macmillan Company, 1899).

34 Ahmed Midhat, *Felatun Bey il Rakım Efendi*, ed. Tacettin Şimşek (Ankara: Akçağ Yayınları, 2000), 96.

35 This scene reflects the ubiquitous misogyny of the era in addition to a criticism of ostentation. Ali Bey, in his satirical dictionary, defines profligacy (*sefahat*) as "a valuable defect in the eyes of women" (Ali Bey, *Lehçet ül-Hakâik* (Mısır: Matbaa-yı Osmaniye, 1897), 21.). In the same dictionary, the devil (*şeytan*) is defined as "the friend of women" (*sadîk-i nisvân*) (Ibid., 23).

36 Ahmed Midhat, *Felatun Bey il Rakım Efendi*, 133.

37 Ibid., 131. For a more detailed analysis of Ahmed Midhat's notion of conspicuous consumption, see Kılınçoğlu, "Weber, Veblen ve Ahmed Midhat Efendi," 448–460.

38 Ahmed Midhat, *Felatun Bey il Rakım Efendi*, 200.

39 Ahmed Midhat, *Letaif-i Rivayat On Birinci Cüz'ü, (Bahtiyarlık) İsmiyle Bir Hikayeyi Havîdir* (İstanbul, 1885), 37.

40 Ibid., 175.

41 Ibid., 190–3.

42 Ahmed Midhat, *Letaif-i Rivayat On Yedinci Cüz'ü, (Para!) İsmiyle Bir Hikayeyi Havîdir* (İstanbul: Kırkanbar Matbaası, 1887), 23.

43 Ibid.

44 Ibid., 51. These words remind us of Ali Suâvi's complaints (1867) about Muslims' investing in land rather than commerce and industry, and thus losing economic and social status while non-Muslims rise in Ottoman society.

45 Ibid., 151.

46 Zweig, *Master Builders*, 46.

47 Ahmed Midhat, *Ekonomi Politik* (İstanbul: Kırkanbar Matbaası, 1879), 44.

48 For the relationship between his characters and his own biography, see Sema Uğurcan, "Ahmet Midhat Efendi'nin Hatıratı İle Romanları Arasındaki Münasebet," *Türklük Araştırmaları Dergisi*, no. 2 (1986): 185–99.

49 Due to the popularity of *Felatun Bey il Rakım Efendi*, Rakım has been analyzed by many scholars of the Ottoman novel as the ideal Ottoman depicted in late Ottoman literature. For analyses of Rakım character as the first Ottoman *Homo economicus*, see Tanpınar, *Türk Edebiyatı Tarihi*, 411–412; Robert P. Finn, *Türk Romanı, İlk*

Dönem: 1872–1900 (Ankara: Bilgi Yayınevi, 1984), 31–2; Evin, *Origins and Development of the Turkish Novel*, 87–92. However, Şinasi's story has been ignored despite its importance as being one of the quasi-utopian narratives of late Ottoman literature.

50 Ahmed Midhat, *Bahtiyarlık*, 5–6.
51 Okay, *Batı Medeniyeti Karşısında*, 39.
52 Ahmed Midhat, *Bahtiyarlık*, 55.
53 Mardin, *Jön Türkler*, 174–5.
54 Ahmed Rıza, *Meclis-i Mebusan ve Ayân Reisi Ahmed Rıza Bey'in Anıları* (İstanbul: Arba Yayınları, 1988), 9.
55 Max Weber, *The Protestant Ethic and the Spirit of Capitalism*, trans. Talcott Parsons (New York: Charles Scribner's Sons, 1958), 71.
56 Ahmed Midhat, *Bahtiyarlık*, 47–8.
57 Ibid., 75.
58 See for example his article, "Bereket Yerde midir, Gökde midir? Yahud Bir Cahil Çiftçinin Mütâlaât-ı Fenniyesi," *Müntahabât-ı Tercüman-ı Hakikat*, Vol. 2 (1884), 289, in which he relates his discussions with the gardener of his farm. Ahmed Midhat's article also reminds us of the modernist Ottoman elite character in the novel of one of his followers, Hüseyin Rahmi Gürpınar (1864–1944). Dehri Efendi in Hüseyin Rahmi's novel *Mürebbiye* (1899) is a farcical character sketch of an Ottoman vanguard of modernism. Even his name, which literally means "materialist," reflects the dominant worldview of the people he represents. Dehri tries to teach lessons from political economy and the science of midwifery (and others) to his illiterate gardener and housekeeping woman whenever he catches them off guard. As usual, Hüseyin Rahmi's scenes reflect highly ironic and mostly ludicrous encounters between the traditional and the modern, as these "simple" people try to get away from Dehri's highly didactic discourses. (Hüseyin Rahmi Gürpınar, *Mürebbiye* (Dersaadet [İstanbul]: İkdam Matbaası, 1897), 65.) Nevertheless, Hüseyin Rahmi also notes how these forced lessons sharpen the gardener's intellect as he builds an effective scarecrow, which was then imitated by the gardeners of neighboring farms. (Ibid., 75–6).
59 Jale Parla, "Rakım Efendi'den Nurullah Bey'e Cemaatçi Osmanlılıktan Cemiyetçi Türk. Milliyetçiliğine Ahmet Mithat'ın Romancılığı," in *Merhaba Ey Muharrir!: Ahmet Mithat Üzerine Eleştirel Yazılar*, ed. Nüket Esen and Erol Köroğlu (İstanbul: Boğaziçi Üniversitesi Yayınevi, 2006), 21–3.
60 "*Alafranga çiftçilik olmaz*!" (Şerafeddin Mağmumî, *Seyahat Hâtıraları* (Cairo, 1908), 91.).
61 Ibid.
62 Ahmed Midhat, *Bahtiyarlık*, 144–5.
63 Weber, *The Protestant Ethic*, 68.
64 "[A] *roman à thèse* is a novel written in the realistic mode (that is, based on an aesthetic of verisimilitude and representation), which signals itself to the reader as primarily didactic in intent, seeking to demonstrate the validity of a political, philosophical, or religious doctrine." (Susan Rubin Suleiman, *Authoritarian Fictions: The Ideological Novel as a Literary Genre* (New York: Columbia University Press, 1983), 7).
65 Ahmed Midhat, *Sevda-yı Sa'y ü Amel* (İstanbul: Kırkanbar Matbaası, 1879), 56–57.
66 See Evin, *Origins and Development of the Turkish Novel*, 86.
67 Ahmed Midhat, "Tesellî-i Miskinan," in *Kıssadan Hisse*, 31–4 (İstanbul, 1870). *Kıssadan Hisse* consists of fables translated from Aesop (*c.*620–564 BC) and François Fénelon (1651–1715), in addition to a few others which are written by Ahmed Midhat himself. After each story, Ahmed Midhat summarizes its critical message.
68 For an Ottoman rags-to-riches story, see Mehmed Tahir, *Netice-i Sa'y* (Dersaadet [İstanbul]: Mahmud Bey Matbaası, 1893), in which the protagonist comes to Istanbul as a poor boy and struggles to survive simply through his hard work and

intellectual and entrepreneurial skills. However, although we see that the boy keeps his head above the water with his persistence and hard work, we do not see him attaining riches in the end.

69 See Chapter 4 for major late Ottoman approaches to and discussions about economic development.

70 Ahmed Midhat, "Hikâye Tasvir ve Tahriri," in Mehmet Kaplan *et al.*, eds., *Yeni Türk Edebiyatı Antolojisi*, vol. 3 (İstanbul: İ.Ü. Edebiyat Fakültesi Yayınları, 1979), 57.

71 Robin Buss, "Introduction," in Émile Zola, *Au Bonheur Des Dames*, trans. Robin Buss (London: Penguin Books, 2001), xii.

72 By contrast, his anti-heroes have affairs with immoral, uneducated, and unskilled French or culturally alienated Ottoman women.

73 For an analysis of Ahmed Midhat's understanding of family as an economic unit in his fiction, see A. Holly Shissler, "The Harem as the Seat of Middle-Class Industry and Morality: The Fiction of Ahmed Midhat Efendi," in *Harem Histories: Envisioning Places and Living Spaces*, ed. Marilyn Booth (Duke University Press, 2010), 319–41.

74 Uğurcan, "Ahmed Midhat."

75 Tanpınar, *Türk Edebiyatı Tarihi*, 411.

76 For his influence on the following generation of press entrepreneurs, see Ahmet İhsan Tokgöz, *Matbuat Hatıralarım, 1888–1923*, vol. 1 (İstanbul: Ahmet İhsan Matbaası, 1930), 52–3, et passim.

77 For a short biography of Murad Bey, see Abdullah Uçman, "Mizancı Murad," *T.D.V. İslam Ansiklopedisi* (İstanbul: Türkiye Diyanet Vakfı, 2005). For a more detailed analysis of his political and intellectual life, see Birol Emil, *Mizancı Murad Bey: Hayatı ve Eserleri* (İstanbul: İ.Ü. Edebiyat Fakültesi, 1979); Şerif Mardin, *Jön Türklerin Siyasi Fikirleri, 1895–1908* (İstanbul: İletişim Yayınları, 2004), 77–135.

78 Emil, *Mizancı Murad*, 79–82.

79 For the organization and activities of the Committee of Union and Progress under the direction of Murad Bey, see M. Şükrü Hanioğlu, *The Young Turks in Opposition* (New York: Oxford University Press, 1995), 90–109.

80 For his term at *Duyûn-i Umûmiye* see Mehmed Murad, *Meskenet Ma'zeret Teşkil Eder Mi?: Mücahede-yi Milliyeden: Mizan-ı Kadim ve Düyun-ı Umumiye Komiserliği Devirleri* (Dersaadet [İstanbul]: Matbaa-yı Âmedî, 1913), 173–253.

81 In his memoirs, he notes that some students from the Mekteb-i Mülkiye asked him to join and lead the Committee of Union and Progress, but he responded that he still believed in the sultan and legitimate ways of reform. (Emil, *Mizancı Murad*, 93–4).

82 Mehmed Murad, *Turfanda Mı, Turfa Mı?* (İstanbul: Mahmud Bey Matbaası, 1890), 3.

83 Ibid., 3–4.

84 For an analysis of the romantic hero in the early Turkish novel, see Finn, *Türk Romanı*, 40–65.

85 Mehmed Murad, *Meskenet.*

86 Murad Bey himself was not from Algeria, but from Dagestan, yet he had a very similar life story. See Uçman, "Mizancı Murad," 214.

87 Mehmed Murad, *Turfanda Mı, Turfa Mı?*, 19.

88 Ibid., 23.

89 Ibid., 117. For Murad Bey's cultural Turkism, see Mardin, *Jön Türkler*, 114–16.

90 Murad Bey calls his novel a *millî roman* (national novel), but he notes that this term is also used of some other novels to indicate that the novel in question is not a translation but it is written by an Ottoman author. He questions the alleged national character of such novels and emphasizes that his novel is national in terms of its identity and spirit (Mehmed Murad, *Turfanda Mı, Turfa Mı?*, 2).

91 Some examples are as follows: Ottoman bureaucracy, Ibid., 117–32; the importance of hard work and the problem of laziness and indifference, 187–91; an empire-wide

educational organization, 214–15; the difference between Europe and the Ottomans, 294–8; financial policies, 299–307; problems of the Ottoman tax system, 395–9. These are direct reflections, or fictionalized versions, of Murad's ideas on these topics that he presented in his articles in *Mizan* and other publications. Cf. Emil, *Mizancı Murad*, 288–91 (on bureaucracy); 275–8 (on economics and public finance); 278–86 (on education).

92 Cf. Ahmed Midhat's arguments on civil service employment above.

93 Mehmed Murad, *Turfanda Mı, Turfa Mı?*, 100–1.

94 Ibid., 118. The same scene appears in his memoirs as a real event. Cf. Mehmed Murad, *Meskenet*, 64.

95 Mehmed Murad, *Turfanda Mı, Turfa Mı?*, 118.

96 Ibid., 121–4.

97 Ibid., Cf. Mehmed Murad, *Meskenet*, 46–52.

98 In fact, Mansur does not resign officially, nor does he inform anyone of his decision. He simply stops going to the office. More interestingly, no one asks about his whereabouts. This is another detail that testifies to the loose administration at the office.

99 Mehmed Murad, *Turfanda Mı, Turfa Mı?*, 294–307. Evin argues that Murad Bey was influenced by Turgenev's *Fathers and Sons* (1861), which has similar scenes of heated arguments between different generations on social and political issues (Evin, *Origins and Development of the Turkish Novel*, 125). It is important to note, however, that Turgenev successfully blends such scenes into his literary work and gives a realistic and complex picture of the tensions in a changing society, whereas Mansur's abrupt tirades and Murad Bey's black-and-white picture give away the author's purely political aims in writing this novel.

100 Mehmed Murad, *Turfanda Mı, Turfa Mı?*, 293–4.

101 Ibid., 261.

102 Ibid.

103 Ibid.

104 Ibid., 263.

105 Ibid., 296–7.

106 Ibid., 297.

107 Ibid.

108 Ibid., 297–8.

109 Ibid., 299.

110 Ibid., 299–300.

111 Ibid., 300.

112 Ibid.

113 Ibid.

114 Ibid., 301.

115 Ibid., 302.

116 Ibid., 303.

117 Ibid., 303. Here, we see another manifestation of Murad Bey's own political stance. In his *Mizan*, he harshly criticized the government while praising the sultan's excellent statesmanship. (Mardin, *Jön Türkler*, 82).

118 Mehmed Murad, *Turfanda Mı, Turfa Mı?*, 304.

119 Ibid., 368–9.

120 For example, the American Bible Society obtains a permission to found a missionary school near Diyarbakır. (Ibid., 369).

121 Ibid., 371–2.

122 Ibid., 373.

123 Emil, *Mizancı Murad*, 101; for a transcribed copy of the memorandum see Kaplan *et al.*, *Yeni Türk Edebiyatı Antolojisi*, 3: 486–508.

124 Mehmed Murad, *Turfanda Mı, Turfa Mı?*, 372–3. Evin argues that Mansur's rural life resembles that of Levin of *Anna Karenina* (1877). According to Evin, "Murat,

in fact, had derived his ideas on rural reform from the debates of Russian intelligentsia on the issues related to serfdom, and *Turfanda* is the first Turkish novel to pay attention to the village." (Evin, *Origins and Development of the Turkish Novel*, 125).

125 Murad Bey was closely interested in the Ottoman fiscal system and wrote articles about its problems in his *Mizan* before the publication of his novel. (See Emil, *Mizancı Murad*, 275–8.) He later became an inspector of the *Duyûn-ı Umûmiye* (Ottoman Public Debt Administration), shortly after the publication of this novel.

126 Mehmed Murad, *Turfanda Mı, Turfa Mı?*, 395–6.

127 Ibid., 397.

128 Ibid.

129 Ibid.

130 Ibid., 398–9.

131 Ibid., 398.

132 Ibid., 373.

133 Cf. Ahmed Midhat's example of a paper factory in *Teşrik-i Mesa'î, Taksim-i Mesa'î* (İstanbul: Kırkanbar Matbaası, 1879), 131.

134 Cf. Sabahaddin, "Terbiye-i Milliye ve Islahat-i Şahsiye," *Terakki*, no. 19–20 (June 1908): 8. Sabahaddin Bey, in this article that he wrote 20 years after the publication of *Turfanda*, complains about the lack of entrepreneurial spirit among the Anatolian peasants. He states that the "moral purity" of the Anatolian peasantry is a result of the simplicity of rural life. This life also leads people "to observe tradition instead of adopting entrepreneurship and to cling to the past instead of [planning] the future." Therefore, he concludes, "the productive power of the nation is not improving."

135 1 *kuruş* = 40 *paras*

136 Mehmed Murad, *Turfanda Mı, Turfa Mı?*, 399–400.

137 In the post-1908 (i.e., the Young Turk) era, the idea of cooperation was to dominate nationalist economic thought as well as the government's economic policies, see Zafer Toprak, *Türkiye'de Ekonomi ve Toplum (1908–1950), Milli İktisat, Milli Burjuvazi* (İstanbul: Tarih Vakfı Yurt Yayınları, 1995), 125–44.

138 The Memleket Sandıkları later evolved into the Ziraat Bankası (Agricultural Bank) in 1888.

139 For more information on the Memleket Sandıkları, see Seçil Akgün, "Midhat Paşa'nın Kurduğu Memleket Sandıkları: Ziraat Bankası'nın Kökeni," in *Uluslararası Midhat Paşa Semineri: Bildiriler ve Tartışmalar, Edirne: 8–10 Mayıs 1984* (Ankara: Türk Tarih Kurumu, 1986).

140 For more information on Kâmil Pasha's *köy bakkalları* (village grocers) project and favorable reactions to the project in the local press, see Zeki Arıkan, "İzmir'de İlk Kooperatifleşme Çabaları," *Tarih İncelemeleri Dergisi*, no. 4 (1989): 31–42.

141 Kâmil Pasha (1832–1913) served several times as grand vizier from 1885 to 1913. When he started the *köy bakkalları* project, he was governor of the province of Aydın. He was also the lifelong patron of Şair Eşref.

142 Eşref and Alpay Kabacalı, *Çeşitli Yönleriyle Şair Eşref: Hayatı, Sanatı, Yergileri* (İstanbul: Özgür Yayın Dağıtım, 1988), 387–9.

143 Pertev Naili Boratav, "İlk Romanlarımız," in *Folklor ve Edebiyat*, vol. 1 (İstanbul: Adam Yayınları, 1982), 316.

144 It is important to note that although Murad Bey was able to publish his novel, it was later banned and existing copies were confiscated by the government.

145 For more information on censorship in the Hamidian era, see Cevdet Kudret, *Abdülhamit Devrinde Sansür* (İstanbul: Milliyet Yayınları, 1977).

146 For examples of such stories and novels, see Boratav, "İlk Romanlarımız," 313–15.

147 Hüseyin Cahid Yalçın, *Edebî Hatıralar* (İstanbul: Akşam Kitabhanesi, 1935), 102.

148 For an example of the illegal printing and distribution of Namık Kemal's works such as *Rûya*, see Kudret, *Abdülhamit Devrinde Sansür*, 29.

Conclusion

> The bourgeoisie, by the rapid improvement of all instruments of production, by the immensely facilitated means of communication, draws all, even the most barbarian, nations into civilisation. The cheap prices of its commodities are the heavy artillery with which it batters down all Chinese walls, with which it forces the barbarians' intensely obstinate hatred of foreigners to capitulate. It compels all nations, on pain of extinction, to adopt the bourgeois mode of production; it compels them to introduce what it calls civilisation into their midst, i.e., to become bourgeois themselves. In one word, it creates a world after its own image.[1]
>
> (Karl Marx and Friedrich Engels, 1848)

These words written by the famous radical internationalist intellectuals of the mid-nineteenth century provides us with a succinct summary of the paradigm that shaped the economic and social thought and the historiography of the age. Obviously, even these anti-capitalist and anti-bourgeois thinkers celebrated the "civilizing mission" of capitalism and the bourgeoisie through the expansion of the capitalist mode of production to the so-called "barbarian" parts of the world. Late nineteenth-century Ottoman economic mindset and thus the socio-economic aspects of Ottoman modernization were informed by the same paradigm. Looking from this particular perspective, the assumed place of the Ottoman Empire was among the backward and "barbaric" nations due to its pre-capitalist economy. This understanding constituted the major impetus behind Ottoman economic modernizaiton efforts to catch up with the so-called "civilized" (meaning, industrialized) nations. In this respect, in the late nineteenth century, economic development was as much a question of identity for the Muslim Ottoman elite as it was a question of the country's material well-being.

The question of identity and the notion of economic society

The question of identity had never been a problem for the Muslim elite of the Ottoman Empire before the nineteenth century, as they had been the ruling class of a mighty empire. The conditions began to change, however, with the rise of capitalist modernity. Following the socio-economic and political transformations as a result of the Scientific and Industrial Revolutions, the nineteenth century brought about a new episteme in European social and economic thought. The consequent Eurocentrist, Orientalist, and industrial-capitalist paradigm in European thinking began to diffuse worldwide. One such example was that the world was divided into the industrialized—thus culturally as well as economically advanced, or simply "civilized"—European nations and the backward (and "barbarian") nations. Although the Ottoman ruling elite pragmatically embraced modernity with its political and economic features as early as in the late eighteenth century, such exclusionist Eurocentric discourses of the age was not very encouraging for Muslim reformists in their efforts to join the ranks of the so-called civilized nations. Against all odds, however, the strategy for modernization in the late Ottoman Empire was crystallized as a nation-building project that was defined by the same epistemological (i.e., industrialist, Orientalist, and Eurocentrist) parameters that constituted the ideological challenge to Muslim-Ottoman modernity in the late nineteenth and early twentieth centuries.

Ottoman modernization was a full-fledged struggle waged at the cultural, social, economic, and political levels both externally and internally. A significant internal challenge for the Ottoman political elite was the emergence of the notions of economy and society as self-regulating systems. From the perspective of the pre-nineteenth century Ottoman ruling elite, the notion of Ottoman subjects (i.e., *re'aya*, flock) was a hazy entity, whose only feature was to keep the state alive and well through taxation and conscription. The traditional circle of justice mentality was based on the assumption that if the ruler secured order and justice, his subjects would supply the state with the necessary financial means to govern through taxation. The modernization process, however, demanded extraordinary measures at the societal level. Ottoman modernists realized that being a civilized country necessitated an economic society with its advanced forms of production mechanisms, along with industrious and skillful citizens. Accordingly, the issue of the salvation of the empire, which haunted the nineteenth- and early twentieth-century Ottoman reformist mind, was tightly linked to the question of economic development and an accompanying societal transformation in capitalistic terms.

The notion of economic development as a cooperative and comprehensive imperial project paved the way for the denunciation of individualism in favor of communitarian approaches to society in the Hamidian era. Notwithstanding Sakızlı Ohannes and Mehmed Cavid Bey's influential economic liberalism and Sabahaddin Bey's "decentralization and private initiative," communitarian approaches to the question of social reform dominated Hamidian-era social and economic thought. From the perspective of Hamidian communitarianists, such as Münif Pasha and Ahmed Midhat, economic development necessitated mobilizing masses for the common goal of building a new country. Despite the conspicuously liberal theoretical roots of their social projections, altruism and patriotism were put before private interests. In other words, Hamidian modernists promoted private enterprise and free (domestic) market, and they expected modern Ottoman citizens to become wealthy through entrepreneurship. It is important to note, however that, according to this perspective, the main motivation behind getting wealthy at the individual level was to make the country more affluent. This notion was simply an adaptation of Adam Smith's understanding of private interest to Ottoman modernization by giving it an evident altruistic tint. According to Smith, "By pursuing his own interest he [an individual] frequently promotes that of the society more effectually than when he really intends to promote it."[2] The objective of building a new society on such an ideal patriotic and solidarist entrepreneurial behavior marked the Ottoman modernist social and economic thought in the late nineteenth and early twentieth centuries. It is also important to note that similar communitarian approaches to the question of economic development shaped many other national modernization projects of the era, Japan being the most prominent example.[3]

The biggest obstacle to economic development in the Ottoman Empire was the lack of adequate capital in all forms. As a result, concern about the inadequacy of human, physical, and financial capital shaped Hamidian modernization plans. Hamidian-era Ottoman modernism sought the salvation of the empire through education (to produce human capital) and economic development (to enhance physical and financial capital). Even the education policies of the state were shaped in accordance with such economic concerns, as they emphasized preventing the waste of domestic resources through corruption, immorality, and indolence. These policies have so far been analyzed by scholars of the Hamidian era in relation to the sultan's Islamist ideology. I argue, however, that economic concerns regarding the formation of human capital and the preservation of national wealth constituted a decisive factor that shaped the ostensibly Islamic discourse of Hamidian ideology. In short, the question of capital (and especially the lack thereof) marked Hamidian ideology, and it manifested itself in the government's moral-educational as well as socio-economic policies. Therefore, Hamidian era *encyclopedists*' efforts for formation of moral, industrious, punctual, and educated citizens should be understood within this economic-intellectual context.

Limited resources for economic development led the Ottoman modernists to embrace two basic organizational principles of Adam Smith's economics: cooperation and division of labor. As a disappointing fact for the reformists, a financially powerful, economically dynamic, and politically patriotic (preferably Muslim) Ottoman entrepreneurial class with sufficient accumulated capital for large-scale investments did not exist. Besides, Ottoman statesmen did not consider state-led capitalism an option, favoring the free-market system (at least in theory) in the Ottoman Empire. Therefore, cooperation among small producers and investors to gather large amounts for large-scale investments emerged as a potential solution to the problem of capital accumulation. In addition to theorizing about this idea, popular intellectuals, such as Ahmed Midhat, provided their readers with practical suggestions and hypothetical examples (e.g., establishing a paper factory through cooperation) to inspire and encourage the readers to put these economic principles in practice. The existence of real-life examples of such enterprises shows us that these ideas did not remain within the boundaries of intellectual speculation. Cooperation and division of labor thus constituted a main intellectual axis of Ottoman economic modernization in the late nineteenth and early twentieth centuries, and gained an even more important position with the elaboration of the National Economy (*Millî İktisat*) program of the Young Turks. In short, the material and intellectual roots of the solidarist and corporatist economic ideology of the Young Turks, which shaped modern Turkey of the twentieth century, rest in the second half of the nineteenth century.

Economic nationalism, protectionism, and mercantilism

As the economic proto-nationalistic aspects of late Ottoman modernization evolved, the notion of "foreigner" began to change its meaning for the Muslim elite. The increasing European economic and financial control of the Ottoman economy and the rise of a comprador non-Muslim bourgeoisie paved the way for the emergence among the Muslim elite of an anxiety of losing social and political power in the empire. Especially after the establishment of the Ottoman Public Debt Administration in 1881, and along with an increasing sense of grievance towards the capitulations, Muslim-Turkish proto-nationalism began to supplant the Ottomanism of earlier decades. In the early twentieth century, economic and political Muslim-Turkish proto-nationalism began to crystallize as Turkism and later as Turkification in the nation-building project of the Young Turks in the late imperial and early Republican eras.

Despite the conspicuous rise of economic nationalism, we must question the deeply rooted assumption in the existing literature regarding the dominance of mercantilist and neo-mercantilist tendencies in late Ottoman Empire. Following Listian theses, Ottoman protectionists suggested limiting international competition in the short run to protect nascent domestic industries. However, Hamidian-era protectionism did not lay any emphasis on a positive trade balance, and Ottoman protectionists did not suggest a closed economic system or a command economy. In accordance with the Listian approach, they simply suggested that in order to join the international market on equal terms, the Ottoman economy should attain a level of economic development and industrial infrastructure similar to that of European economies. Otherwise, they concluded, Ottoman producers could not stand the cut-throat competition with European industries, and the Ottoman production system would be destroyed, something that had already been experienced in the pre-Hamidian era. In short, Hamidian era Ottoman protectionists proposed moderate protectionism (*himâye-i ma'kûle*) as Akyiğitzade Musa Bey put it, with an eye on the complete opening up of the Ottoman market in the long-run in order to benefit from global markets to the fullest possible extent. It is also important to note in passing that, before 1908, the Ottoman protectionist reaction against British liberalism was never dominated by any autarkic, anti-market, pro-central planning, or even anti-European discourses.

Storytelling for economic development

Hamidian-era Ottoman modernists considered economics an essential instrument for social transformation. In other words, they believed that building a modern Ottoman industrial society necessitated a change in popular economic mentality and work ethics. In order for modern economic ideas to have such a popular impact, some modernist intellectuals used the novel, especially the *roman feuilleton*, as a tool. In my analyses of the Ottoman novel as a source for understanding economic mentality of an era, I was inspired by the New Historicist approach to literary theory:

> Taking their cue from [Clifford] Geertz's method of 'thick description' they [the New Historicists] seize upon an event or anecdote ... and re-read it in such a way as to reveal through the analysis of tiny particulars the behavioral codes, logics, and motive forces controlling a whole society.[4]

However, thanks to Ottoman modernists' not-so-subtle use of the novel as a means of modernization, I did not even have to rely on "tiny particulars." In the novels of Ahmed Midhat Efendi and Mizancı Murad Bey, for example, I have found fictionalized versions of the bottom-up economic development strategy and social engineering vision of Hamidian-era reformism. In this context, Ahmed Midhat Efendi has a special place as the most prolific and influential Ottoman novelist of the era. The rational, industrious, and entrepreneurial protagonists of several of Ahmed Midhat's works represent the ideal modern Ottoman citizen in the minds of Ottoman modernists. Mizancı Mehmed Murad Bey was another immensely influential intellectual of the era, and, like Ahmed Midhat, his concern for popular impact led him to present his social reform project in the form of a novel. His *Turfanda mı, Turfa mı?* appeared in 1890 as a manifesto novel, which delineated a bottom-up modernization strategy for the Ottoman Empire. In both Ahmed Midhat and Murad Bey's works, the effort of changing popular economic mentality with obvious entrepreneurial-bourgeois values, thereby generating an Ottoman capitalist spirit as a first step towards the salvation of the empire through economic development.

Ottoman "Islamic" economics

Ottoman economists of the late nineteenth century presented earlier examples of Islamic economics in the course of their modest attempts to reconcile principles of modern economics with the traditional sources of Islamic knowledge. First, Ottoman economists legitimized bourgeois economic principles and notions (such as the self-help spirit, and the idea of the free market) with references to the Qur'an and the *hadith* literature. Second, Ottoman economists responded to the European claim of ownership of the modern sciences by attempting to dig out (or rather to invent) a long tradition of Islamic economics, using examples from the Rightly Guided Caliphs as well as Muslim scholars such as Ibn

Khaldun. Islamic economics of the twentieth century is a product of the ideas of Adam Smith and his followers as well as (and probably more than) those of the Prophet Muhammad and his tradition, and Ottoman economists were the first Muslim intellectuals who supplied the discipline with Islamic content.

Ottoman pragmatist reformism

Just as the strategy of bottom-up economic development marked Hamidian-era Ottoman modernization, so also intellectual and political pragmatism shaped Ottoman economic mindset. My critique of the "aping the West approach" to Ottoman modernization does not entail attributing any originality to Ottoman economic literature in theoretical terms. On the contrary, I acknowledge that Ottoman economists hardly contributed to economic theory. Yet, instead of a normative interpretation of this phenomenon, I have explained it through the most conspicuous aspect of the late Ottoman intellectual sphere: pragmatism. The main concern for popular Ottoman modernist intellectuals was the education of the Ottoman public. Ottoman *encyclopedists* were writing for an audience largely unaware of modern sciences and philosophies. Thus, the primary role of the Ottoman intellectuals of the era was to serve as society's first teachers, as in the case of Ahmed Midhat. This led the intellectuals to translate, adapt, or simply cite the simplest and plainest sources available. In short, I argue, no Ottoman economist ever aimed to become the next Adam Smith. Instead, the objective was to adapt pragmatically useful economic knowledge to Ottoman economic conditions. In other words, Ottoman economists considered economics as an essential instrument for modernization, but not as a field of pure intellectual inquiry.

All in all, this book offers an alternative view also about the nature of Ottoman modernization itself. It has been suggested, as a comparison of Middle Eastern modernization processes with those of Western European examples, that—in the Iranian and Ottoman-Turkish cases,

> The failure of some early attempts during the first half of the nineteenth century in both countries to implement change and reform from below enabled the intelligentsia to pursue modernization exclusively from above. Bureaucrats and military officers were sturdily convinced that, in the presence of colonial powers, any endeavour to seek change and reform from below was nothing but a cause of political chaos, jeopardizing their country's sovereignty.[5]

Although this seems to be the case in political modernization, in economic modernization we need a more nuanced approach. This book demonstrates that the failure of top-down industrialization attempts in the first half of the nineteenth century showed the Ottoman elites that economic modernization should be built on a supporting societal base. They realized that without entrepreneurially-minded and industrious middle-classes, and skillful workers and managers, top-down enterprises for economic modernization was basically futile. As a result, economic education at all levels, and inoculating masses and the elites alike with bourgeois values began to occupy a central place in modernization efforts, especially in the Hamidian era.

The approach was still in a sense top-down, since the elites decided the need for a change towards a more economically-minded society and they led the education process. However, the change itself was to be realized bottom up, thanks to the cultural and behavioral impact of modern economic knowledge and the self-help spirit of the age. More specifically, compared to state-led industrialization efforts of the earlier decades, the Hamidian-era reformists put the emphasis on creating entrepreneurially-minded and hard-working citizens who were expected to materialize the desired economic modernization in the empire. In this context, the government included economics and economy-related courses in school curriculum both to inform students about this new discipline and to encourage (especially Muslims) to pursue entrepreneurial careers, instead of civil service. Many public intellectuals joined these efforts by promoting self-help values in popular periodicals, writing, translating or adapting relevant books, and even fictionalizing these ideas to further popularize them among the masses. In this respect, another point that this book makes is that regardless of their political positions regarding the government (including its staunchest critics), reformist intellectuals and the government of the era were on the same side against their struggle to build a new economic society on similar capitalist principles.

Notes

1 Karl Marx and Frederick Engels, *Manifesto of the Communist Party*, trans. A.M. Simons and Marcus Hitch, Authorized English Translation; Edited by Frederick Engels (Chicago: Charles H. Kerr, 1906), 18–19.
2 Smith, *The Wealth of Nations*, 184.
3 Byron K. Marshall, *Capitalism and Nationalism in Prewar Japan; the Ideology of the Business Elite, 1868–1941* (Stanford: Stanford University Press, 1967), 3–4.
4 H. Aram Veeser, "Introduction," *The New Historicism*, ed. H. Aram Veeser (New York: Routledge, 1989), xi. For Geertz's method of "thick description," see Clifford Geertz, "Thick Description: Toward an Interpretive Theory of Culture," in *The Interpretation of Cultures: Selected Essays* (New York: Basic Books, 1973) 3–30.
5 Touraj Atabaki, *The State and the Subaltern: Modernization, Society and the State in Turkey and Iran*, (London: I. B. Tauris, 2007), xiv.

Bibliography

Primary sources

Archives

Başbakanlık Osmanlı Arşivi (İstanbul) – Yıldız Esas Evrakı
Österreichischen Nationalbibliothek

Periodicals

Dağarcık
Envâr-ı Zekâ
Hürriyet
İbret
İktisadiyat Mecmuası
Journal de la Chambre de Commerce de Constantinople
Hakayık el-Vaka'i
Hanımlara Mahsus Gazete
İktisadiyat Mecmuası
Kırkanbar
The Levant Herald and Eastern Express
Mecmua-i Ebüzziya
Mecmua-i Fünûn
Mecmua-i Umûr-ı Nâfia
Mîzan
Le Moniteur Ottoman
Servet-i Fünûn
Tarih-i Osmânî Encümeni Mecmuası
Takvîm-i Vekâyi'
Tercümân-ı Hakîkat
Vakit

Articles, manuscripts, and books

Abdelhaleem, M.A.S. (Translator). *The Qur'an.* Oxford: Oxford University Press, 2004.
Abdurrahman Şeref. "Ahmed Midhat Efendi." *TOEM*, no. 18 (1913): 1112–19.

Abdurrahman Vefik. *Tekâlif Kavaidi*. 2 vols. Dersaadet [İstanbul]: Matbaa-yı Kader, H. 1328–30 [1910–12].
Abdülhamid II. *Abdülhamit Han'ın Muhtıraları (Belgeler)*. Edited by Mehmet Hocaoğlu. İstanbul: Oymak Yayınları, 1975.
Abdülhamid II. *Devlet ve Memleket Görüşlerim*. Edited by A. Alâaddin Çetin and Ramazan Yıldız. İstanbul: Çığır Yayınları, 1976.
Ahmed Cevdet [Pasha]. *Tarih-i Cevdet*. 12 vols. İstanbul: Matbaa-yı Âmire and Matbaa-yi Osmaniye, 1854–84.
Ahmed Cevdet [Pasha]. *Ma'rûzât*. Edited by Yusuf Halaçoğlu. İstanbul: Çağrı Yayınları, 1980.
Ahmed Midhat. "Tesellî-i Miskinan." In *Kıssadan Hisse*, 31–4. İstanbul, H. 1287 [1870].
Ahmed Midhat. "Te'âvün ve Tenâsür." *Dağarcık* 2 (1871): 54–63.
Ahmed Midhat. "Fakr ü Gınâ." *Dağarcık* 7 (1871), 194–9.
Ahmed Midhat. *Kâinat: Kütübhane-yi Tarih*. İstanbul: Kırkanbar Matbaası, 1871–81.
Ahmed Midhat. "Hikâye Tasvir ve Tahriri." *Kırkanbar* 4 (1873): 107–12.
Ahmed Midhat. *Menfa*. İstanbul: Kırkanbar Matbaası, 1876.
Ahmed Midhat. *Felatun Bey il Rakım Efendi*. Ankara: Akçağ Yayınları, 2000.
Ahmed Midhat. *Üss-i İnkılâb*. 2 vols. İstanbul, H. 1294–5 [1877–78].
Ahmed Midhat. *Tarih-i Umûmi*. 2 vols. İstanbul: Kırkanbar Matbaası, H. 1294–5 [1877–78].
Ahmed Midhat. *Sevda-yı Sa'y ü Amel*. İstanbul: Kırkanbar Matbaası, H. 1296 [1879].
Ahmed Midhat. *Teşrik-i Mesai, Taksim-i Mesai*. İstanbul: Kırkanbar Matbaası, H. 1296 [1879].
Ahmed Midhat. *Ekonomi Politik*. İstanbul: Kırkanbar Matbaası, H. 1296 [1879].
Ahmed Midhat. "Bereket Yerde midir, Gökde midir? Yahud Bir Cahil Çiftçinin Mütâlaât-ı Fenniyesi." *Müntahabât-ı Tercüman-ı Hakikat*. Vol. 2 (1884): 289.
Ahmed Midhat. *Letaif-i Rivayat On Birinci Cüz'ü, (Bahtiyarlık) İsmiyle Bir Hikayeyi Havîdir*. İstanbul: Kırk Anbar Matbaası, H. 1302 [1885].
Ahmed Midhat. *Letaif-i Rivayat On Üçüncü Cüz'ü, (Obur) İsmiyle Bir Hikayeyi Havîdir*. İstanbul: Kırk Anbar Matbaası, H. 1302 [1885].
Ahmed Midhat. *Mufassal Tarih-ı Kurun-ı Cedide*. 3 vols. İstanbul, 1886.
Ahmed Midhat. *Letaif-i Rivayat On Yedinci Cüz'ü, (Para!) İsmiyle Bir Hikayeyi Havîdir*. İstanbul: Kırk Anbar Matbaası, H. 1304 [1887].
Ahmed Midhat. *Müsâbahât-ı Leyliye, Birinci Müsâhabe: Vakit Geçirmek*. İstanbul, H. 1304 [1887].
Ahmed Midhat. *Mufassal Tarih-i Kurun-i Cedide*. İstanbul. 3 vols. H. 1303–05 [1886–88].
Ahmed Midhat. *Fennî Bir Roman yâhut Amerika Doktorları*. İstanbul, H. 1305 [1888].
Ahmed Midhat. *Hallü'l-'Ukad*. Dersaadet [İstanbul], H. 1307 [1890].
Ahmed Midhat. *Müşahedat*. İstanbul. H. 1308 [1891].
Ahmed Midhat. *Ahmed Metin ve Şirzad*. İstanbul: Tercüman-ı Hakikat Matbaası, H. 1309 [1892].
Ahmed Midhat. *Avrupa Âdab-ı Muaşereti yâhud Alafranga*. İstanbul: İkdam Matbaası, H. 1312 [1894].
Ahmed Midhat. *Dar ül-Fünûn Dersleri: Tarih-i Umumi*. Darülhilâfe [İstanbul]: Sırat-ı Müstakim Matbaası, H. 1328 [1912].
Ahmed Rasim. *Arabların Terakkiyât-ı Medeniyesi*. İstanbul, H. 1304 [1887].
Ahmed Rasim. *Terakkiyât-ı İlmiye ve Medeniye*. Kostantiniye: Matbaa-yı Ebüzziya. H. 1304 [1887].

Ahmed Rasim. *Tarih-i Muhtasar-ı Beşer*. İstanbul: Matbaa-yı Ebüzziya, 1887.

Ahmed Rasim. *Resimli ve Haritalı Osmanlı Tarihi*. İstanbul: Şems Matbaası, H. 1326–30 [1908–12].

Ahmed Rasim. *Küçük Tarih-i İslâm*. Dersaadet [İstanbul]: Şirket-i Mürettibiye Matbaası, 1910.

Ahmed Rıza. *Meclis-i Mebusan ve Ayân Reisi Ahmed Rıza Bey'in Anıları*. İstanbul: Arba Yayınları, 1988.

Akarlı, Engin D., ed. *Belgelerle Tanzimat: Osmanlı Sadrıazamlarından Âli ve Fuad Paşaların Siyasî Vasiyyetnâmeleri*. İstanbul: Boğaziçi Üniversitesi, 1978.

Akçuraoğlu Yusuf. *Üç Tarz-ı Siyaset*. İstanbul: Kader Matbaası, R.1327 [1911].

Akçuraoğlu Yusuf. *Eski "Şura-yı Ümmet"de Çıkan Makâlelerimden*. İstanbul: Tanin Matbaası, R. 1329 [1913].

Akçuraoğlu Yusuf. "Türk Milliyetçiliğinin İktisadi Menşe'lerine Dâir." In *Siyaset ve İktisad Hakkında Birkaç Hitabe ve Makale*, 141–68. İstanbul: Kitabhane-i Hilmi, 1924.

Akyiğitzade Musa. *İktisad yahud İlm-i Servet: Azadegi-i Ticaret ve Usul-i Himaye*. İstanbul: Karabet Matbaası, H. 1314 [1896].

Akyiğitzade Musa. *Avrupa Medeniyetinin Esâsına Bir Nazar*. İstanbul: Cemal Efendi Matbaası, H.1315 [1897].

Ali Bey. *Lehçet ül-Hakaik*. Mısır: Matbaa-yı Osmaniye, H. 1315 [1897].

Ali Kemal. *Çölde Bir Sergüzeşt*. Kostantiniye [İstanbul]: Esseyid Mehmed Tahir, H. 1316 [1898].

Ali Kemal. *Ömrüm*. Edited by Zeki Kuneralp. İstanbul: İsis Yayımcılık, 1985.

Ali Vahbi Bey, ed. *Avant la débâcle de la Turquie: Pensées et souvenirs de l'ex-sultan Abdul-Hamid, recueillis par Ali Vahbi Bey*. Paris: Attinger Frères, *c*.1913.

Andı, Fatih and Mustafa Çiçekler, eds. *Yeni Harflerle Hanımlara Mahsus Gazete (1895–1908) Seçki*. İstanbul: Kadın Eserleri Kütüphanesi ve Bilgi Merkezi Vakfı, 2009.

Arşizen, Serandi. *Tasarrufât-ı Mülkiye: Osmanlı İmparatorluğu'nda Bir Politik Iktisat Kitabı*. Edited by Hamdi Genç and M. Erdem Özgür. İstanbul: Kitabevi, 2011.

Baudrillart, Henri. *Manuel d'économie politique*. Paris: Guillaumin, 1857.

Beauregard, Paul. *Éléments d'économie politique*. Paris: Quantin, 1889.

Beauregard, Paul. *Mebadi-i İlm-i Servet-i Milel*. Translated by Mahmud Hayri. İstanbul: Mahmud Bey Matbaası, H. 1317 [1899].

Block, Maurice. *Petit Manuel d'économie pratique*. Cinquième édition. Paris: J. Hetzel, 1878.

Block, Maurice. *Amelî İktisad Dersleri*. Translated by Ahmed Muhtar. İstanbul: Mahmud Bey Matbaası, H. 1324 [1906].

Bourdonné, Philippe-Louis. *Simples Notions d'économie politique*. Paris: E. Thorin, 1869.

Coqueline, Charles. *Dictionnaire de l'économie politique contenant l'exposition des principes de la science*. 2 vols. Paris: Librairie de Guillaumin et Cie, 1852–53.

De Brouckère, Georges. *Principes généraux d'économie politique*. Bruxelles: Société pour l'émancipation intellectuelle, 1850.

Ebüzziya Tevfik. *Benjamin Franklin*. Kostantiniyye [İstanbul]: Matbaa-i Ebüzziya, H. 1299 [1882].

Ebüzziya Tevfik. "Avrupa Şarkı Bilmez," *Mecmua-i Ebüzziya* 49 (1886), 1551–52.

Ebüzziya Tevfik. "Biz Nasıl Çalışıyoruz, Başkaları Nasıl Çalışıyor ve Ahmed Midhat Efendi." *Mecmua-i Ebüzziya* 80 (1898).

Engels, Friedrich. "Preface." In Karl Marx, *Free Trade: A Speech Delivered before the Democratic Club, Brussels, Belgium, Jan 9, 1848*. Translated by F.K. Wishnewetsky, 2–24. Boston: Lee and Shephard Publishers, 1888.

Fahrünnisa. "İki Aile Levhası." *Hanımlara Mahsus Gazete* 3 (1895): 1–3.

Fatma Aliye. *Ahmed Cevdet Paşa ve Zamanı*. Dersaadet [İstanbul]: Kana'at Matbaası, R. 1332 [1914].

Fehmi. "Istılahat-ı Fenniye Vaz'ı." In *Müntehabât-ı Tercüman-ı Hakikat*, Vol. 2. İstanbul: Tercüman-i Hakıkat, 1884.

Franklin, Benjamin. *Poor Richard Improved; Being an Almanack and Ephemeris ... for the Year of Our Lord 1758*. Philadelphia: Franklin and Hall, 1757.

Franklin, Benjamin. *Tarik-i Refah*. Translated by Reşad Bey. Paris, 1286 [1869].

Franklin, Benjamin. *Tarik-i Servet ez Hikmet-i Rikardos*. Translated by Bedros Hocasaryan. Dersaadet [İstanbul]: Mühendisoğlu Ohannes Matbaası, H. 1286 [1869].

Franklin, Benjamin. *Tarik-i Refah: Franklin'in Servet Hakkındaki Nesayihi ve Tercüme-i Hali*. Translated by Bedros Hocasaryan. Saraybosna, Sultan Bayezid Sa'adet Kütübhanesi, H. 1326 [1908].

Galib Haldun. "Tanzimat Devrinde Matbuât ve Neşriyat-ı İktisadiye." *İktisadiyat Mecmuası* 30 (1916), 6–7.

Galib Haldun. "Tanzimat Devrinde Neşriyat-ı İktisadiye." *İktisadiyat Mecmuası* 37 (1916), 3–4.

Garabed Bey. "El movimiento literario en Turquía." *La España Moderna* 77 (1895): 154–70.

Gasprinski, İsmail Bey. *Avrupa Medeniyetine Bir Nazar-ı Muvazene*. Kostantiniye [İstanbul]: Matbaa-yı Ebüzziya, H. 1302 [1885].

Gürpınar, Hüseyin Rahmi. *Mürebbiye*. Dersaadet [İstanbul]: İkdam Matbaası, H. 1315 [1897].

Gürpınar, Hüseyin Rahmi. *Şık*. İstanbul: Pınar Yayınevi, 1964.

Gürpınar, Hüseyin Rahmi. *Gazetecilikte Son Yazılarım*. Edited by Abdullah Tanrınınkulu and Gülçin Tanrınınkulu. İstanbul: Özgür Yayınları, 2001.

Hamsun, K. and H.C. Andersen. *İstanbul'da İki İskandinav Seyyah*. Translated by B. Gürsaler-Syvertsen. İstanbul: Yapı Kredi Yayınları, 2009.

Hübner, Otto. *Il Piccolo Economist*. Translated by Luigi Cossa. Milano, 1855.

Hübner, Otto. *Petit Manuel Populaire d'économie Politique, imité de l'ouvrage allemand intitulé Der kleine Economist*. Translated by Ch. Le Hardy de Beaulieu [*sic*]. Second edition. Bruxelles and Leipzig: A. Lacroix; Paris: Guillaumin, 1862.

Hübner, Otto. *Ekonomi Tercümesi: Fenn-i İdare*. Translated by Mehmed Midhat. İstanbul: Cemiyet-i İlmiye Matbaası, 1869.

Karaosmanoğlu, Yakup Kadri. *Bir Sürgün*. İstanbul: İletişim Yayınları, 1987.

Karaosmanoğlu, Yakup Kadri. *Hep O Şarkı*. İstanbul: İletişim Yayınları, 2004.

Leroy-Beaulieu, Pierre-Paul. *Traité de la science des finances*. Paris: Guillaumin et cie, 1877.

Leroy-Beaulieu, Pierre-Paul. *İlm-i Usul-i Maliye*. Translated by Hüseyin Kâzım. İstanbul: Mihran Matbaası, H. 1297 [1880].

Leroy-Beaulieu, Pierre-Paul. *Traité théorique et pratique d'économie politique*. 4 vols. Paris: Guillaumin et cie, 1896.

List, Friedrich. *National System of Political Economy*. Translated by G.A. Matile. Philadelphia: J.P. Lippincott & Co., 1856.

Mahmud Es'ad. *İlm-i Servet*. İstanbul: Mekteb-i Sanayi, H. 1302 [1885].

Mahmud Es'ad. *İktisad*. 4 vols. Istanbul: Matbaa-i Hayriye, H. 1325–27 [1907–09].

Marx, Karl. *A Contribution to the Critique of Political Economy*. Translated by N.I. Stone. Chicago: Charles H. Kerr & Company, 1904.

Marx, Karl, and Frederick Engels. *Manifesto of the Communist Party*. Translated by A.M. Simons and Marcus Hitch. Authorized English Translation; Edited by Frederick Engels. Chicago: Charles H. Kerr, 1906.

Mehmed Cavid. *İlm-i İktisad*. 4 vols. Vols. 1–3, İstanbul: Karabet Matbaası; Vol. 4, İstanbul: Âlem Matbaası, H. 1315–17 [1897–99].

Mehmed Cavid. *İhsâiyat*. İstanbul, H. 1318 [1901].

Mehmed Cavid. *İlm-i İktisad: Mekâtîb-i İdâdîyeye Mahsus*. İstanbul: Matbaa-i Amire, H.1326 [1908].

Mehmed Cavid. *Ma'lumât-i İktisâdiye: Mekâtib-i İdadiyenin En Son Programlarına Muvâfık Olarak Tertib Edilmişdir*. İstanbul: Kana'at Matbaası, H. 1329 [1911].

Mehmed Cavid. *İktisat İlmi*. Edited by Orhan Çakmak. İstanbul: Liberte Yayınları, 2001.

Mehmed Enisi, *Avrupa Hatıratım*. Vol. 1 (Kostantiniye [İstanbul]: Matbaa-yı Ebuzziya, R. 1327 [1911].

Mehmed Hilmi. *Benjamin Franklin*. Kostantiniye [İstanbul]: İstepan Matbaası, 1307 [1890].

Mehmed Murad. *Tarih-i Umûmi*. İstanbul, H. 1298–1302 [1881–85].

Mehmed Murad. *Muhtasar Tarih-i Umûmi*. İstanbul: Garabet, H. 1302 [1884].

Mehmed Murad. "Müdahelat-ı Ecnebiyyeyi Men' İçün En Kısa Tarik." *Mîzan* 34 (1887): 279–80.

Mehmed Murad. "İmtiyazat-ı Ecnebiye." *Mîzan* 48 (1888): 424–5.

Mehmed Murad. "Defter-i Muktesid." *Mîzan* 104 (1889): 999.

Mehmed Murad. *Turfanda mı, Turfa mı?: Millî Roman*. İstanbul: Mahmud Bey Matbaası, H. 1308 [1890].

Mehmed Murad. Meskenet Ma'zeret Teşkil Eder mi? Mücâhede-yi Milliyeden: Mizân-ı Kadîm ve Düyûn-ı Umûmiye Komiserliği Devirleri. Dersaadet [İstanbul]: Matbaa-yı Âmedî, R. 1329 [1913].

Mehmed Rakım, and Mustafa Nail. *Hayat-ı Düvel*. İstanbul: A. Maviyan Şirket-i Mürettebiye Matbaası, H. 1306 [1889].

Mehmed Şerif. "Sanayi' ve Ziraatden Kangısının Hakkımızda Hayırlı Olduğuna Dairdir." *Tercüman-ı Ahval* 68 and 69 (1861).

Mehmed Şerif. "Ekonomi Politik 'İlminin Tarîkiyle Hudûd-ı Tabî'iyesinin Tahdîdi Beyânındadır." *Tercüman-ı Ahval*, no. 75 (September 5, 1861): 2–3.

Mehmed Şerif. *İlm-i Emvâl-i Milliye*. İstanbul: Tab'hane-i Âmire Litoğrafya Destgâhı, H. 1279 [1863].

Mehmed Tahir. *Netîce-i Sa'y*. Dersaadet [İstanbul]: Mahmud Bey Matbaası, H. 1311 [1893].

Mikael Portakal. *Usûl-i Maliye*. İstanbul: Mekteb-i Mülkiye-yi Şâhâne Litografya Destgâhı, H. 1306 [1889].

Münif. *Muhaverât-ı Hikemiye: Fransa Hükema-yı Benâmından Voltaire ve Fenelon ve Fontenelle'in Telifâtından*. İslambol [İstanbul]: Ceridehane Matbaası, H. 1276 [1859].

Münif. "San'at ve Ticaretin Mâhiyetine ve Bunların Tesir-i Menfa'atine Dair," *Ruzname-i Ceride-i Havadis* 33 (2 Cemaziyelevvel 1277 [1860]).

Münif. "Mukayese-i İlm ü Cehl," *Mecmua-i Fünûn* 1 (1862): 21–35.

Münif. "Karıncaların San'at ve Medeniyeti," *Mecmua-i Fünûn* 30 (1864): 230–6.

Münif. *Destân-ı Âl-i Osman*. İstanbul: Mihran Matbaası, H. 1299 [1882].

Mustafa Nail. *Muhtasar İlm-i Servet*. İstanbul: Matbaa-i Âmire, H. 1317 [1899].

Namık Kemal. "İbret." *İbret* 3 (1872): 1–2.

Namık Kemal. "Sanat ve Ticaretimiz." *İbret* 57 (1872): 1–2.

Namık Kemal. "Avrupa Şarkı Bilmez," *İbret* 7 (1872): 2.

Namık Kemal. *Osmanlı Tarihi*. 2 vols. Kostantiniye: Matbaa-yı Ebüzziya, H. 1305 [1888].

Nigâr bint-i Osman. "Sa'y ü Amel." *Hanımlara Mahsus Gazete* 61 (1896): 1–2.

Nuri. *Mebahis-i İlm-i Servet*. İstanbul: Mahmud Bey Matbaası, H. 1299 [1882].

Nys, Ernest. *Researches in the History of Economics*. Translated by N.F. [Dryhurst] and A.R. Dryhurst. London: A. & C. Black, 1899.

[Sakızlı] Ohannes. "İlm-i Servet-i Milel." *Mecmua-i Fünûn* 2 (1863): 86–92; 6 (1863): 243–9.

[Sakızlı] Ohannes. *Mebadi-i İlm-i Servet-i Milel*. Dersaadet [Istanbul]: Mihran Matbaası, H. 1297 [1880].

Rambaud, Joseph. *Sommaire détaillé du Cours d'économie politique professé à la Faculté catholique de droit de Lyon*. Lyon: Impr. du Nouvelliste, 1892.

Rambaud, Joseph. *Éléments d'économie politique*. Paris: L. Larose, 1895.

Rambaud, Joseph. *Histoire des doctrines économiques*. Paris: L. Larose, 1899.

Rambaud, Joseph. *Cours d'économie politique*. Paris: Librairie de la Société du recueil Sirey, 1910–11.

Rambaud, Prosper. *Précis élémentaire d'économie politique: à l'usage des facultés de droit et des écoles*. Paris: Ernest Thorin, 1880.

Rambaud, Prosper. *Telhis-i İlm-i Servet*. Translated by Su'ad. İstanbul: Mihran Matbaası, H. 1305 [1888].

Recaizade Mahmud Ekrem. *Araba Sevdası*. İstanbul: Âlem Matbaası, Ahmed İhsan ve Şürekâsı, H. 1314 [1896].

[Refik]. "Esbâb-ı Servet." *Mir'at* 1 (1863): 5–11.

Reşad. "Fenn-i Servet," *İbret* 10 (1872): 1.

Reşad. "İstikraz." *İbret* 19 (1872): 1.

Sabahaddin. *Teşebbüs-i Şahsî ve Tevsi'-i Me'zuniyyet Hakkında Bir İzah*. Dersaadet [İstanbul]: Kütübhane-i Cihan, R. 1324 [1908].

Sabahaddin. "Terbiye-i Milliye ve Islahat-ı Şahsiye," *Terakki* 19–20 (June 1908): 7–8.

Sabahaddin. *Türkiye Nasıl Kurtarılabilir?Meslek-i İctimâ'î ve Programı*. İstanbul: Kader Matbaası, R. 1334 [1918].

Sâdık Rıfat Pasha. *Müntehâbât-ı Âsâr*. İstanbul: Ali Bey Matbaası, n.d.

Safa, Peyami. *Fatih-Harbiye*. İstanbul: Semih Lütfü Sühulet Kütüpanesi, 1931.

Say, Jean-Baptiste. *Traité d'économie politique, ou, simple exposition de la manière dont se forment, se distribuent et se consomment les richesses*. 2 vols. Paris: Chez Deterville, 1803.

Say, Jean-Baptiste. *A Treatise on Political Economy or the Production, Distribution, and Consumption of Wealth*. Translated by C.R. Prinsep. Philadelphia: J.B. Lippincott & Co., 1857.

Seniha Vicdan. "Moda-İsraf." *Hanımlara Mahsus Gazete* 26 (1895): 2–3.

Senior, Nassau W. *A Journal Kept in Turkey and Greece in the Autumn of 1857, and the Beginning of 1858*. London: Longman, Brown, Green, Longmans, and Roberts, 1859.

Şerafeddin Mağmumî. *Seyahat Hâtıraları*. Cairo, 1909.

Serçe, Erkan, ed. *Bir Osmanlı Aydınının Londra Seyahatnamesi*. İstanbul: İstiklal Kitabevi, 2007.

Şerif Mehmed. "Sultan Selim Han-ı Sani Devrinde Nizam-ı Devlet Hakkında Mütâla'at." *TOEM* 7, no. 38 (1916): 74–88.

Smith, Adam. *An Inquiry into the Nature and Causes of the Wealth of Nations*. Edinburgh: Thomas Nelson, 1843.

Smith, Adam. *Milletlerin Zenginliği*. Translated by Haldun Derin. 2 vols. İstanbul: Millî Eğitim Basımevi, 1948.

Suavi. "Memalik-i Osmaniye'de Ticaret," *Ulûm* 12 (1869).

Sulṭān Valad. *Valadnāmah, az Sulṭān Valad*. Edited by Jalāl al-Dīn Humāyī and Māhdukht Bānū Humāyī. Tehrān: Mu'assasah-i Nashr-i Humā, 1376 [1997].

Süleyman Sûdi. "Mebâhis El-Mâliye Fi'd-Devleti'l-Osmaniyye – VII." *Vakit*. September 5, 1881.

Süleyman Sûdi. "Mebâhis El-Mâliye Fi'd-Devleti'l-Osmaniyye – XI." *Vakit*. October 17, 1881.

Süleyman Sûdi. *Defter-i Muktesid*. 3 vols. Dersaadet [İstanbul]: Mahmud Bey Matbaası, H. 1306–07 [1889–90].

Süleyman Sûdi. *Osmanlı Vergi Düzeni (Defter-i Muktesid*). Edited by Mehmet Ali Ünal. Isparta, 1996.

Süleyman Sûdi. *Tabakât-ı Müneccimîn*. İstanbul: Fatih Üniversitesi, 2005.

Tatarcıkzâde Abdullah Molla Efendi. "Sultan Selim Han-ı Sani Devrinde Nizam-ı Devlet Hakkında Mütâla'at." *TOEM* 7, no. 41 (1916): 257–84; 7, no. 42 (1917) 321–346; 8, no. 43 (1917): 15–34.

"Tedbîr-i ʿÜmran-ı Mülkî," n.d. Mxt. 1169. Österreichischen Nationalbibliothek.

Tokgöz, Ahmed İhsan. *Avrupa'da Ne Gördüm?* İstanbul: Âlem Matbaası, H. 1307 [1890].

Tokgöz, Ahmed İhsan. *İlm-i Servet*. Kostantiniye [İstanbul]: Âlem Matbaası, H. 1309 [1892].

Tokgöz, Ahmed İhsan. *Matbuat Hatıralarım: 1888–1923*. 2 vols. İstanbul: Ahmet İhsan Matbaası, 1930–31.

Tūnisī, Khayr al-Dīn. *Kitāb Aqwām Al-Masālik Fī Ma'rifat Aḥwāl Al-Mamālik*. Tūnis: Maṭba'at al-Dawlah, 1867.

Tūnisi ̄, Khayr al-Dīn. *Mukaddime-yi Akvam ül-Mesâlik fi Marifet-i Ahval il-Memâlik Tercümesi*. Translated by Abdurrahman Süreyya. İstanbul: Elcevaib Matbaası, H. 1296 [1879].

Tūnisī, Khayr al-Dīn. *The Surest Path; the Political Treatise of a Nineteenth-century Muslim Statesman. A Translation of the Introduction to the Surest Path to Knowledge Concerning the Condition of Countries*. Translated by L. Carl Brown. Cambridge: Harvard University Press, 1967.

Turan, Fikret, ed. *Seyahatname-i Londra: Tanzimat Bürokratının Modern Sanayi Toplumuna Bakışı*. İstanbul: Tarih Vakfı, 2009.

Türk Hukuk Kurumu. *Büyük Türk Hukukçusu Seydişehirli İbn-il Emin Mahmut Esat Efendi*. İstanbul: Türk Hukuk Kurumu, 1943.

Ubicini, M.A. *Letters on Turkey: An Account of the Religious, Political, Social, and Commercial Condition of the Ottoman Empire, the Reformed Institutions, Army, Navy, etc., etc*. Translated by Lady Easthope. London: John Murray, 1856.

Urquhart, David. *Turkey and Its Resources: Its Municipal Organization and Free Trade, the State and Prospects of English Commerce in the East, the New Administration of Greece, its Revenue and National Possessions*. London: Saunders and Otley, 1833.

Uzer, Tahsin. *Makedonya Eşkiyalık Tarihi ve Son Osmanlı Yönetimi*. Ankara: Türk Tarih Kurumu Yayınları, 1979.

Vambéry, Arminius. *The Story of My Struggles: The Memoirs of Arminius Vambéry*. Third Impression. London: T. Fisher Unwin, 1905.

Yalçın, Hüseyin Cahit. *Edebi Hatıralar*. İstanbul: Akşam Kitaphanesi, 1935.

Yetimzade M. Tevfik Hamdi. *Bürokrat Tevfik Biren'in Sultan II. Abdülhamid, Meşrutiyet ve Mütareke Hatıraları*. Edited by F. Rezan Hürmen. 2 vols. İstanbul: Pınar Yayınları, 2006.

Walsh, R. *A Residence at Constantinople, during a Period Including the Commencement, Progress, and Termination of the Greek and Turkish Revolutions*. London: F. Westley & A.H. Davis, 1836.

Wells, Charles. *İlm Tedbiri Milk: "The Science of the Administration of A State", or An Essay on Political Economy, in Turkish: Being the First ever Written in that Language*. London: Williams and Norgate, 1860.

Zeyneb Sünbül. "Kızların Tahsili Hakkında Bir Mütala'a." *Hanımlara Mahsus Gazete* 7 (1895): 2–4; 21 (1895): 1–2.

Zola, Émile. *Au Bonheur Des Dames*. Translated with an Introduction by Robin Buss. London: Penguin Books, 2001.

Secondary sources

Acemoglu, Daron, and James Robinson. *Why Nations Fail: The Origins of Power, Prosperity, and Poverty*. Crown Business, 2012.

Adas, Michael. *Machines as the Measure of Men: Science, Technology, and Ideologies of Western Dominance*. Ithaca: Cornell University Press, 1989.

Ahmad, Feroz. "Ottoman Perceptions of the Capitulations 1800–1914." Journal of Islamic Studies 11, no. 1 (2000): 1–20.

Akarlı, Engin Deniz. "The Problems of External Pressures, Power Struggles, and Budgetary Deficits in Ottoman Politics under Abdülhamid II (1876–1909): Origins and Solutions." Unpublished PhD dissertation. Princeton University, 1976.

Akarlı, Engin Deniz. "Gedik: Implements, Mastership, Shop Usufruct, and Monopoly among Istanbul Artisans, 1750–1850." *Wissenschaftskolleg Jahrbuch* 1986 (1987): 223–31.

Akarlı, Engin Deniz. "Economic Policy and Budgets in Ottoman Turkey, 1876–1909." *Middle Eastern Studies* 28, no. 3 (1992): 443–76.

Akgün, Seçil. "Midhat Paşa'nın Kurduğu Memleket Sandıkları: Ziraat Bankası'nın Kökeni." In *Uluslararası Midhat Paşa Semineri: Bildiriler ve Tartışmalar, Edirne: 8–10 Mayıs 1984*. Ankara: Türk Tarih Kurumu, 1986.

Akın, Adem. *Münif Paşa ve Türk Kültür Tarihindeki Yeri*. Ankara: Atatürk Kültür Merkezi, 1999.

Akkaya, Rukiye. *Prens Sabahaddin*. İstanbul: Liberte Yayınları, 2005.

Aktar, Ayhan. "Economic Nationalism in Turkey: The Formative Years, 1912–1925." *Boğaziçi Journal: Review of Social, Economic and Administrative Studies* 10, no. 1–2 (1996): 263–90.

Alatas, Hussein Syed. *The Myth of the Lazy Native: A Study of the Image of the Malays, Filipinos and Javanese from the 16th to the 20th Century and Its Function in the Ideology of Colonial Capitalism*. London: F. Cass, 1977.

Allen, Robert C. *The British Industrial Revolution in Global Perspective*. Cambridge University Press, 2009.

Arık, Şahmurad "'*Ahmed Metin ve Şirzad'* Romanının Sultan II. Abdülhamid'e Takdimi ve Bir Maruzat," *Atatürk Üniversitesi Türkiyat Araştırmaları Enstitüsü Dergisi* 35 (2007): 157–65.

Arıkan, Zeki. "Tanzimat'tan Cumhuriyet'e Tarihçilik." In *Tanzimat'tan Cumhuriyet'e Türkiye Ansiklopedisi*, vol. 6, 1584–1594. İstanbul: İletişim Yayınları, 1985.

Arıkan, Zeki. "İzmir'de İlk Kooperatifleşme Çabaları." *Tarih İncelemeleri Dergisi* 4 (1989): 31–42.

Asiltürk, Baki. *Osmanlı Seyyahlarının Gözüyle Avrupa*. İstanbul: Kaknüs Yayınları, 2000.

Augello, Massimo M, and Marco E.L Guidi. *The Spread of Political Economy and the Professionalisation of Economists: Economic Societies in Europe, America and Japan in the Nineteenth Century*. Routledge studies in the history of economics 50. London: Routledge, 2001.

Aslanoğlu, Mehmet. "II. Abdülhamid'in İktisadi ve Mali Politikalar Üzerindeki Etkisi." Toplumsal Tarih, no. 63 (1999): 25–32.

Atabaki, Touraj. *The State and the Subaltern: Modernization, Society and the State in Turkey and Iran*. London: I.B. Tauris, 2007.

Ayalon, Ami. *The Press in the Arab Middle East: A History*. New York: Oxford University Press, 1995.

Baeck, L. *The Mediterranean Tradition in Economic Thought*. London New York: Routledge, 1994.

Baer, Gabriel. "The Administrative, Economic and Social Functions of Turkish Guilds." International Journal of Middle East Studies 1, no. 1 (January 1, 1970): 28–50.

Bairoch, Paul. "European Trade Policy, 1815–1914." Translated by Susan Burke. In *The Cambridge Economic History of Europe*. Edited by Peter Mathias and Sydney Pollard. Vol. 8, 51–69. Cambridge: Cambridge University Press, 1989.

Balcı, Sezai. "Bir Osmanlı-Ermeni Aydın ve Bürokratı: Sahak Abro (1825–1900)." In *Osmanlı Siyasal ve Sosyal Hayatında Ermeniler*, edited by İbrahim Erdal and Ahmet Karaçavuş, 304:105–38. İstanbul: IQ Kültür Sanat Yayıncılık, 2009.

Barnett, Vincent. *A History of Russian Economic Thought*. New York: Routledge, 2009.

Baskıcı, Mehmet Murat. *1800–1914 Yıllarında Anadolu'da İktisadi Değişim*. Ankara: Turhan Kitabevi, 2005.

Bayur, Hilmi Kâmil. *Sadrazam Kâmil Paşa: Siyasî Hayatı*. Ankara: Sanat Basımevi, 1954.

Beetham, David. "Max Weber." In *The New Palgrave Dictionary of Economics*. Second Edition. Edited by Steven N. Durlauf and Lawrence E. Blume. Vol. 8, 715–17. New York: Palgrave Macmillan, 2008.

Béraud, Alain, and Steiner, Philippe. "France, Economics in (before 1870)." In *The New Palgrave Dictionary of Economics*. Second Edition. Edited by Steven N. Durlauf and Lawrence E. Blume. Vol. 3, 475–80. New York: Palgrave Macmillan, 2008.

Berg, Maxine. *The Machinery Question and the Making of Political Economy, 1815–1848*. Cambridge: Cambridge University Press, 1980.

Berger, Stefan. *A Companion to Nineteenth-Century Europe: 1789–1914*. Wiley-Blackwell, 2009.

Berkes, Niyazi. *Türkiye'de Çağdaşlaşma*. Edited by Ahmet Kuyaş. İstanbul: Yapı Kredi Yayınları, 2006.

Berkes, Niyazi. "Ekonomik Tarih ile Teori İlişkileri Açısından Türkiye'de Ekonomik Düşünün Evrimi." In *Türkiye'de Üniversitelerde Okutulan İktisat Üzerine*. Edited by Fikret Görün, 39–55. Ankara: Orta Doğu Teknik Üniversitesi, 1972.

Birdal, Murat. *The Political Economy of Ottoman Public Debt: Insolvency and European Financial Control in the Late Nineteenth Century*. London: Tauris Academic Studies, 2010.

Blaisdell, Donald C. *European Financial Control in the Ottoman Empire: A Study of the Establishment, Activities, and Significance of the Administration of the Ottoman Public Debt*. New York: Columbia University Press, 1929.

Blaug, Mark. *Economic Theory in Retrospect*. Fifth Edition. Cambridge: Cambridge University Press, 1996.

Blaug, Mark. "British Classical Economics." In *The New Palgrave Dictionary of Economics*. Second Edition. Edited by Steven N. Durlauf and Lawrence E. Blume. Vol. 1, 562–76. New York: Palgrave Macmillan, 2008.

Blaug, Mark. "Invisible Hand." In *The New Palgrave Dictionary of Economics*. Second Edition. Edited by Steven N. Durlauf and Lawrence E. Blume. Vol. 4, 564–6. New York: Palgrave Macmillan, 2008.

Bonner, Michael. "The *Kitāb al-Kasb* Attributed to al-Shaybānī: Poverty, Surplus, and the Circulation of Wealth." *Journal of the American Oriental Society* 121, no. 3 (2001): 410–27.

Boratav, Pertev Naili. *Folklor ve Edebiyat*. Istanbul: Adam Yayınları, 1982.

Bölükbaşı, Ö. Faruk. *Tezyid-i Varidat ve Tenkih-i Masarifat: II. Abdülhamid Döneminde Mali İdare*. İstanbul: Osmanlı Bankası Arşiv ve Araştırma Merkezi, 2005.

Brown, Leon Carl. "An Appreciation of *The Surest Path*." In Tunisi, Khayr al-Din. *The Surest Path; the Political Treatise of a Nineteenth-century Muslim Statesman. A Translation of the Introduction to the Surest Path to Knowledge Concerning the Condition of Countries*. Translated by L. Carl Brown, 3–64. Cambridge: Harvard University Press, 1967.

Brummett, Palmira Johnson. *Image and Imperialism in the Ottoman Revolutionary Press, 1908–1911*. Albany: State University of New York Press, 2000.

Budak, Ali. *Batılılaşma Sürecinde Çok Yönlü Bir Osmanlı Aydını: Münif Paşa*. İstanbul: Kitabevi, 2004.

Carr, Edward Hallett. *What Is History?* New York: Vintage Books, 1961.

Cezar, Yavuz. *Osmanlı Maliyesinde Bunalım ve Değişim Dönemi: XVIII. Yy'dan Tanzimat'a Mali Tarih*. İstanbul: Alan Yayıncılık, 1986.

Chakrabarty, Dipesh. *Provincializing Europe: Postcolonial Thought and Historical Difference*. Princeton: Princeton University Press, 2000.

Chang, Ha-Joon. *Kicking Away the Ladder: Development Strategy in Historical Perspective*. London: Anthem, 2002.

Clark, Edward C. "The Ottoman Industrial Revolution." *IJMES* 5, no. 1 (1974): 65–76.

Czygan, Christiane. "On the Wrong Way: Criticism of the *Tanzimat* Economy in the Young Ottoman Journal Hürriyet (1868/1870)." In *The Economy as an Issue in the Middle Eastern Press*. Edited by Gisela Procházka-Eisl and Martin Strohmeier, 41–54. Vienna: Lit Verlag, 2008.

Çakır, Coşkun. "Tanzimat Dönemi'nde Ticaret Alanında Yapılan Kurumsal Düzenlemeler: Meclisler." *Sosyal Siyaset Konferansları Dergisi*, no. 43–44 (2000): 363–79.

Çakır, Coşkun. *Tanzimat Dönemi Osmanlı Maliyesi*. İstanbul: Küre Yayınları, 2001.

Çakır, Serpil. *Osmanlı Kadın Hareketi*. İstanbul: Metis Yayınları, 1994.

Çankaya, Ali. *Yeni Mülkiye Tarihi ve Mülkiyeliler*. 8 vols. Ankara: S.B.F. 1968–69.

Çavdar, Tevfik. *Türkiye'de Liberalizmin Doğuşu*. İstanbul: Uygarlık Yayınları, 1982.

Çelik, Hüseyin. *Türk Dostu, İngiliz Türkolog Charles Wells: Hayatı, Eserleri ve Osmanlı Türkleri ile İlgili Düşünceleri*. Ankara: T.C. Kültür Bakanlığı, 1996.

Çiçek, Nazan. *The Young Ottomans: Turkish Critics of the Eastern Question in the Late Nineteenth Century*. London: Tauris Academic Studies, 2010.

Çizakça, Murat. *Islamic Capitalism and Finance: Origins, Evolution and the Future*. Cheltenham: Edward Elgar, 2011.

Dallal, Ahmad. *Islam, Science, and the Challenge of History*. New Haven: Yale University Press, 2010.

Darling, Linda T. "Islamic Empires, the Ottoman Empire and the Circle of Justice." In *Constitutional Politics in the Middle East: With special reference to Turkey, Iraq, Iran and Afghanistan*. Edited by Said Amir Arjomand, 11–32. Oxford: Hart, 2008.

Demir, Kenan. "Osmanlı Basınında İktisadi Kavram Ve Süreç Üzerine Yaklaşımlar (1860–1873 Dönemi)." Unpublished MA Thesis, Marmara University, 2008.

Deringil, Selim. *The Well-Protected Domains: Ideology and the Legitimation of Power in the Ottoman Empire, 1876–1909*. London: I.B. Tauris, 1998.

Devellioğlu, Ferit. *Osmanlıca-Türkçe Ansiklopedik Lûgat*. Ankara: Doğuş Ltd. Şti. Matbaası, 1970.

Dino, Güzin. *Türk Romanının Doğuşu*. İstanbul: Cem Yayınevi, 1978.

Doğan, İsmail. *Tanzimatın İki Ucu: Münif Paşa ve Ali Suavi: Sosyo-Pedagojik Bir Karşılaştırma*. İstanbul: İz Yayıncılık, 1991.

Doğan, İsmail. "Münif Mehmed Paşa." In *T.D.V. İslam Ansiklopedisi*. Vol. 32, 9–12. İstanbul: Türkiye Diyanet Vakfı, 2006.

Dowler, Wayne. "The Intelligentsia and Capitalism." In *A History of Russian Thought*. Edited by William Leatherbarrow and Derek Offord, 263–85. Cambridge University Press, 2010.

Durusoy, Mustafa. "Sultan II. Abdülhamid'e Sunulan Layihalar Işığında Dönemin İktisadi Özellikleri." Unpublished MA Thesis, Marmara University, 1995.

Eisenstadt, S. N. *Comparative Civilizations and Multiple Modernities*. 2 vols. Leiden: Brill, 2003.

Ekelund, Robert B., Jr. and Robert F. Hébert. *A History of Economic Theory and Method*. Third Edition. New York: McGraw-Hill, 1990.

El-Ashker, Ahmed A.F. and Rodney Wilson. *Islamic Economics: A Short History*. Leiden: Brill, 2006.

Eldem, Vedat. *Osmanlı İmparatorluğu'nun İktisadi Şartları Hakkında Bir Tetkik*. Ankara: Türk Tarih Kurumu, 1994.

Emil, Birol. *Mizancı Murad Bey: Hayatı ve Eserleri*. İstanbul: İ.Ü. Edebiyat Fakültesi, 1979.

Ergin, Osman. *İstanbul Mektepleri ve İlim, Terbiye, ve San'at Müesseseleri Dolayısiyle Türkiye Maarif Tarihi*. 5 vols. İstanbul: Osmanbey Matbaası, 1939–43.

Ermiş, Fatih. "Ottoman Economic Thinking Before the 19th Century." Unpublished PhD Dissertation, Universität Erfurt, 2011.

Ermiş, Fatih. *A History of Ottoman Economic Thought: Developments Before the Nineteenth Century*. Routledge, 2014.

Erreygers, Guido. "Economics in Belgium." In *The New Palgrave Dictionary of Economics*. Online Edition. Edited by Steven N. Durlauf and Lawrence E. Blume. Palgrave Macmillan, 2009. www.dictionaryofeconomics.com/article?id=pde2009_B000343. Accessed on January 29, 2010.

Esen, Nüket. *Hikâye Anlatan Adam: Ahmet Mithat*. İstanbul: İletişim Yayınları, 2014.

Esen, Nüket and Erol Köroğlu, eds. Merhaba Ey Muharrir!: Ahmet Mithat Üzerine Eleştirel Yazılar. İstanbul: Boğaziçi Üniversitesi Yayınevi, 2006.

Eşref and Kabacalı, Alpay. *Çeşitli Yönleriyle Şair Eşref: Hayatı, Sanatı, Yergileri*. İstanbul: Özgür Yayın Dağıtım, 1988.

Evin, Ahmet. *Origins and Development of the Turkish Novel*. Minneapolis: Bibliotheca Islamica, 1983.

Fahmy, Ziad. *Ordinary Egyptians: Creating the Modern Nation through Popular Culture*. Stanford: Stanford University Press, 2011.

Faroqhi, Suraiya. *Artisans of Empire: Crafts and Craftspeople under the Ottomans*. London: I.B. Tauris, 2009.

Faroqhi, Suraiya. "Guildsmen Complain to the Sultan: Artisans' Disputes and the Ottoman Administration in the 18th Century." In *Legitimizing the Order: The Ottoman Rhetoric of State Power*. Edited by Hakan T. Karateke and Maurus Reinkowski, 177–93. Leiden: Brill, 2005.

Fındıkoğlu, Z. Fahri. "Bizde Avrupavari İktisatçılığın Başlangıcı." *İş* 1 (1934): 45–8.

Fındıkoğlu, Z. Fahri. *Türkiyede İktisat Tedrisatı Tarihçesi ve İktisat Fakültesi Teşkilâtı*. İstanbul: Akgün Matbaası, 1946.

Fındıkoğlu, Z. Fahri. "Türk İktisadi Tefekkür Tarihi Ve Mehmed Şerif." In *III. Türk Tarih Kongresi, Ankara 15–20 Kasım 1943, Kongreye Sunulan Tebliğler*, 260–8. Ankara: Türk Tarih Kurumu, 1948.

Fındıkoğlu, Z. Fahri. "İktisadi Tefekkür Tarihimizden Bir Parça." In *Ordinaryüs Profesör*

İbrahim Fazıl Pelin'in Hatırasına Armağan. 221–30. İstanbul: İstanbul Üniversitesi İktisat Fakültesi, 1948.

Fındıkoğlu, Z. Fahri. "İktisadi Tefekkür Tarihimize Ait Yeni Bir Vesika." *Kongreye Sunulan Tebliğler, IV. Türk Tarih Kongresi*, 340–6. Ankara: Türk Tarih Kurumu, 1952.

Fındıkoğlu, Z. Fahri. "Türkiye'de İbn Haldunizm." In *60. Doğum Yılı Münasebetiyle Fuad Köprülü Armağanı*, 153–63. İstanbul: İstanbul Dil ve Tarih-Coğrafya Fakültesi, 1953.

Field, Alexander J. "Economic History." In *The New Palgrave Dictionary of Economics*. Second Edition. Edited by Steven N. Durlauf and Lawrence E. Blume. Vol. 2, 694–7. New York: Palgrave Macmillan, 2008.

Findlay, Ronald. "Comparative Advantage." In *The New Palgrave Dictionary of Economics*. Second Edition. Edited by Steven N. Durlauf and Lawrence E. Blume. Vol. 2, 28–33. New York: Palgrave Macmillan, 2008.

Findley, Carter V. *Ottoman Civil Officialdom: A Social History*. Princeton: Princeton University Press, 1989.

Findley, Carter V. "Competing Autobiographical Novels, His and Hers." In *Many Ways of Speaking about the Self: Middle Eastern Ego-Documents in Arabic, Persian, and Turkish (14th-20th Century)*. Edited by Ralf Elger and Yavuz Köse, 133–40. Otto Harrassowitz Verlag, 2010.

Finn, Robert P. *Türk Romanı, İlk Dönem: 1872–1900*. Ankara: Bilgi Yayınevi, 1984.

Fortna, Benjamin. "Islamic Morality in Late Ottoman 'Secular' Schools." *IJMES* 32, no. 3 (2000): 369–93.

Fortna, Benjamin. *Imperial Classroom: Islam, the State, and Education in the Late Ottoman Empire*. Oxford: Oxford University Press, 2002.

Fortna, Benjamin. *Learning to Read in the Late Ottoman Empire and the Early Turkish Republic*. New York: Palgrave Macmillan, 2011.

Foucault, Michel. "Governmentality." In *The Foucault Effect: Studies in Governmentality, with Two Lectures by and an Interview with Michel Foucault*. Edited by Graham Burchell, Colin Gordon, and Peter Miller, 87–104. Chicago: University of Chicago Press, 1991.

Frierson, Elizabeth Brown. "Unimagined Communities: State, Press, and Gender in the Hamidian Era." Unpublished PhD Dissertation, Princeton University, 1996.

Frierson, Elizabeth Brown. "Women in Late Ottoman Intellectual History," in *Late Ottoman Society: The Intellectual Legacy*. Edited by Elisabeth Özdalga. London: RoutledgeCurzon, 2005.

Fuzûlî. *Fuzûlî Divânı*. Edited by Abdülbâki Gölpınarlı. 2nd ed. İstanbul: İnkılâb Kitabevi, 1961.

Gallagher, Catherine. *The Body Economic: Life, Death, and Sensation in Political Economy and the Victorian Novel*. Princeton: Princeton University Press, 2006.

Gallagher, Catherine and Stephen Greenblatt. *Practicing New Historicism*. Chicago: University of Chicago Press, 2000.

Geertz, Clifford. "Thick Description: Toward an Interpretive Theory of Culture." In *The Interpretation of Cultures: Selected Essays*, 3–30. New York: Basic Books, 1973.

Gellner, Ernest. *Nations and Nationalism*. Ithaca: Cornell University Press, 1983.

Genç, Mehmet. "Ottoman Industry in the Eighteenth Century: General Framework, Characteristics, and Main Trends." In *Manufacturing in the Ottoman Empire and Turkey, 1500–1900*, edited by Donald Quataert, 59–86. Albany: State University of New York Press, 1994.

Genç, Mehmet. *Osmanlı İmparatorluğu'nda Devlet ve Ekonomi*. İstanbul: Ötüken, 2000.

Georgeon, François. "L'économie politique selon Ahmed Midhat." In *Première Rencontre Internationale Sur l'Empire Ottoman et La Turquie Moderne*. Edited by Edhem Eldem, 461–79. Varia Turcica 13. Istanbul: ISIS, 1991.

Georgeon, François. *Abdülhamid II: le sultan calife, 1876–1909*. Paris: Fayard, 2003.

Georgeon, François. "Ahmed Midhat'a Göre Ekonomi Politik." In *Osmanlı-Türk Modernleşmesi 1900–1930: Seçilmiş Makaleler*. Edited by Ali Berktay, 141–57. İstanbul: Yapı Kredi Kültür Sanat Yayıncılık, 2006.

Gerschenkron, Alexander. *Economic Backwardness in Historical Perspective: A Book of Essays*. Cambridge: Belknap Press of Harvard University Press, 1962.

Ghazanfar, Shaikh M., ed. *Medieval Islamic Economic Thought: Filling the "Great Gap" in European Economics*. London: RoutledgeCurzon, 2003.

Ghazanfar, Shaikh M. "Medieval Islamic Socio-Economic Thought: Links with Greek and Latin-European Scholarship." In *Medieval Islamic Economic Thought: Filling the "Great Gap" in European Economics*. Edited by Shaikh M. Ghazanfar, 147–58. London: RoutledgeCurzon, 2003.

Göçek, Fatma Müge. *Rise of the Bourgeoisie, Demise of Empire: Ottoman Westernization and Social Change*. New York: Oxford University Press, 1996.

Göçer, Kenan. "Cumhuriyet Öncesi İslamcı Akımın İktisadi Görüşleri–Kavramsal Bir Yaklaşım." Unpublished MS Thesis, Marmara University, 1993.

Göçer, Kenan. "Son Dönem Osmanlı İktisat Düşüncesinde Birey (Ulum-ı İktisâdiye ve İctimâiye Mecmuası ile İktisâdiyat Mecmuası Dergisi Örnekleri)." Unpublished PhD Dissertation, Marmara University, 2002.

Göçgün, Önder. *Ziya Paşa'nın Hayatı, Eserleri, Edebi Kişiliği ve Bütün Şiirleri*. Ankara: Kültür ve Turizm Bakanlığı, 1987.

Gökçek, Fazıl. *Küllerinden Doğan Anka: Ahmet Mithat Efendi Üzerine Yazılar*. İstanbul: Dergah Yayınları, 2012.

Green, Anne. "The Nineteenth Century (1820–1880)." In *Cassell Guide to Literature in French*. Edited by Valerie Worth-Stylianou. London: Cassell, 1996.

Grimmer-Solem, Erik. "Germany: From Sciences of State to Modern Economics." In *Routledge Handbook of the History of Global Economic Thought*. Edited by Vincent Barnett, 86–94. New York: Routledge, 2015.

Groenewegen, Peter. "Division of Labor." In *The New Palgrave Dictionary of Economics*. Second Edition. Edited by Steven N. Durlauf and Lawrence E. Blume. Vol. 2, 517–26. New York: Palgrave Macmillan, 2008.

Güran, Tevfik. *19. Yüzyıl Osmanlı Tarımı Üzerine Araştırmalar*. İstanbul: Eren, 1998.

Haddad, Mahmoud. "Ottoman Economic Nationalism in the Press of Beirut and Tripoli (Syria) at the End of the Nineteenth Century." In *The Economy as an Issue in the Middle Eastern Press*. Edited by Gisela Procházka-Eisl and Martin Strohmeier, 75–84. Vienna: Lit Verlag, 2008.

Halmwood, John. "Functionalism." In *Cambridge Dictionary of Sociology*. Edited by Bryan S. Turner, 218–20. Cambridge: Cambridge University Press, 2006.

Hanioğlu, M. Şükrü. *Bir Siyasal Düşünür Olarak Doktor Abdullah Cevdet ve Dönemi*. İstanbul: Üçdal Neşriyat, 1981.

Hanioğlu, M. Şükrü. *The Young Turks in Opposition*. New York: Oxford University Press, 1995.

Hanioğlu, M. Şükrü. *A Brief History of the Late Ottoman Empire*. Princeton: Princeton University Press, 2008.

Hanna, Nelly. *Artisan Entrepreneurs in Cairo and Early-Modern Capitalism (1600–1800)*. Syracuse, N.Y: Syracuse University Press, 2011.

Hébert, R.F. "Leroy-Beaulieu, Pierre-Paul (1843–1916)." In *The New Palgrave Dictionary of Economics*. Second Edition. Edited by Steven N. Durlauf and Lawrence E. Blume. Vol. 5, 92. New York: Palgrave Macmillan, 2008.

Heilbroner, Robert L. *The Worldly Philosophers: The Lives, Times, and Ideas of the Great Economic Thinkers*. Seventh Edition. New York: Touchstone, 1999.

Henderson, W.O. *Friedrich List, Economist and Visionary, 1789–1846*. London: F. Cass, 1983.

Hobsbawm, Eric J. *The Age of Revolution, 1789–1848*. London: Weidenfeld and Nicolson, 1962.

Hobsbawm, Eric and Ranger, Terence, eds. *The Invention of Tradition*. Cambridge: Cambridge University Press, 1983.

Hodgson, Geoffrey M. *How Economics Forgot History: The Problem of Historical Specificity in Social Science*. New York: Routledge, 2001.

Hoell, Margaret Stevens. "The Ticaret Odasi: Origins, Functions, and Activities of the Chamber of Commerce of Istanbul, 1885–1899." Ohio State University, 1974.

İlhan, Attila. *Dersaadet'te Sabah Ezanları*. Ankara: Bilgi Yayınevi, 1988.

İnalcık, Halil. "Ottoman Economic Mind and the Aspects of Ottoman Economy," in *Studies in the Economic History of the Middle East: From the Rise of Islam to the Present Day*. Edited by M.A. Cook. 207–18. London: Oxford University Press, 1970.

İnalcık, Halil. *The Ottoman Empire; the Classical Age, 1300–1600*. Translated by Norman Itzkowitz and Colin Imber. London: Weidenfeld & Nicolson, 1973.

İnsel, Ahmet. "Milliyetçilik ve Kalkınmacılık." In *Modern Türkiye'de Siyasi Düşünce 4 – Milliyetçilik*, edited by Tanıl Bora, 4:763–76. İstanbul: İletişim, 2002.

Irwin, Douglas A. "Infant-Industry Protection." In *The New Palgrave Dictionary of Economics*, Second Edition. Edited by Steven N. Durlauf and Lawrence E. Blume. Vol. 4, 291–3. New York: Palgrave Macmillan, 2008.

İskit, Server R. *Türkiyede Matbuat Rejimleri*. İstanbul: Ülkü Matbaası, 1939.

İskit, Server R. *Türkiyede Neşriyat Hareketleri Tarihine Bir Bakış*. İstanbul: Devlet Basımevi, 1939.

İslamoğlu-İnan, Huri, and Peter C. Perdue, eds. *Shared Histories of Modernity: China, India and the Ottoman Empire*. London: Routledge, 2009.

Issawi, Charles Philip. *The Economic History of Turkey, 1800–1914*. Chicago: University of Chicago Press, 1980.

Issawi, Charles Philip. "Economic Legacy." In *Imperial Legacy: The Ottoman Imprint on the Balkans and the Middle East*. Edited by L. Carl Brown. New York: Columbia University Press, 1996.

Jay, Elisabeth and Jay, Richard. *Critics of Capitalism: Victorian Criticism of "Political Economy."* Cambridge: Cambridge University Press, 1986.

Jefferies, Mathew. "The Age of Historism." In *A Companion to Nineteenth-Century Europe: 1789–1914*. Edited by Stefan Berger, 316–32. Malden, MA: Wiley-Blackwell, 2009.

Kafadar, Cemal. "When Coins Turned into Drops of Dew and Bankers Became Robbers of Shadows: The Boundaries of Ottoman Economic Imagination at the End of the Sixteenth Century." Unpublished PhD dissertation, McGill University, 1986.

Kafadar, Cemal. "A Death in Venice (1575): Anatolian Muslim Merchants Trading in the Serenissima." *Journal of Turkish Studies* 10 (1986): 191–217.

Kahan, Arcadius. "Nineteenth-Century European Experience with Policies of Economic

Nationalism." In *Economic Nationalism in Old and New States*. Edited by Harry G. Johnson, 17–30. Chicago: University of Chicago Press, 1967.

Kaplan, Mehmet, İnci Enginün, Birol Emil, and Zeynep Kerman, eds. *Yeni Türk Edebiyatı Antolojisi*. 5 vols. İstanbul: İ.Ü. Edebiyat Fakültesi Yayınları, 1974–89.

Karakartal, Oğuz. "Ahmed Midhat Efendi ve Para." Unpublished MA Thesis, Marmara University, 1990.

Karaman, Deniz. *Cavid Bey ve Ulûm-ı İktisadiye ve İçtimâiye Mecmuası*. Ankara: Liberte Yayınları, 2001.

Karpat, Kemal H. "Traditionalist Elite Philosophy and the Modern Mass Media." In *Political Modernization in Japan and Turkey*. Edited by Robert E. Ward and Dankwart A. Rustow. Princeton: Princeton University Press, 1964.

Karpat, Kemal H. *Ottoman Population, 1830–1914: Demographic and Social Characteristics*. Madison: University of Wisconsin Press, 1985.

Karpat, Kemal H. *The Politicization of Islam: Reconstructing Identity, State, Faith, and Community in the late Ottoman State*. Oxford: Oxford University Press, 2001.

Kasaba, Reşat. "Treaties and Friendships: British Imperialism, the Ottoman Empire, and China in the Nineteenth Century." *Journal of World History* 4, no. 2 (1993): 215–41.

Kerim, Sadi. *Türkiye'de Sosyalizmin Tarihine Katkı*. Second Edition. Edited by Mete Tunçay. İstanbul: İletişim Yayınları, 1994.

Keynes, John M. *The General Theory of Employment, Interest and Money*. London: Macmillan, 1973.

Kılınçoğlu, Deniz T. "Weber, Veblen ve Ahmed Midhat Efendi'nin Kahramanları," in *Kurumsal İktisat*. Edited by Eyüp Özveren (Ankara: İmge Yayınevi, 2007), 441–72.

Kırtekin, Ahmet. "Tanzimat ve İktisadi Liberalizm." Unpublished MS Thesis, Marmara University, 2006.

Kırmızı, Abdulhamit. "Authoritarianism and Constitutionalism Combined: Ahmed Midhat Efendi Between the Sultan and the Kanun-I Esasi." In *The First Ottoman Experiment in Democracy*. Edited by Christoph Herzog and Malek Sharif, 53–65. Ergon in Kommission, 2010.

Kinmonth, Earl H. *The Self-Made Man in Meiji Japanese Thought: From Samurai to Salary Man*. Berkeley: University of California Press, 1981.

Koloğlu, Orhan. "Osmanlı Devleti'nde Liberal Ekonominin Savunucusu: Blacque (Blak) Bey (1792–1836)." *Tarih ve Toplum* 10, no. 57 (1988): 15–19.

Köprülü, M. Fuad. "Osmanlı Müelliflerinde Ekonomik Düşünceler." *Ülkü*, July 1936, 339–44.

Kudret, Cevdet. *Abdülhamit Devrinde Sansür*. İstanbul: Milliyet Yayınları, 1977.

Kunt, I. Metin. "Dervis Mehmed Pasa, Vezir and Entrepreneur: A Study in Ottoman Political-Economic Theory and Practice." *Turcica* 9, no. 1 (1977): 197–214.

Kuran, Timur. *Islam and Mammon: The Economic Predicaments of Islamism*. Princeton: Princeton University Press, 2004.

Kuran, Timur. *The Long Divergence: How Islamic Law Held Back the Middle East*. Princeton: Princeton University Press, 2011.

Kurdakul, Necdet. "19. Yüzyılda İktisat Kitapları." *Tarih ve Toplum* 75 (1990): 57–60.

Kurdakul, Necdet. *Tanzimat Dönemi Basınında Sosyo-Ekonomik Fikir Hareketleri*. Ankara: T.C. Kültür Bakanlığı, 1998.

Kushner, David. *The Rise of Turkish Nationalism, 1876–1908*. London: Frank Cass, 1977.

Kütükoğlu, B. "Vekayinüvis." In *İslam Ansiklopedisi*. Vol. 13, 271–87. İstanbul: Kültür ve Turizm Bakanlığı, 1986.

Lai, Cheng-chung, ed. *Adam Smith Across Nations: Translations and Receptions of The Wealth of Nations*. Oxford: Oxford University Press, 2000.

Lee, Frederic S. "Heterodox Economics." In *The New Palgrave Dictionary of Economics*. Second Edition. Edited by Steven N. Durlauf and Lawrence E. Blume. Vol. 4, 2–6. New York: Palgrave Macmillan, 2008.

Lemay, J.A. Leo. *The Life of Benjamin Franklin*. 2 vols. Philadelphia: University of Pennsylvania Press, 2006.

Lewis, Bernard. *The Emergence of Modern Turkey*. London: Oxford University Press, 1961.

Lewis, Bernard. *Islam in History: Ideas, People, and Events in the Middle East*. New Edition, Revised and Expanded. Chicago: Open Court, 1993.

Makdisi, Ussama. "Ottoman Orientalism." *The American Historical Review* 107, no. 3 (2002): 768–96.

Maloney, J. "Historical Economics, British." In *The New Palgrave Dictionary of Economics*. Second Edition. Edited by Steven N. Durlauf and Lawrence E. Blume. Vol. 4: 42–5. New York: Palgrave Macmillan, 2008.

Mandaville, Jon E. "Usurious Piety: The Cash Waqf Controversy in the Ottoman Empire." *International Journal of Middle East Studies* 10, no. 3 (1979): 289–308.

Marchi, N. de. "Senior, Nassau William (1790–1864)." In *The New Palgrave Dictionary of Economics*. Second Edition. Edited by Steven N. Durlauf and Lawrence E. Blume. Vol. 7, 428–30. New York: Palgrave Macmillan, 2008.

Mardin, Şerif. *The Genesis of Young Ottoman Thought: A Study in the Modernization of Turkish Political Ideas*. Princeton: Princeton University Press, 1962.

Mardin, Şerif. "Super Westernization in Urban Life in the Last Quarter of the Nineteenth Century." In *Turkey: Geographical and Social Perspectives*. Edited by Peter Benedict *et al.*, 403–46. Leiden: Brill, 1974.

Mardin, Şerif. "Tanzimat'tan Cumhuriyet'e İktisadi Düşüncenin Gelişimesi (1838–1918)." *Tanzimat'tan Cumhuriyet'e Türkiye Ansiklopedisi*. Vol. 3, 618–34. İstanbul: İletişim Yayınları, 1984.

Mardin, Şerif. "Tanzimat'tan Sonra Aşırı Batılılaşma." In Şerif Mardin. *Türk Modernleşmesi*, 23–81. İstanbul: İletişim, 1991.

Mardin, Şerif. *Jön Türklerin Siyasî Fikirleri, 1895–1908*. İstanbul: İletişim Yayınları, 2004.

Marshall, Byron K. *Capitalism and Nationalism in Prewar Japan: The Ideology of the Business Elite, 1868–1941*. Stanford: Stanford University Press, 1967.

Masters, Bruce. *The Origins of Western Economic Dominance in the Middle East: Mercantilism and the Islamic Economy in Aleppo, 1600–1750*. New York: New York University Press, 1988.

Mears, E.G., ed. *The Modern Turkey: A Politico-Economic Interpretation, 1908–1923 inclusive, with Selected Chapters by Representative Authorities*. New York: The Macmillan Company, 1924.

Milgate, Murray and Shannon C. Stimson. *After Adam Smith: A Century of Transformation in Politics and Political Economy*. Princeton: Princeton University Press, 2009.

Mitchell, Timothy. *Colonising Egypt*. Berkeley: University of California Press, 1991.

Mitchell, Timothy. *Questions Of Modernity*. Minneapolis: University Of Minnesota Press, 2000.

Mitchell, Timothy. *Rule of Experts: Egypt, Techno-Politics, Modernity*. Berkeley: University of California Press, 2002.

Moran, Berna. *Türk Romanına Eleştirel Bir Bakış*. Vol. 1. Cağaloğlu Istanbul: İletişim Yayınları, 1983.

Muller, Jerry Z. *The Mind and the Market: Capitalism in Modern European Thought*. New York: Alfred A. Knopf, 2002.

Nackenoff, Carol. *The Fictional Republic: Horatio Alger and American Political Discourse*. New York: Oxford University Press, 1994.

Nasar, Sylvia. *Grand Pursuit: The Story of Economic Genius*. New York: Simon & Schuster, 2011.

O'Donnell, Margaret G. "Harriet Martineau: A Popular Early Economics Educator." *The Journal of Economic Education* 14, no. 4 (October 1, 1983): 59–64.

Offord, Derek. *The Russian Revolutionary Movement in the 1880s*. Cambridge: Cambridge University Press, 1986.

Oğuz, Mustafa. "II. Abdülhamid'e Sunulan Lâyihalar." Unpublished PhD Dissertation, Ankara University, 2007.

Okay, M. Orhan. *Batı Medeniyeti Karşısında Ahmed Midhat Efendi*. Ankara: Baylan Matbaası, 1975

Okay, M. Orhan. "Ahmed Midhat Efendi (1844–1912)." In *T.D.V. İslam Ansiklopedisi*. Vol. 2, 100–103. İstanbul: Türkiye Diyanet Vakfı, 1989.

Okay, M. Orhan. "Teşebbüse Sarfedilmiş Bir Hayatın Hikayesi." *Kitap-Lık*, no. 54 (2002): 130–36.

Ortaylı, İlber. "Osmanlılarda İlk Telif İktisat Elyazması." *Yapıt* October 1983: 37–44.

Ortaylı, İlber. *İmparatorluğun En Uzun Yüzyılı*, İstanbul: Alkım Yayınevi, 2006.

Önsoy, Rıfat. *Tanzimat Dönemi Osmanlı Sanayii ve Sanayileşme Politikası*. Türkiye İş Bankası Kültür Yayınları, 1988.

Önsoy, Rıfat. "Tanzimat Döneminde İktisadi Düşüncenin Teşekkülü." In *Mustafa Reşid Paşa ve Dönemi Semineri, Bildiriler, Ankara, 13–14 Mart 1984*, 91–6. Ankara: Türk Tarih Kurumu, 1994.

Özçelik, Tarık. "Modern İktisadın Osmanlı'ya Girişi ve Ceride-i Havadis (1840–1856)." Unpublished PhD Dissertation, Marmara University, 2003.

Özçelik, Tarık. "Ceride–i Havadis'de Ziraat, Ticaret ve Sanayi Tartışmaları." *İstanbul Üniversitesi Sosyal Siyaset Konferansları Dergisi*, no. 56 (2009): 469–518.

Özdalga, Elisabeth. *Late Ottoman Society: The Intellectual Legacy*. London: Routledge-Curzon, 2005.

Özgür, Erdem M. and Hamdi Genç. "An Ottoman Classical Political Economist: Sarantis Archigenes and His Tasarrufat-ı Mülkiye." *Middle Eastern Studies* 47, no. 2 (2011): 329–42.

Özön, Mustafa Nihat. *Türkçede Roman Hakkında Bir Deneme*. İstanbul: Remzi Kitabevi, 1936.

Özsoy, İsmail. "Süleyman Sûdi'nin Osmanlı Mâliyesi ve Vergi Sistemi Ile İlgili Görüş ve Tesbitleri (1881)." *Akademik Araştırmalar Dergisi* 2, no. 4–5 (July 2000): 611–56.

Öztürk, Yusuf Kemal. "Osmanlı Devleti'nin Son Döneminde İktisadi Düşünce Akımları (1838–1914)." Unpublished PhD dissertation, Gazi University, 2007.

Özveren, Eyüp. "Ottoman Economic Thought and Economic Policy in Transition: Rethinking the Nineteenth Century." *Economic Thought and Policy in Less Developed Europe, The Nineteenth Century*. Edited by Michalis Psalidopoulos and Maria Eugénia Mata. London: Routledge, 2002.

Özveren, Eyüp. "Economic Agents, Rationality and the Institutional Setup: The Advent of Homo Œconomicus in the Representations of the Levant." *History of Economic Ideas* 14, no. 3 (2006): 9–34.

Pakalın, Mehmet Zeki. *Sicill-i Osman Zeylî: Son Devir Osmanlı Meşhurları Ansiklopedisi*. 19 vols. Ankara: Türk Tarih Kurumu, 2008.

Pamuk, Şevket. "The Ottoman Empire in the 'Great Depression' of 1873–1896." *The Journal of Economic History* 44, no. 1 (1984): 107–18.

Pamuk, Şevket. *The Ottoman Empire and European Capitalism, 1820–1913: Trade, Investment, and Production*. Cambridge: Cambridge University Press, 1987.

Pamuk, Şevket, and Jeffrey G. Williamson. "Ottoman De-Industrialization 1800–1913: Assessing the Shock, Its Impact and the Response." *NBER Working Papers*, no. 14763 (2009).

Parla, Jale. *Babalar ve Oğullar: Tanzimat Romanının Epistemolojik Temelleri*. İstanbul: İletişim Yayınları, 1990.

Parla, Jale. "Rakım Efendi'den Nurullah Bey'e Cemaatçi Osmanlılıktan Cemiyetçi Türk. Milliyetçiliğine Ahmet Mithat'ın Romancılığı." In *Merhaba Ey Muharrir!: Ahmet Mithat Üzerine Eleştirel Yazılar*. Edited by Nüket Esen and Erol Köroğlu, 17–51. İstanbul: Boğaziçi Üniversitesi Yayınevi, 2006.

Parla, Taha. *Ziya Gökalp, Kemalizm ve Türkiye'de Korporatizm*. Edited by F. Üstel and S. Yücesoy. İstanbul: İletişim Yayınları, 1989.

Pearson, Heath. "Historical School, German." In *The New Palgrave Dictionary of Economics*. Second Edition. Edited by Steven N. Durlauf and Lawrence E. Blume. Vol. 4, 5–48. New York: Palgrave Macmillan, 2008.

Piketty, Thomas. *Capital in the Twenty-First Century*. Translated by Arthur Goldhammer. Cambridge, MA: Belknap Press, 2014.

Polanyi, Karl. *The Great Transformation*. Boston: Beacon Press, 1957.

Pomeranz, Kenneth. *The Great Divergence: Europe, China, and the Making of the Modern World Economy*. The Princeton Economic History of the Western World. Princeton, N.J: Princeton University Press, 2000.

Psalidopoulos, Michalis M. and Nicholas J. Theocarakis. "The Dissemination of Economic Thought in South-Eastern Europe in the Nineteenth Century." In *The Dissemination of Economic Ideas*, 161–91. Cheltenham, UK: Edward Elgar, 2011.

"Putin Reaffirms Commitment to Military Modernization in Speech to Officers." *The Moscow Times*, November 4, 2014. www.themoscowtimes.com/business/article/putin-reaffirms-commitment-to-military-modernization-in-speech-to-officers/510601.html.

Quataert, Donald. "Ottoman Reform and Agriculture in Anatolia, 1876–1908." Unpublished PhD Dissertation, University of California, 1973.

Quataert, Donald. *Social Disintegration and Popular Resistance in the Ottoman Empire, 1881–1908: Reactions to European Economic Penetration*. New York: New York University Press, 1983.

Quataert, Donald. *Ottoman Manufacturing in the Age of the Industrial Revolution*. Cambridge: Cambridge University Press, 1993.

Quataert, Donald. "The Age of Reforms, 1812–1914." In *An Economic and Social History of the Ottoman Empire, 1300–1914*. Edited by Halil Inalcik and Donald Quataert, 761–943. Cambridge, New York: Cambridge University Press, 1994.

Quataert, Donald. ed. *Manufacturing in the Ottoman Empire and Turkey, 1500–1950*. Albany, NY: State University of New York Press, 1994.

Quataert, Donald. "Ottoman Manufacturing in the Nineteenth Century." In *Manufacturing in the Ottoman Empire and Turkey, 1500–1900*. Edited by Donald Quataert, 87–121. Albany: State University of New York Press, 1994.

Rabinbach, Anson. *The Human Motor: Energy, Fatigue, and the Origins of Modernity*. New York: Basic Books, 1990.

Ravndal, G. Bie. "Capitulations." In *The Modern Turkey: A Politico-Economic Interpretation, 1908–1923 inclusive, with Selected Chapters by Representative Authorities*. Edited by E.G. Mears, 430–47. New York: The Macmillan Company, 1924.

Rodinson, Maxime. *Islam and Capitalism*. Translated by Brian Pearce. Austin: University of Texas Press, 1978.

Sarc, Ömer Celâl. "Tanzimat ve Sanayiimiz." In *Tanzimat: Yüzüncü Yıldönümü Münasebetile*, 423–40. İstanbul: Maarif Matbaası, 1940.

Sayar, Ahmed Güner. *Osmanlı İktisat Düşüncesinin Çağdaşlaşması*. Second Edition. İstanbul: Ötüken, 2000.

Schumpeter, Joseph A. *History of Economic Analysis*. Edited from manuscript by Elizabeth Boody Schumpeter. New York: Oxford University Press, 1961.

Scott John and Marshall, Gordon, eds. *A Dictionary of Sociology*. Third Edition. Oxford: Oxford University Press, 2005.

Shaw, Stanford J. *Between Old and New: the Ottoman Empire under Sultan Selim III, 1789–1807*. Cambridge, Harvard University Press, 1971.

Shissler, A. Holly. *Between Two Empires: Ahmet Ağaoğlu and the New Turkey*. London: I.B. Tauris, 2003.

Shissler, A. "The Harem as the Seat of Middle-Class Industry and Morality: The Fiction of Ahmed Midhat Efendi." In *Harem Histories: Envisioning Places and Living Spaces*, edited by Marilyn Booth, 319–41. Duke University Press, 2010.

Smetanin, Stanislav I. *Istorija Predprinimatel'stva v Rossii : Kurs Leksij*. Moskva: MTFER, 2008.

Somar, Ziya. *Yakın Çağların Fikir ve Edebiyat Tarihimizde İzmir*. İzmir: Nefaset Matbaası, 1944.

Somar, Ziya. *Bir Şehr'in ve Bir Adam'ın Tarihi: Tevfik Nevzat: İzmir'in İlk Fikir ve Hürriyet Kurbanı*. İzmir: Ahenk Matbaası, 1948.

Sombart, Werner. "Economic Theory and Economic History." *The Economic History Review* 2, no. 1 (1929): 1–19.

Somel, Selçuk Akşin. *The Modernization of Public Education in the Ottoman Empire, 1839–1908: Islamization, Autocracy, and Discipline*. Leiden: Brill, 2001.

Stanković, F. "Conspicuous Consumption." In *The New Palgrave Dictionary of Economics*. Second Edition. Edited by Steven N. Durlauf and Lawrence E. Blume. Vol. 2, 118–19. New York: Palgrave Macmillan, 2008.

Strauss, Johann. "Who Read What in the Ottoman Empire (19th-20th Centuries)?" *Middle Eastern Literatures* 6, no. 1 (January 1, 2003): 39–76.

Strohmeier, Martin. "Economic Issues in the Turkish-Cypriot Press (1891–1931)." In *The Economy as an Issue in the Middle Eastern Press*. Edited by Gisela Procházka-Eisl and Martin Strohmeier, 171–85. Vienna: Lit Verlag, 2008.

Suleiman, Susan Rubin. *Authoritarian Fictions: The Ideological Novel as a Literary Genre*. New York: Columbia University Press, 1983.

Şirin, İbrahim. *Osmanlı İmgeleminde Avrupa*. Ankara: Lotus, 2006.

Tanpınar, Ahmed Hamdi. *XIX. Asır Türk Edebiyatı Tarihi*. Edited by Ahmet Kuyaş. İstanbul: Yapı Kredi Yayınları, 2006 [1949].

Thompson, E.P. "Time, Work-Discipline, and Industrial Capitalism." *Past & Present* 38 (1967): 56–97.

Toprak, Zafer. *Türkiye'de "Millî İktisat", 1908–1918*. Ankara: Yurt Yayınları, 1982.

Toprak, Zafer. *Türkiye'de Ekonomi ve Toplum (1908–1950), Milli İktisat – Milli Burjuvazi*. İstanbul: Tarih Vakfı Yurt Yayınları, 1995.

Tribe, K. "List, Friedrich (1789–1846)." In *The New Palgrave Dictionary of Economics*. Second Edition. Edited by Steven N. Durlauf and Lawrence E. Blume. Vol. 5, 160–62. New York: Palgrave Macmillan, 2008.

Tribe, Keith and Hiroshi Mizuta. *A Critical Bibliography of Adam Smith*. London: Pickering & Chatto, 2002.

Tripp, Charles. *Islam and the Moral Economy: The Challenge of Capitalism*. Cambridge: Cambridge University Press, 2006.

Tuna, Orhan. "Türkiye'de İlk Tercüme İktisat Kitabı." In *III. Türk Tarih Kongresi, Ankara 15–20 Kasım 1943, Kongreye Sunulan Tebliğler*, 700–3. Ankara: Türk Tarih Kurumu, 1948.

Tütel, Eser. *Şirket-i Hayriye*. İstanbul: İletişim Yayınları, 1994.

Uçman, Abdullah. "Türk Romanında İlk Alafranga Tip: Felatun Bey." *Kitap-lık* 54 (2002): 140–7.

Uçman, Abdullah. "Mizancı Murad." In *T.D.V. İslam Ansiklopedisi*. Vol. 30, 214–16. İstanbul: Türkiye Diyanet Vakfı, 2005.

Udovitch, Abraham. *Partnership and Profit in Medieval Islam*. Princeton: Princeton University Press, 1970.

Uğurcan, Selma. "Ahmet Midhat Efendi'nin Hatıratı ile Romanları Arasındaki Münasebet." *Türklük Araştırmaları Dergisi* 2 (1986), 184–99.

Us, Hakkı Tarık, ed. *Bir Jübilenin İntiba'ları: Ahmed Midhat'ı Anıyoruz!*. İstanbul: Vakit, 1955.

Ülgen, Erol. *Ahmet Midhat Efendi'de Çalışma Fikri*. İstanbul: Ahilik Araştırma ve Kültür Vakfı, 1994.

Ülgener, Sabri. "Ahmed Cevdet Paşa'nın Devlet ve İktisada Dair Düşünceleri." *İş* 76 (1947): 5–23.

Ülgener, Sabri. *İktisadi İnhitat Tarihimizin Ahlâk ve Zihniyet Meseleleri*. İstanbul: İstanbul Üniversitesi İktisat Fakultesi, 1951.

Ülgener, Sabri. *Dünü ve Bugünü ile Zihniyet ve Din: İslâm, Tasavvuf ve Çözülme Devri İktisat Ahlâkı*. İstanbul: Derin Yayınları, 2006.

Ülken, Hilmi Ziya. *Türkiye'de Çağdaş Düşünce Tarihi*. 2 vols. Konya: Selçuk Yayınları, 1966.

Vanpaemel, Geert and Brigitte van Tiggelen. "Science for the People: The Belgian *Encyclopédie populaire* and the Constitution of a National Science Movement." In *Popularizing Science and Technology in the European Periphery, 1800–2000*. Edited by Faidra Papanelopoulou, Agustí Nieto-Galan and Enrique Perdriguero, 65–88. Aldershot: Ashgate, 2009.

Veblen, Thorstein. *The Theory of the Leisure Class: An Economic Study in the Evolution of Institutions*. New York: The Macmillan Company; London: Macmillan & Co. Ltd., 1899.

Veeser, H. Aram, ed. *The New Historicism*. New York: Routledge, 1989.

Warshaw, Dan. *Paul Leroy-Beaulieu and Established Liberalism in France*. DeKalb: Northern Illinois University Press, 1991.

Weber, Max. *The Protestant Ethic and the Spirit of Capitalism*. Translated by Talcott Parsons. New York: Scribner's, 1950 [1904–5].

Wernick, Andrew. "Le Play, Pierre Guillaume Frédéric Le Play, (1806–1882)." In *Cambridge Dictionary of Sociology*. Edited by Bryan S. Turner. 331. Cambridge: Cambridge University Press, 2006.

Wood, Diane. *Medieval Economic Thought*. Cambridge: Cambridge University Press, 2002.

Yapp, Malcolm. *The Making of the Modern Near East, 1792–1923*. London: Longman, 1990.

Yeniay, İ. Hakkı. *Yeni Osmanlı Borçları Tarihi*. İstanbul: İ. Ü. İktisat Fakültesi, 1964.

Yıldırım, Onur. "The Industrial Reform Commission as an Institutional Innovation During the Tanzimat." *Arab Historical Review for Ottoman Studies* 17–18 (1998), 117–26.

Yıldırır Kocabaş, Özlem. *Türkiye'de Tarımsal Kooperatifçilik Düşüncesinin Gelişimi.* İstanbul: Libra, 2010.

Yinanç, Mükrimin Halil. "Tanzimattan Cumhuriyete Kadar Bizde Tarihçilik." In *Tanzimat: Yüzüncü Yıldönümü Münasebetile*, 573–95. İstanbul: Maarif Matbaası, 1940.

Zanasi, Margherita. *Saving the Nation: Economic Modernity in Republican China.* Chicago: University Of Chicago Press, 2006.

Zweig, Stefan. *Master Builders: A Typology of the Spirit.* New York: Viking Press, 1939.

Index